AF352533

CONSTRUCTING POLICY CHANGE

Early Childhood Education and Care
in Liberal Welfare States

For a list of books published in the series, see page 335.

LINDA A. WHITE

Constructing Policy Change

Early Childhood Education and Care in Liberal Welfare States

UNIVERSITY OF TORONTO PRESS
Toronto Buffalo London

© University of Toronto Press 2017
Toronto Buffalo London
www.utppublishing.com
Printed in the U.S.A.

ISBN 978-1-4875-0203-4

∞ Printed on acid-free, 100% post-consumer recycled paper with
vegetable-based inks.

Library and Archives Canada Cataloguing in Publication

White, Linda A. (Linda Ann), 1967–, author
Constructing policy change : early childhood education and care
in liberal welfare states / Linda A. White.

(Studies in comparative political economy and public policy ; 52)
Includes bibliographical references and index.
ISBN 978-1-4875-0203-4 (cloth)

1. Early childhood education – Government policy – Developed
countries.   2. Child care – Government policy – Developed countries.
I. Title.   II. Series: Studies in comparative political economy and
public policy ; 52

LB1139.3.D48W55 2017   372.2109172'2   C2017-901062-X

This book has been published with the help of a grant from the Federation
for the Humanities and Social Sciences, through the Awards to Scholarly
Publications Program, using funds provided by the Social Sciences and
Humanities Research Council of Canada.

University of Toronto Press acknowledges the financial assistance to its
publishing program of the Canada Council for the Arts and the Ontario
Arts Council, an agency of the Government of Ontario.

Contents

Figures and Tables

Preface and Acknowledgments

Writing a book is much like raising children: the process forces one to think in terms of very long time horizons, and it is very difficult to see through the weeds, but once finished, one can look back and admire what has grown.

I began this project while on a research leave as Fulbright faculty fellow in Washington, DC. I was affiliated with the Georgetown Institute of Public Policy and working with William T. Gormley, Jr, with the intention of studying comparative paid family leave policy. The buzz around Washington, though, was all about universal pre-kindergarten (UPK). When I returned to Canada, I noticed a similar buzz surrounding early childhood education in the province of Ontario after the election there of a Liberal government under Dalton McGuinty. In Ontario and in a number of other provinces, provincial ministries of education or dedicated children and youth ministries were assuming responsibility for child care programs, which for decades had been housed in social service or health ministries. My curiosity was piqued regarding the fundamental shifts in early childhood education and care that I sensed were occurring on both sides of the border. Those shifts were signalled by the shift in language to describe these programs: early childhood education and care, pre-school, pre-k, or UPK, as opposed to child care or day care. That switch in language signalled a change both in the content of policy (education *and* child care as opposed to education *or* child care) and in the scope of policy (*universal* pre-kindergarten). Just at a time when policy makers on Capitol Hill in the United States were passing Temporary Assistance for Needy Families legislation that included child care funding to support parental employment, pre-k initiatives were starting to crop up in a number of states; and just as the Canadian federal Liberal government was eliminating child care funding as part of the Canada Assistance Plan, concerns about the early years were percolating across the provinces and territories. Why? And what explained the variation in policy adoption across jurisdictions?

It was not until I read Thomas Rochon's *Culture Moves* (1998) that I understood the phenomenon I was studying. What I was observing was not simply a policy shift but a "culture move," much like the women's rights movement or green movements around the globe. As this book documents, a sea change in cultural views regarding childhood and the family is occurring. The early years are increasingly seen as key years in the development of the whole child, as emphasized in the catchy slogans of child organizations such as "the years before five last the rest of their lives." The scope and form of policy change, however, is really intriguing … and really puzzling.

My interest in this topic is both personal and professional. I have been a scholar of child and family policy since my doctoral work. When I was conducting doctoral research on comparative child care policy, I occasionally ventured into the Ontario Institute for Studies in Education library to read about Head Start, the Perry Preschool Project, and so on. But child care and education were treated as separate policy topics. That these two fields have come together represents an incredible change in thinking.

I regard this book project as building on the magisterial book by Sally Cohen, *Championing Child Care* (2001). The final chapters of her book hinted at the direction that child care policy was taking in the United States at the state and national levels. In so saying I cannot claim to have covered the topic with the same richness of detail as Cohen's book. I only hope that others will see this book as a worthy companion to hers and to other single-country studies such as those by Maris Vinovskis and Barbara Beatty. The cross-national lens I lend to this project reveals that the idea of universal early childhood education is not confined to the United States. By grouping child care and early childhood education together in a single study, I am not trying to imply that these changes are universally embraced as socially desirable. I worry, for example, about the excessive "schoolification" of some early years curricula and the loss of the core play-based principles of early years programs found in the highest-quality child care centres in Europe and North America. Other scholars have reflected on this schoolification, including Alison Gopnik.

I wish to thank the many interviewees in both the United States and Canada who gave of their time and generously shared their own research and policy work. I thank the funding agencies and granting councils that made this research possible: Fulbright Canada and the Social Sciences and Humanities Research Council of Canada.

I had the benefit of working with fantastic graduate student research assistants over the project's duration: Caitlin Cavanagh Halferty at Georgetown University and Safiyyah Ally, James Farney, Olivia Magilny, and Kate Mulligan at the University of Toronto provided excellent research help in the early stages of the project. In the latter stages of the project, I had the greatest pleasure to work with Adrienne Davidson, Heather Millar, Milena Pandy, and Juliana Yi, four extremely bright and talented doctoral students with whom I have co-authored. Other doctoral students, whose interest in child care and education inspired me to keep researching in these fields, have come through the doctoral program and have since moved on to wonderful careers: Celine Mulhern, Amy Nugent, Luc Turgeon, and Jennifer Wallner.

I also wish to thank the delightful, intelligent, and incredibly fun colleagues with whom I have the privilege of working. Martha Friendly, the Director of the Childcare Resource and Research Unit, along with Michal Perlman and Susan Prentice – when she is town – have talked about things ECEC over many dinners and coffees. Martha in particular has worked tirelessly for decades to see realized a national system of early years programming that puts children first and supports working parents. She started up a child care centre when her own children were small (she now has grandchildren), and she has worked tirelessly to help parents throughout Canada gain access to the same high-quality programs as her own children did. She never compromises on her demands for quality, which makes her a great advocate (but a challenging co-author, as nothing slips by her!).

The Department of Political Science at the University of Toronto provides the ideal intellectual environment in which to pursue creative scholarly research. Intellectually situated between American, British, and Continental schools of thought (what one esteemed chair, Louis Pauly, calls "the U of T uniqueness," and another esteemed chair, Robert Vipond, has identified as the "Canadian political tradition"), our Department lets researchers engage in eclectic yet rigorous and systematic research pursuits. It also provides a culture of professionalism and collegiality that allows researchers to thrive. I would especially like to thank Antoinette Handley, Matt Hoffmann, Grace Skogstad, Phil Triadafilopoulos, Rob Vipond, and Joseph Wong, colleagues and moreover friends, who read and commented on many aspects of this project over the years, and the very active Comparative and International Relations book club.

The inter-disciplinary nature of the School of Public Policy and Governance (my second scholarly home) challenges one to ask, is my research relevant outside of my own discipline and my own subject area? The school was established during the nascence of this project, and I have reaped the benefit of its provision of excellent colleagues such as Michael Baker, Mark Stabile, Carolyn Tuohy, and wonderful professors of practice who always ask the toughest questions, including, "What is this project's policy relevance?," and, most importantly, "Is the book finished yet?" A special thanks also to the founding director, Mark Stabile, whose leadership at SPPG provided the interdisciplinary space to write significant chunks of this book.

I also wish to extend special thanks to the editorial and production team at the University of Toronto Press. I was very fortunate to work with Daniel Quinlan, whose talent and expertise made the entire review process a dream. He solicited extremely thoughtful and constructive reviewers and ensured that the review process moved swiftly and effectively. Wayne Herrington ably managed the manuscript through the editorial and production processes.

My incredible family – my two wonderful girls, who are blessed (?) with growing up in a two-academic household, and especially my ever loving and patient husband, Steven, whose commitment to equal parenting allows me to do what I do – supported and sustained me through the entirety of the research and writing process.

I have had the benefit of observing first-hand what high-quality early childhood education and care mean to children through my own children's lives, first at our neighbourhood child care centre and then at the Jackman Institute of Child Study at the University of Toronto's Ontario Institute for Studies in Education. Jackman ICS is the very model of what high-quality and integrated early childhood education and care looks like and shows what deeply caring and nurturing environments can achieve for all children. I only wish that every child could experience a similarly intellectually rich, warm, creative, and nurturing environment.

Over the period it took to research and write this book, a profound change occurred in Ontario early childhood education policy. In 2007, when my eldest daughter was slated to attend kindergarten at our local public school, integrated early years services did not exist at that school. Children younger than age six were not eligible to attend the school's before- and after-school programming. It was a relief when Charles Pascal's early years report proposed just such a system of integrated service provision for all schools in Ontario for wrap-around play-based programming for children enrolled in junior and senior kindergarten delivered by and in the school. Although the school principal at the time assured me that wrap-around services for JK and SK children in that school would surely happen by the time my youngest was beginning senior kindergarten, education and care remain distinct services within the confines of a single building. As policy makers struggle to marry different organizational cultures and create a seamless day of early childhood education and care for all, it brings home the very message of this book: cultures move, but slowly.

PART ONE

Assessing the Scope of Policy Change in Liberal Welfare States

Constructing Policy Change in Early Childhood Education and Care: Scientific Avenues and Cultural Impediments in Liberal Welfare States

A remarkable expansion in early childhood education and child care (ECEC) programs has occurred in many OECD countries since the 1980s and 1990s, even while governments have instituted austerity measures in other areas. This book is about that transformation: Why is it happening? And what is the scope and substance of that change? Government spending on child care and early childhood education programs has increased especially dramatically as a percentage of GDP in the traditionally austere liberal welfare states of Australia, New Zealand, and the United Kingdom, and, within Canada, in the province of Quebec, relative to Canada's overall spending (see Figure 1.1). In Australia and the United Kingdom, per child spending on child care has increased dramatically as well (see Figure 1.2). ECEC spending in Canada and the United States has remained stagnant or even declined over this time period, even while those welfare states, along with Australia, New Zealand, and the United Kingdom, have witnessed increases in overall ECEC enrolment rates (see Figure 1.3).

While liberal welfare states still lag their Nordic counterparts on these measures, their "catching up" is a puzzle that requires explanation, especially given that empirical studies find little evidence of widespread cross-national policy expansion in other social policy areas (with the exception of family policies such as maternity and parental leave) (Emmenegger et al., 2012; Heichel, Pape, and Sommerer, 2005; Starke, Obinger and Castles, 2008; White, 2009b). Puzzling too is the relative laggardness of the United States and Canada, even compared to their other liberal counterparts. But most striking is the variation in the choices governments make at both the national and sub-national levels to invest in more educationally based

Figure 1.1. Variation in public expenditure on ECEC services (0–6 Years) as % GDP in selected OECD countries, 2000 and 2011

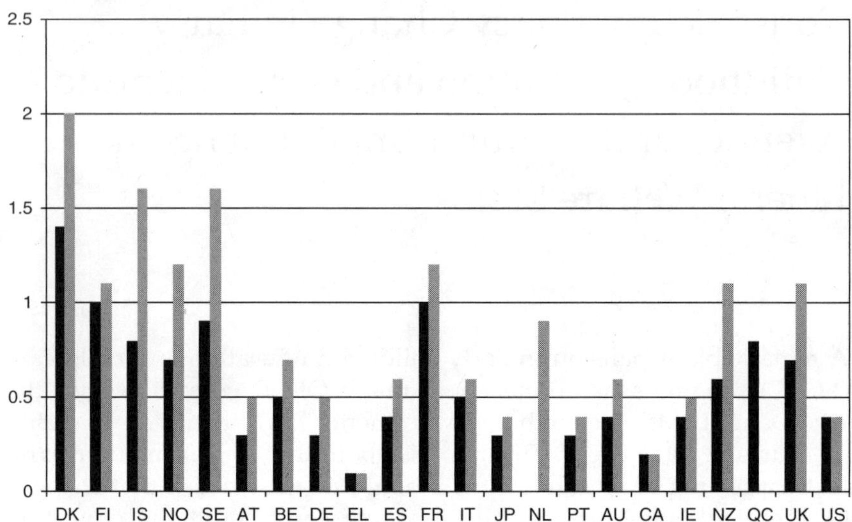

Sources: OECD (2014b, *Family Database* PF 3.1); 2003 Quebec data from OECD (2005, pp. 17, 109) and are from 2001.
Country key: AT = Austria; AU = Australia; BE = Belgium; CA = Canada; DE = Germany; DK = Denmark; EL = Greece; ES = Spain; FI = Finland; FR = France; IE = Ireland; IS = Iceland; IT = Italy; JP = Japan; NL = Netherlands; NO = Norway; NZ = New Zealand; PT = Portugal; QC = Quebec; SE = Sweden; UK = United Kingdom; US = United States

pre-primary programs or more care-based programs structured around parents' workdays (see Figure 1.4). What explains why governments choose to devote public resources to, and expand spaces in, one program or both or none at all?

This book explores these questions in two parts. The first part investigates the sources of the policy ideas that triggered these policy changes, and their promoters, and what explains their increasing salience in liberal welfare states. The second part examines what accounts for cross-national and within-country variation in the implementation of these ECEC policy ideas in the United States and Canada, where, for decades, public investment in these services for all but the poorest families has faced significant opposition. Recent investments reveal huge variation in the scope, delivery mechanisms, and financing between and within these national jurisdictions.

Figure 1.2. Public expenditure per child on child care and pre-primary education[a] in US$ (PPP converted) in selected countries, 1998 and 2011

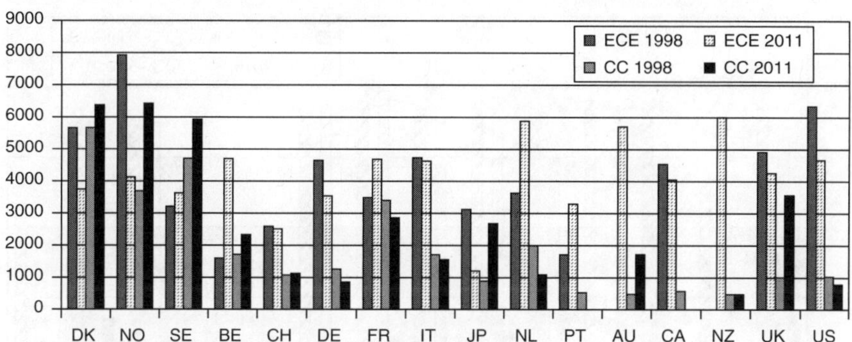

Sources: 1998 pre-primary data from OECD (2001b, p. 190); 2011 pre-primary data from OECD (2014b, *Family Database* PF3.1.B). Pre-primary data for Canada for 2003 are from Friendly et al. (2007, p. 80) and represent spending per child in the province of Ontario only for 2005–6. Figures across provinces and territories vary quite widely and are often not reported by the provinces and territories in comparable form. See Friendly et al. (2007, pp. 203–4). Pre-primary data for Australia not available.
1998 child care data calculated from OECD (2011) www.oecd.org/els/social/expenditure; Stats OECD: http://stats.oecd.org/wbos/default.aspx?datasetcode=SOCX_AGG. 2011 child care data from OECD (2014b, *Family Database* PF3.1.B). 2011 child care data for Canada not available.
Note: data are missing for some years
Country key: AU = Australia; BE = Belgium; CA = Canada; CH = Switzerland; DE = Germany; DK = Denmark; FI = Finland; FR = France; IS = Iceland; IT = Italy; JP = Japan; NL = Netherlands; NO = Norway; NZ = New Zealand; PT = Portugal; SE = Sweden; UK = United Kingdom; US = United States
[a] Data on pre-primary programs are limited to "organized centre-based programmes designed to foster learning and emotional and social development in children for 3 to compulsory school age. Day care, play groups and home-based structured and developmental activities may not be included in these data."

The choice to focus on these two countries – laggards in ECEC investment compared to the United Kingdom, Australia, and New Zealand, and indeed to most other welfare states – helps illuminate this book's principal argument: the primary mechanisms for policy change are not simply rational – that is, grounded in evidence-based arguments and instrumentally rational calculations about the costs and benefits of early years programs – but also cultural. Early years programs and services are part of contemporary cultural debates as they raise larger questions regarding the family and particularly the role of mothers in the family

Figure 1.3. Enrolment levels in child care and early childhood education services in selected OECD countries, 1998 and 2010

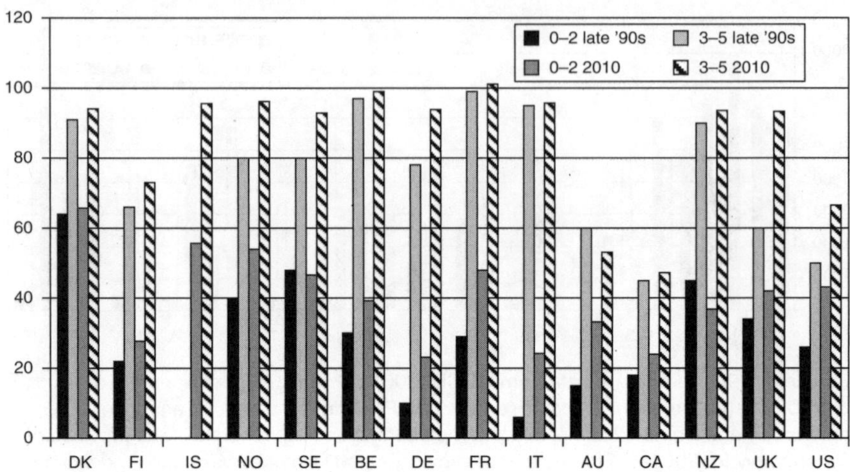

Sources: Late 1990s figures from OECD (2001a, p. 144); 2008 figures from OECD (2014b, *Family Database* PF 3.2.A); data for late 1990s for Canada are from HRDC (1997, p. 12) but do not include kindergarten figures; data for United States for late 1990s are from Kamerman (2000, p. 21) and figure is for 3–4-year-olds.
Note: OECD child care enrolment data include public and private child care centres, family day care homes, and child minders for children ages 0–3 and thus may include some pre-school programs. Early childhood education enrolment data include all organized centre-based programs that are designed to foster learning and emotional and social development in children from 3 to compulsory school age.

and the labour market. Gender norms regarding the appropriateness of women's labour market participation remain powerfully persuasive in some quarters, making child care and early learning still-contested policy areas, even while changing scientific beliefs about early childhood have altered both government and societal beliefs about the acceptability of early years programs.

Shifts in scientific understandings of childhood, as well as policy leadership to implement policies based on human capital development arguments, have encouraged shifts in both cognitive beliefs and principled beliefs with regard to the economic and social benefits that arise from high-quality early years programs. Since the 1970s, research on specific early years interventions, much of it based on longitudinal experimental studies in the United States, has demonstrated that

Figure 1.4. Public expenditure per child on early childhood education and child care in US$ (PPP converted), 2011

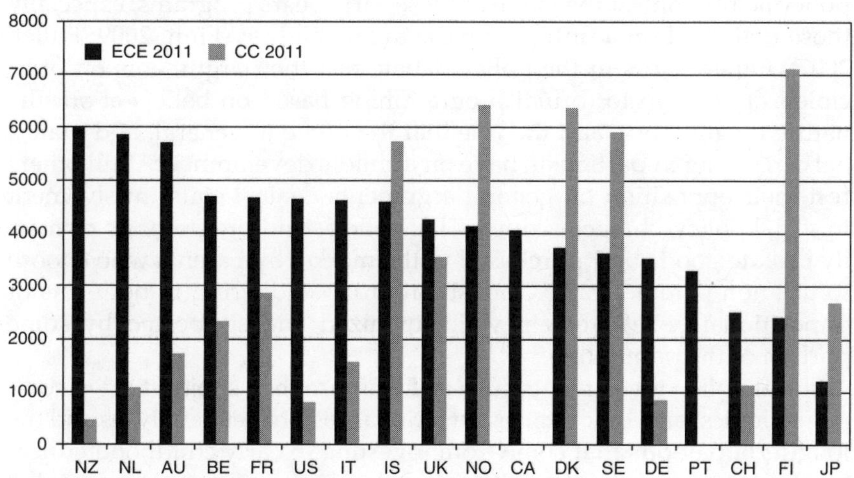

Souroo: OECD (2014b, *Family Database* PF 3.1.B).
Note: Child care figures are missing for Canada and Portugal.

specific early years interventions can mitigate young children's cognitive and non-cognitive deficits. Three of the most widely cited US-based longitudinal studies are the Perry High Scope study (Belfield et al., 2006; Schweinhart et al., 2005), the Carolina Abecedarian study (Campbell et al., 2012; Ramey et al., 2000), and the Chicago Child–Parent Centers study (Reynolds et al., 2011; Temple and Reynolds, 2007). Taken together, these studies point to the positive impact of high-quality early interventions on vulnerable populations of children on a number of cognitive and non-cognitive measures, beginning with demonstrated higher IQ scores, better performance in school, higher high school completion rates, and, in later years, higher incomes earned, fewer arrests, higher rates of homeownership, higher rates of ownership of a second car, lower use of welfare and other social assistance, longer marriages, and fewer births outside marriage. These and other research findings and their popularization in various media have helped shift policy makers' and societal beliefs.

Policy changes, however, are not inevitable, nor are they consistent across jurisdictions. Indeed, the pattern of policy adoption bears little resemblance to rational policy diffusion. Research pointing to the benefits of these program interventions is accumulating (Shonkoff and Phillips, 2000; Reynolds et al., 2010); even so, some researchers and policy actors contest the value of these early years programs, especially those delivered on a universal basis to all children (Finn, 2009; Fuller, 2007). Other actors in the policy debate rest their arguments on principled opposition to formal programming based on beliefs about the nature of childhood and the role that the home in general, and maternal caregiving in particular, have on a child's development.[1] Still others rest their opposition on general arguments against state involvement in social policy, characterizing ECEC policies and programs as primarily private goods best purchased in the market by parents who choose to use non-parental care. Opposition groups adhering to both sets of oppositional beliefs remain well organized and supported by some portion of the population.[2]

Social policy investments such as ECEC are thus subject to two competing logics: one logic focuses on rational cost–benefit analyses and the long-term pay-offs that come from investing in early childhood education and care over the long term; the other logic is rooted in principled beliefs and focuses on values and norms around state investment vis-à-vis markets and the family. Social policy investments differ, therefore, from other policy areas that also have a policy investment logic underpinning them, such as pension policy. As Alan Jacobs (2011) argues, pension investments are subject to inter-temporal trade-offs ("Should I spend now and reap the immediate satisfaction from that spending, or should I save and reap the benefits in future from having made that investment?"). The main challenge in the pension policy field is convincing people to make those inter-temporal trade-offs and to engage in rational discounting of the benefits of investment. Once those inter-temporal investment debates are resolved, policy discussions then turn to questions of instrument choice (e.g., defined benefit versus defined contribution pension schemes) and policy settings.

Similarly in the field of environmental policy, policy makers and the public are subject to inter-temporal logics as well as concerns about risk and potential environmental harms that come from the negative externalities of economic and other development (e.g., should we make investments in resource extraction where there are potential environmental harms, or should we adopt a precautionary approach that compromises economic development?).

The social policy investment model of policy change developed in this book posits that some policy debates occur at both the cognitive level ("What is the evidence basis to achieve the largest returns on human capital investments?") and at the normative level ("What 'ought' the state to do, given principled beliefs about the appropriate relationship between the state and family and children within the family?"). ECEC policy discussions centre not only on the role of the state in funding and delivering social programs but also on the role of the family and the connection to parenthood and mothers' roles in particular. Policy change requires a shift in values more fundamental than simply persuading policy decision makers to act based on some evidentiary claims. Overcoming previously strongly held views about the appropriate role of the state vis-à-vis markets and families is equally important.

Early years policy change is thus more equivalent to what Rochon (1998) labels "culture moves," those societal shifts that involve changes in the perception of issues confronting policy makers. Rochon (1998) developed the concept of "culture move" to capture the importance of observed changes in cultural values in the United States in the late twentieth century regarding civil rights and desegregation, women's rights (including reproductive rights), environmentalism, and so on. The acceptability of marriage between partners of the same sex, the appropriateness of teaching evolution in schools, and the value of abstinence-only education all centre on principled beliefs about what the family is, what values should be inculcated in children, and what values should guide teachers and student learning (Berkman and Plutzer, 2010; Brennan, 2006; Davison Hunter, 1991; Zimmerman, 2002). Some contemporary cultural battles centre on religious issues indirectly rather than directly and involve debates over science and the weight that should be granted to scientific expertise in policy making (Byers, 2011; Drori et al., 2003; Pielke, 2007). Debates over the permissibility of stem cell research (Ho, Brossard, and Scheufele, 2008), and the scepticism evidenced in some quarters – especially in the United States – over the human causes of climate change (Hoffman, 2011a, 2011b) all rest to some extent on principled *and* cognitive beliefs.

A culture move is said to occur when something that was seen as morally "bad" becomes morally "good" or at least societally acceptable (e.g., women working outside the home), or when something that was seen as morally acceptable becomes bad (e.g., segregation). Shifts in norms that are widespread are the best measure of culture change and are revealed not just in policy enactments but also in public support for those enactments. As will be seen with regard to both Alberta and California, initial efforts to enact universal early childhood education programs failed in the face of public opposition. The process by which culture moves occur, therefore, is often not rational and systematic; instead it is slow, as well as contingent on the confluence of particular actors, institutional opportunities, and events; over time, this confluence brings about changes in beliefs and practices. Small events can bring about large changes in policy discussions; for example, the media's attention to and popularization of a particular study can help transform the public's and policy makers' principled beliefs.[3] When those principled beliefs are transformed so as to become widely held, and reflected in public opinion and in policy discussions, cultural shifts can result.

This book acknowledges the often contingent nature of this change process and unveils a more complex account of successful policy investments that focuses on three key causal mechanisms: (1) science and the role of experts in shifting cognitive *and* principled beliefs around early childhood, (2) the role and autonomy of political leadership and policy advocates promoting those new norms, and (3) the framing strategies of those political leaders and policy entrepreneurs and the frame dynamics that arise during public discussion, particularly around the credibility and legitimacy of the state when it comes to delivering programs that supplant the family or market.

Choice of Cases

This book tracks policy responses in the liberal welfare states of Australia, Canada, New Zealand, the United States, and the United Kingdom, but focuses in particular on the United States and Canada.[4] Both of these countries have evidenced rather rapid policy change at the state/provincial level over the past decade but exhibit huge variation in policy choices. Given the size and scope of policy investment in other policy areas such as health care and parental leave, we would have predicted more rapid growth in Canada (Swank, 2002, p. 239; see also comparative data in Alesina and Glaeser, 2004; Pontusson, 2005). However, governments in the United States have increased both child care and pre-school program investments earlier and more extensively than in Canada. Since the late 1990s, the vast majority of US states – forty out of fifty as of 2013, according to the National Institute for Early Education Research (Barnett et al., 2013, p. 6) – have introduced or expanded early childhood education programs, and these programs enrol children younger than age 5. Over one-quarter (28 per cent) of all 4-year-olds in the United States attend a pre-school program, and 4 per cent of 3-year-olds (Barnett et al., 2013, p. 9). That is in addition to the more than 75 per cent of children who attend a full-day kindergarten program in the United States, according to the Children's Defense Fund (2014). Eleven states and the District of Columbia have in place a statutory requirement to provide full-day kindergarten programs, ensuring the same level of funding as grade one. Child care spending per child has increased in that time period as well in the United States.

Canada – with the exception of the province of Quebec – in contrast, remained throughout most of the 2000s an outlier among OECD countries in terms of ECEC program investment (see Figure 1.1). Nationally, child care policy development froze entirely in the same time period (Friendly and White, 2012). In terms of both pre-school enrolment expansion and national spending on a per child basis and as a percentage of GDP, Canada lags the United States. Provincially, however, in the late 2000s, a number of governments – British Columbia, Ontario, Prince Edward Island, and most recently Newfoundland – invested in universal full-day kindergarten for children aged 5 and, in Ontario, aged 4 as well.[5] That investments vary both cross-nationally and between states/provinces is a puzzle to be investigated.

It is perhaps not surprising that US governments would pursue pre-school programs more enthusiastically than Canadian governments. The United States has long valued public education as a means to support individual equality of opportunity as well as collective social stability (Garfinkel et al., 2010; Hochschild and Scovronick, 2003; Kaestle, 1983), even when it has neglected to develop other robust welfare state programs such as health care and paid maternity and parental leave. The United States also faces greater pressure than Canada to address poor educational outcomes (see, e.g., the report of the National Commission on Excellence in Education, 1983; as well as the Program for International Student Assessment [PISA] results of cross-national student educational performance throughout the 2000s). In addition, the US Educate America Act of 1994, the No Child Left Behind Act of 2001, and Common Core state educational standards have placed pressure on public schools to improve overall student performance and close achievement gaps between more and less advantaged students (Manna, 2006; Manna and McGuinn, 2013; McGuinn, 2006; Vinovskis, 2009). The expectation therefore would be for states to adopt or expand targeted programs that focus on the most at-risk children. Instead, a number of state-led initiatives over the past decade have emphasized *universal* pre-k. Why? And why has the notion of universal pre-kindergarten (UPK) been accepted and implemented in some states, such as Georgia and Oklahoma, but not in others, such as California? And why has UPK been much slower to develop in Canada, although full-day kindergarten is catching on?

This book explores policy changes over a large time span (the 1960+ period) but with more specific attention paid to the 1995–2010 period. The early 1960s saw the advent of the second wave feminist movement (Freedman, 2002), the contemporary upward trend in women's labour market participation, and the concomitant emergence of some child care services in North America, and in liberal welfare states generally. Despite the increase in women's labour market participation, child care availability remained uneven, with varying degrees of state funding and delivery. Those developments form the backdrop to more recent policy changes.[6] The year 1996 saw a revolution in social assistance policy in North American welfare states – in the United States, with the move from Aid to Families with Dependent Children (AFDC) to Temporary Assistance for Needy Families (TANF), and in Canada, with the move from the Canada Assistance Plan (CAP) to the Canada Health and Social Transfer (CHST) (Mink, 1998; Timpson, 2001).[7] The post-TANF period also saw increased policy attention to early childhood education and a shift in attention to "pre-k," especially in the United States (Bushouse, 2009; Cohen, 2001; Kirp, 2007; Rose, 2010).

Policy Changes and Culture "Moves"

In both the United States and Canada, governing elites and organized interest groups have mobilized around all sides of the policy issue, especially as a number of transnational and domestic epistemic communities (Haas, 1992), advocacy organizations, charitable foundation projects, and research institutes have emerged (Bushouse, 2009; Karch, 2013). The general public is attentive to ECEC debates as well, but opinion is divided – sometimes deeply so – because those debates are linked to broader opinions about family and the relationship between family and the state. Organized interest groups, advocacy associations, policy experts, and government officials have played key roles in shaping the debate over policy and have affected public opinion on the issue. But the configuration of interest groups and interest group politics cannot on its own account for the variations in program adoption.

The argument developed in this book is that one cannot fully understand the pattern of ECEC policy provision and policy change in these countries without understanding the beliefs, both principled and scientific (i.e., rational cognitive), that inform public opinion and policy decision making, as well as shifts in those beliefs. As documented in this book, there has been a sea change in how experts, policy makers, and practitioners talk about the education and care of young children. This change has been driven in part by the scientific research described in chapter 4 and by the transnational networks described in chapter 5. It makes sense to conceptualize this change as a "culture move" if we understand culture as a "logic of appropriateness" that constrains the range of legitimate solutions available to policy makers. The framing of policy investments around scientific evidence does much to shift policy actors' cognitive and principled beliefs around ECEC. This framing's success in significantly shifting policy, however, depends on institutions and politics: policy making in this area still invokes a conflict between evidence-based arguments and principled beliefs about the appropriate role and scope of government. I outline below the main causal factors contributing to policy change.

Science and the Role of Experts in Informing Cognitive
and Principled Beliefs

Culture moves first require normative shifts in policy makers' thinking. Part of that shift has occurred in the ECEC policy area as a result of science and scientific expertise. The agents of science are *epistemic communities* – communities of scientific experts (Haas, 1992) – who are influential because of the weight of scientific authority they carry. They are linked to the policy system as advisers or decision makers, and they ground their recommendations primarily in scientific knowledge rather than in social critique (Rochon, 1998, p. 25). Campbell and Pedersen (2011, p. 167) label the sets of actors, along with the organizations with which they are affiliated, and the connected institutions, as a "knowledge regime" that "produce[s] and disseminate[s] policy ideas that affect how policy-making and production regimes are organized and operate." These knowledge regimes, Campbell and Pedersen (2011, p. 167) argue, "are important because they contribute data, research, theories, policy recommendations, and other ideas that influence public policy."

Dobbin and colleagues (2007, p. 452) observe that broader "social acceptance of a policy approach can happen in three different ways:

(a) leading countries serve as exemplars (follow-the-leader); (b) expert groups theorize the effects of a new policy, and thereby give policy makers rationales for adopting it; or (c) specialists make contingent arguments about a policy's appropriateness, defining it as right under certain circumstances."

Those patterns of policy change can be observed in a number of liberal welfare states regarding ECEC programs. The science tended to be ignored for long periods. Then, as policy makers started to face domestic crises – in the United States, declining educational performance, and in the United Kingdom, labour market and poverty problems (Waldfogel, 2010) – they began to adopt these programs, even if the particular policy "solutions" that emerged did not completely match those found in scientific and social scientific studies.

In contrast to a model of policy making that assumes comprehensive rationality on the part of policy makers, however, this book uncovers evidence of a more bounded rationality at work. First, policy makers work within organizations and share interpretive frameworks that create ways of thinking that are akin to what Blyth (2001) labels cognitive locks (see also Blyth 2002). As Skogstad and Schmidt (2011, p. 6) argue, "'normal' policy-making is guided by more or less coherent interpretive frameworks that consist of beliefs about how the world works and should work in a policy domain." Policy actors are governed by shared logics regarding their policy goals and by their methods for achieving those goals; these logics then structure their thinking and limit the range of policy responses. The comparative politics literature refers to these shared logics as *policy paradigms* (Hall, 1993). These shared understandings of cause and effect dominate a wide range of policy areas and professions such as economics and finance (Hall, 1989), agricultural policy (Skogstad, 2008), and biotechnology (Montpetit, Allison, and Varone, 2007), as well as, as we will see, early childhood education and child development. The wide variation in the starting age of compulsory education, for example – from age 5 in the United Kingdom to age 7 in some Nordic countries – highlights the cognitive lock-in that occurs around developmental scientists' assumptions about young children's reasoning ability, as well as the variation in those shared norms. Dodd (1994, p. 332) argues that policy makers and other participants in the policy process hold tightly to these views "until informational stimuli pass a critical threshold of change, whereupon societal participants engage in an experimental search for a new strategy of action." Once that happens, Weyland (2008, p. 287) argues, policy change can often be "disproportionate in both directions. For a long time decision makers do less than a rational assessment of [what] the situation calls for and instead try to muddle through; but when problems get out of hand, they finally confront the ongoing deterioration, act with full force, and effect a breakthrough. This lengthy hesitation and eventual boldness gives rise to the 'punctuated equilibria' that scholars have observed." Thus policy change "is likely to be asymmetrical: many minor adjustments are occasionally punctuated by major restructuring" (Weyland, 2008, p. 287).

In other words, policy change does not occur in a comprehensively rational way. Scientific findings can emerge in such a way that participants recognize the limitations of their theories of how the world works with reality. If participants easily recognize the gap between their shared understandings (epistemology) and how the world really works (ontology), this can lead to an epistemological reconstruction (Dodd, 1994, p. 335). But if the gap between epistemology and ontology grows wide, then epistemological reconstruction may take longer and be more difficult and will result in major cultural clashes, such as the debate over the "reality" of climate change (Hoffman, 2011a, 2011b). Negative reactions to new policy ideas can impede policy change. At the same time, worshipful embrace of new ideas can be seen in those who want change. A logic of appropriateness can then come to dominate policy discussions.

Culture: Informing Principled Beliefs

The same cognitive locks that constrain policy makers' decision making also encourage a logic of appropriateness and not just logic of consequence in society at large (March and Olsen, 1989; Powell and DiMaggio, 1991). Societal and government actors are motivated by rational beliefs about best practices to achieve the public good, but also by subjective beliefs about appropriate action. In other words, actors are not simply self-interested and utility maximizing; they are also governed by a kind of rationality that has cognitive, moral, and subjective aspects (Dryzek, 1992, p. 401). This means that both policy makers and the public can be swayed by emotion, habit, appeals to authority, and similar factors. Accepting this view of decision making leads us to consider the impact of principled beliefs, culture, and norms in policy making.

Culture refers to "shared conceptions of reality, institutionalized meaning systems, and collective understandings that guide policy making" (Campbell, 2001, p. 163). Cultural theorists have long argued that if we accurately understand human decision making, then we will take seriously the interaction between preferences and norms (Ross, 1997). Wilson (2000) argues, for example, that "individual preferences continuously affect the normative order while the norms themselves are one of the influences that shape preferences." But preferences and culture are not identical and thus cannot be derived simply by aggregating individual preferences (Wilson, 2000, p. 264). Furthermore, as Wildavsky (1987, p. 4) argues, human beings do not have a full smorgasbord of preferences laid out for them at birth. Rather, the available combinations of values and preferences have already been prepared for us. We do not choose à la carte; rather, we choose from a set menu. Thus "only second-level choices (which of the available ways of life do I prefer?) and third-level choices (which policies do I believe are efficacious in supporting my preferred way?) are potentially available to choice." All of these "worldviews, ethical positions, and identity contribute[] to and help[] constitute an individual's rationality" (Dryzek, 1992, p. 401). Wilson (2000, p. 264) argues that cultures are "the product of both *social* (for example, rules that coordinate role relationships within organizations) and *psychological* (for example, the preferences of individuals) influences but are not reducible to either." "Culture" has both subjective and inter-subjective or shared aspects. However, there is not always agreement on the shared beliefs. A culture can contain many contradictory ideas and traditions (Phillips and Hardy, 2002, pp. 1–2; Wedeen, 2002, p. 715).

Unlike other cultural theorists, I am not using the term culture to refer to national orientations of citizens towards political objects (Almond and Verba, 1963; Lockhart, 2003; Thompson et al., 1990); nor do I define culture as comprising simply individual orientations towards objects (Inglehart, 1990). Rather, I see culture as comprising shared patterns of meaning making that "constrain the normative range of legitimate solutions available to policy makers" (Campbell, 2001, p. 166; see also Legro, 2000, p. 420; Wedeen, 2002, p. 714). A logic of appropriateness, rather than a logic of consequence, can sometimes dominate decision making even when policy makers are striving to be rational (March and Olsen, 1989; 1996). Culture is distinguishable from *ideologies*, which are coherent sets of shared beliefs, values, and principles, typically expressed by political groupings, about social, political, and economic relations (Gerring, 1997). Unlike cultural beliefs, ideologies usually contain both diagnoses of problems and recommended policies for solving them. Cultural beliefs around childhood, family, and maternal employment become normative – inviolable – and the moral "goods" and "bads" of policy become detectable in the responses to their violation or challenge.

Policy Frames and Culture Moves

This book asserts that policy decision making is often grounded both in appeals to science- or evidence-based arguments and in norms and other principled beliefs. One must therefore observe the value connections that government officials and the public articulate in policy debates through their particular word choices. Are ECEC policies part of a progressive politics to rehabilitate poor families and thus crucial to welfare reform? Are they vital to promote gender equality? Are they educational and developmental? Or are they negative, undermining crucial ways of life? Words and arguments inform ways of thinking about an issue as well as possible solutions to policy challenges.

Language becomes the key marker of our views and understanding of a policy area (Fairclough, 1995; Phillips and Hardy, 2002). The scope and substance of cultural shifts can be uncovered through the study of language in general and of specific policy frames in particular. Frames are "symbols and concepts that help policy makers to legitimize policy solutions to the public" (Campbell, 2001, p. 166).[8] To frame, as Entman (1993, p. 52) argues, is to "select some aspects of a perceived reality and make them more salient in a communicating text, in such a way as to promote a particular problem definition, causal interpretation, moral evaluation, and/or treatment recommendation." Frames provide the crucial levers of policy change within extant norms because they have the power to alter beliefs and preferences. Framing ideas "in the right way" by applying linguistic and other cues can alter people's perceptions of problems or issues and can influence their judgment of a situation and their choices (Druckman, 2010; Fischer, 2003; Tversky and Kahneman, 1981; Lakoff and Johnson, 1980; Schneider and Ingram, 1993). Successful policy change is therefore highly contingent on the framing strategies of proponents and detractors.

Which frames are used is key to understanding why certain ideas diffuse (Dobbin, Simmons, and Garrett, 2007, p. 452). The language of "child care" conjures up images of institutionalized care and "warehousing" of children and, concomitantly, the weakening of the family and parental influences (Dorfman and Woodruff, 1999; McManus and Dorfman, 2002). "Early childhood education," in contrast, connects to already strong principled beliefs about the value of education and tacks on to images of the school as (potentially) a place of learning. When those "school" images are positive, then early childhood education is also viewed positively and as instrumental to other societal goals. "Universal pre-k" can be persuasive language to sell the idea of extending pre-school to all young children. However, when schools are perceived as poor in quality, early childhood education may be regarded in a negative light.

Framing Strategies That Lead to Policy Change and,
Ultimately, Culture Moves

Successful policy change occurs when policy advocates manage to shift the terms of debate to accept the principle of early years investments. A key mechanism for transforming policy debates involves shifting the language used to describe the policy. This can mean substituting a negative principled belief for a positive one, or substituting a principled belief for an instrumentally rational reason rooted in the perceived benefits of policy change. ECEC debates often fall within the category of what Mucciaroni (2011, p. 193) calls "hybrid" cases, where often one side in a policy debate focuses on the instrumental rational benefits of adopting a particular policy instrument or setting and the other side focuses on principled beliefs about appropriate levels of state involvement in the economy and social policy.

In policy debates in which all sides draw on instrumentally rational arguments about the "best" course of action to achieve a given policy end, successful frames are those that make the best case in utilitarian terms. "Rational course of action" thus becomes a strategic means to frame arguments, along with appeals to strategic or material benefits. The ability to draw on the imprimatur of "science" also is helpful. ECEC advocates have gradually recognized the appeal of science and shifted their arguments from ones that rest on normative claims about gender equality and support for mothers' labour market participation (White, 2001b) to "these policies are good for children and the economy" (Prentice, 2009; Warner, 2009). The frame shifts are reflected even in the language used to describe programs: from "child care" or "day care" to "early childhood education and care" or "educare" or "pre-school" or "pre-kindergarten" (White, 2004b).

Shifting the policy debate from appeal to first principles to appeal to rational policy investment logics places greater weight on evidentiary claims and can act as a bulwark against attacks based on appeals to principles and norms. But if policy makers initiate discussions about the specifics of a policy – the instruments and settings[9] – while opponents are still questioning the legitimacy of state action, this *asymmetry* in framing favours oppositional principled beliefs over instrumentally rational policy investment arguments. Only after the public accepts a policy goal can debate move to questions of instrument choice, policy settings, and other rational implementation concerns. And while instrumentally rational arguments grounded in evidence are a necessary condition for policy reform, they are not sufficient to ensure successful and sustained implementation without *autonomous and credible political leadership* and *perceived trustworthiness or legitimacy of state institutions*. Because social policy investments differ from policies that involve technical rational discussions, they raise fundamental and principled debates about goals; they are thus vulnerable to attacks focused on the legitimacy of state action and/or political leadership, and this can ultimately detract from discussion of instrumentally rational policy implementation.

A Roadmap to What Follows

The rest of this book maps the shifts in policy makers' and the public's perceptions of early childhood education and care and documents the varied success in enacting policy change across the two country cases. It begins with an examination of the ECEC policies and programs that have emerged over time in liberal welfare states. Drawing on a variety of descriptive statistical data as well as primary and secondary sources comprised of government documents, and the secondary and scholarly literature, chapter 2 outlines the policies and programs in place in a broad set of OECD countries that are revealing of core beliefs around early childhood and motherhood. The chapter then traces the broad policy changes, shifts in practices, and institutional shifts evident in liberal welfare states over the past decade. The chapter uses these observations of institutional and policy change to build the case that a "culture move" is in progress across liberal welfare states. The policy changes under way suggest that policy makers' attitudes are shifting such that child care (and, concomitantly, maternal employment) is no longer regarded as "bad" and early childhood education and care is sometimes seen as "good."

Observing trends does not reveal *why* policy changes occur and why certain policy ideas are adopted or rejected. Chapter 3 examines alternative explanations for these changes. Actor-centred accounts and those that focus on transnational diffusion are found to be important albeit insufficient to account for the scope and substance of domestic policy change. Nor can political factors such as partisanship or the demographic composition of state and provincial legislatures account for the variation observed in the United States and Canada at the state/provincial levels; nor can political-economic factors such as GDP levels and/or growth, budget size, and deficit size; nor can population effects such as population homogeneity.

The remaining chapters focus, therefore, on the additional factors at work – ideas, norms, and policy frames, as well as the actions of particular sets of actors – in influencing policy choices. Using a variety of primary and secondary sources, including interview data, public opinion data, political speeches, and government and interest group documents, chapters 4 and 5 examine the idea carriers – that is, the epistemic and advocacy communities that initiated the shift in thinking ("child care isn't bad; it's good"!) within the broader policy community. These largely domestic epistemic communities and their knowledge regimes then helped provide the impetus to policy diffusion and policy change at a transnational and international level. Chapter 4 documents the domestic sources of the policy ideas, and chapter 5 documents the concomitant ideational transformation at the level of international organizations (IOs).

Those "push" factors are not sufficient to transform domestic policies, however, contrary to what international relations or transnational advocacy theories may expect (Finnemore and Sikkink, 1998; Meyer et al., 1997; Risse, Ropp, and Sikkink, 1999). While IOs' and transnational advocates' research and advocacy provided means to further transmit and popularize ideas about ECEC, they alone did not cause policy changes in advanced industrialized states such as the United States and Canada. Chapters 6 and 7 present empirical evidence of a more complex model of social policy change. They document the scope of change in the United States and Canada, focusing on the national as well as state and provincial levels. After reviewing a number of changes at the state and provincial levels, the chapters focus on a number of critical cases at the state and provincial level in the United States and Canada. Florida and Ontario provide the strongest evidence of the success of political leaders' appeals to policy investment frames that focused on evidence-based arguments and instrumentally rational calculations regarding the costs and benefits of early years investments; in California and Alberta, by contrast, policy leaders advocated for universal policies even while public sentiment challenged the very role of the state in delivering universal early childhood education programs. The concluding chapter reflects more on whether the breadth and depth of policy change is sufficient to support a claim of a "culture move" in ECEC.

The process of uncovering the explanatory factors for policy change involves mainly qualitative methods; it also involves performing "an archaeology of archival and textual material" (Campbell and Pedersen, 2001, p. 12) to reveal how policy makers and the broader public describe a policy and what value connections they make through the rhetoric they use (positive, negative). I use the analytic techniques of process tracing as well as thematic and discourse analysis[10] of documents and press releases to determine whether and to what extent the meanings attached to early childhood education and care changed among policy makers and the public. Drawing on material gathered from interviews, policy documents, and media reports, I document how the arguments used to justify program intervention shifted (or not). Interviews with relevant policy officials and organized interests help us discern, through interviewees' own self-assessments, how policy ideas emerged and key policy changes occurred, and what factors most influenced those changes.

Why Write This Book

This book offers a corrective to the comparative welfare state literature, which tends to focus on either structural accounts of policy change or agential accounts, ranging from power resources theories (Huber and Stephens, 2001; Korpi, 2006) to social movement theories and feminist analyses (O'Connor, Orloff, and Shaver, 1999). These accounts focus on the political opportunity structures that actors face and what actors do to extract resources from the state. These actor-centred approaches underemphasize that actors are also "acted upon" ideationally and institutionally. That is, actors exist in a normative context. Powerful cultural narratives work to discipline actors in a certain policy direction. Thus, policy outcomes are as much about contests over meaning and identity as they are about interests.

This book also provides evidence that ideas matter – not just specific programmatic ideas but *normative* ideas as well: people are motivated by the values they attach to things. The tools for studying meaning making in a systematic way, however, remain elusive. The public policy literature is dominated by materialist approaches such as rational choice that lead to, as Benford (1997, p. 419) argues, an overly cognitive conception of policy. Given the passionate debate surrounding a number of policy issues that seem on the surface to be well-grounded in science, such as health policy reform (Béland, Rocco, and Wadden, 2016; Morone, 2011) and climate change (Hoffman, 2011a, 2011b), policy researchers are remiss in neglecting the role of principled beliefs, norms, and values in policy making and the factors that can cause a shift in values.

Furthermore, analysis of early years programs and policies contributes to our theoretical and empirical understanding of the factors that contribute to the growth, shrinkage, or stagnation of the contemporary welfare state in general. Governments are facing major choices such as whether to spend money at all on social programs and, if so, on what kinds of programs and policy delivery mechanisms. A crucial policy research question is why governments make one choice over another. ECEC policy debates reveal a complex mix of policy logics: the inter-temporal trade-offs evidenced in pensions policy or infrastructure investment; the intertemporal trade-offs and risk logics in the area of climate change and environmental policy generally; and the redistributive conflicts that arise in debates over targeted versus universal social programs. In addition to the budgetary challenges and distributive questions raised in ECEC policy debates are complex inter-temporal and risk considerations (should we invest in *this child* in order to reap the possible future individual *and* societal rewards from that human capital investment?) – as well as questions of *who* should be entrusted to perform the function of care and education. Do we trust the state? Or do we trust families? Or markets (White et al., 2015)? The book uncovers and documents factors that underpin a *social investment model* of policy change.

Finally, are these policy changes simply adjustments to policy instruments and existing program settings, or is more fundamental paradigmatic change occurring in liberal welfare states? This book finds evidence of the beginnings of a profound policy paradigm change, but within fundamentally liberal welfare norms. There are glimmerings of more fundamental shifts in norms around parental employment. But gender norms regarding the appropriateness of women's labour market participation remain powerfully persuasive for some societal and government actors, making both child care and early childhood education still deeply contested policies.

Chapter Two

The Idea of Childhood and the Idea of Motherhood in Liberal Welfare States

The key question this book explores is how governments in liberal welfare states – which once conceptualized child care as a necessary evil for single parents and low-income families so that that they could participate in the labour market (Michel, 1999), and early childhood education as an optional program for the middle class and well-to-do (Beatty, 1995) – transformed their thinking so that they viewed integrated early childhood education and care programs as "good" for most if not all children and families (Liberal Party of Canada, 2006; White House Office of the Press Secretary, 2013). This chapter focuses in particular on liberal welfare states, but contrasts those policies and programs with other (mainly continental European) welfare states. The chapter documents policy makers' treatment of these policies and programs historically and then documents the policy and programmatic changes that have occurred, as indicated by changes in enrolment rates, levels of public funding, institutional procedures and organizational practices, and legislation and regulation. All of this will provide an empirical basis for the argument that a culture move is under way in ECEC policy making across liberal welfare states.

Historical Development of Early Childhood Education and Care Policies and Programs[1]

A plethora of programs and practices are captured under the ECEC label; however, some discernible patterns of provision can be observed in OECD countries that fall broadly under what Esping-Andersen (1990) labels welfare state regimes. The concept of welfare regime captures the view that industrialized countries' social policy provisions are governed by certain logics regarding the appropriate roles of the state, the family, and the market; those logics then underpin choices in social policy provision and affect social and economic outcomes (see also Esping-Andersen, 1999).[2] These patterns of provision rest on shared norms regarding the structure of waged work, the nature of citizenship, poverty and the value of redistribution, and the relationship between the state, the market, and the family. *Social democratic welfare regimes* tend to "decommodify" citizens in the sense that they do not always link eligibility for social policies directly to employment; also, their programs are often universally available and are sufficiently generous to provide viable options for those not earning income in the labour market. Governments in social democratic welfare states have assumed a great deal of responsibility for social reproduction[3] in order to promote social citizenship as well as, in more recent decades, gender equality (Lewis, 1992; O'Connor, 1993; Sainsbury, 1999). *Conservative welfare regimes*, in contrast, link a number of social entitlements to employment. Benefits may vary by occupation and income group. Corporatist arrangements sometimes include some support for social reproduction, but the state generally presumes that caregiving is primarily a family responsibility. Thus government programs for mothers and children have tended to support and reinforce women's caregiving (Kremer, 2007). *Liberal welfare regimes* have traditionally been less generous than those in other industrialized states in terms of public funding for and availability of social services, relying instead on markets to provide services and on families to provide care. Liberal welfare regimes traditionally conceive of social reproduction largely as a choice and thus as the responsibility of families themselves, with the state stepping in to assist only the very poor and other disadvantaged families. State-provided social supports tend to be need-based and subject to means tests (Orloff, 1993; 1996).

A number of scholars have built on the notion of regime clustering to identify how capitalist economies tend to cluster according to industrial relations regime, corporate governance, and labour relations. Hall and Soskice (2001) identify a similar clustering of liberal market economies (LMEs: Australia, Canada, Ireland, New Zealand, the United Kingdom, and the United States) and what they label coordinated market economies or what others (Rueda and Pontusson, 2000) label social market economies (CMEs: e.g., Austria, Belgium, Denmark, Finland, Germany, Japan, Sweden, and Switzerland). This research similarly reveals that countries with a particular configuration of industrial relations tend to develop complementary institutions; hence, LMEs and CMEs tend to share a number of characteristics on such indicators as union density and reliance on market mechanisms.

Furthermore, scholars have noted that in LMEs and CMEs, the configuration of the political economy affects the pattern of social service provision. Morgan (2005), for example, argues that the low-wage, low-skill pattern of employment in LMEs tends to foster markets for child care that is not state-subsidized. However, in unionized higher-wage economies that suffer from skills shortages, governments tend to provide services such as child care in order to encourage maternal participation in the labour market. And because of the high delivery costs for such services, governments also subsidize the costs of provision.

Liberal welfare regimes and liberal market economies are presumed to share a number of characteristics regarding care. For much of the twentieth century in the main liberal welfare states of Australia, Canada, New Zealand, the United Kingdom, and the United States,[4] middle- and upper-income families were expected to manage the tasks of social reproduction by themselves, either through mothers' own caregiving or through the purchase of private services in the market. Governments generally provided some income support for very poor families, as well as some funding of child care services; and gradually, early childhood development programs were targeted to highest-risk families, including Aboriginal and African American families. Otherwise, the market was expected to deliver services, mostly through low-wage formal (e.g., centre-based) and informal (at-home) service delivery.[5]

Liberal Welfare State Norms of Childhood, Motherhood, and Schooling

Interwoven with these labour market norms, traditional gender norms in each of these countries reinforced the notion that maternal care is best for young children and that non-maternal care structured around the parental workday "harms" children.[6] Those norms led to government reluctance or indifference when it came to funding services that would encourage white middle- and upper-class women with children in particular to participate in the labour market; yet governments did encourage the labour market participation of poor, minority, and immigrant women (Ladd-Taylor, 1994; Mink, 1995; Skocpol, 1992).

These norms around maternal caregiving clashed somewhat with norms regarding the age at which the education of young children should start and who should be responsible for socializing children. Middle- and upper-class women were discouraged from working, yet those same women saw the value of educational socialization, and this led to the development of a private nursery school movement in liberal welfare states (Beatty, 1995; Wollons, 2000); meanwhile, the state took on the role of socializing the poor, immigrants, and so on (May, 1997). That socialization was provided through a variety of services, though, and not just education; for example, social services programs were provided in child health, early childhood development, and proper child-rearing techniques.

Antipathy to the education of young children grew even as the notion of mass primary and secondary education spread. A number of researchers have documented how industrialized countries came increasingly to view mass education as part of an "articulated cultural project" of the modern state (Meyer, Ramirez, and Soysal, 1992, p. 131; see also, e.g., Alexander, 2000; Benavot et al., 1991; Ramirez and Boli, 1987). Governments in Europe and North America began to assume responsibility for providing its citizens with primary and secondary education.[7]

Deeply entrenched views of the appropriate age at which children should enter school, however, limited the breadth and depth of programs that states offered for children younger than compulsory school age. Beatty (1995, p. 23) argues that "in the 19th century, Americans were ready to accept the idea of privately controlled extra-familial education for young children but not the extension of public schooling to children under the age of six." The rationale for the age cut-off (discussed in more detail in chapter 4) stemmed from beliefs about the age at which children develop sufficient cognitive capacity to benefit from education. Ironically, prior to the development of common schools run by the state, there were no strict age cut-offs prior to which children could not attend school. For example, in the United States, Kaestle (1983, p. 15) reports that in many rural schools, children as young as age two or three attended for some months of the year. Kaestle (p. 15) also reports that many rural and farm families in America would send younger children to school to keep them from being underfoot, even while pulling older children from school to help with farmwork during busy periods.

Hulbert (2003, p. 25) points out that with industrialization, and certainly by the turn of the twentieth century, "home began to be conceived as the special, 'separate sphere' of women, who were no longer partners with men in productive household labour, nor part of the new world of more organized, increasingly mechanized work. Instead, they were expected to be soothing presences in an emotional, spiritual 'haven.'" Mothers took on the primary responsibility for raising children – for the domestic "science" of childrearing – a division of labour encouraged, of course, by experts who reinforced arguments that women were primary caregivers by nature (Grant, 1998).

Continental Europeans, in contrast, did not link childrearing and socialization exclusively to mothers and were more willing to embrace the formal educational socialization of younger children, first under church-run or voluntary organizations and then under state-run programs. Those programs did not necessarily promote explicitly educational goals or "schoolification." Instead, their guiding principle was that children could flourish in play-based programs in a group setting (Beatty, 1995). Some governments (e.g., Sweden in 1836, Britain in 1870, and France in 1881) recognized the value of these programs early on and took over responsibility for "infant schools" – programs for children below the age of compulsory school (Randall, 2000, p. 21; Bennett, 2008, p. 1). These programs were popular among the wealthy and the expanding middle class but were not generally options for poor families, which tended to rely on voluntary and often religious institutions for child care.

But in both North America and Europe, child care and early childhood education grew increasingly distinct. The two were viewed as separate functions and delivered by different types of service providers (Bennett, 2003). Different bureaucracies arose to administer programs, and different organizational cultures and personnel emerged. When a government took over regulatory authority for child care, it usually placed it under a health or social services ministry. Kindergarten or pre-school, in contrast, tended to be delivered by educational authorities. In the public's mind and in the minds of many policy makers, "care" was something that went on in non-parental, non-school-delivered child care services or in the home; "education" was what went on in school-based kindergartens and pre-schools. Even in countries where the educational socialization of young children was deemed more acceptable, such as in Belgium and France, formal programs tended to emphasize readiness for school (Jensen, 2009). Only in social democratic welfare states like Sweden and Denmark did a tradition of strong, play-based programs develop along with full-day programs (Bennett, 2003; Jensen, 2009).

This division of policies and programs has led to the emergence of two different organizational cultures that reflect but also shape societal views of these programs. For teachers, a school's educational culture does not consist of a seamless day but rather instructional chunks interspersed with long breaks for lunch and part days off during the week.[8] Many primary schools encourage children to go home for lunch rather than remain at school. Child care centres, in contrast, tend to operate for full days and long hours. From a societal, school, centre, and administrative perspective, meshing these cultures has been difficult.[9]

Table 2.1 captures some of the current variation in ECEC provision in OECD countries. Variation can be seen in the age at which children begin attending school on a compulsory basis (ranging from age 5 in Hungary, the Netherlands, New Zealand, and the United Kingdom, to age 6 in most other liberal and conservative welfare states, as well as Finland and Iceland, and to age 7 in the rest of the Nordic welfare states as well as in some Eastern European countries such as Poland and Romania) (Plantenga and Remery, 2009, p. 74). The length of the pre-school and primary school day varies enormously as well. In Germany, for example, school tends to begin between 7:30 and 8:30 a.m. and end between 11:30 a.m. and 1:30 p.m.; in France and England, school tends to begin at 9:00 a.m. and end between 3:00 and 4:00 p.m. with a break for lunch; in Spain, until recently, a long break of two-and-a-half hours in the school day was typical; in Italy, primary schools sometimes run only in the morning (Kamette, 2011). Such schedules are not easily compatible with full-time parental employment.

Variation can be observed as well in the degree of state involvement in educating, socializing, and funding care for children prior to their entry to compulsory school. Some governments tend to conceive of services for children ages 0 to 3 as "care" services, and services for children ages 3 to age of compulsory school as "educational" "pre"-school services (OECD 2001b; 2006). In other countries – mainly the Nordic countries – a single, public "pre-school" system cares for and socializes children for a much longer period of time before public school begins at age 6 or 7; the programs tend to be full-time centre-based services delivered by municipalities and other organizations as opposed to school-based education services; but they also deliver a strong pedagogy. In the United States, in contrast, "pre-school" is used to describe a variety of programs from Head Start, to kindergarten programs in schools, to full-day centre-based programs delivered by for-profit and not-for-profit operators, even to programs housed in private homes. Programs may be delivered by local authorities such as municipalities

Table 2.1. Typology of child care and early childhood education services in selected OECD countries

	Centre-based care			Family child care		Pre-school		Compulsory school	
Public*									
Private*									
Age	0	1	2	3	4	5	6	7	
Liberal ECEC regimes									
Australia	Accredited centres and family child care available part-time (20 hours) or full-time (up to 50 hours)				Reception/pre-school classes, with primary school (full-time, out-of-school-hours care also provided)			Compulsory schooling	
Canada	Centre-based and family child care				Junior Kindergarten Ontario	Kindergarten/ Maternelles in Quebec		Compulsory schooling	
New Zealand	Child care centres and some home-based services (family child care)		Community-based Kindergarten, Playcentres			Compulsory schooling			
UK	Nurseries, child minders, and playgroups		Playgroups and nurseries part-time	Reception class, with primary school		Compulsory schooling			
United States	Child care centres and family child care		Educational programs, including Head Start, pre-k			Compulsory schooling			
Liberal mimicking ECEC regimes									
Austria	Tagesmutter (family child care) and Krippen (centers), part-time (25 hrs)		Kindergarten (part-time, 25 hrs). Out-of-school care provision under development					Compulsory schooling	
Czech Republic	Crèche (centres), full-time		Materska skola (state kindergarten)						
Ireland	Regulated family child care and nurseries (centres)			Early Start and Infant school (pre-school) with primary school				Compulsory schooling	
Japan	Centre-based care							Compulsory schooling	
	Family child care		Kindergartens						

(Continued)

Table 2.1. Typology of child care and early childhood education services in selected OECD countries (Continued)

	Centre-based care	Family child care	Pre-school	Compulsory school
Public*				
Private*				
Liberal mimicking ECEC regimes				
Netherlands	Gastouderopvang (family child care), Kinderopvang (centres), and playgroups	Group 1, with primary school	Compulsory schooling (group 2 onwards)	
Poland	Nurseries	Pre-school/nursery schools		Compulsory schooling
Portugal	*Creche familiare* (family child care) and centres	*Jardins de infancia* (pre-school)		Compulsory schooling
Switzerland	*Creche, Krippen*, varies across cantons (centres)	Pre-school, mandatory in some cantons		Compulsory schooling
Continental ECEC regimes				
Belgium	*Kinderdagverblif* (centres) and family child care; *crèches*, and *gardiennes encdarées* (family child care)	*Kleuterschool*, pt or ft, with out-of-school-hours care; *école maternelle*, pt or ft, with out-of-school-hours care		Compulsory schooling
France	*Crèche* (centres) and *Assistant maternelles* (family child care),	*École maternelle* (pre-school)		Compulsory schooling
Germany	*Krippen* (centres)	Kindergarten (pre-school)		Compulsory schooling
Greece	*Vrefonipiaki stahmi* (*crèche* for children < 2.5 and nursery school for > 2.5	*Nipiagogeia* (kindergarten)		Compulsory schooling
Hungary	*Bolcsode* (*crèche*), ft (40 hrs)	*Ovoda* (kindergarten)		Compulsory schooling
Italy	*Asili nidi* (*crèches*) pt (20 hrs) and ft (< 50 hrs)	*Scuola dell-infanzia* (pre-school)		Compulsory schooling

Korea	Child care centres			Compulsory schooling
		Kindergartens		
		Hakwon (pre-school)		
Luxembourg	*Crèche* (centres) and *Tagesmutter* (family child care)	*Enseignement pre-scholaire* (pre-school)		Compulsory schooling
Mexico	*Educación inicial* (centres)		Compulsory *educación prescholar* (pre-school)	Compulsory schooling
Slovakia	Nursery schools	Kindergarten		Compulsory schooling
Spain	*Educación Pre-scolar* (centers)	Education infantile (pre-school) with primary school		Compulsory schooling

Nordic ECEC regimes

Denmark	*Dagpleje* (family child care) and *Vuggestuer* (crèches) ft (> 32 hrs)	*Bornenaver* (kindergarten) ft (> 32 hrs)		Compulsory schooling
	Adlersintegrer (age-integrated facility) full-time (> 32 hrs)		*Borne-haver* (> 32 hrs)	
Finland	*Perhepaivahoito* (family child care) and *Paivakoti* (municipal early child development centres), ft (< 50 hrs)		*Esiopetus* (pre-school)	Compulsory schooling
Iceland	Day-care centres and "day mothers" (family child care)	Pre-school	Compulsory schooling	
Norway	*Barnehage*, including rural *Familiebarnhager*, ft (40 hrs)		Compulsory schooling	
Sweden	*Forskola* (pre-school), ft (30 hrs), some *Familiedaghem* (family child care) particularly in rural areas		*Forskole-klass* (pre-school), pt	Compulsory schooling

* Provision is largely publicly funded and managed (more than 50 per cent of enrolments are in publicly operated facilities).
** Provision is largely managed by private stakeholders (both for-profit and not-for-profit providers) and is publicly and privately financed.
Source: OECD (2014b, *Family Database PF4.1*).

or schools, or by state or federal governments, or by child care centres or self-employed operators (Hustedt and Barnett, 2011).

Policy Changes Post-1960

Until the 1960s in both Europe and North America, mothers did not participate in the labour market in large numbers, albeit maternal employment rates varied across the OECD countries. After the late 1960s and early 1970s, rates of maternal employment increased tremendously, again with significant variation across OECD countries. A number of European countries began to establish or expand already existing child care and early childhood education services so that by the late 1980s, many continental European countries were providing child care and early childhood education programs, increasingly on a full-time basis (OECD, 2006).

At the same time, many governments moved towards integrating these services under a single administrative umbrella. In the early 1980s, most EC countries still placed programs for very young children (0 to 3 or 4) under ministries of health or social affairs, while placing programs for children ages 4 to the age of compulsory school under education ministries (Pichault, 1984, Table 1). Most liberal welfare states followed this model (Meyers and Gornick, 2003, p. 387), although in England and Wales, the education and science ministry traditionally was in charge of programs from age 3 (Pichault, 1984, Table 1). Note that the Nordic welfare states, especially Denmark and Sweden, had integrated their ECEC services decades earlier under their welfare ministries (Moss, 2006b, pp. 160–1).

In what Moss (2006b) calls a "second wave" of integration, a number of countries have integrated their ECEC administrations under their education ministries. New Zealand was the first country to transfer child care services from welfare to education in 1986, followed by Spain in 1990, Slovenia in 1993, Sweden in 1996, and England and Scotland in 1998 (but not Northern Ireland or Wales) (Moss, 2006b, pp. 161–4). In the United States, a number of states have established single administrative ECEC departments. For example, in 2004 Georgia founded the Department of Early Care and Learning; and Massachusetts in 2005 and Washington State in 2006 founded consolidated offices for early education and care from their old education and child care offices (OECD, 2006, p. 48). Other states have integrated responsibility for child care and early childhood education under a variety of governance models. For example, North Carolina has established an Office of School

Readiness, Connecticut has established an early childhood cabinet, and Ohio has established a public–private partnership called the Partnership for Continued Learning (OECD, 2006, p. 435).

As part of that integration, a number of countries and sub-national governments have developed national or state-level curriculum frameworks of the sort that exist for primary and secondary school: New Zealand, Norway, and Finland in 1996, Queensland and other state governments in Australia in 1997, Sweden in 1998, Scotland in 1999, and England in 2000 (Oberhuemer, 2005, p. 30).[10] Some of these curriculum frameworks, such as Sweden's, emphasize a whole package of social pedagogical goals (Bennett, 2005; Moss, 2006a, 2006b). Other national governments, such as Britain and the United States, concerned about student educational performance on cross-national education assessments, place more emphasis on school readiness (Jensen, 2009; Miller and Almon, 2009; Oberhuemer, 2005, p. 32).

Measuring the Extent of Norm Change in Liberal Welfare States

If we understand norms to mean rules or principles of "right" or appropriate action (Opp, 2001, p. 10,714; see also generally Finnemore and Sikkink, 1998), then measuring the extent of norm and policy change in liberal welfare states involves analysing the extent to which those rules and principles of appropriate action have changed, as revealed in government statements and policy pronouncements as well as legislation and program provision. The key sets of norms related to ECEC are those surrounding (a) *maternal employment* (i.e., whether states encourage or discourage maternal employment in law and policy); (b) *ECEC financing and program delivery* (state/market/family responsibility) as well as levels of financing; and (c) *ECEC system integration* (separate or integrated service delivery and system administration, including across orders of government). To track the extent of norm change, I have developed indicators of each of these sets of norms based on best practices identified, for example, in OECD reports (e.g., OECD, 2001b, p. 7; OECD, 2006, p. 3) (see Table 2.2).

Gender norm change can be measured by the extent to which a country provides labour market- and family-supportive family policies such as maternity and parental leave rights and paid leave provisions, as well as how effective that parental leave is (i.e., the extent to which the length of maternity/parental leave, combined with the wage replacement rate, usefully allows parents to take a leave from paid employment) (Plantenga and Siegel, 2004). Another indicator of gender norm

Table 2.2. Indicators of norm change in liberal welfare states

Policies supportive of maternal employment		Policies supportive of building an ECEC system		Policies supportive of ECEC system integration	
Paid maternity/ parental leave	Yes: CA, NZ, UK, AU No: USA	**Public spending on child care and ECE service operations and not just parent subsidies**	Yes: AU for certain specialized services, NZ, UK Minimal: USA federal and state No: CA at federal level; min at prov'al level	**All services administered under a single administrative authority within a level of govt**	Yes: AU: national Office of Early Childhood Education and Child Care NZ: Min of Education UK: Dept. of Education and Employment Some: CA, USA at state/ prov'al level No: CA, USA at federal level
Effective parental leave	Median: QC < median: AU, CA, NZ, UK, USA	**Universal versus targeted programs**	Yes: AU, NZ, UK for ECE NZ: govt. funding for all ECEC services but not for all parents Some universal ECE in USA states, CA provs QC: $7 per day child care where available; universal full-day kindergarten for age 5	**Service delivery coordination between levels of govt. (in federal systems)**	Yes: some recent attempts in AU Some: USA Minimal: CA since 2006
% employed mothers with children ages 3–5	> 60%: CA, NZ, USA < 60%: UK < 50%: AU	**Not-for-profit service delivery**	Yes: some provisions in CA Both: NZ govt. funds all forms of services but provides grants for not-for-profit services No: AU, UK, USA	**Involvement outside constitutional jurisdiction (in federal systems)**	Yes: AU, USA No: minimal in CA

% employed mothers with 3 or more children	> 60%: CA < 60%: AU < 50%: NZ, UK USA N/A	National regulations to improve quality	Yes: AU (National Quality Framework), NZ (Education (Early Childhood Services) Regulations), UK (Childcare Act) No: CA, USA
% women who work part-time	35% or more: AU, NZ, UK < 30%: CA < 20%: USA	National staffing standards	Yes: AU, NZ Commitment by 2015: UK No: CA, USA
Child care availability for younger age groups	> 40%: UK < 40%: NZ, USA < 20%: AU, CA	National curriculum	Yes: AU (Early Years Learning Framework), NZ (*Te Whariki*), UK (*Curriculum Guidance for the Foundation Stage*) No: CA, USA
Funding emphasis on universal full-day rather than part-day programs for younger children	More: AU, QC Both: NZ Less: CA, UK, USA	Public delivery of universally accessible services w/ costs assumed by state	None

Sources: Data amassed from chapter evidence; see also tables in this chapter.

change is the extent to which the state provides ECEC programs that are structured around the parental workday and for younger as well as older children. The extent to which government investment provides an effective system of parental employment support can be measured by the percentage of wage replacement provided and the percentage of ECEC program costs that parents assume, as well as the extent to which mothers with young children return to work after having a baby, or return to work full-time as opposed to part-time.

Measuring the extent of change regarding the norms around ECEC program delivery requires digging deeper than the indicators typically used, which include levels of public spending as a percentage of GDP or overall enrolment rates. Those measures reveal little about the kinds of services in place, the mandate (educational or otherwise) of those services, the length of time per day programs operate, the duration of the program in the year, and so on, all of which reveal a country's norms around ECEC. ECEC program spending may be low compared to other countries, but the programs that spending goes to may be of high quality because of high levels of investment historically or high regulatory standards. Similarly, a country's ECEC spending may be high or may have increased significantly, but programs may not be of high quality because of lack of regulatory standards. Australia, New Zealand, Quebec, the United Kingdom, and even the United States devote significant public resources to "educationally based" child care and pre-school programs, but as detailed below, they allow that funding to be spent on a variety of care providers in a variety of settings and with varied standards.

Kamerman (2000) has developed a number of additional indicators that draw attention to what Hall (1993) has labelled *policy instruments* and *policy settings*. Kamerman's indicators, which are revealing of changing norms around ECEC provision, include the following: ownership and agent responsible for delivery (government; private sector – either community-based organization or commercial, and if commercial, small-business or corporate); funding strategies (government; employer-based; parents; or combination); funding targets (the ECEC services themselves, or the users of services, e.g., parent vouchers); age group served (infants and toddlers; pre-schoolers; primary school-aged); other issues regarding scope and eligibility criteria (e.g., universal or targeted program delivery for the poor, children with working parents, and so on); locus of care (pre-primary school, child care centre, family child care, in-own-home); primary caregiver (professional; paraprofessional; parent); program philosophy and curriculum framework, if any, and scope (national/regional/local; mandatory or voluntary); quality and effectiveness indicators (e.g., child/staff ratios; indicators such as "school readiness" versus a focus on the whole child's social and emotional development); and accountability measures used to maintain quality and other policy goals.

ECEC system-building indicators identified include the following: the extent of state versus private funding of services; the degree to which services are universally available or targeted; the degree to which public spending supports service delivery (supply) and not just parental subsidies (demand); the extent of funding for formal as opposed to informal forms of care; the extent of government regulatory oversight and the imposition of standards such as staff training, child/staff ratios, and curriculum frameworks; and the extent of government delivery of services. Child care and early childhood education measures are tracked separately, even though one of the dimensions of norm change is coordination and integration of services, given that services are still functionally distinct in many liberal welfare states and that changes are often occurring at a different pace in each policy sector.

The extent of ECEC system integration can be discerned using a number of measures, including these: the extent to which administrative authority is being vested in a single administrative unit within a level of government; the degree to which service delivery is coordinated between levels of government; and the degree to which services are delivered by one level of government in federal systems. Which administrative unit has primary administrative authority is an important indicator of whether the integration is primarily care-focused or educationally focused (e.g., full-day child care centres or part-day preschool services). The substantive nature of the integration can also be discerned by considering the curriculum frameworks adopted – that is, whether they emphasize the child's overall development or narrower school readiness concerns. Findings from the case analyses below and accompanying tables and figures are summarized in Table 2.2.

Case Analyses

Indicators of Gender Norm Change: Policies Supportive of Maternal Employment

Until very recently, most liberal welfare states were notable for their lack of maternal employment policies such as paid maternity or parental leave. Australia, New Zealand, and the United Kingdom also had notably low levels of maternal employment and high levels of female part-time employment, and they neither funded nor provided extensive ECEC provision to encourage maternal employment. Throughout the UK, levels of part-time work were also high among mothers.

Australia, for example, did not have a national paid maternity or parental leave scheme in place until 2011 (Broomhill and Sharp, 2012), although the Commonwealth government and some private sector employers introduced paid leave provisions in the 1970s. Australia lacked a national statutory paid leave program until the late 2000s; the government did, however, provide a few family-related benefits programs that assisted in the costs of bearing and raising young children. In 1996 (Baker and Tippin, 1999, p. 143), for example, the Commonwealth government introduced a lump sum maternity payment (a "baby bonus") to assist families with the costs of birth or adoption of a first child, based on the mother's prior income, payable for up to five years (Klapdor, 2017). The government also provided a maternity allowance, equivalent to about one week's wages, to assist in the costs of having a baby. Low-income families were also eligible for Family Tax Benefits, which provided means-tested payments to defray the costs of having children (OECD, 2006, p. 265).

In more recent decades, public policy at the national level in Australia has focused on expanding child care services (called "long day care" in Australia) and family child care in an effort to encourage maternal labour market participation (Brennan, 2004, p. 212). Australian family policy underwent a sea change regarding paid parental leave after the Labor Party won the 2007 national election. Soon after that, in February 2008, the government appointed the federal Productivity Commission to examine the issue of paid maternity, paternity, and parental leave (Australian Government Productivity Commission, 2009). In 2009, based largely on the recommendations in that commission's final report, the Labor government introduced paid parental leave, to commence on 1 January 2011 (Australian Government, 2009, p. 1).

The government's stated goals in introducing the paid leave scheme were to stimulate women's labour market participation and to achieve "greater gender equity and balance between paid work and family life" (Australian Government, 2009, p. 3). The government noted as well the "compelling evidence of child and maternal health and development benefits from a period of absence from work for the primary caregiver of around six months" (Australian Government, 2009, p. 3). Under the scheme, a parent who has worked at least ten of the thirteen months prior to the birth or adoption of a child and for a minimum of 330 hours is eligible for eighteen weeks of leave paid at the rate of the federal minimum wage (Australian Government, 2009, p. 3). The scheme does not cover high-income earners, nor does it allow parents who collect parental leave benefits to also collect the baby bonus or Family Tax Benefits, but it does cover the self-employed and casual workers.

Similar to Australia, until the late 1980s, New Zealand resembled many other liberal welfare states in not providing a statutory maternity or parental leave program or benefits. Then, in 1987, the New Zealand government introduced an unpaid twelve-month parental leave and job protection program for eligible parents. In 2002, with the election of a Labour government, the state introduced a paid parental benefit as part of its parental leave program. That leave was of twelve weeks' duration, up to a maximum payment (Levin-Epstein, 2004, p. 3). The paid parental leave benefits are financed through general revenues rather than the much more common contributions by employers or employees (Levin-Epstein, 2004, p. 3), and the number of weeks' duration has increased in recent years (New Zealand Ministry of Labour, 2016).

In the United Kingdom, the election of a Labour government led by Prime Minister Tony Blair triggered a number of policy changes, including some related to paid leave, the goal of which was to promote maternal employment. There had been some maternity leave provisions before then, including the ones introduced in 1975 under the Employment Protection Act. Also, some employees were entitled to maternity benefits, and other, lower-income women had access to a maternity allowance (Baker, 1995, p. 178). But many women did not meet the eligibility criteria, and the Conservative government under Margaret Thatcher had eroded many of the maternity leave provisions (Baker, 1995, pp. 178–9).

In the 1998 document *Meeting the Childcare Challenge* (DfEE, 1998, para. 1.6) the government stated that it "welcomes women's greater involvement and equality in the workplace and wants to ensure that all those women who wish to can take up these opportunities." Soon after the election, the Labour government committed itself to implementing the EU's Parental Leave Directive; this would give all parents the right to unpaid leave for three months (thirteen weeks) after the birth or adoption of a child (DfEE, 1998, p. 6). In 2003 it introduced a paid paternity leave program of two weeks for those workers who had worked for the same employer for twenty-six weeks; it also extended its maternity leave program from eighteen to twenty-six weeks. It also allowed a further twenty-six weeks' unpaid leave if the parent had worked for an employer for longer than twenty-six weeks. It increased the compensation rate for maternity allowances and for statutory maternity provisions. It also allowed parents with young children to request more flexible work arrangements (HM Treasury, 2004, para. 3.5). It further set the goal of twelve months' paid maternity leave for 2010, a portion of which could be taken by the father (OECD, 2006, p. 415), with an interim plan to establish nine months' paid maternity leave by 2007 (HM Treasury, 2004, p. 1). The government also created an unpaid parental leave entitlement of thirteen weeks and established the right to a flexible work schedule for parents with children under the age of 6 (Morgan, 2012, p. 159). These leave policies continued with the coalition Conservative/Liberal Democratic government led by Conservative Prime Minister David Cameron (and influenced greatly by Deputy Leader Nick Clegg of the LibDems).

Canada was a leader among liberal welfare states in introducing a national paid scheme in 1971. In Canada, ECEC services are exclusively a provincial responsibility; however, the federal government enjoyed exclusive constitutional responsibility for maternity and parental leave programs as part of its federal authority over employment insurance. Workers are eligible for paid maternity and parental benefits if they are salaried or waged employees entitled to federal EI benefits. The current rate of compensation includes fifteen weeks of maternity leave paid at 55 per cent of earnings to a cap, plus a two-week unpaid waiting period at the outset; and thirty-five weeks of parental leave that can be taken by either parent and is paid at 55 per cent of earnings to a cap. In 2006 the Quebec government implemented its own more generous maternity and parental leave program, which covers both salaried and self-employed parents (federal EI rules, by contrast, do not cover the self-employed). The length of paid leave and the amount of salary replacement varies depending on the plan the worker chooses (i.e., a longer leave period at a lower level of salary replacement or better benefit levels for a shorter period of leave). The Quebec plan provides far better compensation and longer leave periods than the federal plan (for details, see Friendly et al., 2007, p. 62).

With the introduction of paid leave in Australia, New Zealand, and the United Kingdom in the 2000s, the United States remains the only liberal welfare state that provides no national paid parental leave program. The federal Family and Medical Leave Act, enacted in 1993, mandates that twelve weeks of unpaid job-protected leave be available within a twelve-month period for reasons that include the employee's illness, the birth and care of a newborn or newly adopted or fostered child, or the care of a seriously ill child, parent, or spouse. However, the numerous eligibility restrictions mean that the act covers about half or fewer of all US workers (White, 2006; 2009b).

At the state level, a few states have mandated that companies that offer temporary disability insurance (TDI) programs must also allow new mothers to apply for TDI (Wisensale, 2003, p. 142).[11] Temporary disability programs allow for partial wage replacement for the time period that a woman is medically unfit to work after giving birth. The average leave time under TDI is about six weeks (Hartmann and Yoon, 1996). The state of California implemented a paid family leave program in 2002 funded under the State Disability Insurance Program and paid for entirely by employee contributions rather than employer taxes (Labor Project for Working Families, 2003). In addition, some employers provide workplace benefits that include some paid leave provisions. However, many of the occupations in which women are typically employed provide few workplace benefits, and as mentioned above, it is even difficult to qualify for unpaid leave.

The lack of paid benefits means that US women return to the labour force relatively soon after giving birth compared to other countries. In the 1996–9 period, nearly 65 per cent of first-time mothers in the United States returned to work one year after giving birth and 45 per cent after the first three months (US Census Bureau, 2005, Table 8). In contrast, in Canada, about 47 per cent of women in 2001 returned to work after one year, and less than 10 per cent returned to work after 0–2 months or 3–4 months (Marshall, 2003, pp. 6–7). Because maternal employment rates have traditionally been higher in Canada and the United States than in Australia, New Zealand, and the United Kingdom, however, the shifts in norms around maternal employment have been most dramatic in the latter countries and particularly so around state provision of ECEC services, as detailed below.

Indicators of Norm Change: Policies to Support ECEC System Building

Shifts in norms around state support for ECEC can be observed by tracking broad policy changes in each of the liberal welfare states regarding finance and delivery, as well as specific choices of policy instruments and settings. Review of these changes focuses largely on Australia, New

Zealand, and the United Kingdom, with the United States and Canada sketched only in brief as they are the subject of substantial analysis in later chapters.

In all liberal welfare states, private for-profit and community-based child care and philanthropic pre-schools existed for many decades prior to state involvement in funding and provision. Australia, New Zealand, and the United Kingdom have arguably witnessed the most dramatic shift among liberal welfare states in terms of ECEC funding, while at the same time expanding and subsidizing the private market for ECEC services.

The Commonwealth government of Australia became increasingly involved in child care services in the early 1970s with the 1972 passage of the Commonwealth Childcare Act (Brennan, 1998). While education and child care services remain the substantive responsibility of state governments, the Commonwealth government has become the predominant funder of children's services (Ashby, Kennedy, and Mellor, 2002, pp. 7–8). By 2006–7, the Commonwealth government accounted for approximately 78 per cent of all government expenditures on children's services (SCRGSP, 2008, p. 3.7). The Commonwealth government provided financial assistance to community-based not-for-profit child care centres that met defined standards of quality such as specified child/staff ratios (Baker and Tippin, 1999, p. 138; Brennan, 2004, pp. 212–213). Parents still had to pay fees to the centres but the Commonwealth government provided grants to centres in the form of wage subsidies that covered the majority of their expenses (Ashby, Kennedy, and Mellor, 2002, p. 9; Baker, 1995, p. 208). Because the government committed to paying a certain portion for each space in centres, child care expansion was subject to a needs-based planning process (Baker, 1995, p. 208; Press and Hayes, 2000, p. 31). That policy was a departure from government practice in many other liberal welfare states at the time because it provided subsidies directly to services (in addition to parents), and it encouraged the development of not-for-profit services. As analysed below, that system came under increasing pressure from market actors and from within government itself.

Pre-schools in Australia are largely the responsibility of state and territorial governments[12] and operate mostly on a full-time (i.e., five to six hours per day) basis during the school year for children one year before beginning primary school, and part-day for children two years before beginning primary school (Press and Hayes, 2000, pp. 76–7).[13] There is huge variation in the provision of these services across the states and territories, however. For example, pre-school services are provided free of charge to parents in some parts of the country, with funding provided either through direct funding of services or via fee subsidies to families, while in other parts of the country some fees are charged, depending on the service provider (Press and Hayes, 2000, pp. 32, 34; see also Dowling and O'Malley, 2009, p. 4). Programs are delivered in a variety of settings, including school premises but also stand-alone programs, programs within child care centres, and so on (Press and Hayes, 2000, p. 32; Dowling and O'Malley, 2009, p. 2).

As in Australia, while the majority of ECEC services in New Zealand have been delivered by the private sector – although with some government subsidies – most (but not all) of the private sector services are community-based (many with religious affiliation), not corporate (Meade and Podmore, 2002, p. 5). The number of for-profit services has increased over the years, however, as it has in Australia. As of the mid-2000s, 58.4 per cent of children attended for-profit non-denominational child care centres (which are called "education and care centres" in New Zealand) and 41.6 per cent were in community-based services (New Zealand Ministry of Education, 2007a). State oversight of the system is much stronger than in other liberal countries, however. For example, the vast majority of early learning and child care services in New Zealand are licensed, including family child care (called home-based networks) (OECD, 2004a, p. 104), unlike in other liberal countries, where a large number of informal and unregulated care services exist.

New Zealand is somewhat of an outlier among liberal welfare states in that it was an early innovator in establishing an educational focus for its early years programs. This commitment can be traced back to the 1947 Bailey Report, which recommended that the state be responsible for a part-day early childhood education program for 3- and 4-year-olds (May, 1997, p. 6). In 1988, the Before Five Report made the case for early childhood programs to be a "political priority for social policy" for all children from birth to school entry. For much of the twentieth century in New Zealand, as in other liberal welfare states, the use of child care was stigmatized and public opinion reflected the belief that young children were best off at home; even so, the New Zealand government supported the development of community-based kindergarten (or "free kindergarten"), providing subsidies to them as far back as the early decades of the twentieth century. After the Second World War, the government also agreed to fund play centres (Meade and Podmore, 2002, p. 8).

In 1960, after a child care scandal, the New Zealand government introduced child care centre regulations (Meade and Podmore, 2002, p. 7) that extended to community and commercial child care centres and even private kindergartens (May and Mitchell, 2009, p. 7). But while the government agreed to regulate, it did not agree to pay for child care. Only in 1974 did the government introduce fee subsidies for low-income families to help them with the cost of child care. In 1983 it introduced financial incentives for centres to employ trained staff (Meade and Podmore, 2002, p. 8; May and Mitchell, 2009, p. 7).

It was not until the 1989 funding reforms, however, that similar levels of funding for child care and kindergarten services were established. Meade (2000, p. 83) reports that in 1989 (just before the New Zealand government embarked on major reforms to its ECEC system), about 90 per cent of children aged 4, 61 per cent of 3-year-olds, and 40 per cent of all children under the age of 5 were attending an early years program. Those numbers reflect care in a diversity of programs, including community-based and commercial education and care centres (which include some sessional, some full-day, and some flexible-hours programs (drop-in crèches) for children from birth to school age – Meade and Podmore, 2002, p. 6); sessional free kindergarten programs for 3- and 4-year-olds, which are usually community- rather than government-run;[14] parent-supervised and managed parent and child play centres; home-based services (i.e., family child care); and Maori (*nga kohanga reo*) and Pacific Islander language, cultural immersion, and school readiness services, which operate for six hours (Goelman, 2004). All of these received some kind of government funding (Meade, 2000, p. 83; Moss, 2006b, p. 163). Government support included some fee subsidies for low-income families to use child care services, as well as grants for trained staff for child care centres (Meade, 2000, p. 85).

In terms of government spending on ECEC services, the United Kingdom[15] has arguably experienced the most dramatic transformation not only among liberal welfare states but also among all countries in the industrialized world (Moss, 2006b, p. 165; see also the data in Figure 1.1). The sweeping changes include the massive development of child care spaces so that "all families with children aged up to 14 who need it" have access to "an affordable, flexible, high quality childcare place that meets their circumstances" (HM Treasury, 2004, p. 1); a universal part-day pre-school entitlement for 3- and 4-year-olds (with compulsory education beginning at age 5); a large-scale Sure Start program for disadvantaged children, with more than five hundred local programs in place currently; and a pledge to develop integrated child care / ECE Children's Centres in every locality (Moss, 2006b, p. 165; Lewis, 2003; Wincott, 2005). These programs are designed, as Ball and Vincent (2005, p. 558) argue, to address several goals: "increasing social inclusion and in particular combating child poverty, revitalizing the labour market, and raising standards in education."

Prior to the reforms launched in 1997, the government's principal role in child care had been to regulate private services, while funding child care for children deemed to be in need (Cohen et al., 2004, p. 52). Otherwise, parents were responsible for the costs of care if they chose to work (Moss, 1991, p. 133). Playgroups organized by parents (mothers), which required a great deal of parental involvement, were the predominant form of care for pre-school children until the 1990s, but the short hours and the focus on 3- and 4-year-olds meant they could not care for children of full-time working parents (Moss, 1991). Parents in need of full-day child care tended to rely on social networks such as relatives or on the private market of childminders (Melhuish and Moss, 1991). England is distinctive, though, in that schools permitted children to begin primary school as early as age 4 (Moss, 2006a, p. 71). School-based services provided education for even earlier ages – 3- and 4-year-olds – either as nursery classes (part-day) or reception classes (full-day) (Moss, 2006a, p. 71).

By the late 1980s, however, increases in maternal employment in families with young children had increased demand for child care – mainly for private "day nursery" services (Cohen et al., 2004, p. 52; Moss, 2006a, p. 71). Most of that demand was met by the expansion of private, for-profit child care centres, with the government introducing a regulatory regime governing those centers as part of the Children Act, 1989 (Moss, 2006a, p. 71). Concerns about a shrinking labour force and labour shortages, and the severe economic and social inequalities that emerged as a result of earnings inequalities, drew the Conservative government's attention to child care and early childhood education.

The Conservative government introduced two child care programs in the early 1990s: one to support the start-up costs of school-age child care (the Out of School Childcare initiative), and the other to provide some financial support for low-income families' child care costs so as to encourage parental employment in those families (Cohen et al., 2004, p. 53). Both programs originated in the Employment Department but were placed under the administrative umbrella of the newly created Department of Education in 1995, portending a transfer of authority for child care, which the Labour government undertook in 1997 (Cohen et al., 2004, p. 54). The Conservatives introduced a national curriculum and national standards, national student assessments, and national inspection of facilities as part of the 1986 Education Act, signalling increased attention to education (Cohen et al., 2004, p. 54). Finally, in 1994, the Conservative government committed itself to universal nursery education for 3- and 4-year-olds. The new funds would be directed not just to school-based programs but to *any* provider that met certain standards (Cohen et al., 2004, p. 54). The government distributed these funds in the form of vouchers rather than as grants to providers.

Tony Blair's Labour government, elected in 1997, continued with education reforms, some of them major. Indeed, Cohen and colleagues (2004, p. 56) argue that "for the first time in peacetime, childcare became a recognised policy priority, alongside education." Increasing child care provision was thought to be a means to "bring women back into the workforce, thereby increasing productivity as well as lifting families out of poverty, modeling child-rearing skills to parents understood as being in need of such support, and giving children the skills and experience they need to succeed in compulsory education" (Ball and Vincent, 2005, p. 558).

Just before the 1997 national election, the Office of Standards in Education (Ofsted) commissioned a report to review all of the international studies measuring educational achievement that included England. The published report (Reynolds and Farrell, 1996) noted England's relatively poor performance, especially in science and math, although Alexander (2000, p. 36) notes that the study surveyed some studies that were considered methodologically flawed and that England showed improved performance on the TIMSS study. Even so, the study helped justify New Labour's focus on math and science. Soon after the 1997 election the Labour government introduced a Numeracy Strategy to accompany science and literacy emphases (Alexander, 2000, p. 36). Gordon Brown, Chancellor of the Exchequer at the time, stated in Parliament in July 2004 that "while the nineteenth century was distinguished by the introduction of primary education for all and the twentieth century by the introduction of secondary education for all, so the early part of the twenty first century should be marked by the introduction of pre-school provision for the under-fives and childcare available to all" (as quoted in Vincent, Braun, and Ball, 2008, p. 5).

US governments have been similarly motivated in recent decades to attend to early childhood education. As in all other liberal welfare states, child care and early childhood education policies and programs have developed along separate paths, with child care primarily regarded as a private matter of parental responsibility and choice and with little government role beyond funding programs for disadvantaged families (Michel, 1999). State and local governments have traditionally played a strong role in funding and delivering public education. Haskins (2005, p. 141) notes that despite the lack of formal constitutional responsibility for education and child care, the federal government is involved in at least seventy or eighty major and minor programs. And despite states' jurisdictional responsibility for early care and education programs, as of 2002, "federal spending still outpace[d] state spending on early care and education by about a 3:1 ratio" (Olson, 2002, p. 12).

Federal ECEC programs include Head Start, Early Head Start, Title 1, the Individuals with Disabilities Education Act, and the Child Care and Development Fund (CCDF). States can also use money from the Temporary Assistance for Needy Families (TANF) program to finance welfare reduction efforts such as providing child care for parents who are pursuing work or training (Olson, 2002, p. 12). Also, federal and state tax codes provide credits or deductions so that families can write off a portion of their child care expenses. Thus, while the federal government provides no comprehensive early learning and child care program, it has helped fund a number of programs for families, mainly targeted to low-income or at-risk families.

Administrative responsibility for major programs is divided between the federal Department of Education (which funds some early years programs such as early reading, special education, and pre-school grants); Health and Human Services (which funds the Child Care and Development Fund [CCDF] programs as well as Head Start and the Social Services Block Grant (Title XX); and the Department of Agriculture, which funds the federal Child and Adult Care Food Program (Haskins, 2005, p. 142). These federal agencies have responsibility for areas that are constitutionally under the authority of the states. Given the lack of substantive jurisdiction, federal authorities must achieve their goals through "persuasion and lobbying," often accompanied by financial incentives, rather than through coercion (Alexander, 2000, p. 103).

The largest federal early childhood education and development program is Head Start and Early Head Start. Head Start began in 1965 as a summer program for children of poor families that provided pre-school enrichment. It expanded into broader programs providing early childhood education, health, and social services targeted to children of low-income families. Despite a large federal funding allocation for the programs, far more children are eligible than are funded. In 2003–4, for example, 21 per cent of children under age 5 lived in poverty in the United States, but Head Start reached only 7 per cent of children age 3 and only 11 per cent of children age 4 (OECD, 2006, p. 427).

Since the late 1990s, the most remarkable ECEC program expansion has occurred at the state level. As of 2015, 42 states plus the District of Columbia offered some kind of state-funded pre-kindergarten program, according to the National Institute for Early Education Research (Barnett et al., 2016, p. 6). These programs enrol children younger than age 5: enrolment levels for children age 4 in state-funded pre-kindergarten were 29 per cent in 2015 and nearly 5 per cent for children age 3. Additionally, more than 75 per cent of children attend a kindergarten program, according to the Children's Defense Fund (2014). Some states even mandate the offering of full-day kindergarten and the provision of funding at the same level as grade one. The NIEER reports overall spending on pre-k at $6.2 billion in 2015 (Barnett et al., 2016, p. 6).

The scope of program delivery varies widely across states and regions, however (Barnett and Yarosz, 2007, p. 10). The NIEER defines pre-school quite broadly so as to include all private and public child care and pre-kindergarten programs, but that definition does not include children age 4 in kindergarten or in home-based programs (Barnett and Yarosz, 2007, pp. 5, 15n4). Because of the broad definition used, these data are not comparable to other countries' specific program participation rates; they do, however, give a sense of the extent to which American children are in some kind of formal program, although most of them are part-day. Children in families with modest incomes (i.e., who do not qualify for government-funded programs, but who do not earn enough to pay themselves) have the least access to pre-school (Barnett and Yarosz, 2007, p. 1). Georgia and Oklahoma, in contrast, have developed universal pre-k programs that cover all children age 4, although Oklahoma is the only state to deliver universal pre-school through the public school system.

In Canada, jurisdictional authority for both child care and education services rests with the provinces and territories, although the federal government is directly responsible for services related to certain populations, such as Aboriginal people and military personnel. There is no federal Ministry of Education. The federal government has at times been responsible for funding child care services through the instrument of the federal spending power, although it has not funded primary and secondary education.

In Canada, major federal involvement in funding care services began in 1966 with the introduction of the Canada Assistance Plan (CAP). This program provided subsidies for low-income families on a shared-cost basis with the provinces and territories for regulated public and not-for-profit child care services. As Friendly and colleagues (2007, p. xiv) argue, while the shared cost nature of the federal CAP program encouraged provinces and territories to develop child care programs, the targeted nature of the funding meant that "regulated child care emerged as a welfare rather than a universal or educational service."

Federal funding specifically directed at child care programs ended in 1996, with the cancellation of the CAP and the introduction of the Canada Health and Social Transfer (CHST), a block grant which does not specifically earmark monies for child care. Federal, provincial, and territorial governments in 2000 signed the Agreement on Early Childhood Development (ECDA), which provided a federal transfer of $2.2 billion over five years to programs deemed to be part of a "child development" agenda: healthy pregnancy, birth and infancy; parenting and family supports; early childhood development, learning and care; and community supports (Friendly and White, 2007). Then in 2003 the federal, provincial, and territorial governments signed the Multilateral Framework Agreement on Early Learning and Child Care (MFA), under which the federal government agreed to provide $900 million over five years, beginning in 2003, to support provincial and territorial government investments specifically in early learning and child care (Friendly and White, 2007).

In 2004–5 the federal government reached agreements with the provinces and territories to spend even more money on ECEC services. The 2006 federal election brought in a change of government, however, after which the new Conservative government cancelled these agreements. Instead it created a $1,200 per year taxable allowance for families for each child under age 6; also, in an effort to encourage the development of child care spaces, it provided $250 million in tax credits to employers and not-for-profit associations to create 125,000 child care spaces. In the 2007 federal budget, that $250 million was converted into an explicit transfer to the provinces as part of the Canada Social Transfer to support the development of child care spaces (Department of Finance Canada, 2007). These funds, as well as the federal Child Care Expense Deduction, which allows working parents to deduct a certain portion of their child care expenses ($7,000 per child under age 7 currently) on their income taxes, and a few other programs targeted to specific populations, represented the extent of federal involvement in child care provision under the Harper government.

At the provincial level, early education and care services developed along separate tracks, as in other liberal welfare states. Within the provinces and territories, responsibility for child care and education tended to rest with two different ministries – typically the Ministry of Education (for kindergarten), and a ministry of health, or community services, or children's services (for the rest of the ECEC file). Some provinces, though, are now merging administrative authority (Beach et al., 2009, p. xiii). The vast majority of child care programs are sustained in large part through parent fees rather than government funding – almost 50 per cent, according to a 1998 study (Friendly et al., 2007, p. xvii). Every province and territory provides fee subsidies to low-income families to cover some portion of child care fees. Some provinces also provide wage grants and other funds to support the operation of child care services, but these funds represent only a small portion of the overall budgets of these services.

The only province that provides a significant amount of funding for both parental subsidies and capital funds is Quebec. In 1997 the Quebec government began to phase in its publicly funded universal early learning and child care program, beginning with expansion of kindergarten to full day for all 5-year-olds. It then gradually implemented a C$5 per day parent fee for all child care centres (raised to $7 a day in 2003 by a provincial Liberal government and to $7.30 per day as of 2014), and provided capital funding to encourage the expansion of child care spaces in not-for-profit *centres de la petites enfances* – centre-based and family child care (Jenson, 2009; Tougas, 2002).

By the mid-1980s, most Canadian 5-year-olds were enrolled in public kindergarten programs, but usually part-day (Friendly et al., 2007, p. xiv). New Brunswick since 1992 and Nova Scotia since 1997 have offered full-day kindergarten for 5-year-olds. BC and PEI introduced full-day kindergarten programs in public schools in 2010. Only in Ontario is full-day kindergarten offered for children younger than 5. Most provinces have now shifted responsibility for child care services from ministries of community and social services to ministries of education (Ferns and Friendly, 2014, p. 3).

Indicators of Norm Change: Policy Instruments and Settings

The preceding analysis demonstrates the extent to which liberal welfare states have shifted to fund and support the development of ECEC services. Changes in financing, delivery mechanisms, scope of provision, and regulatory oversight are important indicators of norm change. Battles over policy instruments and settings help uncover the extent of norm change around early childhood education and care. Case analysis reveals significant variation among liberal welfare states regarding public financing versus public or not-for-profit delivery as well as some differential treatment of early childhood education and child care. Governments in Australia, New Zealand, the United Kingdom, and the United States have all, through government subsidies, encouraged the growth of child care markets; Canada (more specifically, some provincial and territorial governments) remains an outlier in some cases directing public funds to not-for-profit providers and in delivering early childhood education services through schools.

In Australia, federal public investment in ECEC services has been increasingly directed at subsidizing the cost of child care that is purchased in the market. Controversy over public funding of child care arose in the 1980s in Australia (Brennan, 2004, p. 216). The left raised concerns over the subsidy system, specifically with regard to whether all families had access to affordable care. The right raised concerns over the restriction of subsidies to not-for-profit child care services. In 1988, in an attempt to quell the controversy, the Commonwealth government agreed to offer tax deductions to private child care services (Baker and Tippin, 1999, p. 139). In 1991, after extensive lobbying from private child care operators and – ironically[16] – the Australian Council of Trade Unions, the government further agreed to extend parental subsidies to the users of for-profit child care centres (Press and Hayes, 2000, p. 18; Brennan, 2004, 216).

According to Brennan (2004, p. 218), the Labor government thought this strategy of opening up subsidy eligibility to parents who placed their children in for-profit care would be more cost-effective for the government and would expand the child care supply because commercial centres would absorb the capital outlay costs but would not be eligible for operational subsidies. Commercial centres, however, were not subject to the needs-based planning process that not-for-profit centres had to undergo. Press and Hayes (2000, p. 31) report that "uneven and unforeseen growth resulted, with some areas experiencing an oversupply of places, whilst demand and gaps in supply, such as places for children aged 0-2, still existed in some regions."

Then, in 1996, under a "level playing field" strategy, the federal government withdrew operational subsidies altogether from not-for-profit child care centres and before- and after-school child care programs, although it retained subsidies for indigenous and other special services, including family child care, occasional care centres, multifunctional children's services, and not-for-profit services in rural areas and disadvantaged urban areas (Baker and Tippin, 1999, p. 141; Press and Hayes, 2000, p. 31; OECD, 2006, p. 273). The government again thought that this would encourage the development of competition in service delivery.

The decision, in fact, has had the opposite effect. Australia has seen increased domination of child care service delivery by for-profit providers at great expense to the federal government and great profit for for-profit child care providers, yet services are now lower in quality (Brennan, 2004, p. 218; Brennan, 2007a; Dowling and O'Malley, 2009). The number of places in commercial child care centres rose 233 per cent between 1991 and 1996 while places in community-based not-for-profit services grew by only 15 per cent (Australian Senate, 2009, p. 21). As Brennan (2004, p. 218) points out, "to qualify for child care assistance, a service simply had to open for a certain number of hours per day and weeks per year, be licensed by the relevant state or territory authority and be registered with the Quality Improvement and Accreditation System."

The decision to withdraw operational subsidies also made the cost of delivering not-for-profit child care more expensive. Centres could make up for the loss of operational subsidies only by reducing costs (e.g., staff wages) or increasing parent fees. In 1994 the Commonwealth government had established the Child Care Cash Rebate to provide a rebate to working families for their work-related child care costs that could be used to purchase formal and informal care (including care by a family member) (Baker and Tippin, 1999, p. 139). But parents still experienced a fee gap between the price of care and the amount of government subsidy provided under either the Child Care Cash Rebate program or the Childcare Assistance program.

In 2000, in response to the high fees, the Commonwealth government amalgamated these two programs into the Child Care Benefit (CCB), a more generous program that provided subsidies to parents according to income, number of children, and type of care used. Then in

2004 it introduced the Child Care Tax Rebate (CCTR) program, which provides parents with a tax offset of 30 per cent of their out-of-pocket child care expenses for approved child care, minus the amount of Child Care Benefit received, up to a certain maximum. In 2008 that rebate increased from 30 to 50 per cent to a maximum of $7,500 per child (Australian Government, 2010, p. 8). Unlike the CCB, which delivers the biggest benefits to lower-income families, the CCTR provides the biggest tax benefits to parents who pay the most for child care (Brennan, 2007a). In 1997 the Commonwealth government had introduced a planning mechanism to cap the number of new centres for which fee subsidies would be available; later, though, it discontinued the cap (Press and Hayes, 2000, p. 31). Instead, the government resorted to providing information to potential investors regarding supply issues. Thus the commercial child care sector continued to grow.

By the late 1990s the private for-profit sector was providing over 70 per cent of centre-based child care (Press and Hayes, 2000, p. 21). That trend continued throughout the 2000s so that by 2008, the proportion of services delivered by the commercial child care sector had reached 75 per cent, albeit with huge variation between states/territories regarding the proportion of services delivered by the private for-profit sector (Australian Government, 2010, p. 5). The proportion of services provided by community-based agencies declined throughout the 2000s to 22 per cent by 2008 (with government provision at 3 per cent) (Australian Government, 2010, p. 5). The 2000s also saw the concentration of child care and related services under the umbrella of a single company, ABC Learning Centres, which listed itself on the Australian stock exchange in 2001 (Australian Senate, 2009, p. 9; Press and Woodrow, 2009). ABC Learning Centres held about 20 per cent of the spaces across Australia before it collapsed in 2008; in some municipalities, though, it had effectively cornered the market on child care, reducing parental choice in child care services.

Brennan (2004, p. 220) contends that the dominance of the commercial child care sector has led to pressures to deregulate so as not to create barriers to profit. Regulation in the form of child care licensing falls under state authority (Australian Senate, 2009, p. 4), and this has led to a variety of licensing standards as well as government supervision of the industry (Australian Senate, 2009, p. 5). The Commonwealth government has introduced a Quality Improvement and Assurance System, an accreditation system covering both commercial and not-for-profit child care centres. The system operates separately from state-based licensing requirements and looks specifically at the quality of child/staff interactions (Brennan, 2004, p. 216). Under the system, services that do not meet standards of accreditation are not eligible to receive public funding. The OECD (2006, p. 272) reports, however, that "despite state regulation and national monitoring," "low pay, low status and training levels of ECEC staff undermine quality."

The collapse of ABC Learning Centres in 2008 led to a national re-evaluation of the ECEC system as a whole, as well as pressure to introduce stronger national regulations; it also drew attention to the quality of care provided, especially in programs deemed "educational" (Australian Senate, 2009, pp. 19, 35; Early Childhood Australia, 2011). In cooperation with state governments, which had to pass enabling legislation, the Commonwealth government implemented a National Quality Framework on a phased basis, with enforcement beginning in January 2012 (Early Childhood Australia, 2011). The framework has established compulsory national standards for registered services, in tandem with a quality rating system; a national oversight agency ensures that ECEC services meet those standards. It has increased child/staff ratios (1 staff for 4 children ages 0–24 months; 1:5 for children ages 25–35 months; 1:11 for children ages 36 months to school age) (Early Childhood Australia, 2011, p. 3). The framework has also raised staff qualifications – for example, it requires an ECE-qualified teacher to be in attendance at least part-time in services with fewer than twenty-five children, and full-time in services with twenty-five children or more (Early Childhood Australia, 2011, p. 3).

In New Zealand, enrolment in formal full-day ECEC increased throughout the 1990s, while the proportion of children in part-day kindergartens and play centres declined. Those enrolment trends have continued into the 2000s. By 2006, full-day services comprised 60 per cent of all enrolments in ECEC programs, compared to 42 per cent in 1998, and wait times have increased for access to those programs (New Zealand Ministry of Education, 2008b). Nearly 100 per cent of 3- and 4-year-olds participate in some kind of ECEC service, about 60 per cent of 2-year-olds, about 35 per cent of 1-year-olds, and nearly 20 per cent of children under the age of 12 months. Parents cover approximately 15 per cent of the fees in child care centres, while kindergarten services are free or have nominal fees (Goelman, 2004).

By the early 1990s, government ECEC funding included grants for licensed early childhood services and charters based on a per hour and per child formula (capped at thirty hours per week), with a higher rate for infants and toddlers (Meade, 2000, p. 86). These grants were demand-driven, which meant that government spending on these services increased dramatically over the years, as did enrolment levels in early childhood services. Thus in 1992, the government began to reduce subsidies for infants and toddlers as a way to decrease government expenditures. Some service providers, such as kindergartens, found that the only way to make up lost government grants was to increase enrolments (Meade, 2000, p. 88). Throughout the 1990s, the government continued to provide fee subsidies to low-income families for child care, although it had to institute a cap on fee subsidies as the number of applicants increased when the government restricted early childhood service grants (Meade, 2000, p. 87). The government also encouraged the growth of community-based services specifically through a program of discretionary grants (New Zealand Ministry of Education, 2008a).

In 2007 the government committed to provide up to twenty hours of free early childhood education per week for children ages 3 and 4 participating in all teacher-led ECE services and *kohanga reo* in addition to the hours for which subsidies were already provided (New Zealand Ministry of Education, 2007b). New Zealand has not followed the social democratic and continental European welfare states, however, in that services are delivered mainly privately, not publicly. After protests from private operators, the government agreed that these services could be delivered in a variety of settings so long as the service was teacher-led (Mitchell, 2012; New Zealand Ministry of Education, 2007b). According to Mitchell (2012, p. 10), privately owned services increased from 41 per cent in 1992 to 64 per cent in 2010.

The decision to promote "free ECE" through mixed markets, Mitchell (2012, p. 7) argues, is the "Achilles heel" in building a high-quality ECEC system in New Zealand. Mitchell (2012, p. 7) notes that the New Zealand government's commitment to fund a mix of ECEC services has encouraged the growth of private ownership, resulting in "duplications and gaps in ECEC provision, inequities in access particularly for low income, ethnically diverse and rural families" and the expansion of corporate providers as well, including – until its collapse – the Australian giant, ABC Learning. New Zealand, Australia, and the United Kingdom have all experienced a similar trend: for-profit providers are targeting higher-income communities for their services, with resulting erosions in quality as for-profit providers employ fewer qualified teachers and provide fewer employment supports (2012, p. 11).

The New Zealand government has tried to improve quality in centres. In 2002 the Ministry of Education released a Ten-Year Strategic Plan, which outlined goals for early childhood education quality improvement. New Zealand also passed national regulations in 2008 (Education [Early Childhood Services] Regulations). Those regulations include the requirement to increase the number of registered teachers delivering ECEC services; by the target year of 2012, all regulated staff in teacher-led ECE services are to be registered ECE teachers or enrolled in approved education programs. The government's goals also include improving child/staff ratios and group sizes. As of 2006, 50 per cent of ECE teachers' qualifications in all ECE services met those registration requirements, which represented an increase from 39 per cent in 2002. Mitchell (2012, p. 13) notes a poorer record in for-profit and community-based services in reaching these targets.

The UK government has used similar tools (i.e., parental subsidies and grants) for a variety of ECEC services to vastly expand the child care market. The Labour government's 1998 National Childcare Strategy established the Childcare Tax Credit for low- and middle-income working families to cover a certain portion of child care costs, depending on the number of children in the family (DfEE, 1998, para. 3.4). That program was replaced by the child care element of the Working Tax Credit in 2003 (HM Treasury, 2004, para. 3.4), which pays up to 70 per cent of child care costs to a certain maximum. Eligibility is limited to parents in low-wage occupations working a minimum of sixteen hours per week; the money can be used for both for-profit and not-for-profit services and can pay for pre-school outside of the free portion. However, the provider must be registered and must permit the Office of Standards in Education to inspect services. Also, providers must work towards government-specified learning goals (OECD, 2006, p. 420).

In 1998 the government also established the New Opportunities Fund, consisting of lottery-generated money to develop integrated before- and after-school ECEC programs. These grants cover part-time provision (twelve hours per week over three eleven-week terms) and are given to programs that agree to work towards the early learning goals outlined in the document *Curriculum Guidance for the Foundation Stage* (DfEE, 2000), which became statutory in 2002 (DfEE, 2000, p. 68). The government has encouraged some planning around child care: the 1998 National Childcare strategy required local Early Years Development and Childcare Partnerships, made up of a variety of public, private, and community-based agencies, to scrutinize child care needs in their area and draw up plans (Randall, 2004, p. 4). The government has also engaged in "pump priming" spending to encourage businesses to start up child care centres (Cohen et al., 2004, p. 58; DfEE, 1998, para. 5.2).

These two policy choices – parental subsidies for many forms of care, and grants for various ECE programs – have encouraged the development of a largely private child care market. The United Kingdom currently has the highest percentage of private for-profit providers in Europe: 97 per cent of services for children under 3 are delivered through private providers, and 40 per cent of services to children ages 3 to 5 (Gaunt, 2011).

Further encouraging the growth of this child care market was the Blair government's guarantee of a universal part-time (12.5 hours per week for the thirty-three-week academic year) early education program for 4-year-olds in 1998 (DfEE, 1998, para. ES 9, 12), with a commitment to expand entitlement to 3-year-olds as well (para. 4.0). In 1998 the Blair government abolished the early childhood education voucher introduced by the Conservative government and set up a grant system for all ECE services (the Nursery Education Grant) (Lewis, 2003, p. 224). This grant system covered not just schools but also playgroups, nurseries, and child minding (Cohen et al., 2004, p. 67). The grant covers part-time provision (twelve hours per week over three eleven-week terms) and is given to programs that agree to work towards the early learning goals. In 2004 the government further expanded that guarantee to twenty hours per week for thirty-eight weeks of "high quality care" for all 3- and 4-year-olds, with the first step to provide fifteen hours per week for thirty-eight weeks per year for all children by 2010; it further guaranteed an out-of-school child care place for all children ages 3 to 14 by 2010 (HM Treasury, 2004, p. 1; OECD, 2006, pp. 415, 418).

Given the guarantee of hours, space availability was crucial. The government thus decided that early education programs could be delivered through a variety of settings, not just schools but also private and community-based service providers (HM Treasury, 2004, para. 3.5). By the 2005–6 academic year, 64 per cent of 3- and 4-year-olds were in what are known as maintained nursery and primary schools, compared to 20.5 per cent in 1970–1 (However, "35 per cent of three and four-year-olds attending early years education were enrolled in other non-school settings such as playgroups in the private and voluntary sectors, either instead of, or in addition to, their school place" (UK Office for National Statistics, 2007, Figure 3.1; appendix 3). In fact, the number of children in state-maintained nurseries and schools has increased only marginally since 1997–8. The UK Office for National Statistics (2000) reports that by 1999, 98 per cent of all 4-year-olds in England were in early years provision, and 78 per cent of those children were in maintained nursery and primary schools. But by 2011, despite near universal attendance of 3- and 4-year-olds in some kind of early education program, approximately 44 per cent were attending programs provided by private and voluntary providers or independent schools (DfE, 2011).

The government provides regulatory oversight of these early education services. In addition to a national curriculum, the government established national standards of care for children under the age of 8. It transferred regulatory authority from local authorities to Ofsted and made it responsible for accreditation and regulation of these services (HM Treasury, 2004, para. 3.27). It also sought to better integrate early childhood education and care by moving children's services, including child care and early childhood education, into the Department of Education and Employment (Moss, 2006b, p. 165). The government also established twenty-five Early Excellence Centres to act as models for integrating early childhood education and care.

Despite these rules, researchers and government agencies tracking child care quality have found variation in quality between private for-profit, voluntary, and public sector providers. Ofsted has rated almost all of the ECEC services as at least satisfactory (HM Treasury, 2004, para. 3.29); the government admits, however, that the lower-qualified and lower-paid staff are concentrated in the private and community-based child care and nursery services and that "around 30 per cent of staff in day nurseries were unqualified and … the staff turnover rate is around 20 per cent" (HM Treasury, 2004, para. 3.34). The 2008 Ofsted report of 90,000 inspection visits to 84,000 providers (including child care, out-of-school clubs, and childminders) over the previous three-year period rated only 57 per cent of providers as good and only 3 per cent as outstanding, with huge variation in quality across the country (Ofsted, 2008, pp. 7, 11). Mathers and colleagues (2007) and Mathers and Sylva (2007), using different data sets, concluded that across all settings (private for-profit, private voluntary, and "maintained" by local education authorities), "the maintained settings were providing the highest quality provision overall, particularly with regard to the 'learning' aspects of provision" (Mathers, Sylva, and Joshi, 2007, p. 6).

In comparing these three liberal welfares with the United States, a similar pattern of provision emerges, although unlike in Australia, New Zealand, and the United Kingdom, US governments have not invested as much to finance system growth as a percentage of GDP (see Figure 1.1). From the start, most ECEC services in the United States have been delivered by the private sector, including philanthropic agencies (Michel, 1999). A great portion of ECEC services are delivered on a for-profit basis. The OECD (2006, p. 429) estimates that by the early 2000s, 90 per cent of early childhood services, including child care centres and family child care, were being delivered by the private sector, and of those, one-third were for-profit. While the federal government funds Head Start programs and provides subsidies to low-income and working families, and states are increasingly funding kindergarten and pre-kindergarten programs, parents assume the bulk of the cost of programs. The OECD (2006, p. 426) reports that "overall, the federal government underwrites 25% of costs, state and local government 15% and parents the remaining 60%."

In comparison to other liberal countries, Canada is emerging as an outlier on a few ECEC policy dimensions. First, and most significantly, one Canadian province – Quebec – has been *sui generis* in pursuit of its own made-in-Quebec early learning and child care policy (Albanese, 2011; Jenson, 2009; Tougas, 2002). Second, unlike in other liberal states, Canadian provinces that fund full-day kindergarten programs do so exclusively through the public school system. Third, unlike in most other liberal welfare states, a much greater proportion of services are provided on a not-for-profit rather than a for-profit basis (only 30 per cent of services were for-profit in 2012 nationally), although with significant variation across provinces and territories (from a high of 80 per cent of services provided on a for-profit basis in PEI and 65 per cent in Newfoundland and Labrador in 2012 to nearly 0 per cent in Saskatchewan, the Northwest Territories, and Nunavut (Friendly et al., 2013, p. 69).

Indicators of Norm Change: Policies Supportive of
ECEC System Integration

The extent of integration of early childhood education and care systems is visible in the administrative units established to administer programs, the degree of coordination among units and between orders of government, and the degree of integration of curriculum frameworks. At the Commonwealth level of government in Australia, currently two offices are responsible for ECEC services: the Department of Education, Training, and Youth Affairs (for pre-school and other forms of school), and the Department of Family and Community Services and

Indigenous Affairs (for child care and other family services other than education) (Press and Hayes, 2000, p. 22). Service administration at the state government level is also characterized by dichotomous service delivery, usually involving departments of education as well as health and/or community services, although the primary area of state and territorial expenditure is on pre-school services (approximately 82 per cent in 2006–7 – SCRGSP, 2008, p. 3.7).

Pre-school attendance in stand-alone programs (paid for by state governments as opposed to parent fees in long day care) is increasing in popularity in Australia (Dowling and O'Malley, 2009, p. 6). All jurisdictions except Victoria allow children to begin pre-school before the age of 4 in certain circumstances (e.g., if they are Aboriginal, or are children for whom English is a second language), although the percentage of children who access the programs two years before primary school is much lower (17 per cent) than that of children who access them one year before primary school (84 per cent) (OECD, 2006, p. 269; SCRGSP, 2008, p. 3.7).[17] Parents perceive that the quality regulations for stand-alone pre-school programs are stronger than those for long day cares because the former tend to employ qualified teachers who are higher paid and who work shorter hours (Dowling and O'Malley, 2009, p. 6).

The Council of Australian Governments (COAG), an institution of multi-level governance, has tackled the integration of formal child care and early childhood education services (Dowling and O'Malley, 2009; Early Childhood Australia, 2011). In a number of states, governments have transferred responsibility for early childhood education from children's services departments to education (Australian Senate, 2009, p. 13). The Commonwealth government did so as well in 2008 with the creation of the Office of Early Childhood Education and Child Care (OECECC). The Australian Government (2010, p. 2) acknowledges a change in policy emphasis post-2005: "Child care is now seen as both a mechanism to support labour force participation and as an important form of early learning and education."

In its 2007 election platform the Australian Labor Party committed to "ensure every four year old child has access to fifteen hours a week and 40 weeks a year of high quality preschool delivered by a qualified early childhood teacher" – a promise that state governments committed to as well in 2008 (Dowling and O'Malley, 2009). The Commonwealth government is agnostic regarding the site of service delivery – in 2007 the Labor government platform included a commitment to fund delivery via pre-schools, kindergartens, and public, private, and community-based child care providers; as well, the Labor government continued to be willing to provide tax rebates to both for-profit and not-for-profit child care services. All of this likely means that the market for commercial child care services delivering "early childhood education" will not shrink.

Administratively, New Zealand was an early leader in integrating early care and education. In 1986 the government moved all early childhood services, including child care, from the education, social welfare, and Maori affairs ministries into a single department – the Ministry of Education (Meade and Podmore, 2002, p. 7). This was more than ten years before countries such as Sweden and the United Kingdom did the same (Cohen et al., 2004). Then, in 1988, the government introduced an early childhood training program in teachers' colleges for both kindergarten and child care staff, portending a number of other changes outlined in the government's *Education to Be More* (New Zealand Ministry of Education, 1988) and *Before Five* (Lange, 1988) reports. These documents advocated improving the educational standards in child care centres. In 1989 the government established a Teacher Registration Board for ECE teachers. By 1994, head teachers and directors of nearly all early childhood services required a teaching diploma in early childhood education (Meade, 2000, p. 87, 89); teaching requirements have increased still more since then.

New Zealand was also the first country to introduce a national curriculum, *Te Whariki* (New Zealand Ministry of Education, 1996), which applies to children age 0 to 5. However, given the variety of programs that deliver ECEC services, a multitude of regulatory regimes exist, which the government is working to streamline (see, for example, New Zealand Ministry of Education, 2004). The government implemented a number of other reforms to improve quality in ECEC services, including an Early Childhood Development Unit (ECDU) (later integrated with the Ministry of Education in 2003), which provided development, advice, and coordination (Meade 2000, pp. 86, 90). It established an Education Review Office to conduct annual audits, although with the proliferation of centres and the decline in government funding, those reviews occurred less frequently as time passed (Meade, 2000, p. 86, 90). And in 1996 it instituted "quality funding" incentives so that "services with better than minimum standards with regard to staff qualifications and staff to child ratios ... receive a higher per child grant" (Meade, 2000, p. 87). It also gave charter status – and higher levels of funding – to child care centres that met additional quality guidelines (Meade, 2000, p. 89).

Education in the United Kingdom is administratively decentralized, with separate school administrations in Scotland and Northern Ireland and semi-separate administration in Wales (Alexander, 2000, p. 120). Also, much of educational administration – including finance – is decentralized to local authorities, although national governments have centralized curriculum, assessment, and teacher training and accompanied those reforms with monitoring agencies, including the Office for Standards in Education (established in 1993), the Qualifications and Curriculum Authority (QCA), and the Teacher Training Agency (TTA) (Alexander, 2000, p. 122, 142). The Blair government added a Standards and Effectiveness Unit (SEU) within the Department for Education, tasked with ensuring the teaching of literacy and numeracy.

In the United States, as mentioned above, federal departments do have responsibility for major ECEC programs despite the fact that these areas are largely under state authority. Administrative responsibility is divided mainly between the federal Department of Education, Health and Human Services and the Department of Agriculture (Haskins, 2005, p. 142). Given the lack of substantive jurisdiction, federal authorities must achieve their goals through "persuasion and lobbying" – often accompanied by financial incentives – rather than through coercion (Alexander, 2000, p. 103). At the state level, a number of states have consolidated responsibility for child care and early childhood education in a number of ways; examples of this include the Office of School Readiness in North Carolina, an early childhood cabinet in Connecticut, and a public–private partnership called the Partnership for Continued Learning in Ohio (OECD, 2006, p. 435). In addition, some states have created a single administrative ECEC authority. For example, Georgia in 2004 established a Department of Early Care and Learning, and Massachusetts in 2005 and Washington State in 2006 created consolidated offices for early education and care from their old education and child care offices (OECD, 2006, p. 48).

In contrast, in Canada, provincial and territorial governments retain much more authority over ECEC services, although various federal departments such as National Health and Welfare and (more recently) Human Resources Development Canada have had administrative responsibility for child care. Each province and territory has established an education ministry and assigned it responsibility for child care regulations and licensing requirements. Those regulatory regimes vary widely across jurisdictions (Beach et al., 2009, p. 190). Separate regulations exist for kindergarten services, which means, for example, that classroom sizes for kindergartens can be much bigger than the maximum allowable group sizes for children in child care.

All provinces and territories specify maximum group sizes as well, but again, these vary widely across jurisdictions – for example, from a maximum group size of six for infants in nearly half the provinces and territories, to ten in Nova Scotia and Ontario and twelve in BC (Beach et al., 2009, p. 191). All provinces and one of the territories specify minimum standards regarding staff training, but again, these vary widely – for example, from a one-year ECE certificate for one member of the teaching staff in a group of children to two-thirds of all staff needing to have an ECE certificate. Some provinces also require centre directors to have certain training (Beach et al., 2009, pp. 188–9). The most recent data available indicate that as of 1998, 66 per cent of staff in regulated child care centres had a two-year ECE credential or more, typically from a community college, while 29 per cent had one year or less of ECE training (OECD, 2006, p. 301). No national curriculum framework or quality standards exist in Canada for either child care or early childhood education.

Conclusion

This chapter has demonstrated the extent of norm change in liberal welfare states in recent decades with regard to maternal employment and ECEC funding, provision, and administration. It has also demonstrated the diversity of provision within those liberal welfare states. While governments in all of these countries have put new money into programs, and while there has been an increase in the overall provision of child care and early childhood education services in each of these countries since the early 1990s, very different policy choices are being made as to the kinds of programs that are being supported and the ways the money is being spent.

First, with regard to liberal gender norms regarding women's workforce participation, the most remarkable policy development over the past decade has been the establishment of paid leave schemes in Australia, New Zealand, and the United Kingdom, making the United States a sharp outlier in comparison, for it has no national paid leave scheme. Overall female employment rates have increased in all of these liberal welfare states – except, again, in the United States (see Tables 2.3a and 2.3b). Part-time employment rates between 2002 and 2012 have declined slightly in all of these countries, except, again, in the United

Table 2.3a. Female employment rates in liberal welfare states for women ages 25 to 54 by presence of children, 2000 (%)

Country	Women's overall employment rate	Women with no children	Women with one child	Women with two or more Children
Liberal w/s				
Australia	66.8	68.4	55.3	50.1
Canada	74.0	76.5	74.9	65.5
NZ (2001)	70.6	80.7	66.9	56.3
UK	73.1	79.9	72.9	63.3
USA (1999)	74.1	78.6	75.6	69.3

Source: OECD (2002, p. 77).

Table 2.3b. Female employment rates in liberal welfare states for women ages 25–54 by age and presence of children, 2011 (%)

Country	Overall female employment rate	Employment rate by age of youngest child			Employment rate by number of children < 15		
		< 3	3–5	6–14	1 child	2 children	3 or more children
Australia	72.1	48.7		73.9	65.7	63.5	50.1
Canada	78.0	64.5	70.4	78.8	70.1	73.2	66.3
NZ	74.2	42.2	61.3	78.0	62.4	62.8	45.9
UK	74.5	56.9	61.2	72.6	71.5	66.1	38.2
USA	69.0	53.9	73.8	69	N/A	N/A	N/A

N/A = not available
Source: OECD (2014b, Family Database, LMF1.2).

States, which saw a slight increase. It is not clear whether the introduction of paid leave schemes has positively affected maternal employment, given that employment rates for mothers with one child in each of these countries have also declined over the past decade, although employment rates for mothers with two children have increased. Researchers in Quebec have found a positive relationship between the introduction of the $7 per day child care scheme and maternal employment (Baker, Gruber, and Milligan, 2008; Lefebvre and Merrigan, 2008). The level of part-time employment in Australia, New Zealand, and the United Kingdom also remains high compared to Canada and the United States, despite the comparatively higher levels of ECEC spending (see Table 2.4 and Figure 1.1).

Especially in the United Kingdom and the United States, a significant shift has occurred with regard to the importance of supporting at least low-income mothers' paid labour market participation. Lewis (2003,

Table 2.4. Female part-time employment as a percentage of female employment in liberal welfare states, 1999 and 2012

Country	2002	2012
UK	40.8	39.4
Australia	39.1	38.4
New Zealand	35.7	34.9
Canada	27.2	26.6
USA	18.0	18.3

Sources: OECD (2014b, Family Database LF1.6).

p. 221) argues that the UK government's 1998 National Childcare Strategy represented "radical" change in the United Kingdom because, by providing public funding for child care services, it was acknowledging for the first time "the desirability of collectively provided childcare" and a model of the family where all adults are wage earners. A similar concern to transform low-income single mothers in the United States into wage earners drove the US government to include child care funding as part of welfare reforms in 1996 (Orloff, 2005).

In both countries there seems to be a growing consensus that low-income and single parents especially need child care in order to participate in the paid labour market, but that has not translated into an acknowledgment of the need for comprehensive child care services for *all* families. The extent to which one can claim that the UK and US governments have moved away from male breadwinner/female caregiver norms to the adult wage earner norm for *all* women is limited by the fact that parental subsidies for child care remain targeted in both countries, and the US government has not instituted a labour-market-supportive paid parental leave program. Out-of-pocket expenses for child care services remain very high in the United Kingdom, the United States, and New Zealand (see Figure 2.1). In contrast, the province of Quebec, through its universal $7 per day child care program, and the government of Australia, through its heavy subsidization of child care expenses, have reduced the child care costs borne by parents. These policy changes seem to signal those governments' willingness to play a role in ensuring labour market participation for *all* parents rather than for targeted groups.

The case analyses reveal a continued emphasis on parental responsibility and parental choice in the delivery of child care services in all liberal welfare states. However, there clearly has been a shift in some

Figure 2.1. Out-of-pocket child care costs for dual-earner families with full-time earnings of 150% of average wage for full-time care at a typical child care centre, 2012

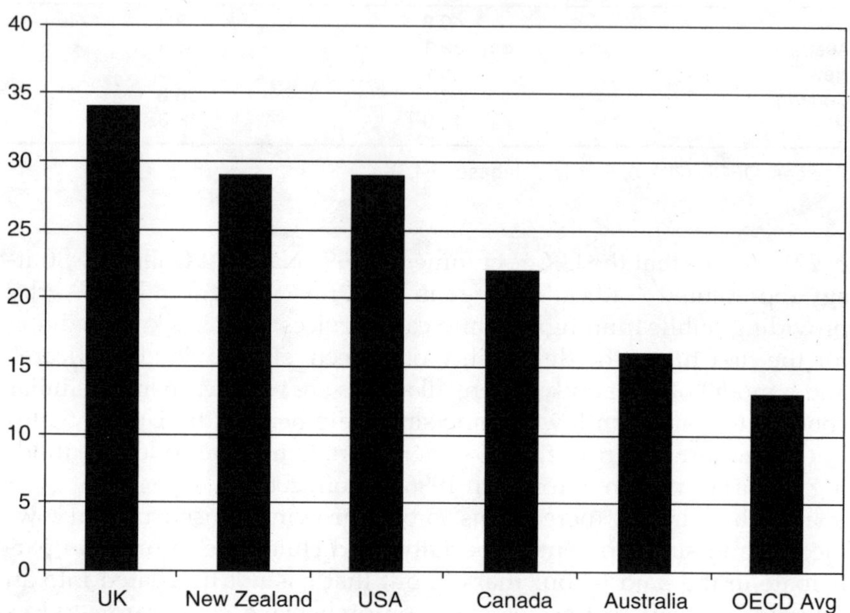

Source: OECD (2014b, Family Database PF3.4)

countries regarding the responsibility for funding those services, with large infusions of funding in Australia, the United Kingdom, and New Zealand in particular. While governments are increasingly concerned about the cognitive or developmental "deliverables" of these ECEC programs, most remain wholly agnostic as to who delivers the programs. In all countries, governments have encouraged through subsidy systems program delivery in a variety of settings: schools, child care centres, family child care, and so on, although the New Zealand government especially has attempted to manage and regulate delivery of these services through, for example, teacher training requirements. And in all countries, governments have always been or have become agnostic as to whether those services can be delivered in for-profit or not-for-profit settings. The New Zealand government has gone much further than other countries in trying to manage the

ECEC system – for example, by instituting national regulations, staff standards, and a national curriculum – but it has not moved away from contracting service delivery.

Alber (2010) and other researchers (e.g., Scruggs and Allan, 2008) have observed that liberal welfare states appear to be becoming more classically liberal – in terms of reliance on markets for delivery of social services – even as ECEC spending is sustained or is even increasing. Child care still seems to be viewed as a private service to be purchased on the market; in early childhood education, however, a decidedly mixed market seems to be emerging, worthy of public financing but not necessarily public delivery.

In most jurisdictions there seems to be a growing awareness of the value of high-quality educational experiences for children at a younger age. Governments in many of the jurisdictions reviewed here are committing themselves to developing universal pre-primary or blended care and education programs. But there is huge variation both between countries and within countries as to age of eligibility for publicly delivered services and the regulatory rules in place. In New Zealand and the United Kingdom, the "free ECE" programs must be teacher-led and follow a curriculum but can be offered in a variety of settings. In the United States, "pre-school" is a very broad term that covers a plethora of programs with varying regulatory standards. In Canada, in contrast, as of 2016, all seven provincial governments – New Brunswick, Newfoundland, Nova Scotia, PEI, Quebec, Ontario, and British Columbia – that have expanded kindergarten for children into full-day programs have done so through the public school system.

The growing consensus around the educational focus of early years programs is also evident in the administrative apparatus established to deliver these programs. New Zealand and the United Kingdom (both unitary states) have integrated early learning and care services under a single administrative apparatus within departments of education, and governments in Australia, and in Canada and the United States sub-nationally, are working to integrate child care and early childhood education program administration as well. In Australia and the United States, furthermore, the federal government seems to be willing to spend money in areas of substantive state jurisdiction, whereas in Canada, federalism still exerts a strong veto when it comes to developing a nationally integrated and jurisdictionally coordinated system of ECEC. The factors that account for these shifts in both public policy and public opinion are explored in the next chapter.

Explaining the Shift in Norms Surrounding Early Childhood, Motherhood, and the State in the Twenty-First Century

Despite increases in women's labour market participation in the United States and Canada especially in the post–Second World War period, and despite examples of strong state investment in such programs in other OECD countries, particularly the Nordic and continental European welfare states, the idea of public investment in child care and early childhood education faced decades of opposition in liberal welfare states. What accounts for that opposition, and why has it diminished? And what accounts for the continued variation in program implementation within liberal welfare states?

Variation in policy adoption does not correspond with typical explanatory factors such as political partisanship. In the United States and Canada, for example, policies and programs are being established and expanded in both conservative and liberal states and provinces, and in both small and large jurisdictions such as Oklahoma and New York in the United States and Prince Edward Island and Ontario in Canada. These policies and programs have involved a variety of change agents, including state governors in Georgia and Illinois (Raden, 1999, 2002; Sheppard, 2007) and legislatures in New York, Oklahoma, and West Virginia (Fuller, 2007; Ryan, 2006, pp. 55, 78); lawsuits that succeeded in New Jersey but failed in Arkansas, Massachusetts, and North Carolina (Ryan, 2006, p. 52); and ballot initiatives that succeeded in Florida (Hampton, 2004) but failed in California (Jacobson, 2009).

Why have a variety of governments, including conservative governments, been amenable to these policy ideas in the late 1990s and early 2000s rather than in previous time periods? Shifts in the global economy have made labour-market-enhancing policies increasingly important, and actors and organizations have played a crucial role in promoting these policy ideas. But while these more functional and actor-centred advocacy models can account in part for the changes observed, none of these arguments fully explain the complexity of patterns of investment observed in liberal welfare states. This chapter reviews the evidence for alternative explanations and then outlines the social investment model of policy change.

Explanatory Factors behind ECEC Provision

The comparative welfare state literature in general has neglected pre-primary and even primary education policy research. In the major political science and sociology research on comparative welfare states in recent years, only a few scholars (Ansell, 2010; Busemeyer, 2007; Castles, 1989; Garfinkel, Rainwater, and Smeeding, 2010; Hega and Hokenmaier, 2002; Heidenheimer, 1973, 1981; Lindert, 2004; Wolf, 2009) discuss education spending and the development of mass schooling as an important part of the development of the welfare state[1] – and none focus on pre-primary education.[2]

Much of the literature on ECEC provision has been largely descriptive, comparing ECEC policies and services across OECD countries and documenting cross-national variations (Kamerman and Kahn, 1991; Lamb et al., 1992; Melhuish and Moss, 1991; Melhuish and Petrogiannis, 1996; Olmsted and Weikart, 1989). More recent research has begun to explore the causal factors underpinning that cross-national variation (Gauthier, 1996; Morgan 2005, 2006; Pedersen, 1993), but the literature lacks consensus regarding the principal explanatory factors. Much of the literature mirrors the policy distinctions noted in the previous chapter, focusing on either pre-compulsory school policy development or child care provision, but rarely both.

Because of the complexity of the policy area, and the lack of easily available comparable policy indicators, much of the research focuses on comparing a few country cases and provides empirical detail regarding specific national models, with less focus on generalizable theory beyond the cases (Bock and Thane, 1991; Jenson and Sineau, 2001; Koven and Michel, 1993; Michel and Mahon, 2002). Insofar as gender policy literature has paid attention to these areas, the causal arrow is reversed such that research focuses on women's labour market participation, with women's equality as the factor to be explained, and with welfare state policies and programs, including ECEC provision, as one of the factors affecting the extent to which women can achieve equality

(England, 1996; Gornick and Meyers, 2003; Jenson and Sineau, 2001; Lewis, 1993; Michel, 1999; Timpson, 2001).

*Functional Arguments Related to Demographic and
Labour Market Changes*

More recently, scholars have turned their attention to the human capital functions of education – in particular, to early education investment (Esping-Andersen, 2002; Esping-Andersen et al., 2002; Hemerijck, 2013; Kenworthy, 2008) – and are including early years investments in analyses of welfare states and production regimes (Iversen and Stephens, 2008; Jensen, 2011a, 2011b). The linkages between state investment and human capital follow from some of the earlier functionalist[3] literature that examines countries' workforce needs (Jordan, 2006; Peng, 2002) or the impact of other demographic changes such as fertility levels on states' decisions to invest in ECEC policies and programs (Gauthier, 1996; Peng, 2002). Research on historical developments in ECEC policy notes, for example, that variation in state investment in work and family policies reflected the extent to which these countries faced labour shortages and had to rely on women's labour as opposed to immigrant or migrant labour (Jordan, 2006). Thus, Jordan (2006, p. 1110) notes "where immigrants were incapable of resolving labor shortages, women became the primary source of reserve labor requiring the state to adopt policies designed to promote women's employment and support dual-earner families." Jordan (2006) suggests, therefore, that norms around maternal employment had little to do with conservative or egalitarian cultural philosophies and more to do with the positions that states took on immigration. Germany was much more open to migrant labour after the Second World War, and this dampened its need for women's paid labour, whereas Sweden and France relied less on migrant labour and more on women's labour. According to Peng (2002), with regard to Japan, similar concerns about population decline and a shrinking workforce have motivated contemporary policy developments. Some scholars of contemporary policy development have observed that even governments with a strong male breadwinner tradition are reversing course and supporting maternal employment as a means of countering declining birthrates or labour shortages (Orloff, 2005; Plantenga and Remery, 2009).

Functional explanations do not carry well beyond the particular countries studied, however, or for all aspects of ECEC policy. Jordan's (2006) argument regarding labour market strategies assumes that governments have only two options in response to labour shortages: hire more women, or allow more immigration. In fact, government responses can be more complex, and even contradictory. For example, in the United States in the early twentieth century, policy makers needed labour but also feared "race suicide" – that is, the decline of the white population. So US governments simultaneously imposed immigration restrictions and some eugenicist measures, such as sterilization of the "feebleminded," and adopted a number of measures designed to support the health of white women and children and to discourage white women's labour market participation (Berry, 1993; Ladd-Taylor, 1994; May, 1995; Michel, 1999; Mink, 1995; Skocpol, 1992). Other country governments responded by providing increased cash and in-kind benefits to families to encourage childbearing, and still others resorted to more coercive measures such as restricting access to contraception and abortion (Gauthier, 1996; Pedersen, 1993). While fear of population decline has been well-documented as a motivating factor in government policy making in a number of country studies, Gauthier's (1996; 2007) comparative work demonstrates that demography is a very complex issue, one that is further complicated by concerns about poverty, social exclusion, and labour market issues. This makes it hard to identify demography as the sufficient causal factor. As well, given that countries respond very differently to their population concerns, researchers need to look beyond demography in order to understand the complex patterns of ECEC provision.

Furthermore, while concerns regarding women's labour market participation may provide analytic leverage when it comes to understanding patterns of state ECEC provision in some countries for children ages 0 to 3, they account less well for patterns of provision for children ages 3 to compulsory school age. Some countries – such as Belgium, France, and Italy, where traditionally there have been lower rates of women's and mothers' labour market participation than in social democratic and some liberal welfare states – have nearly universal pre-primary provision (see Tables 2.3a and b and Figure 1.3). In other words, pre-primary program provision bears very little relationship to labour market conditions. Functional explanations also cannot account for why countries such as the United States and Canada did not introduce child care policies in the 1970s when workplace conditions changed to permit women's labour market participation in ever greater numbers. One can assume that employers had an interest in facilitating those skilled and unskilled workers' participation, yet neither employers nor governments responded with increased public child care provision. Nor did parental demand shift along with employment increases. Barnett and Yarosz (2007, p. 3) note that "over the past half century, preschool participation has increased at the same pace for children whether or not their mothers are employed outside the home."

Barnett and Yarosz (2007, p. 3) posit instead that the primary reason for the contemporary increase in ECEC programs and services is increased demand on the part of all parents for the education of young children. Part of that increased demand for educational experiences for young children comes from increased policy attention to human capital development or what some literature labels "social investment" (Jenson, 2010; Jenson and Saint Martin, 2003; Morel, Palier, and Palme, 2012). Jensen (2011a, 2011b) argues that deindustrialization, and the resulting demand for reskilling, as well as recognition among policy makers that the demand for highly skilled workers in increasing, have together led governments in industrialized countries to focus on programs that generate human capital. In this regard, accumulating research has found that ECEC programs can yield tremendous long-term economic gains, not just in terms of workforce investment but also in terms of benefits to those who participate in high-quality programs. Longitudinal and mainly US-based studies such as the Perry High Scope study (Schweinhart et al., 2005), the Abecedarian study (Ramey et al., 2000), and the Chicago Child–Parent Centres study (Reynolds et al., 2001) have noted the impact of high-quality early interventions on vulnerable populations of children over long periods of time.

More recent studies of newer programs such as New Mexico's pre-k program, New Jersey's Abbott pre-school program, and Oklahoma's pre-k program (Fitzpatrick, 2008; Frede et al., 2007; Gormley et al., 2005; Hustedt, Barnett, and Friedman, 2010) all claim similar positive effects from these programs: they make children better prepared for school and increase their chances of academic success. Economic analyses demonstrating the positive economic impacts that early childhood intervention can have in promoting student success later in life (Heckman and Masterov, 2007; Lynch, 2004; Temple and Reynolds, 2007) have certainly helped draw attention to ECEC initiatives. The policy changes observed in liberal welfare states may thus simply be the result of matching a policy problem – such as poverty or educational inequities – to a policy solution – early years intervention.

While the eradication of poverty and inequality may have been the motivation behind programs such as Head Start in the United States in the 1960s (Vinovskis, 2005) and the British Labour government's Sure Start program in the late 1990s (Waldfogel, 2010), current ECEC

Figure 3.1. Relative child poverty rates in selected OECD countries, 2009*

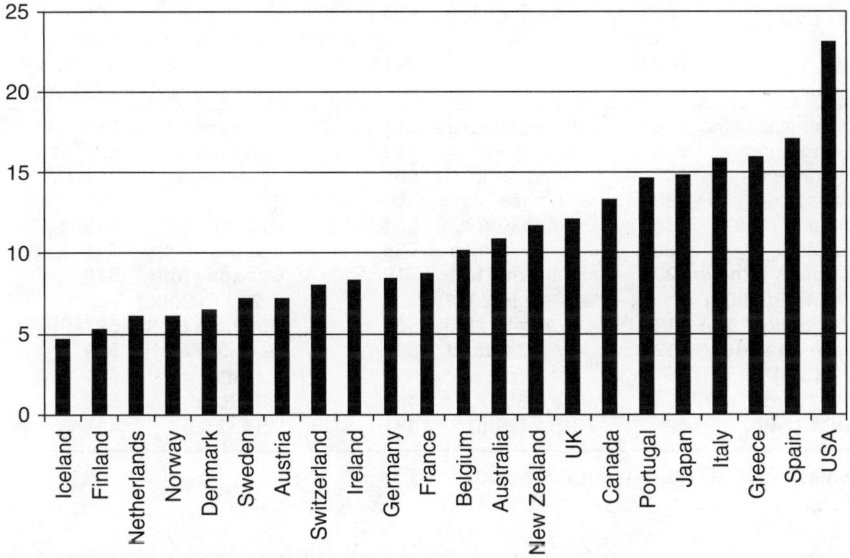

*The Innocenti Research Centre's definition of relative child poverty is the percentage of children age 17 or under who live "in a household in which disposable income, when adjusted for family size and composition, is less than 50% of the national median income" (UNICEF 2012, p. 3).

programs go well beyond serving countries' most vulnerable groups and are emerging as well in liberal countries with lower child poverty rates, such as New Zealand (see Figure 3.1). Efforts to expand early childhood education to the general population seem to coincide with concerns about student performance in cross-national educational assessments such as the PISA (what is known as "PISA shock") (Grek, 2009; Martens, Rusconi, and Leuze, 2007). PISA assessments have revealed that students who had attended pre-primary education programs perform better than peers who had not, even after controlling for socio-economic background (OECD PISA, 2011). The publication of these results, as well as other research on educational outcomes, has drawn attention to early years programs in a number of countries, including the United Kingdom and the United States, where PISA rankings are low compared to those of other industrialized countries (see Table 3.1 as well as Bieber and Martens, 2011; Woessmann, and Peterson, 2007).

Table 3.1. PISA country rankings in selected countries, 2012

Country	Reading mean scores, PISA 2012	Country	Mathematics mean scores, PISA 2012	Country	Science mean scores, PISA 2012
Shanghai-China	570	Shanghai-China	613	Shanghai-China	580
Hong Kong	545	Singapore	573	Hong Kong	555
Singapore	542	Hong Kong	561	Singapore	551
Japan	538	Chinese Taipei	560	Japan	547
South Korea	536	South Korea	554	Finland	545
Finland	524	Macao-China	538	Estonia	541
Canada (7th; 2nd in 2000)	**523**	**Canada (13th; 5th in 2003)**	**518**	**Canada (10th; 2nd in 2006)**	**525**
Australia (13th)	**512**	**Australia (19th)**	**504**	**Australia (16th)**	**521**
New Zealand (13th)	**512**	**New Zealand (22rd)**	**500**	**New Zealand (18th)**	**516**
UK (23rd)	**499**	**UK(26th)**	**494**	**UK (20th)**	**514**
USA (24th)	**498**	**USA (36th)**	**481**	**USA (28th)**	**497**

Sources: OECD PISA (2001, 2004, 2007, 2013)

Given the generally held belief in the importance of a highly skilled and highly educated workforce to compete in an increasingly globalized economy, how countries perform on cross-national educational assessments has become increasingly important in swaying policy opinion. Since the introduction of the US Department of Education's Trends in International Mathematics and Science Study (TIMSS), and especially since 2000 with the introduction of the OECD's PISA, cross-national benchmarking in educational performance has been possible. Countries that perform relatively poorly on these international rankings may therefore be more willing to invest public funds in early childhood education as a means to improve student test scores. In the case of Australia and Canada, "PISA complacency" as opposed to "PISA shock" could explain why there is less domestic outcry for early childhood education programs than in the United Kingdom and the United States, although that would not account for the expansion of early childhood education in both countries at the state/provincial level.

The interesting puzzle is why so many governments have begun to emphasize integrated early learning programs, even in the Nordic welfare states, with their strong social pedagogical traditions, and in countries that do well on cross-national educational assessments, such as Finland. Jensen (2009, p. 15) argues that countries with strong readiness-for-school curriculum traditions such as the liberal welfare states have seen ECEC expansion because governments can increasingly see the demonstrable connections between pre-primary education and the generation of human capital. But it is important to understand how that curriculum tradition has developed and changed. In the past, kindergartens, at heart, were play-based (Wollons, 2000), and child care centres often did not have a strong educational focus (although many had a pedagogical focus) (Bennett, 2003). Both sets of programs are increasing their focus on education.

Curriculum traditions alone cannot account for the cross-national variation observed. Nordic welfare states are generally continuing to increase investments in ECEC programs on a per child basis, even though their overall expenditures as a percentage of GDP are declining (see Figures 1.1 and 1.2). In contrast, some countries, such as Switzerland, have experienced PISA shock (Bieber and Martens, 2011; Grek, 2009) but are still underinvesting in ECEC programs (see Figures 1.1 and 1.2). Still other governments in some continental European countries such as Belgium and Italy had already supported very robust preschool services (Scheiwe and Willekens, 2009). Thus, while these broad human capital concerns may be one part of the explanation for recent ECEC investment, they cannot account entirely for patterns of provision. As Pierson (2000b, p. 477) points out, needs may exist, but the particular policy choices made to respond to those needs, and the institutions that arise to support those policy choices, require explanation as well (see also Pierson, 2000a, 2000c).

Domestic Political Institutions and Policy Advocates

Policy process models focus on the role that policy entrepreneurs and other actors play in garnering attention for a policy issue. Kingdon (1984) argues, for example, that problem identification triggers a complex process of policy debate during which policy advocates and entrepreneurs work with policy makers to explore particular policy solutions in a particular institutional context. A number of scholars have focused on the role that women political activists play in promoting ECEC policies, a role that includes their institutional links to political parties and governing party politics (Hobson and Lindholm, 1997; Huber and Stephens, 2001). Other researchers point to the role that powerful advocacy organizations such as teachers' unions and charitable foundations have played in the universal pre-k movement in the United States (Bushouse, 2009; Fuller, 2007; Kirp, 2007; Knott and McCarthy, 2007). But this research does not provide a full account as to why *particular* ECEC policy ideas are persuasive and why policy advocates supportive of these policies are having success currently (Bushouse, 2009; Cohen, 2001; Kirp, 2007).

Powerful oppositional interests of long standing continue to oppose the adoption of ECEC policies in the United States and in Canada. But oppositional interest-based explanations cannot account for patterns of ECEC provision, either. Both France and the United States, for example, have had fairly strong religious- and familial-based conservative social movements that call for women to remain in the home (Klaus, 1993; Pedersen, 1993; Michel, 1999). In France, strong religious, pro-natalist, and familial conservative organizations were influential politically during much of the pre– and most of the post–Second World War period (Cova, 1991; Offen, 1991). That period was marked by a great deal of socially conservative legislation but also by an expansion of social policies to support families, which provided the basis for program development in the 1960s and beyond (White, 2004a, 2009a). In the United States, socially conservative groups were not dominant in the 1960s and 1970s but have grown in strength politically since the 1980s (Diamond, 1995); yet child care programs have expanded at the same time. As Cohen (2001, pp. 17–18) points out, some of the most significant changes in US child care policy making were in fact enacted under divided partisan government – that is, under a Republican president and a Democratic Congress (e.g., the Child Care Development Block Grant under George H.W. Bush in 1990), or under a Democratic president and a Republican Congress (TANF-related child care funding in 1996), with little happening in periods of unified Democratic governments (under President Carter, 1977–80; President Clinton, 1993–94) (Cohen, 2001, p. 286). A major expansion of child care services in France occurred in the post-1960s period, under mainly centre-right governments (White, 2004a, 2009a), with a major slowing of policies under the left-wing Mitterrand government (Jenson and Sineau, 2001).

Other scholars examine the impact of partisan factors such as confessional parties in explaining cross-national variation in ECEC provision (Castles, 1994; Morgan, 2006; Van Kersbergen, 1995; Van Kersbergen and Manow, 2009). Morgan (2006, p. 2), for example, argues that state provision of ECEC policies and programs depends on political dominance by secular authorities within the state decision-making apparatus as well as societal acceptance "that mothers should work while their children are young and that the state should influence family care arrangements." Morgan (2006, pp. 2–3) thus argues that "organized religion has played a critical role in shaping political ideologies about gender roles and the appropriate relationship between the state and the family" and that "patterns of church-state relations and religious conflict had an enduring impact on early family and educational politics, as well as the way religion would be incorporated into politics." In Sweden and France, state authorities usurped the power of religious authorities, which meant they could secularize family policies and play a more active role in delivering those programs. In the Netherlands and the United States, in contrast, social conservative religious groups gained greater influence in politics and thus could ensure that state policy reinforced traditional gender roles. Korpi (2000) argues that countries with strong religious traditions manifest in confessional party dominance tend to adopt more family-focused social policies than secular conservative parties, which tend to adopt more market-oriented policies, and left parties, which tend to adopt dual-earner reinforcing policies.

There are strong exceptions, however, to the argument that confessional party dominance limits ECEC provision, and that strong left party dominance, often tied with feminist organizations, promotes ECEC provision (Hobson and Lindholm, 1997). While it is true that the Netherlands, along with Ireland, Italy, Switzerland, Germany, and Austria, historically have weak levels of child care provision, and that they all have strong confessional and/or conservative centrist party traditions, Belgium, which Korpi (2000) rates as having strong confessional party dominance, and France, with its conservative centrist party dominance, have greater pre-primary provision compared to Sweden, and this is despite having weaker feminist organizations (Duchen, 1986; Gelb, 1989; Hobson and Lindholm, 1997). Belgium and Italy have also developed near-universal pre-primary programs, despite having strong confessional parties (Korpi, 2000). This evidence suggests that strong educational norms can develop even in religious-dominated polities, and leads us to consider the more complex connections between the development of ECEC programs and that of other social programs.

A number of researchers have examined the connection between weak ECEC provision and weak educational institutional structures resulting from federalism or decentralization (Evers, Lewis, and Riedel, 2005; Rauch, 2005). Federalism and decentralization clearly play a role in contemporary ECEC provision, although the causal relationships are difficult to determine. There is some scholarly dispute about the impact of federal structures and levels of decentralization on public policies. Treisman (2007) argues that the claim that decentralization encourages more effective policies and accountable government does not hold up under theoretical or empirical scrutiny in his cases examined (mainly Russia, China, and other developing countries). However, in a more historical and case-focused analysis of federal countries in the developed world, Leibfried, Castles, and Obinger (2005, p. 308) found that "federalism does indeed have inhibitory effects on welfare state development, but that these effects have crucial temporal and contextual limitations ... under certain circumstance[s], federalism may actually serve to encourage the growth of social expenditure." Henderson and White (2004), in an analysis of child care, early childhood education, and maternity/parental leave provision in developed welfare states, found that an increased number of veto points – measured in terms of presidential, bicameral, and federal systems – produced less extensive early childhood education provision over the 1980–2000 period and that this was also true for child care provision by the late 1990s. However, system vetoes were a significant and positive predictor for maternity/parental leave only in 1998, which suggests that for policies already in place, system vetoes can provide a bulwark against welfare state retrenchment (see also Leibfried, Castles, and Obinger, 2005). And while White (2001a) argues that federalism appeared to hamper Canadian child care policy development in the late 1990s, by the mid-2000s, federalism proved less restrictive to policy development than did partisan ideological factors (Friendly and White, 2007).

Some scholars have thus turned away from federalism per se and scrutinized more explicitly the relationship between central and local governments to explain variation in ECEC provision. Rauch (2005), for example, argues that greater institutional decentralization in Norway absent fiscal autonomy allowed for more veto opportunities among municipal players, including non-governmental organizations (NGOs), and accounts for why child care provision for children under age 3 and rates of full-time provision lag behind the unitary Scandinavian countries of Sweden and Denmark. At the same time, local autonomy with concomitant fiscal capacity is also useful in encouraging both expansion and experimentation. Cohen and colleagues (2004, p. 32) argue that the United Kingdom has experienced greater centralization of authority over education and that this has prevented local authorities from developing ECEC services themselves, which in turn has fuelled a vast but unstable market in ECEC services. Evers, Lewis, and Riedel (2005) note, in contrast, that while the development of ECEC services has been slower in Germany, the subsidiarity model has allowed for steadier growth based on community-based service provision. Cohen and colleagues (2004, p. 33) argue that a similar decentralized approach in Sweden facilitated integration and good relations between schools, pre-schools, and school-age services and more choices for parents (see also Wincott, 2005). Thus, administrative centralization/decentralization does not yield a generalizable explanation for provision.

Ideas and Their Diffusion

The institutional literature offers some insight into the complex processes of policy change but does not reveal why particular policy ideas get chosen over others; nor, given its claims regarding the contingent nature of policy change, does it account for widespread policy change, including the transfer of ideas across borders. The ideational literature, in turn, focuses attention on the role that particular ideas can play in influencing policies. Programmatic ideas can provide specific policy solutions, while policy frames can shape actors' responses to ideas (Blyth, 2001; Schmidt, 2008; White, 2009a). In other words, ideas can shape and transform interests; thus they function as more than merely a "hook" on which actors hang their interests, or focal points around which actors' interests converge, as some ideational literature claims (Garrett and Weingast, 1993; Goldstein and Keohane, 1993; Weingast, 1995).

A model of policy change that takes the substance of ideas seriously needs to focus on the endogenous impact of ideas. The accumulation of new ideas over time can eventually challenge entrenched policy thinking and trigger policy change even absent a major crisis or rupture. Thelen (2003) and others (Streeck and Thelen, 2005) identify some of these endogenous processes of policy change: layering (of some new elements onto an existing institutional structure); conversion (of certain institutional goals to other ends); drift (or erosion in the absence of institutional maintenance); and displacement as "new models emerge and diffuse and … call into question existing, previously taken-for-granted organizational forms and practices" (Streeck and Thelen, 2005, p. 19).

Scholars such as Haas (1992) examine the role that knowledge accumulation in particular and new experiences and events in general have on one's beliefs and preferences; through rational updating, this process can lead to learning and ultimately to policy change. In the case of ECEC, as neurobiological, behavioural, and social scientific knowledge has accumulated regarding the positive impact of early years programs on children's subsequent developmental, social, and economic success (Shonkoff and Phillips, 2000), policy makers' views of early childhood may have shifted as well as their understandings of best policy practices. As that knowledge accumulates and becomes more widespread, policy learning can occur that can "transfer" across jurisdictions through processes of policy diffusion (Dolowitz and Marsh, 2000; Marsh and Sharman, 2009). In order to demonstrate that policy learning is occurring, one must demonstrate that policy makers were aware of and informed about policies elsewhere and that this knowledge influenced their decision making through a process of policy transfer (Mossberger and Wolman, 2003, p. 430).

The fact that policy shifts are occurring in a number of countries simultaneously suggests a need to explore whether ideational diffusion can account for simultaneous adoption across jurisdictions. Learning could result from direct interpersonal contact between policy transmitters and adopters – what McAdam and Rucht (1993, p. 59) label a relational model of ideational diffusion – or through non-relational channels such as the mass media or think tanks McAdam and Rucht (1993, p. 59). The sources of the learning, therefore, could be domestic or transnational/international or both.[4] The literature on transnational policy diffusion points to myriad sources of policy ideas, including international organizations (IOs) (Barnett and Finnemore, 2004), transnational advocacy networks (Keck and Sikkink, 1998), networks of state actors (Slaughter, 2004), and epistemic communities – that is, communities of experts who share "a commitment to a common causal model and a common set of political values" (Haas, 1990, p. 41) and who spread these ideas by attending conferences and sharing their ideas with one another and with policy makers (knowledge regimes) (Campbell and Pedersen, 2011).

Simmons, Dobbin, and Garrett (2008, p. 10) then argue that diffusion of policy ideas occurs as the result of four mechanisms: learning, coercion, competition, and emulation. The latter mechanism can be divided into blind emulation for strategic reasons (e.g., imitation of the most powerful or successful actors), or socialization towards principles of "right" action. Governments may adopt similar policy ideas as an instrumentally rational means to compete with other countries.

Governments may also experience coercion from powerful countries or from international organizations. They may also adopt similar policies through unreflective emulation. Finally, they may be persuaded to adopt a particular policy because they come to believe it is the "right" thing to do.

Recent scholarship (Orenstein, 2008; Weyland, 2006) demonstrates that domestic uptake of international and transnational ideas is contingent on a number of factors. Domestic factors may make the transfer of policy ideas difficult (Lenschow, Liefferink, and Veenman, 2005). For example, the political elite at one level or branch of government may embrace a particular idea, but competing elites either within another branch of government in a congressional system or at another level of government in a federal system may act as veto players (Ha, 2008; Kastner and Rector, 2003; Tsebelis, 1995). So too can recalcitrant bureaucracies. Partisan shifts in key players – for example, the election of a political party with a different partisan agenda – may stymie policy adoption. Also, domestic civil society may respond negatively to policy initiatives at the elite level, and threaten policy makers with electoral loss (Linos, 2013). All of these factors can impede the transfer and uptake of ideas in any setting.

Rational Diffusion and Learning … or Something Else?

Diffusion models thus suggest three sources of policy change, which can in fact operate simultaneously (Koh, 2005–6, pp. 745–6):

- Policy change as a result of international norm development that interacts with domestic policy factors to affect domestic policy making.
- Policy change as a result of government-to-government policy transfer assisted by domestic and transnational groups but absent international forces.
- Policy change as a result of domestic factors that contribute to within-country policy diffusion but not cross-national policy diffusion.

The constraints imposed by domestic institutions on the diffusion of transnational ideas lead us to consider the factors that make domestic uptake more likely. Some research suggests that proximity may influence governments' choices. That is, countries "that are culturally, institutionally or economically close may be expected to adopt similar ideas, instruments or settings in public policy" (Lenschow, Liefferink, and Veenman, 2005, p. 797; see also Simmons and Elkins, 2004; Strang and Meyer, 1993). The geographic proximity of Canada and the United States could lead governments in those countries to adopt similar policy ideas. Other scholars observe the influence that dominant states can have in either encouraging policy harmonization (Drezner, 2005) or imposing it (Busch, Jörgens, and Tews, 2005), suggesting that US policy action would be mimicked elsewhere. Diffusion models of policy change often explore the role of transfer agents – that is, the actions of organized interests, either as policy entrepreneurs (Schneider, Teske, and Mintrom, 1995), or in advocacy coalitions (Sabatier and Jenkins-Smith, 1993), policy networks (Coleman and Skogstad, 1990), or epistemic communities whose influence stems from their scientific expertise (Lindvall, 2009) and whose activities extend across subnational borders.

All would suggest that Canada and the United States would be prime candidates for cross-national policy learning, either nationally or at the state/provincial level. Other political, economic, and social factors that could affect policies – such as ideological parties, trade union density, country wealth, veto points such as federalism, electoral system effects, and female and maternal employment rates (Jahn, 2006; see also Borges Sugiyama, 2008; Brooks, 2005; Busch, Jörgens, and Tews, 2005; Kopstein and Reilly, 2000; Lenschow, Liefferink, and Veenman, 2005) – are similar across the two countries. As subsequent chapters will reveal, however, there is little evidence of cross-national policy learning. US state governments' adoption of early childhood education programs occurred at the same time as, or even prior to, internationalization of these ideas at the IO level. Early adopters were not emulating foreign models; rather, they were figuring out solutions to their own perceived policy problems.

Sub-national country case analysis reveals some major limitations of the rational diffusion and learning literature as well. As Figure 3.2 and Table 3.2 reveal, no regional clustering in western, eastern, midwestern, and southern states can be observed, as would be predicted by rational diffusion models that argue that political processes are affected by events in neighbouring polities (Berry and Berry, 1999; Gray, 1973; Walker, 1969) or that polities tend to become more like neighbouring polities over time, often for reasons of economic competition (Brinks and Coppedge, 2006; Kopstein and Reilly, 2000; Skrede Gleditsch and

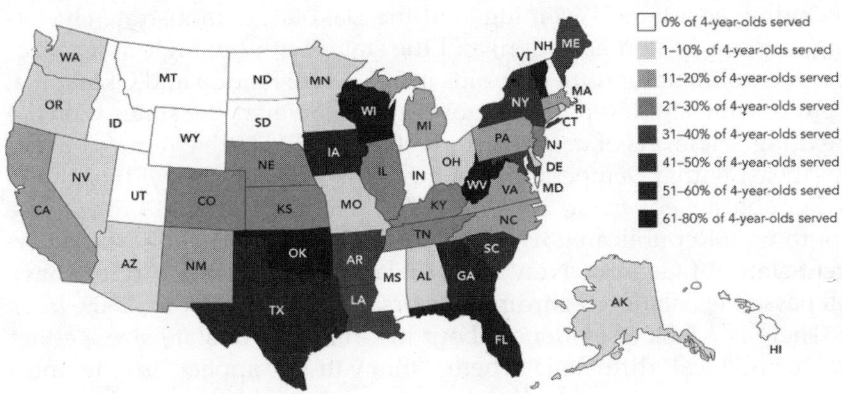

Source: Barnett et al. (2013, p. 9)

Table 3.2. Top 10 states 2013 by census region and governor's party affiliation

Access for 4-year-olds	State spending	Quality**	All resources ranking
Florida (south; R)*	New Jersey (northeast; R)*	Alabama (south; R) [10]	Connecticut (northeast; D)*
Oklahoma (south; R)	Connecticut (northeast; D)	Alaska (west; R)	New Jersey (northeast; R)
Vermont (northeast; D)	Rhode Island (northeast; I)	North Carolina (south; D)	West Virginia (south; D)
Wisconsin (Midwest; R)	Oregon (west; D)	Rhode Island (northeast; I)	Rhode Island (northeast; I)
West Virginia (south; D)	Minnesota (Midwest; D)	Arkansas (south; D) [9]	Oregon (west; D)
Iowa (Midwest; R)	Alaska (west; R)	Kentucky (south; D)	Oklahoma (south; R)
Georgia (south; R)	Delaware (south; D)	Minnesota (Midwest; D)	Minnesota (Midwest; D)
Texas (south; R)	Washington (west; D)	Oklahoma (south; R)	Alabama (south; R)
New York (northeast; D)	West Virginia (south; D)	Tennessee (south; R)	Alaska (west; R)
South Carolina (south; R)	Pennsylvania (northeast; R)	Washington (west; D)	North Carolina (south; D)

* As of 2013, DC ranks highest in terms of access, spending, and all resources.
** Quality measures are ranked in alphabetical order, with quality markers scored out of 10.
Source: Barnett et al. (2013); National Governors' Association Roster

Ward, 2006; Volden, 2002; Walker, 1969). The northwestern states, including Montana, Wyoming, and the Dakotas, demonstrate clustering in terms of non-adoption; and the states with the highest levels of pre-k enrolment for four-year-olds in 2013 were Florida and Oklahoma, both of which had Republican governors. However, the states with the next-highest levels of access include those as diverse as Vermont in the northeast with a Democratic governor, Wisconsin in the Midwest with a Republican governor, and West Virginia and Georgia, both in the south with Republican governors. The regionally and politically divergent states of Georgia, New York, Oklahoma, and West Virginia have all passed legislation regarding universal access (Bushouse, 2009, p. 2).

There is a lack of evidence about the influence of state size – either of hierarchical diffusion, where "innovations appear in the most advanced or largest centers and are then adopted by successively less advanced or smaller units" (Collier and Messick, 1975, p. 1306), or, conversely, of what Collier and Messick (1975, p. 1311) describe as "diffusion up a hierarchy," where early adopters are not necessarily the largest and most advanced economically because change in the larger states encounters resistance in those larger states, which leads to later adoption. Two big states – Florida and New York – have committed to UPK, but California has not, because of a failed ballot initiative. In Canada, the largest province, Ontario, has introduced full-day kindergarten for all 4- and 5-year-olds; the smallest province, PEI, has also implemented full-day kindergarten for 5-year-olds in schools. So too has BC, meaning policy reforms have occurred in provinces both large and small, and in the western and eastern parts of the country as well as in central Canada.

Other factors included in the diffusion literature, such as clustering according to wealth of the state (either high-income and therefore resource-rich; or low-income and therefore with greatest need), and homogeneity of the population, do not have explanatory purchase. Two poorer states – Georgia and Oklahoma – proceeded with pre-k reform during bad economic times, while New York declined to proceed with its commitments even during good economic times (Bushouse, 2009; Raden, 1999; Rose, 2010).

There is little evidence of regional emulation either. In the southern states, Georgia was the first state to adopt universal pre-k. Oklahoma currently has the highest coverage for 4-year-olds. Alabama has one of the highest-quality programs and was the first state to provide full-day kindergarten, but only for a very small portion of the student population.

Mississippi, which has the highest poverty rates in the United States, had no publicly financed pre-k program until 2014 (Barnett et al., 2016). Yet these southern states have populations with similar demographic characteristics, including with regard to workforce participation, levels of education, racial diversity, levels of urban versus rural population, and percentages of families on social assistance.

Oklahoma policy makers redirected funds to pre-kindergarten because of declining enrolments in K-12 classrooms as the state faced population decline (Ackerman et al., 2009, p. 5). The Dakotas have experienced population decline but have not invested in pre-k (Barnett et al., 2013, p. 8). DiChiara and Galliher (1994, pp. 44–5) argue that racial concerns about directing resources to minority communities could lead states with relatively homogeneous populations to be early adopters of programs. That could certainly account for early adoption in Oklahoma but not in Florida.

The case of pre-k adoption thus seems to defy a rational diffusion explanation; in this, it stands in contrast to other policy areas such as social assistance, children's health, and other policy areas (Volden, 2006). Soss and colleagues (2001) found that the adoption of punitive TANF reforms in the United States followed similar "get tough" rules adopted by states that had demonstrated similar practices in the past. Legalization of marriage between partners of the same sex also follows standard diffusion theory, with regional clustering in policy innovation as a result of institutional interventions (National Conference of State Legislatures, 2012). The first states to legalize "same sex" marriage and/or domestic partnerships either through litigation or legislation were Connecticut, Massachusetts, New Hampshire, New Jersey, New York, and Vermont, all in the northeast.[5] This striking instance of regional clustering *is* predicted by the diffusion literature, as a result either of emulation or of independent learning because of similar state characteristics (Shipan and Volden, 2008; Volden, Ting, and Carpenter, 2008). No similar pattern of emulation or regional learning is observed in the case of ECEC, however.

In comparative social policy research, political partisanship is hypothesized to play an important role. Karch (2009) found that more liberal states support the funding of pre-school, as do more Democratic states. Policy adoption may thus be a political strategy that policy elites follow in order to get elected or stay elected. But these strategic partisanship models cannot fully account for the patterns of policy change observed. Universal pre-k has found support among both Republican and Democratic state governments. Karch (2010) also argues that movement fragmentation may partly explain the patterns of policy adoption in the United States. Already existing groups may have an interest in maintaining their own programs and resist policy reform even when it is their interest. Karch (2010) has found that the size of a Head Start community, for example, negatively affects state decisions to invest in public pre-school. Head Start dominance, he notes, has a statistically significant effect, but not absent other factors. But in other states, such as Oklahoma, private child care providers did not resist the legislature's decision to deliver kindergarten solely through public schools (Bushouse, 2009). And in California, the California State Teachers Association supported the UPK ballot initiative despite provisions that would have allowed pre-kindergarten to be delivered in public, private, and parochial schools (Rose, 2010, p. 156). These outcomes suggest that something else besides interest politics accounts for the pattern of policy adoption.

A Social Investment Model of Policy Change

The pattern of ECEC diffusion is difficult to observe through parsimonious observations of one or two key variables such as political party identification or neighbouring jurisdiction effects. It is thus more akin to a culture move (Rochon, 1998) than to a "rational" policy response. The process whereby these culture moves occur is often not rational and systematic, but rather slow and contingent on the confluence of particular actors, institutional opportunities, and events. New evidence or changes in the political-economic or demographic context can cause policy makers and the public to re-evaluate their beliefs and preferences regarding particular policies and programs, as well as the role of the state in delivering those programs. But these new ideas compete with existing cultural norms regarding the appropriateness of state involvement in these areas.

Policy experts and advocates therefore must use specific frames to make ECEC policy adoption appear both rational *and* legitimate. At least in the early period of policy change, the work of framing is done on a jurisdiction-by-jurisdiction basis, but over time it can "spill over" into other jurisdictions, leading to a "tipping point" where jurisdictions emulate the actions of others (Boushey, 2010). Shifts in policies may not occur through a rational process of policy diffusion, but rather in fits and starts; policy adoption in one jurisdiction may in fact discourage innovation in other jurisdictions on principled grounds (e.g., "the province of Quebec is not like the Rest of Canada"). This social policy investment model requires that policy change be traced across multiple jurisdictions. The model focuses on three key factors in particular: the role and autonomy of political leadership; the framing strategies of those political leaders and policy entrepreneurs; and frame dynamics that arise during public discussion, particularly around the credibility and legitimacy of the state to deliver public programs. The rest of this chapter outlines, in brief, the principal explanatory factors underpinning the model.

The social policy investment model rests, first, on the assertion that some policy discussions are more vulnerable than others to norm-based arguments. As Mooney and Lee (1995, 1999), Mucciaroni (2011), and others have observed, some policy discussions – which they label morality policy – encompass normative as well as rational–instrumental considerations. Some normative considerations are more widely diffused; these include debates about gender and gender roles such as those over marriage between partners of the same sex, the acceptability of women working outside the home, and child care and early childhood education. Other norms can be more geographically bounded within a country or at a sub-national level, such as debates over gun control in the United States (Melzer, 2009), debates over embryonic stem cell research (Banchoff, 2005), debates over whether climate change is human-induced (Hoffman, 2011a, 2011b), and debates over the abolition of the death penalty (Mooney and Lee, 1999). Policy debates in these areas centre on principled beliefs around the moral goodness or badness of a policy, as well as the best means to achieve given ends.

Social policy discussions that involve these kinds of principled discussions often do not become "virulent," as diffusion theories such as Boushey's (2010) would predict. Success with issues of policy uptake and institutionalization is highly contingent on the framing strategies of proponents and detractors (Gormley, 2012) and is rooted in the interactive effects of *policy investment* and *cultural logics*. Actors are important agents or carriers of these policy ideas as well as promoters of policy logics. But in contrast to actor-centred explanations, which assert that the success of these actors rests on their organizations' characteristics – such as structure, membership, political and other resources, degree and extent of mobilization, and connections to government (Andrews and Edwards, 2004; Haider-Markel, 2001; McCarthy and Zald, 1977; Mintrom, 1997; Mintrom and Vergari, 1998) – this book demonstrates that policy change

occurs because actors *persuade* policy makers to take up specific ideas –
that is, the substance of ideas matters, and so does specific framing.

Policy Investment Logics

As Alan Jacobs (2011, p. 4) argues, a central challenge of democratic governance is "promoting society's long-run welfare in the face of short-run
political imperatives." Policy makers have to determine when to make
costly policy investments in the short term that may have distributional
implications in order to make society collectively better off in the long
run (A. Jacobs, 2011, p. 17). Increasingly, ECEC investments are perceived in that light. In recent decades, increased economic competition
has led governments to focus on human capital development needs,
learning processes, and how to improve educational outcomes (Esping-
Andersen, 2002; Kenworthy, 2008). These concerns, and the evidence
supporting the positive impacts of certain early years program interventions, have led governments and other policy actors to advocate
for these programs based on the results of high-profile longitudinal
studies that have documented the positive impact of high-quality early
interventions on vulnerable populations of children in terms of a number of cognitive and non-cognitive measures. A number of economic
cost–benefit analyses have quantified the effectiveness of spending on
early years programs. They weigh the financial impact of prevention
and early intervention against the costs of subsequent spending on
such things as labour market training, social assistance, and criminal
prosecutions.[6] Such studies, including reanalyses of earlier intervention
studies (e.g., Heckman et al., 2010) have found that early years investments yield major direct returns to society in terms of decreased costs
in health care, social service use, and delinquency.

ECEC investments must thus be viewed as an instrumentally rational
means for a government to improve its human capital and to compete
with other jurisdictions to gain a comparative economic advantage
(Shipan and Volden, 2008). States have an incentive to make these
investments if they are convinced that there is sufficient evidence that
these investments are worthwhile based on an analysis of costs and
benefits. And indeed, in recent years, some states such as Oklahoma
have adopted UPK as a rational response to halt population decline
and "farm flight" (Bushouse, 2009); Georgia similarly approved a state
lottery to fund pre-k because of perpetually poor educational performance in the state (Ackerman et al., 2009, p. 4). Federal introduction of

the US Educate America Act in 1994 and the No Child Left Behind Act in 2001 put pressure on public schools to improve overall student performance and close achievement gaps between more and less advantaged students (Manna, 2006; McGuinn, 2006; Vinovskis, 2009). Other pressures to promote school readiness have arisen out of concern about how well American students perform on cross-national education assessments. New evidence or changes in a state's political-economic context or these federalism pressures, it is assumed, can cause policy makers and the public to rethink or update their beliefs and preferences regarding particular policies and programs, as well as the state's role in delivering those programs.

Cultural Logics

Policy change often requires a shift in thinking more fundamental than simply persuading policy makers to act and the public to accept policy change on the basis of instrumental or evidentiary claims. It is equally important to overcome previously strongly held views about the role of the state vis-à-vis the family, the market, or civil society. These policy investment arguments compete with existing cultural norms regarding the appropriateness of state involvement in these areas. Public opinion surveys in the United States and Canada reveal that a majority of the public believe that "parents should be the primary influence on their children's lives" and that "it is best if mothers can be home to care for the very young" (Sylvester, 2001a, 53). Early childhood education and care debates, like many of the contemporary "culture wars," centre on deeply held and often conflicting beliefs about mothers, family responsibilities, and family forms. The acceptability of divorce, single parenthood, or same-sex marriage as a family form, the permissibility of sex outside marriage, and adoption by couples of the same sex, all focus on principled beliefs about what the family is, and what values should be inculcated in children (Brennan, 2006; Zimmerman, 2002).

How do we know that policy discussions have a cultural dimension instead of or in addition to being rooted in rational learning or power-based politics? Mucciaroni (2011) argues that morality policies (or, more accurately, morality frames) appeal to principled beliefs rather than instrumental rationality and that those principled beliefs can become normative. Norms are detectable when they are violated, as revealed by public responses to a policy action.

Subsequent chapters document the arguments used to justify policy action and whether and to what extent those arguments have shifted over time. Through the analytic techniques of process tracing and thematic and discourse analysis, analyses of policy documents and public debates reveal how policy makers and the broader public describe a policy and also what value connections they make through the rhetoric they use (positive, negative). Interviews with relevant policy officials and organized interests help to discern, through interviewees' own self-assessments, how policy ideas emerged and key policy changes occurred, as well as what factors most influenced those changes. Subsequent chapters demonstrate in particular how "this goes against" kinds of principled policy arguments as well as means/end kinds of framing strategies and frame dynamics unfold over time and can account for variation in policy outcomes across jurisdictions.

The next two chapters trace the involvement of both domestic actors and international and transnational advocates in setting the agenda for ECEC policy change with arguments rooted in both instrumentally rational arguments and principled beliefs. Chapter 4 traces how a domestic epistemic (expert) community, mostly US-based, laid the evidentiary groundwork for state investment in early childhood education and the subsequent creation of a knowledge regime of actors, related organizations, and institutions. The chapter documents how, as part of that regime building, traditional advocacy organizations in both Canada and the United States shifted their arguments quite explicitly to support more integrated early years policies and programs and to highlight in particular the language of early childhood education and then helped diffuse those ideas through policy networks. Chapter 5 traces how those ideas became concomitantly transnationalized and embedded in international organizations through transnational policy networks.

From chapter 6 on, this book then tracks the impact of those ideas and actors on domestic policy implementation in the United States and Canada. It traces the variation in policy uptake, rooted in political leadership factors, as well as the framing strategies of those political leaders and policy entrepreneurs and the frame dynamics that arise during public discussion, particularly around the credibility and legitimacy of the state to deliver public programs.

PART TWO

The Sources of Policy Change

Chapter Four

The Role of Science in the Development of an ECEC Knowledge Regime

This chapter charts the intellectual origins and trends in scholarly research that led to shifts in scientific understanding of early childhood development, and mothers' roles in that development, and the policy interventions that emerged from those changed understandings. It also tracks the creation of what Campbell and Pedersen (2011, p. 167) label a "knowledge regime" that includes the community of experts (epistemic community), supporting organizations, and attendant institutions that emerged in the United States and then spread both transnationally and internationally through policy networks to promote particular cognitive ideas regarding ECEC policies and programs.

Two things can be observed about the early childhood knowledge regime. First, experts played a crucial role in creating and helping to diffuse policy ideas around the early years and mothers' role. Scientific experts and (later) interest and advocacy groups, along with philanthropic foundations, leveraged a great many resources to influence particular policy developments in the United States and then elsewhere. Second, it was not just the organizational strength of those actors but also the content of their ideas that played a crucial role in shifting norms around early childhood and the moral "goodness" of maternal employment. This chapter demonstrates how changes in cognitive ideas around childhood/motherhood prepared the ground for those shifting norms, which, when combined with particular institutional contexts and particular frames, made some jurisdictions particularly amenable to policy adoption. The strongest indicator of cultural change is whether norms are widespread or widely held; the extent of that culture change is thus explored in chapters 6 and 7.

This chapter maps the domestic knowledge regime and the ideas promoted through publications, websites, speeches, testimonies before legislative bodies, and so on. It explores how those ideas (and idea carriers) spread through research and policy networks. It identifies key individuals and organizations involved in various policy venues and the relationships they cultivated through participation in conferences, through their legislative testimony, and so on. Unlike network analysis, however, which attributes policy change to the strength of those ties, I argue that it was the ideas themselves that were persuasive. I conduct an ideational process tracing (Fisher, Leifeld, and Iwaki, 2013; Paterson et al. 2014) in order to demonstrate what ideas were important and how they diffused over time and across borders, namely, to Canada.

Ideational diffusion often begins with a germination phase during which shifts in thinking occur among a relatively small group of scientists; this is followed by the ideational development and fruition stages (Paterson et al., 2014, p. 10). I trace the germination phase mainly through secondary sources. For the development and fruition phases, I use secondary sources but also data gathered from approximately fifty elite interviews conducted in the mid-2000s with members of advocacy organizations and research institutes and think tanks, as well as congressional and other political and Canadian parliamentary staff. These interviews help identify the main ideas and change agents / idea carriers. I also examine advocacy organization reports and other publications to establish a chronology of organization activity and ideational dissemination.

Ideational Germination: Shifts in Scientific Understandings of Childhood

Throughout the nineteenth and early twentieth centuries, the major focus of child development experts and educators was on children's moral education, not their cognitive development (Hulbert, 2003). As Beatty (1995, p. 34) argues:

> Americans in the early nineteenth century were discovering early childhood and finding that infancy, as this period of life was still called, was a critically important stage for education, though of a different kind from traditional schooling. Infancy was particularly important, manual writers argued, because it was the period when moral character was established. Young children's consciences were still "plastic," receptive to instruction about moral discipline.

Nursery school programs in which middle-class children partici-
pated also tended to emphasize social and emotional maturation rather
than cognitive development. Also, a lot of child development research
focused on the middle childhood years, when, psychologist Alexander
Chamberlain (1900) argued, children's cognition changed; until then,
children were like "savages" (Super, 2005, p. 17). G. Stanley Hall also
argued that pre-adolescent children were little "savages," driven by
passion and emotion and incapable of rationality and discipline. Thus
education should focus especially on the adolescent years in the groom-
ing of intelligent citizens (Hulbert, 2003, p. 81). Some researchers, such
as Arnold Gesell at Yale University, believed that children could be educated at an early age (Silver and Silver, 1991, p. 31), but others agreed
with Heinz Werner that "particularly human kinds of higher order
thinking develop[ed] in humans only during middle childhood, do not
develop in lower animals, and are vulnerable to many kinds of mental
disorder" (Super, 2005, p. 17).

Many of the leading child development and testing experts in the late
nineteenth and early centuries also assumed that IQ was hereditary and
fixed at birth (Vinovskis, 2005, p. 9) and that not much could be done
to help overcome "feeblemindedness" except – at its most extreme –
sterilization. G. Stanley Hall, one of the most influential psychologists
of the early twentieth century, was a strong advocate of eugenics, as
were other developmental psychologists of the time. Some dissenting
scholarly research challenged the belief that IQ was fixed at birth. For
example, research from the Child Welfare Research Station (established
in 1917) and pre-school lab (established in 1921) at the State University
of Iowa disputed the idea that human development was determined
solely by nature. That research instead found that early interventions,
specifically in a pre-school setting, could change a child's developmental trajectory through the "deliberate fostering of social relationships, aspects of health and safety, and systematic enquiry into the links
between children's physical and cognitive development" (Silver and
Silver, 1991, p. 31; see also Cravens, 2002).

But a major challenge to the idea of a fixed IQ did not come until the
publication of Donald Hebb's (1949) book, which "stressed that differences in IQ stemmed in large part from differences in early learning
and environment rather than from variations among brains" (Vinovskis, 2005, p. 10). And because "'all learning tends to utilize and build on
any earlier learning' ... 'much early learning tends to be permanent'"
(Silver and Silver, 1991, p. 32). Hebbs argued that environmental factors,

such as parental income and intelligence and exposure to prolonged schooling, had a powerful effect on IQ (Silver and Silver, 1991, p. 33). Experimental evidence stemming from the work of Harold Skeels and Harold Dye on children in orphanages found that positive changes in orphans' environment could lead to dramatic increases in children's IQ scores (Kirp, 2007, p. 120).

By the 1960s, other research had emerged to support these earlier findings. In 1961, J. McVicker Hunt published *Intelligence and Experience*, which also asserted that children's biology as well as experiences both influenced their intellectual development and challenged the idea of "fixed intelligence" (Silver and Silver, 1991, p. 34; Vinovskis, 2005, p. 10). In 1964, Benjamin Bloom (1964) published *Stability and Change in Human Characteristics*, which supported Hunt's (1961) assertion that "both environment and heredity played a key role in establishing IQ" (Vinovskis, 2005, p. 11); Bloom also argued that "intellectual growth occurred most rapidly in the first four or five years of life, tapering off at about the time the child entered grade school" (Zigler and Anderson, 1979, p. 7). Some child development studies emerged that demonstrated through experimental research that early intervention could alter the educational results for children from disadvantaged backgrounds (Zigler and Anderson, 1979, p. 10. By the late 1950s, other research was emerging that supported the idea that intellectual "retardation" because of deprivation could be reversed (Silver and Silver, 1991, p. 35).

This new knowledge and awareness of the effects of environmental factors on child development led researchers to suggest that "it might be possible to enhance IQ by focusing on improving the learning environment" (Vinovskis, 2005, p. 11). According to Vinovskis (2005, p. 11), these theories and experiments set the stage for a profound change in the way policy makers thought of programs for disadvantaged children. Silver and Silver (1991, pp. 36–7) document how a number of these researchers came together at scientific conferences in the early and mid-1960s to share their findings, and garnered greater attention in other academic disciplines such as sociology. The results of scientific studies suggested to policy specialists that if the child's environment was so important, early education was necessary in order to mitigate the cultural deprivation faced by economically disadvantaged children. Silver and Silver (1991, p. 2) argue that "the second half of the 1960s in the United States witnessed intense interest and investment in, mainly preschool and early childhood education and a variety of related measures designed to 'combat poverty,'" with the federal government involved in commissioning and funding research and promoting discussion.

Project Head Start marked the first major national policy shift in response to this child development research. In 1965 the Johnson administration agreed to fund nationwide summer school readiness programs (Zigler and Anderson, 1979, 5–6). While most of the US government's efforts in the War on Poverty targeted adults, Sargent Shriver, the chief strategist for that war, "decided that a good use of some of the funds … would be to prepare young children of the poor for school" (Phillips and Styfco, 2007, p. 14; Vinovskis, 2005, p. 40).[1] The project's original budget was $17 million and was earmarked to provide early academic enrichment for about 100,000 children. But on the advice of developmental psychologists and others on the planning team,[2] the project expanded to think more broadly about the nutritional, health, and parental education needs of disadvantaged children. The project served more than 500,000 children with an actual cost of $84 million in the first summer (Vinovskis, 2005, p. 91). The administration committed to spend $150 million for a year-round program in the fiscal year 1966, targeted at severely disadvantaged children (Vinovskis, 2005, p. 88, 91). This provided children with free meals, physical examinations including eye exams, hearing tests and vaccinations, and dental care, and social services for parents (Vinovskis, 2005, p. 91).

Early evaluations of the program, though, found that the IQ gains were only temporary and that they faded by the time children entered grade school (Jensen, 1969; Vinovskis, 2005, ch. 5; Westinghouse Learning Corporation, 1969). Some, however, criticized the quality of those evaluations (Rose, 2010, ch. 1). And evaluations did find noticeable non-cognitive benefits from program participation. Despite the mixed results, funding for Head Start remained steady throughout the 1980s, topping $1 billion by 1985 (Woodhead, 1988, p. 445).

Rose (2010, p. 37) notes one further knock-on effect of Head Start: she attributes much of the increased popularity of kindergarten to the implementation of Head Start. The latter program was restricted to the poor, but parents from higher-income families saw the value of such programs, and they began to demand access to similar programs. As early as 1966, the American Association of School Administrators called for the universal provision of kindergarten for 4-year-olds; some called for programs for 3-year-olds as well (Rose, 2010, p. 38). Public kindergarten programs for 5-year-olds, funded and delivered through public schools, grew enormously in the late 1960s and early 1970s, as did private nursery schools (Rose, 2010, pp. 36–7).

The effectiveness of Head Start itself, though, has continued to be challenged, particularly because it is not clear whether the program – or, more accurately, the vast set of programs – is designed to yield cognitive benefits or more broadly developmental or even community-supportive goals (White and Phillips, 2001, pp. 83–5). As Vinovskis (2005, p. 99) reports, Head Start programs vary in type and quality, given that Project Head Start did not mandate or recommend a specific pre-school curriculum; also, as Rose (2010, p. 21) notes, it does not require teachers to have a college degree or teacher certification (Rose, 2010, p. 22). Because the program is funded through the Office of Economic Opportunity, some communities prioritize the job opportunities Head Start provides rather than educational quality. Over time, greater scholarly attention has been directed to the results of other pre-school programs.

Ideational Development: The Proliferation of Scientific Studies

Prior to the introduction of Head Start, some experimental pre-school programs for poor disadvantaged children were in operation, but they were not common, for much of the field was still convinced that IQ was fixed at birth (Haskins, 2005, p. 143; Kirp, 2007, p. 51; Rose, 2010, p. 15; White and Phillips, 2001, p. 93). In 1961, then-PhD student David Weikert at the University of Michigan set up a random control experiment based in the Perry Preschool in the working-class town of Ypsilanti, Michigan. Weikert followed 123 children (58 of whom attended the Perry Preschool) for decades and published the results as a longitudinal study. That study demonstrated that specific early years interventions could overcome gaps in cognitive and non-cognitive abilities in children's early years (Barnett, 1992, 1995, 1996; Belfield et al., 2006; Schweinhart et al., 2005). Two other studies, the Abecedarian study (Campbell and Ramey, 1994; Campbell et al., 2002, 2012; Ramey et al., 2000) and the Chicago Child–Parent Centers study (Reynolds et al., 2001, 2011; Temple and Reynolds, 2007), also observed the impact of high-quality early interventions on vulnerable populations of children on a number of cognitive and non-cognitive measures. The Abecedarian program was a year-round program with children starting in pre-school, although some children stayed in the program until they were 8 and were tracked until they were 21 (Kirp, 2007, p. 58). The Chicago Child–Parent Centers project was modelled on the Carolina

Abecedarian project, but unlike Head Start, which is targeted to the most disadvantaged children, the Chicago centres allow all children who live in the neighbourhood to attend.

In these studies, while school performance effects tended to fade over the years, the longer-term social differences remained and were startling. The Perry pre-school project, for example, found that students and families in the project had higher graduation or GED attainment rates; fewer overall arrests and drug-related arrests; higher monthly earnings; greater likelihood of homeownership; greater ownership of a second car; less use of welfare and other social assistance; longer marriages; and fewer births outside marriage. The Chicago longitudinal study found that students in the program academically outperformed non-participants; were less likely to be held back in school; were less likely to be placed in special education; and experienced lower rates of official juvenile arrests. The Carolina Abededarian project reported similar results. These and other studies of early intervention programs found that high-quality pre-school programs do have benefits for disadvantaged children.

The Consortium for Developmental Continuity (1977), later renamed the Consortium for Longitudinal Studies, which included researchers such as David Weikart and Edward Zigler, published evaluations that pooled the results of a number of early intervention programs from the 1960s (Consortium for Longitudinal Studies,1978; 1983; see also Darlington et al., 1980; Lazar et al., 1982). Again, the findings reported were that pre-school program attendance boosted children's IQ scores, although the effect was not sustained over the long term; even so, the programs had a long-term effect on the-then teenagers' success in high school.

Table 4.1 summarizes the major influential early childhood development studies conducted in the early and mid-twentieth century. As the Web of Science "topic" citation count reveals, the most frequently mentioned is Project Head Start by a wide margin of 47,962, followed by the Perry Preschool project of 1,046. The Google citation count for the Perry Preschool 1993 study reporting results through age 27 is 1,695; the 2005 study through age 40 already has a Google citation count of 1,345 (as of February 2016).

The Diffusion of Research Results

The early results from these studies were publicized in a number of venues. The OECD, for example, sponsored a conference in January

Table 4.1. Influential research centres and early childhood development studies from the early and mid-20th century with Web of Science study citation scores

Child Welfare Research Station, University of Iowa	Established 1917	44
Perry Preschool/High/Scope, Ypsilanti, Michigan	Established 1961	1,046
Carolina Abecedarian Early Childhood Intervention Project, University of North Carolina	Established 1972	544
Project Head Start	Established 1965	47,962
Consortium for Longitudinal Studies (1983)	Consortium formed 1975	189
Chicago Child-Parent Centers, Chicago Public Schools	Established 1985–1986	336

Sources: List generated from secondary sources cited in this chapter; Web of Science scores based on "topic" mentions.

1969, held at the Ford Foundation in New York, with participants such as Edward Zigler from the United States and Alan Little and George Smith from the United Kingdom (Welshman, 2010, p. 90). Little and Smith (1971) then co-authored a follow-up paper for the OECD documenting educational projects for the disadvantaged in the United States. Around the same time, Alfred J. Kahn and Sheila Kamerman, both at the Columbia University School of Social Work, conducted a comparative nine-country study for the OECD Working Party on the Role of Women in the Economy and the US Department of Health, Education, and Welfare (Kahn and Kamerman, 1976). Later on, Welshman (2010, p. 93) notes, the Perry Preschool project and the short- and long-term evaluations of Head Start were the impetus for the founding of Sure Start in Britain under the Blair government.

The mainly US media also played a major role in popularizing the results of neuroscientific studies, which by then were finding that babies' brains develop tremendously in the first three years of life and that there are sensitive periods in children's brain development (Knudsen, 2004). In 1983, Otto Friedrich wrote a story for *Time* magazine titled "What Do Babies Know?" that publicized the "early years" research and that picked up on the "early years last forever" concern (Friedrich, 1983). In 1984 the *Wall Street Journal* ran an article titled "A Head Start Pays Off in the End" (Crittenden, 1984). The article began: "If ever there was a program for the 1980s, a program that addresses the needs for greater productivity and the needs of women and the problem of poverty, it is – are you ready? – preschool education." In 1996, *Newsweek* ran a cover story titled "Your Child's Brain" (Begley, 1996) that was so popular, Rose (2010, p. 103) reports, that it generated over a million requests for reprints (see also Nash, 1997). Other reports drew explicit links between neuroscientific studies and early years programs (Newberger, 1997; Olson, 2002).

Brain research was also popularized through another important avenue: the "celebrity" endorsement of Rob Reiner and his I Am Your Child Foundation. In 1996, actor and director Rob Reiner and his wife, Michelle Singer Reiner, launched the "I am Your Child" Early Childhood Public Education Campaign. As part of that campaign, ABC aired an hour-long TV special titled "I Am Your Child," written by Reiner and narrated by Tom Hanks (Kirp, 2007, p. 98). The campaign coincided with the 1997 White House Conference on Early Childhood Development and Learning. The conference opened on 17 April with First Lady Hillary Clinton delivering opening remarks that were "beamed live by satellite to nearly a hundred hospitals, universities, and schools in thirty-seven states" (Gladwell, 2000, p. 80). However, Thompson and Nelson (2001) document that these media stories often misinterpreted the research or overgeneralized its results. As Kirp (2007, p. 100) argues, the slogan "use it or lose it" gave the impression to anxious parents that they should be doing more to stimulate their babies' cognitive development; this led to the popularity of products such as Baby Einstein videos.[3]

The media also reported inaccuracies related to the longitudinal analyses of Perry Preschool and related programs. Kirp (2007, ch. 2) notes that the media began to equate the Perry results with Head Start, even though "Head Start classes were twice as large as those at Perry, few Head Start teachers had college degrees, they were paid considerably less than public-school teachers, turnover was high, and the pedagogy was haphazard" (Kirp, 2007, p. 65). Woodhead (1988, p. 446) notes that media coverage of the effects of Head Start "fudged several by no means trivial issues about the relationship between one carefully planned and maintained experimental project [i.e., the Perry Preschool study results] and the 1,200 diverse community-run programs collectively known as Head Start." Even so, those media stories were important in distributing these scientific findings to the broader community at a time when concerns about quality of education were weighing on the minds of policy makers.

As the brief summaries of these reports in Table 4.2 reveal, the US policy community was beginning to make linkages between school readiness and early years interventions. In 1983, a National Commission on Excellence in Education (1983) report argued that the American education system was weak and that this was diminishing the

Table 4.2. Influential publications popularizing early years scientific findings and their Google scholar citations

Sponsoring organization/author	Report	Date; Google Scholar citations	Policy argument (cost–benefit analysis, child development, etc.)
US Federal Department of Education / National Commission on Excellence in Education	*A Nation at Risk: The Imperative for Education Reform*	1983; 339	Concern about high school education system
Committee for Economic Development	*Investing in Our Children: Business and the Public Schools: A Statement*	1985; 332	Takes a cost–benefit analysis approach to education and endorses early education for vulnerable children
National Governors' Association	*Time for Results*	1986; 366	Reviews US education system and raises concerns about school readiness; provides a set of recommendations to improve US education system
Committee for Economic Development	*Children in Need: Investment Strategies for the Educationally Disadvantaged*	1987; 303	Called for coalitions of business, education, parent, and civic groups to press for early intervention programs for at-risk children and teenagers
National Assessment of Educational Progress (NAEP)	*America's Challenge: Accelerating Academic Achievement*	1990; 160	Reviewed data from 1970 to 1990 and noted US poor educational performance, particularly in math and science
National Education Goals Panel	*The National Education Goals Report: Building a Nation of Learners*	1991; 450	First report of the National Education Summit convened by President George H.W. Bush and national governors in 1989 to discuss ways to improve US educational performance and compete in the global economy
Carnegie Corporation of New York	*Starting Points: Meeting the Needs of Our Youngest Children*	1994; 229	Highlights the importance of the first three years of a child's life and calls for good child care choices for children under age 3

National Conference of State Legislatures	*Early Childhood Care and Education: An Investment That Works*	1995; 72	Highlights the benefits of early years programs for school readiness, juvenile justice, and labour force development
Carnegie Corporation of New York	*Years of Promise: A Comprehensive Learning Strategy for America's Children*	1996; 115	Focuses on children ages 3–10 and calls for high-quality early learning opportunities
Rima Shore / Families and Work Institute	*Rethinking the Brain: New Insights into Early Development*	1997; 837	Examines the literature on brain development in children's early years
Committee on Integrating the Science of Early Childhood Development, Board on Children, Youth, and Families, National Research Council and Institute of Medicine / Jack P. Shonkoff and Deborah A. Phillips, eds.	*From Neurons to Neighborhoods: The Science of Early Child Development*	2000; 4,917	Examines the evidence about early childhood "brain wiring" and how children learn; also examines contextual factors that affect child development such as families, communities, and child care
Committee on Early Childhood Pedagogy, Commission on Behavioral and Social Sciences and Education, National Research Council / Barbara T. Bowman, M. Suzanne Donovan, and M. Susan Burns, eds.	*Eager to Learn: Educating Our Preschoolers*	2001; 1,157	Reviews and synthesizes research findings on how young children learn and the impact of early learning on later development
Committee for Economic Development	*Preschool for All: Investing in a Productive and Just Society*	2002; 126	Calls for high quality voluntary pre-k for all children offered by a variety of providers in order to close the perceived achievement gap
Educational Testing Service, Princeton, NJ / Richard Coley	*An Uneven Start: Indicators of Inequality in School Readiness*	2002; 146	Concerned about school readiness and inequalities in children's ability to do well in school

Sources: List generated from secondary sources cited in this chapter.

country's economic competitiveness. Rose (2010, p. 88) notes that the National Commission report spurred a number of education reform efforts among state governors, as well as a 1986 policy statement aptly titled *Time for Results*. The theme that the US education system was failing built up over time. The report for the Educational Testing Service (2002) in Princeton, New Jersey, found, for example, that while 65 per cent of children entering kindergarten in 1998 were able to recognize the letters of the alphabet, there were huge differences depending on socio-economic status and among various ethnic and racial groups in the United States.

In 1989, President George H.W. Bush convened an educational summit with the fifty state governors as well as corporate CEOs to review US educational performance. He followed this with a 1990 State of the Union address in which he outlined a number of goals for American education. In 1994, under President Clinton, the federal government passed Goals 2000 legislation; among its stated goals were to achieve 90 per cent high school graduation rates, to become first in the world in math and science, and to ensure that graduating students had the skills to compete in the global marketplace (Rebell, 2012, p. 62). As Rebell (2012, p. 62) argues, those performance targets were accompanied by an acknowledgment that "to achieve these ends, substantial efforts would be required to prepare economically disadvantaged students to learn at higher levels" including that "'all children in America will start school ready to learn.'"

Kirp (2007, p. 66) argues around this time (the mid-1990s) "was the moment when people stopped focusing on child care (a major concern of the children's lobby during the Reagan and Bush administrations) and started thinking about universal preschool" (brackets in original). The Carnegie Corporation of New York (1994) began to pay attention to the needs of young children in the early 1990s and released its report *Starting Points: Meeting the Needs of Our Youngest Children* in 1994. In June 1996 the Families and Work Institute, the Carnegie Corporation, and other foundations convened a meeting in Chicago that brought together 150 experts in brain science, child development, early childhood education, business, policy, and the media to focus attention on the early years; this led to the release of Rima Shore's (1997) *Rethinking the Brain* in conjunction with the White House Conference on Early Childhood Development in 1997. RAND then released a study in 1998, *Investing in Our Children: What We Know and Don't Know about the Costs and Benefits of Early Childhood Interventions*, which connected early interventions with decreased government costs for programs such as welfare and criminal justice (Karoly et al., 1998; see also Cohen, 2001, p. 212). Cohen (2001, pp. 212–13; see also Thompson and Nelson, 2001) notes that all of these studies were dutifully reported in the media, fueling legislative interest.

Then a series of National Research Council studies emerged, after the Board on Children, Youth, and Families at the Institute of Medicine and National Research Council of the National Academy of Sciences established a blue ribbon Committee on Integrating the Science of Early Child Development. These studies included *From Neurons to Neighborhoods* (Shonkoff and Phillips, 2000), *Eager to Learn: Educating Our Preschoolers* (Bowman, Donovan, and Burns, 2001), *Working Families and Growing Kids* (Smolensky and Gootman, 2003), and *Children's Health, The Nation's Wealth* (Committee on Evaluation of Children's Health, 2004).[4]

These scientific studies were followed by research that uncovered further achievement gaps related to socio-economic status (Blau, 1999; Bowles, Gintis, and Groves, 2005). In their spoken conversations and when reading to children, parents and caregivers in families with high socio-economic status utter far more words than do parents with low socio-economic status (Fernald, Marchman, and Weisleder, 2013). Exposure to language-rich environments has positive effects on IQ and academic performance in school (Rosenberg, 2013 reporting on findings by Hart and Risley, 1995). Reardon (2013) reports that gaps in educational achievement in the United States between higher- and lower-income students have grown substantially, as have gaps in student participation in extra-curricular activities (Reardon, 2013; see also Reardon, 2011; Murnane and Duncan, 2011).

The Role of Economists and Business Leaders in Popularizing Early Years Research

The perceived failures of the public education system caught the attention of business policy organizations such as the Committee for Economic Development (CED). In 1985 the CED issued a statement titled *Investing in Our Children: Business and the Public Schools* (Committee for Economic Development, 1985). It concluded that "the seeds of educational failure are planted early" and argued for early childhood education programs for vulnerable children. It issued a second report in 1987 titled *Children in Need: Investment Strategies for the Educationally Disadvantaged*, which called for business leaders, along with education officials, parents, and civic leaders, to press for federal and state funding for early intervention programs (Committee for Economic Development, 1987); then in 2002 it released *Preschool for All*, which called for pre-school for all 3- and 4-year-olds (Committee for Economic Development, 2002). In 2003, the Business Roundtable and Corporate Voices for Working Families (2003) released a "Call to Action" document. Other business organizations got on board. The Institute for a Competitive Workforce, affiliated with the US Chamber of Commerce, issued a report in 2010 that described early childhood education as an "investment in workforce development" (ICW, 2010, p. 2), citing economic cost–benefit analyses as evidence (2010, p. 6).

Child advocates in the United States acknowledge that business leaders' increasing attention to early childhood education was important, because "it was not just the usual suspects talking about the issue" (Copeland, then-President of Voices for America's Children, commenting on the release of CED's reports). The popularity of early childhood programs among business leaders and policy officials grew significantly as research emerged regarding the economic impact of the small demonstration projects. Well-respected economists began producing numerous cost–benefit analyses, some of these in conjunction with advocacy organizations or think tanks (Karoly, Kilburn, and Cannon, 2005; Kilburn and Karoly, 2008; Lynch, 2004, 2007; Rolnick and Grunewald, 2003). The most noteworthy analyses were produced by Nobel economist James Heckman, whose cost–benefit analyses of active labour market policies (Heckman, Lalonde, and Smith, 1999) led him to turn to early childhood education and to calculate rates of return on those investments (Carneiro and Heckman, 2003; Cunha and Heckman, 2007; Heckman, 2000, 2006; Heckman and Masterov, 2004, 2007). These cost–benefit analyses compare spending on prevention and early intervention against subsequent spending in terms of labour market training, social assistance, criminal prosecutions, and so on. Such studies, including reanalyses of early intervention studies (Heckman et al., 2010), have found that early years investments yield major direct returns to society in terms of decreased costs in health care, social service use, and delinquency.

Other economists, including Steven Barnett and Clive Belfield, provided cost–benefit analyses justifying pre-k investment based on analyses of the Perry Preschool participants (Barnett, 1983, 1993, 1996; Belfield et al., 2006; Schweinhart et al., 2005). Frances Campbell and Craig Ramey published a number of analyses of the Carolina Abecedarian study (Campbell and Ramey, 1994; Campbell et al., 2002, 2012; Ramey et al., 2000). Others have published similar analyses of the Chicago Child–Parent Centers study (Reynolds et al., 2001, 2011; Temple and Reynolds, 2007). More recent studies of newer programs all claim similar good program effects in better preparing children for school and increasing the chances of academic success for disadvantaged populations and, in some cases, for the broader population as well (Cascio, 2009; Magnuson, Ruhm, and Waldfogel, 2007; Wong et al., 2007). Other economic research has emerged that champions the indirect benefits of these programs. Some researchers have tracked the economic stimulus that public investment in infrastructure and workforce employment accrues (Fairholm, 2010; McMillen and Parr, 2004; Warner and Liu, 2005). Others have tracked the labour market gains and especially the stimulation of maternal employment brought about by investments in ECEC (Baker, Gruber, and Milligan, 2008; Lefebvre and Merrigan, 2008). Economic analyses of Quebec's low-fee $5 (later $7) per day child care program have shown that the tax transfer returns that the federal and Quebec governments receive from the increases in maternal employment "significantly exceed" the costs of the program (Fortin, Godbout, and St-Cerny, 2012).

Yet there remains significant disagreement in the scholarly community regarding whether programs should be universal or targeted to vulnerable populations (Baker, 2011; Doherty, 2007; Karoly et al., 1998), whether they should be full-day or half-day, whether they should be delivered in schools or other settings, and whether they should be extended to younger ages of children (for a review of this vast literature, see White, Prentice, and Perlman, 2015). As some researchers have pointed out (e.g. Baker, 2011), small-scale specific studies from the United States that included very specific treatments of very high quality (e.g., excellent child/staff ratios with trained teachers) may not be replicable on a larger scale.[5] Furthermore, the children studied in these longitudinal studies were often extremely high risk (often members of racial minority groups) and probably not typical of other populations. Thus, policy makers may not be able to expect the same benefits for disadvantaged children in universal programs.

And many of the policies and programs created after these scientific and related studies were popularized did not resemble the programs on which the studies were based. As Rose (2010, p. 93) notes, while those working on policies in the US context made frequent reference to the Perry Preschool program, "per-child spending on state pre-kindergarten programs was about one-third of what the Perry Pre-school program cost." Furthermore, "most were small, part-day programs, and the level of resources they had varied widely, as did their requirements for teaching training, group size, curriculum, and other factors that shaped program quality." As later chapters of this book will document, real differences emerged between the evidence base and policy outcomes.

Yet it is stunning how much attention was paid to these longitudinal studies and cost–benefit analyses and how much importance was placed on them. Policy document after policy document cited these longitudinal studies and related analyses; those documents were then cited as evidence to justify policy interventions (see Table 4.2). Rose (2010, p. 126) observes that courts in New Jersey cited the Perry Pre-school study, the Abecedarian study, and the 1996 Carnegie Task Force report on education to support increased access for New Jersey children to pre-school. The latter report was not a peer-reviewed research paper but rather a review of other research that had been conducted. A similar phenomenon occurred in Canada, where the Ontario government commissioned an Early Years Study to review the evidence for early years interventions. That report, co-authored by Margaret McCain and Fraser Mustard (1999), has been cited numerous times subsequently in government and advocacy organizations' reports alike to justify a variety of program interventions. Studies on children's cognitive development in early childhood proliferated in subsequent decades; the OECD's "Learning Sciences and Brain Research" project, launched in 1999, produced two massive reports to document the accumulating research (OECD CERI, 2002, 2007).

Challenges to Early Years Researchers: Opposing Viewpoints

The increased scholarly attention on the first three to five years of children's lives, and particularly the view that certain early childhood experiences are necessary for optimal brain development, led to a pendulum swing in the other direction: concern that too much weight was being placed on children's early experiences. A number of scholars, including John Bruer, president of the James S. McDonnell Foundation in St Louis, Missouri, and creator of the McDonnell–Pew Program in Cognitive Neuroscience, Jerome Kagan, a developmental psychologist at Harvard, and Steven Pinker, a psychologist at Harvard, challenged the idea that the first three years of a child's life are determinative of their later development (Bruer, 1999; Kagan, 2000; Pinker, 2002). Researchers were concerned about the policy conclusions being drawn from the neuroscientific findings regarding dense early synapse formation in the brain in the early years, critical developmental periods, and the effects of enriched or complex environments on vulnerable children. Bruer (1997, 1998) in particular challenged the policy linkages between these cognitive developments that researchers were observing and early childhood education policies, as well as music for babies programs, and so on.

Conservative organizations and foundations also voiced their opposition to early childhood program interventions for any child, low-income or otherwise, as unnecessary state interventions. The Cato Institute, for example, states on its website that "for years, local, state, and federal governments and diverse private sources have funded early intervention programs for low-income children, and benefits to the children have been few and fleeting. There is also evidence that middle-class children gain little, if anything, from preschool" (Cato Institute, 2017; see also Coulson, 2010; Olsen 1997, 1999). A number of other organizations, such as the American Enterprise Institute, the Goldwater Institute, the Thomas B. Fordham Institute, and the Hoover Institution have issued their own reports decrying early years investments such as Head Start and pre-school (Besharov, 2005; Finn, 2009; Olsen, 2005; Whitehurst, 2013). Brian Robertson, a fellow at the Center for Marriage and Family at the Family Research Council, wrote one book decrying centre-based care and another book decrying how "parents" were being driven out of the home and into the workplace because of business practices and government policies (Robertson, 2000, 2003). In an interview posted on National Review Online, he cited Jay Belsky's work as revealing the "detrimental effects of day care on preschool children," despite the efforts of "the cultural gatekeepers" who did not want this information to "get through" to parents (Lopez, 2003).

Even scholars who were sympathetic to early childhood interventions offered measured critiques of universal policy interventions. One of the most interesting academic exchanges occurred in a 1987 issue of *American Psychologist* between Yale psychologist Edward Zigler (first director of the US Office of Child Development and one of the principal architects of Head Start) and then–National Education Association president Mary Hatwood Futrell about extending public schooling to children aged 4. Futrell (1987, p. 251) was strongly supportive of doing so in order "to equip today's preschoolers for the information-based society that will challenge their emotional and intellectual capacities," but she argued for a play-based curriculum that was different from that for 5-year-olds.

Zigler (1987, p. 256), in contrast, argued that the research evidence did not support any conclusion that middle-class children benefited from early education; indeed, he argued that "early schooling is inappropriate for many four-year-olds and may even be harmful to their development" (Zigler, 1987, p. 257). He noted that a number of communities, including New York City, were moving to mandatory full-day kindergarten for 4-year-olds and contended that this was developmentally inappropriate. He noted as well that he was among those who opposed then-President Carter's proposal to move the administrative responsibility for Head Start into the US Department of Education; in his view, it was inappropriate to have a comprehensive development and family support program housed under Education (Zigler, 1987, p. 255). Zigler (1987, p. 256) noted that a more pressing need was to ensure adequate child care for working parents and to recognize that "when the family situation is appropriate, the best place for a preschool child may be at home." Zigler (1987, p. 257) went on to argue that "some four-year-olds can handle a five- or six-hour school day. Many others cannot. Whenever it is best for the children to be at home with their parents, we should not needlessly deprive families of valuable time they could spend together." But "we are driving our young children too hard and thereby depriving them of their most precious commodity – their childhood." And Zigler (1987, p. 257) stated: "The image of the four-year-old in designer jeans, miniature executive briefcase in hand may seem cute, but rushing children from cradle to school denies them the freedom to develop at their own pace. Children are growing up too fast today, and prematurely placing four-year-olds and five-year-olds into full-day preschool education programs will only compound this problem."

Those kinds of arguments, including those of Professor Zigler himself, had largely disappeared by the 1990s. A 2006 book that he co-authored with Walter Gilliam and Stephanie Jones recommended universal preschool with the assertion that "emerging data are now demonstrating the potential value of preschool education for children of all economic groups who attend large-scale public programs" (Zigler, Gilliam, and Jones, 2006, 263). The benefits were listed as "improved school readiness; reduced grade retention; reduced need for costly remedial and special education services; improved educational test scores; increased high school graduation rates and postsecondary education; increased employment rates and family income; reduced criminal activity and likelihood of incarceration; reduced dependence on welfare" (Zigler, Gilliam, and Jones, 2006, p. 262). By the late 1990s, the notion that universal pre-school offered myriad benefits was taking on the air of being commonsensical.

Shifts in Scholarly Opinion Regarding the "Harm" of Maternal Employment

One other major shift both in policy making and in the academic research occurred in the 1980s and 1990s around the question of whether maternal employment was bad for children. For decades, conservative commentators have decried formal child care as "socialist" and "anti-family" and as undermining traditional gender roles. Well-known is President Richard Nixon's flip-flop on child care funding in the early 1970s in the face of intra-party politicking on the part of conservative legislators, who described the reforms as akin to "Soviet-style child-rearing techniques" that threatened to supplant the role of mothers and the traditional family structure (Cohen, 2001, p. 51). Bowlby's (1952) attachment theory – that children in the hands of anyone other than the mother would experience separation anxiety, which would negatively affect their social and emotional development – dominated the child development field and popular culture for decades.

A huge debate in the academic literature in the 1980s and 1990s surrounded the question of whether non-parental (more specifically, non-maternal) care was harmful for children. In 1986, Jay Belsky published an article in the journal *Zero to Three* that claimed that early and extensive non-maternal care posed a risk to mother–infant attachment and fostered aggressive behaviour (Belsky, 1986; see also Belsky, 1987, 1988; Belsky and Eggebeen, 1991; Belsky and Rovine, 1988).[6] The Washington, DC–based organization Zero to Three: The National Association for Clinical Infant Programs published the original study. Because of the controversy it generated, the organization held a one-day workshop to discuss the findings. Then-director of the National Institute of Child Health and Human Development (NICHD) Dr Duane Alexander attended the workshop and decided to fund a research network on the topic of Early Child Care and Youth Development. The research team drew applicants from universities across the United States and designed a longitudinal observational study that followed 1,364 children in ten sites around the United States at five different points from

6 to 54 months in their various child care settings (US Department of Health and Human Services, 2006).

The NICHD produced a number of research studies over the years that reported on findings as the children in the study grew older (see the NICHD Early Child Care Research Network website https://www.nichd.nih.gov/research/supported/seccyd/Pages/biblio.aspx). Phillips and McCartney (2005, pp. 114–15) summarize the results: "With respect to mother-child attachment, there was no evidence that insecurity was associated with child-care experience ... There was, however, some indication that poor-quality child care coupled with poor-quality parenting might pose an increased risk of insecurity." They went on to note that "with respect to behavior problems, there was evidence of risk associated with more hours in child care." The journal *Child Development* devoted the bulk of an issue in 2003 to the NICHD's findings (Early Child Care Research Network, 2003; Watamura et al., 2003). The lead articles were considered controversial within the field, so the editors of *Child Development* published nine commentaries along with the lead articles.

Some researchers have pointed to the highly socially constructed nature of the research question (Scarr, Phillips, and McCartney, 1990). The studies were not investigating the impact of *paternal* employment on child development, after all, but rather only *maternal* employment, the implication being that the natural maternal role for mothers is to be at home. The focus of the research began to shift in the mid-2000s to investigate possible positive effects of maternal employment. Baum (2003, p. 409), for example, in *Journal of Labor Economics*, argued that while maternal employment "in the first year of a child's life has detrimental effects ... the negative effects of maternal marketplace work are partially offset by positive effects of increased family income."

One challenge for parents that the academic research began to identify was the policy context in which parents in the United States made choices about child care. The lack of paid parental leave in the United States federally and in many states meant that children were being placed in non-parental child care settings at a very young age, some at as little as twelve weeks (Capizzano and Adams, 2000). Some of the research thus shifted to highlight the impact of "early" maternal employment with regard to mothers who return to work full-time within twelve weeks of giving birth (Brooks-Gunn, Wen-Jui, and Waldfogel, 2010). Berger, Hill, and Waldfogel (2005), for example, found evidence of declines in breastfeeding and immunization rates and of "externalizing" behaviour in the children (see also Loeb et al., 2007; Ruhm, 2004). These research findings lent support to the importance of providing paid parental leave to families with young children as a way of improving child health and other developmental outcomes (Galtry and Callister, 2005; Tanaka, 2005).

Gregg and colleagues' (2005) study of child cognitive development, drawing on data from the United Kingdom, found that mothers' full-time employment during the child's first eighteen months of life negatively affected children who were in informal care and led to poorer cognitive outcomes, but did not affect children who were in more formal child care; this suggested a link between child care *quality* and cognitive effects. Much of non-parental care in the United States has been found to be of low quality. Many child care centres in the United Staes operate with no federal regulations regarding quality and with great variation in state regulations. Faith-based service providers in some states are not subject to regulation, and the same is true for some part-day and family child care providers (Neuman, 2005, p. 137). As Neuman (2005, p. 137) notes, "about 90% of child-care services are privately operated centres or family child-care homes, and more than half of these operate for profit." Research has shown that there are systemic differences between commercial and not-for-profit child care programs in terms of quality (Sosinsky, Lord, and Zigler, 2007). Research has generally also found that low-quality programs can have negative developmental outcomes (Herbst and Tekin, 2010); conversely, high-quality programs benefit children developmentally (Peisner-Feinberg et al., 2001).

Indeed, studies of child care in other countries were not yielding the same negative results as those in the United States (Andersson, 1992; McMunn et al., 2010; Zachrisson et al., 2013). Havnes and Mogstad's (2009) study of the introduction in 1976 of subsidized, universally accessible child care in Norway found that the program had strong positive effects on children's later educational achievement and also reduced welfare dependency. They concluded the "effect on education stems from children with low educated mothers, whereas most of the effect on labor market attachment and earnings relates to girls," suggesting that "access to subsidized child care levels the playing field by increasing intergenerational mobility and closing the gender wage gap" (Havnes and Mogstad, 2009, p. 3).

More and more research on the United States was finding positive effects for some children in non-parental child care settings as well as improvements in school readiness, especially for children from low-income families (Dearing, McCartney, and Taylor, 2009; Vandell et al., 2010). Loeb and colleagues (2004) reported that young children from poor communities demonstrated positive cognitive effects when in high-quality centre-based care (see also Loeb et al., 2007). Further results from the NICHD study found that high-quality child care led to higher child vocabulary scores (albeit with negative externalizing behaviour also reported) (Belsky et al., 2007). As mentioned earlier, the three most influential longitudinal studies in the United States included very specific treatments of very high quality (such as excellent child/ staff ratios with trained teachers) that were not always replicated in other early years programs (Baker, 2011).

The results of all this research – both positive and negative – were often heavily publicized in the media (e.g., N.A., 2003; McNamara, 2004; Stolberg, 2001). For example, a Proquest Newstand search of English-language newspaper articles for "Jay Belsky" and "day care" found 432 articles published between 1984 and 2016, 142 articles on "NICHD" and "child development," and 25 articles alone on "Deborah Vandell" and "day care."

Media controversy erupted again with the publication of Baker, Gruber, and Milligan's (2008) cohort study of children in Quebec after the introduction of $5-per-day child care and the later follow-up study (Baker, Gruber, and Milligan, 2015). A Proquest Newstand search found sixteen articles on Baker and colleagues' 2008 and 2015 studies, including in the *New York Times* (Leonhardt, 2006). Baker, Gruber, and Milligan's (2008) study found negative behavioural effects among the general cohort of children in Quebec compared to those in the rest of Canada. The study did not explicitly compare children in non-parental child care to those who were not, but rather took advantage of the natural experiment created by the shift in policy to subsidized child care. Still, it generated a wealth of attention from the time of its first publication as an NBER working paper and was then publicized by the C.D. Howe Institute in Canada.[7] Other studies such as Geoffroy and colleagues' (2010) longitudinal study of about 1,800 children in Quebec found contrary effects: children from disadvantaged backgrounds who participated in formal child care earned higher scores on academic readiness and achievement tests at ages 6 and 7 than children cared for by a relative or nanny. And in their longitudinal study of children in the neighbouring province of Ontario, Peters and colleagues (2010) found long-term positive outcomes in terms of school and social functioning among children from economically disadvantaged areas of Ontario who participated in a community-based comprehensive early years program (Better Beginnings, Better Futures).

The general research consensus that has emerged is that quality matters to positive developmental outcomes (Belsky et al., 2007; Love et al., 2003; Sosinsky, Lord, and Zigler, 2007; Sylva et al., 2011). Indeed, the Baker, Gruber, and Milligan (2008) study that found negative behavioural effects among the general cohort of children in Quebec could have simply been an artefact of the fact that much of the care in Quebec is not of high quality (Japel, Tremblay, and Côté, 2005; Japel, 2008). In contrast, Magnuson, Ruhm, and Waldfogel (2007) found that some of the negative behavioural effects of full-day programs on young children did not manifest in children in pre-schools located in public schools. A lot of research attention has thus turned to the question of how participation in pre-school programs of a variety of sorts can improve school readiness (Forry, Davis, and Welti, 2013).

Recent studies have reversed the dependent variable and have found that provision of early years services has significant positive maternal employment effects (Baker, Gruber, and Milligan, 2008; Kenworthy, 2008; Lefebvre and Merrigan, 2008). A much different attitude towards maternal employment is reflected even in government documents. For example, the US Department of the Treasury released a report in April 1998, following from the 1997 White House Conference on Child Care, that highlighted ways that businesses could promote child care access for their employees (US Treasury Working Group on Child Care, 1998).

Ideational Flourishing: The Creation of a Principled Belief in Early Childhood Education

Once a policy consensus was established that maternal employment can be good for the economy, and that child care is important, at least to support low-income women's employment,[8] early childhood researchers and advocates began to envision ways of bringing child care and education together (Finn-Stevenson and Zigler, 1999; Kagan and Cohen, 1996, 1997) and to argue in earnest for more universal programs (Zigler, Gilliam, and Jones, 2006). As can be seen from the review of scientific and social scientific evidence above, however, it is a huge leap from the research claim that child care does not harm children to the claim that universal pre-school is good for all children, especially because the neuroscience would suggest that improving children's experiences in the earliest years of life should be the focus of policy makers' attention.

How, then, did universal (pre-)kindergarten emerge as the predominant policy prescription? Furthermore, as the above sections demonstrate, important scholarly research on early childhood development had begun to emerge as early as the 1960s. Why did it take until the mid- to late 1990s to catch on with policy makers?

Researchers such as Sally Cohen (2001, p. 211) suggest that "what changed was how organizations and advocates interested in child development marketed the information." That is, knowledge transfer efforts and agents became more active. Foundations and policy advocacy groups have been extremely important in promoting the idea of universal early childhood education in particular, which suggests that something about the *idea* of UPK was appealing, whereas the idea of universal child care was not.

The appeal of universal pre-school is partly functional. US policy makers at the national and state levels were increasingly concerned about the quality of education. At the 1990 education summit of fifty state governors and then-President George H.W. Bush, the participants committed to quality improvements that eventually became the Goals 2000: Educate America Act, signed into law by President Clinton in 1994. The goal these policy makers articulated was that by the year 2000, children in the United States would begin school "ready to learn" (Kagan and Cohen, 1996, p. xi). Early childhood education, in part, became the solution to the problem of school readiness.

Advocates for universal early childhood education also could claim to have the imprimatur of science behind them (Kirp, 2007, p. 103), drawing on everything from brain research and neuroscience studies to longitudinal studies to make their case. References to the Perry Pre-school project became ubiquitous in the scholarly and policy literature and among advocates themselves.[9] Universal pre-school gradually shifted from being a policy "idea" to being a "good." That shift from policy idea to principled belief was certainly aided by the concerted efforts of the policy community.

A number of scholars have documented the importance of Pew Charitable Trusts and the incredible financial investments it made in research dissemination as well as advocacy (Bushouse, 2009; Kirp, 2007, ch. 6; Rose, 2010, ch. 5). But a plethora of other foundations besides Pew promoted the idea of UPK (see Table 4.3). Some US foundations, such as the Carnegie Corporation of New York and the Foundation for Child Development, had been involved in funding child care and early childhood education research and advocacy since the beginning of the

Table 4.3. US foundations funding child care/early childhood education policy advocacy

Foundation	Campaign/Fund/Activity	Affiliated Organizations
Buffet Foundation / Susan Thompson Buffet Foundation	National/Nebraska; Buffet Early Childhood Fund (est. 2005)	Alliance for Early Success; First Five Years Fund; Educare Learning Centers; Partnership for America's Economic Success/ReadyNation; Harvard Center on the Developing Child (National Scientific Council on the Developing Child and the National Forum on Early Childhood Program Evaluation); plus a number of Nebraska-based initiatives
Carnegie Corporation of New York	National/New York; Carnegie Task Force on Meeting the Needs of Young Children (1991); Carnegie Task Force on Learning in the Primary grades (1994); Carnegie Commission on Educational Television (1965); pathways to education opportunity (though not focused on early childhood)	School of the 21st Century program; Brookline Early Education Project (BEEP), which existed from 1973 to 1981 and was the nation's first health and developmental program for children from birth to age 3 sponsored by a public school; Children's Television Network
Annie E. Casey Foundation	National/Baltimore; *Kids Count* annual report (1990) and data centre; evidence-based policy making project	Funds a host of state organizations in virtually every state (network est. in 1991 and expanded through 1990s): http://www.aecf.org/work/kids-count/kids-count-network/kids-count-state-organizations
Foundation for Child Development (FCD)	National/New York; PreK-3rd Education (2003); Young Scholars Program to fund early career researchers on early learning; America's Diverse Children (focused on development of children in poverty, low-income); Child Well-Being Index; New American Children (low-income immigrant needs)	FCD funds a number of grants for university and advocacy organization research including the Trust for Early Education (with PEW): https://www.fcd-us.org/about-us/grants/
Bill and Melinda Gates Foundation	Washington State early learning plan; Washington Kindergarten Inventory of Developing Skills; funding program to expand early learning	Alliance for Early Success; Ounce of Prevention Fund; Thrive by Five Washington; Washington Early Learning Foundation; Educare Learning Centers
Gerber Foundation	National/western Michigan; grants to support initiatives on dental and health issues, early childhood education, parenting education, and math, science and technology education	

(Continued)

Table 4.3. US foundations funding child care/early childhood education policy advocacy (Continued)

Foundation	Campaign/Fund/Activity	Affiliated Organizations
William T. Grant Foundation	National/New York/New Jersey/Connecticut; research relating to child care and pre-school education (1961); focus on after-school programs; youth inequality; understanding the uses of research evidence and connecting research, policy, and practice	Primarily funds research/scholars
Irving B. Harris Foundation	Chicago/Illinois; early childhood education; Head Start programs	Alliance for Early Success; Ounce of Prevention Fund; Beethoven Project; Educare Learning Centers; Erikson Institute graduate training of early childhood development teachers (1966); Irving B. Harris Graduate School of Public Policy, University of Chicago (1986); Minding the Baby study at the Early Childhood Study Center at Yale University
Heising-Simons Foundation	National (research)/San Mateo and Santa Clara counties, CA (direct services); founded in 2007 and focuses on early childhood education, education from birth to age 8; early math; transition to kindergarten; family engagement; along with other policy areas including the environment; and science research	Funds a number of initiatives in California related to early math, kindergarten transitions, and so on
I Am Your Child Foundation / Parents' Action for Children	National/California/Nashville; focus on early childhood development and school readiness; I Am Your Child national public awareness campaign and video series (1997); policy promotion	Receives funding from a number of other foundations: http://www.parentsaction.org/partners/
Joyce Foundation	Great Lakes region (e.g., Illinois, Michigan, Wisconsin/ Chicago; focus on education, including early reading and education innovation	Illinois Action for Children
George Kaiser Family Foundation	Tulsa/Oklahoma; founded in 1999 with a major focus on young children; Tulsa Educare; Oklahoma Early Childhood Program; EduCareers University of Oklahoma and Tulsa Community College early childhood training program	Alliance for Early Success; Educare Learning Centers; Community Action Project of Tulsa County; Early Childhood Institute, University of Oklahoma–Tulsa

Ewing Marion Kauffman Foundation	National/Kansas/Missouri; Early Education Exchange funding research on child care and school readiness and an annual conference (since 2001); also focuses on entrepreneurship and innovation	Projects in the Kansas City area on academic achievement and low-income youth
W.K. Kellogg Foundation	National/Michigan and other high-priority states (Mississippi, New Mexico, New Orleans); focused on education and development from birth to age 8, esp. for vulnerable children – GR8by8	Alliance for Early Success; Ounce of Prevention Fund; Educare Learning Centers; Orleans Public Education Network; Edible Schoolyard New Orleans; Native American Community Academy; funds a number of other organizations through mission-driven investments fund, including Charter schools, Head Start programs: http://www.wkkf.org/what-we-do/mission-driven-investments/investments#pp=100&p=1
John D. and Catherine T. MacArthur Foundation	National/Chicago; Research Network on Early Childhood Transitions (1983–92); Research Network on Early Experience and Brain Development (1998–2010); National Scientific Council on the Developing Child (2003, first based at Brandeis University's Heller School for Social Policy and Management, then at Harvard); National Forum on Early Childhood Policy and Programs; the use of economic analyses in policy making	Center on the Developing Child, Harvard University (National Scientific Council on the Developing Child and the National Forum on Early Childhood Program Evaluation); FrameWorks Institute
A.L. Mailman Family Foundation	No info – website not available	School of the 21st Century Program; Mailman School of Public Health, Columbia University; Mailman Segal Center for Human Development, Nova Southeastern University, FL
Edna McConnell Clark Foundation	National/Boston/New York; since 1999, the foundation's exclusive focus has been on economically disadvantaged youth and organizations that support vulnerable youth	Harlem Children's Zone; the SEED Foundation, and a number of other organizations and programs: http://www.emcf.org/grantees
McCormick Tribune Foundation	Chicago/Illinois; goal is to build a quality early care and education system in Illinois for children birth through grade three, along with programs in building strong communities, and civics education	Funds research and children's programs in Illinois such as the DuPage Children's Museum

(Continued)

Table 4.3. US foundations funding child care/early childhood education policy advocacy (Continued)

Foundation	Campaign/Fund/Activity	Affiliated Organizations
Charles Stewart Mott Foundation	National/Michigan; funds after-school programs to promote learning beyond the classroom, especially for traditionally underserved youth under the pathways out of poverty program	Afterschool Alliance; Afterschool All-Stars
David and Lucile Packard Foundation	National/California; funds professional development in the early childhood sector early learning strategy as well as after-school and summer enrichment; also focuses on conservation and science	Funds research and a number of programs and organizations such as the Alliance for Early Success; Council for a Strong America; Fight Crime–Invest in Kids; Children Now; American Federation of Teachers Educational Foundation; Preschool for All
PEW Charitable Trusts	National/state-based initiatives; The National Early Childhood Accountability Task Force (2005)	Trust for Early Education; Pre-K Now; NIEER; Fight Crime–Invest in Kids; Committee for Economic Development; Council of Chief State School Officers; Partnership for America's Economic Success/ReadyNation
JB and MK Pritzker Family Foundation	Pritzker Early Childhood Foundation (2003); Pritzker Children's Initiative; funds social impact bonds for early childhood (Early Childhood Innovation Accelerator Initiative with Goldman Sachs 2013)	Pritzker Consortium on Early Childhood Development, University of Chicago (2006); First Five Years Fund; Ounce of Prevention Fund; Minding the Baby study at the Early Childhood Study Center at Yale University
Schott Foundation for Public Education	Massachusetts and New York; (est. 1991) supports preK-12 public education including state-level allocations for early childhood education (campaign 2006–15); Schott Fellowship in Early Care and Education (2003)	National Women's Law Center; Voices for America's Children; Partnership for America's Economic Success/ReadyNation; plus a number of state organizations, mainly in Massachusetts and New York, including Early Education for All in Massachusetts
The Schumann Fund of New Jersey	Formed in 1988 out of the larger foundation to focus on early childhood education, school reform, and educational innovation and environmental protection	Advocates for Children of New Jersey; Building Responsible, Intelligent Creative Kids; Fight Crime Invest in Kids; NIEER; among others
Spencer Foundation	Supports education research generally, not specifically on early childhood	

Sources: Information compiled from foundation websites and interview data; see also Knott and McCarthy (2007).

twentieth century (Knott and McCarthy, 2007, p. 324); others, such as the William T. Grant Foundation and the W.K. Kellogg Foundation, got involved during the interwar period. More concerted foundation activity began in the late 1950s and 1960s because of developments in the science of child development (Knott and McCarthy, 2007, p. 324). Foundations funded a number of experimental programs and demonstration projects (Silver and Silver, 1991, pp. 37–48; Vinovskis, 2005, pp. 26–31), especially the Ford Foundation through its Great Cities School Improvement Project to help disadvantaged students in urban areas (Vinovskis, 2005, pp. 26–7).

A great deal of policy attention from the late 1960s to the mid-1990s was focused on child care policy, as chapter 6 documents. The year 1995 marked a historic shift in thinking about child care with the end of Aid to Families with Dependent Children (AFDC) and the creation of Temporary Assistance for Needy Families (TANF). The strong work imperative built into the program led policy makers to accept the idea that families needed access to child care in order to participate in the labour market. The inclusion of child care in the final legislation represented a compromise on the part of Democratic and Republican members of Congress and signalled a growing consensus that programs that required single parents to work also required funding for child care (Haskins, 2001, p. 26, Table 2.1). A number of advocates then turned their attention to more universal programs. Knott and McCarthy (2007, p. 323) note that foundations also turned their attention to universal pre-school initiatives as part of their focus on community and neighbourhood development. The Children's Defense Fund, which had been very active on child care, published *First Steps, Promising Futures: State Prekindergarten Initiatives in the Early 1990s* (Adams and Sandfort, 1994). In 1999 it followed up with *Seeds of Success: State Prekindergarten Initiatives* (Schulman, Blank, and Ewen, 1999).

In 2000, economist Steven Barnett of Rutgers University approached the Pew Charitable Trusts to convince Pew to focus its education policy efforts on pre-kindergarten (Kirp, 2007, pp. 156–7). In September 2001, the Pew board of trustees agreed to launch an initiative to support universal pre-school. As part of that effort, it founded the academically based National Institute for Early Education Research (NIEER) at Rutgers University, directed by Steven Barnett, as well as an advocacy organization, the Trust for Early Education (then renamed Pre-K Now), in Washington, DC, which was set up to support state and federal efforts to lobby for universal early education for 3- and 4-year-olds.

NIEER began to publish its annual *The State of Preschool* in 2003. Pew also targeted advocacy efforts at states with experienced advocates and policy makers who would push for initiatives: Arkansas, Illinois, Massachusetts, New York, New Jersey, North Carolina, Oklahoma, and Wisconsin (Trust for Early Education, TEE State Activities). Other foundations developed state-based campaigns, such as the BUILD Initiative, in conjunction with numerous nationwide efforts.

A number of striking observations can be gleaned from the organization and activities of foundations (see Table 4.3). First is the sheer number of US foundations – twenty-four – devoted to funding research in and developing policy and programs in early childhood education and development. Second is the number of relatively new foundations whose founders have chosen to make early childhood education and development one of their primary areas of concern for their US-based philanthropy; these include the Buffet Foundation (2005), the Gates Foundation (2000), the Heising-Simons Foundation (2007), the I Am Your Child Foundation (1996), the George Kaiser Family Foundation (2009), the Pritzker Family Foundation (early 2000s), the Schott Foundation (1991), and the Schumann Fund of New Jersey (1988). Third, a number of these foundations have identified as another area of concern the development and funding of evidence-based policy/scientific research: the William T. Grant Foundation, the Heising-Simons Foundation, the MacArthur Foundation, the Packard Foundation, and PEW all list this as one of their principal areas of concern as of 2014.

The Creation of a Policy Network

Many of these foundations were key to the creation of a network of researchers on early childhood. Those researchers, in turn, have become important idea transmitters as their work gets published and cited in both the scholarly literature and the media and as they present their findings at conferences in the United States and around the world (see Table 4.4).

This survey of researchers demonstrates a research network that is both broad and deep. Scholars affiliated with numerous departments and centres at universities have strong connections with other scholars with diverse scholarly backgrounds and research interests. Much of the research has been and continues to be funded by various federal and state government departments and receives foundation funding as well. The strength of ties among researchers is facilitated by institutes

Table 4.4. Network of US researchers with affiliated university and/or research institutes and foundation sponsorship

Researcher	Institutional Affiliation	Foundation Links
W. Steve Barnett, Director	Professor of Education Economics and Public Policy and Director of the National Institute for Early Education Research (NIEER), Rutgers University	PEW Charitable Trusts
David Blau	Professor of Economics, Ohio State University (formerly at University of North Carolina, Chapel Hill	Member of various NIH and National Research Council committees including Committee on Early Child Care and Education Workforce; adviser to US GAO on study of child care subsidies and employment
Barbara Bowman	Taught at the University of Chicago's lab school; cc-founded the Chicago School for Early Childhood Education / Erikson Institute (1966)	Irving B. Harris Foundation
Jeanne Brooks-Gunn	Professor of Child Development and Education, Teachers College and College of Physicians and Surgeons, Columbia University; Co-director, National Center for Children and Families (with Sharon Lynn Kaçan); Co-director, Columbia University Institute for Child and Family Policy (with Sheila Kamerman); board of NICHD	NCCF funded by the US Department of Health and Human Services, NICHD, some state govts, Carnegie, Pew, Packard, among others; ICFP initially funded by the William T. Grant Foundation; affiliated with the Center for Research on Child Well-Being, Princeton; PI on "Child Care and Parental Employment in Fragile Families," Fragile Families and Child Well-being Study, Princeton/Columbia
Margaret Burchinal	Adjunct Professor, Department of Education, University of California, Irvine, and senior scientist at the Frank Porter Graham Child Development Institute, and Department of Psychology, University of North Carolina at Chapel Hill	Serves on the Board of Trustees of the William T. Grant Foundation (since 2012); (other faculty serving on the Board include Prudence Carter (Stanford); Adam Gamoran (Wisconsin–Madison); Nancy Gonzales (Arizona State); Andrew Porter (UPenn); Kenneth Prewitt (Columbia)
Frances A. Campbell, Richard Clifford, Ellen S. Peisner-Feinberg, Joseph J. Sparling	Frank Porter Graham Child Development Institute, University of North Carolina; Abecedarian Child Care Program begun in 1966; expanded to become a comprehensive, multidisciplinary research project on the effect of full-day early education, health care, and social services on the lives of disadvantaged children	Named after a former university president; institute receives funds from a variety of federal and state agencies and other donors, including universities. Lists foundation support including Buffet Early Childhood Fund; Casey Family Programs; George Kaiser Family Foundation; Kellogg Foundation; Spencer Foundation

(Continued)

Table 4.4. Network of US researchers with affiliated university and/or research institutes and foundation sponsorship (Continued)

Researcher	Institutional Affiliation	Foundation Links
Janet Currie	Professor of Economics and Public Affairs, Princeton University, and Director of Princeton's Center for Health and Well Being; Member of the Institute of Medicine; Director, National Bureau of Economic Research's Program on Children	Affiliated with the Center for Research on Child Well-Being, Princeton; PI on "fragile families study," Princeton/Columbia University
Greg Duncan	Professor of Education, UC Irvine (formerly U of Michigan); Co-chair, Committee on Evaluation of Children's Health, National Research Council and Institute of Medicine; plus other NRC/Institute Committees	Member, MacArthur Network on Family and the Economy 1996–2008
Bruce Fuller	Professor of Education and Public Policy, UC Berkeley	*Growing Up in Poverty Project* (1997–present) with funding from US depts of education and health and human services, and the Casey, MacArthur, Packard and Spencer foundations; *Decentralizing Early Education for Latino Children* (2004–present) funded by the Foundation for Child Development, among other projects
Walter Gilliam	Associate Professor, Child Study Center, School of Medicine and Dept. of Psychology; Director, the Edward Zigler Center in Child Development and Social Policy, Yale University; PI on the National Prekindergarten Study; Board Member, Child Care Aware of America; Zero to Three	Funding from Dept of Children and Families, State of Connecticut; Carnegie; Foundation for Child Development; Mailman; NICHD; NAEYC; PEW, among others
William Gormley	Professor of Public Policy and Co-Director, Center for Research on Children in the US (CROCUS), Georgetown University (with Deborah Phillips)	CROCUS est'd with start-up funds from the Foundation for Child Development; Oklahoma Pre-K Project funded by the Foundation for Child Development; Mailman; NIEER/Pew; NICHD; Packard; Spencer
Neil Halfon	Director Professor, David Geffen School of Medicine at UCLA, Dept. of Pediatrics; Professor, UCLA Fielding School of Public Health, Dept. of Health Policy and Management; Professor, UCLA Luskin School of Public Affairs, Dept. of Public Policy	Board member, Children Youth and Families at the Institute of Medicine and National Research Council, 2001–6

Ron Haskins	Senior Fellow, Economic Studies program and Co-director, Brookings Center on Children and Families and Budgeting for National Priorities Project, Brockings Institution; Former White House and congressional adviser on welfare issues; former senior researcher at the Frank Porter Graham Child Development Center at the University of North Carolina, Chapel Hill	Senior Consultant, Annie E Casey Foundation; affiliated with the Center for Research on Child Well-being, Princeton
James Heckman	Professor of Economics, Director, Center for the Study of Childhood Development, Harris School of Public Policy; Center for the Economics of Human Development, Pritzker Consortium on Early Childhood Development, University of Chicago	Harris Foundation; McCormick-Tribune Foundation; J.B. and M.K. Pritzker Family Foundation
Sharon Lynn Kagan	Professor of Early Childhood and Family Policy; Co-director, National Center for Children and Families (with Jeanne Brooks-Gunn), Columbia University; member Institute of Medicine (various committees)	NCCF funded by the US Department of Health and Human Services, NICHD, some state govts, Carnegie, Pew, Packard, among others
Sheila Kamerman	Professor (now Emerita) of Social Work, Co-director, Columbia University Institute for Child and Family Policy (with Jeanne Brooks-Gunn), Columbia University	Board member of several orgs including Citizen's Committee for the Children of New York, the Children's Rights Division of Human Rights Watch, and the National Partnership of Women and Families; consultant with OECD and other IOs
Lynn Karoly	Senior Economist, RAND	Member, various National Research Council and Institute of Medicine committees; member, Evaluation Advisory Committee, Edna McConnell Clark Foundation; member, Corporate Council, Los Angeles Universal Preschool
Joan Lombardi	Founding Director, the Children's Project; *Huffington Post* columnist; Deputy Assistant Secretary for Early Childhood Development, Department of Health and Human Services, Obama administration (2009–2011); Deputy Assistant Secretary for Policy and External Affairs, Administration for Children and Families, First Commissioner of the Child Care Bureau, Clinton Administration (1993–8)	Founding chair of the Birth to Five Policy Alliance (est'd by the Buffett Early Childhood Fund); State Early Childhood Policy Leadership Forum; among others

(Continued)

Table 4.4. Network of US researchers with affiliated university and/or research institutes and foundation sponsorship (Continued)

Researcher	Institutional Affiliation	Foundation Links
Samuel Meisels	Founding Executive Director, Buffett Early Childhood Institute, University of Nebraska; former president Erickson Institute; Professor Emeritus of Education, University of Michigan	Former member, Pre-K Accountability Task Force, Pew Charitable Trusts; former president of the Board of Directors, Zero to Three; former member, State of Illinois Early Learning Council, 2004–7
Deborah Phillips	Professor of Psychology and affiliated with Public Policy Institute, Georgetown University; Co-director Center for Research on Children in the US (CROCUS) (with William Gormley)	Executive Director of the Board on Children, Youth, and Families, National Research Council and the Institute of Medicine; Study Director for *From Neurons to Neighbourhoods;* former president of the Foundation for Child Development; former Director of Child Care Information Services at the National Association for the Education of Young Children; former Congressional Science Fellow (Society for Research in Child Development) on the staff of Congressman George Miller; served on the Task Force on Meeting the Needs of Young Children, Carnegie Corporation; the National Scientific Council on the Developing Child; the Head Start FACES Redesign Expert Panel; Secretary's (US DHHS) Committee on the Maternal, Infant, and Early Childhood Home Visiting Evaluation
Robert Pianta	Professor of Education and Founding Director, Center for Advanced Study of Teaching and Learning, University of Virginia; Director of the National Center for Research in Early Childhood Education; creator of the Classroom Assessment Scoring System (CLASS); Steering Committee, NICHD Study of Early Child Care	Research funded by a variety of foundations including Gates, Grant, Packard, US Dept of Education and Health and Human Services
Craig Ramey, Sharon Ramey	Both are Professors of Psychology and research scholars Carilion Research Institute, Virginia Tech; Craig Ramey was a founder of the Abecedarian Project, University of North Carolina, Chapel Hill	Early phases of the Abecedarian project were funded by NICHD and the US Dept of Health and Human Development; Dept of Human Resources, State of North Carolina; age-21 follow-up study funded by the Maternal and Child Health Bureau of the US Dept of Health and Human Service, US Dept of Education; Packard; and the Frank Porter Graham Child Development Center

Arthur Reynolds	Professor, Humphrey School of Public Affairs and Institute of Child Development (Dept. of Child Psychology), University of Minnesota; Director of the Chicago Longitudinal Study; Co-Director (with Arthur Rolnick) of the Human Capital Research Collaborative (a partnership of the University of Minnesota and the Federal Reserve Bank of Minneapolis)	Original funding from Title I of the Elementary and Secondary Education Act of 1965; other funding from Waisman Center and School of Social Work, University of Wisconsin-Madison; Dept of Economics, Northern Illinois University; Institute for Research on Poverty, University of Wisconsin–Madison; NICHD and US Dept of Education
Art Rolnick	Economist and Co-director for the Human Capital Research Collaborative (with Arthur Reynolds), University of Minnesota. Former Senior Vice-President and Director of Research, Federal Reserve Bank of Minneapolis	Board member Minnesota Early Learning Foundation, Ready 4 K
Isabel Sawhill	Senior fellow in Economic Studies, Director of the Budgeting for National Priorities project, Director of the Center on Children and Families all at the Brookings Institution; former senior fellow at the Urban Institute; former associate director federal OMB (1993–5)	Has served as Board member on numerous organizations including the National Research Council, the Center for Research on Child Well-Being (Princeton)
Lawrence Schweinhart	Lead researcher on the High/Scope Perry Preschool Study; President of the HighScope Foundation 2003–13	Board member and panel chair on quality, compensation, and affordability at NAEYC; former public policy co-chair for the Michigan Association for the Education of Young Children
Jack Shonkoff	Professor of Child Health and Development, Department of Social and Behavioural Sciences, Harvard School of Public Health and Harvard Graduate School of Education; Professor of Pediatrics, Harvard Medical School and Children's Hospital, Boston; Director, Center on the Developing Child, Harvard University; Chair, National Scientific Council on the Developing Child and National Forum on Early Childhood Program Evaluation; former Chair of the Board on Children, Youth, and Families, which produced *From Neurons to Neighborhoods*	Buffet Early Childhood Fund; Johnson and Johnson Pediatric Institute; MacArthur; Omidyar; McCormick Tribune, among others

(Continued)

Table 4.4. Network of US researchers with affiliated university and/or research institutes and foundation sponsorship (Continued)

Researcher	Institutional Affiliation	Foundation Links
Judy Temple	Associate Professor, Humphrey School of Public Affairs, Department of Applied Economics, and Adjunct Professor, Institute of Child Development, University of Minnesota; involved in the Chicago Longitudinal Study (PI Arthur Reynolds)	NICHD; US Dept of Health and Human Services; McKnight Foundation (Minnesota-based), among others
Jane Waldfogel	Professor of Social Work, Columbia University	PI, "Work, Family Policies and Child and Family Well-Being" project funded by NICHD; Co-PI on "Economic Status, Public Policy and Child Neglect" Fragile Families and Child Well-Being Study, Princeton/Columbia; affiliated with the Center for Research on Child Well-being (Princeton); previous funding from Russell Sage, Casey, PEW, Spencer, among others
Marcie Whitebook	Director, Center for the Study of Child Care Employment, Institute for Research on Labor and Employment, UC Berkeley; founding Executive Director of the Center for the Child Care Workforce	PI, "No Single Ingredient: The Complexity of Early Childhood Teacher Preparation" longitudinal study, among other projects; former scholar in residence, Center for the Future of Children, David and Lucile Packard Foundation
Martha Zaslow	Director, Office for Policy and Communications, Society for Research in Child Development; Senior Scholar, Child Trends; PhD psychology, Harvard	Member, Advisory Committee for Head Start Research and Evaluation; Committee Member, Developmental Outcomes and Assessments of Young Children, National Research Council
Edward Zigler	Professor of Psychology, Zigler Center in Child Development and Social Policy, Yale University	Director, Office of Child Development; Head of the Children's Bureau, US Dept of Health, Education and Welfare 1970–2; member of the Head Start Evaluation Committee; board member of numerous organizations including Fight Crime, Invest in Kids, Institute for Women's Policy Research; advisor to Mailman

Sources: List of names generated from secondary sources as well as review of primary research on early childhood education and search of National Research Council and Institute of Medicine reports and internet searches.

such as NIEER; many of the scholars serve as members of advisory boards. Many others serve or have served in the past on committees of the National Research Council and the Institute of Medicine, the now named Eunice Kennedy Shriver National Institute of Child Health and Human Development (NICHD), the Society for Research on Child Development, the Center for Research on Child Well-being at Princeton, the National Forum on Early Childhood Policies and Programs, and the National Scientific Council on the Developing Child at Harvard. Many researchers consult for the Department of Education or the Department of Health and Human Services federally, and some consult at the state level as well.

The strength of the network becomes even more visible when we observe the broader policy community of advocacy organizations and policy entrepreneurs, many of whom are or were active researchers. As seen from Table 4.5, the early childhood policy community is enormous in the United States and has burgeoned with the active support of foundation funding. Many, many other organizations exist at the state and local levels, and considerable policy effort has been focused on expanding state and local programs and services, as chapter 6 documents.

National policy advocacy has continued to yield incremental gains. In his 2013 State of the Union address, President Obama, as part of his Preschool for All initiative, proposed a ten-year $75 billion federal–state shared-cost program to encourage states to provide pre-school for all 4-year-olds from low- and moderate-income families and to expand programs for middle-class families. The plan also called for quality improvements in child care programs for younger children; quality improvements through the Child Care and Development Block Grant; and support for the Maternal, Infant, and Early Childhood Home Visiting Program (White House Office of the Press Secretary, 2013). The plan called for an increase in the federal tobacco tax to pay for it. Democratic Senator Tom Harkin of Iowa introduced legislation in November 2013 that reflected much of the president's agenda (Harkin, 2013), although with fewer funds pledged; Republican members of Congress were opposed (Pérez-Peña and Rich, 2014).

Very few of the efforts of think tanks and other organizations have been directed to initiatives outside the United States, with some exceptions such as the Children's Project and the New America Foundation. However, policy ideas have spread as a result of experts travelling outside the country and promoting their ideas and research at the transnational and international levels, as documented in the next chapter. The

Table 4.5. Advocacy organizations and policy entrepreneurs that focus on early childhood education and development

Organization	Mission	Lead Actor(s)	Foundation Support
Alliance for Early Childhood Finance	Focuses on strategies for system building and financing of high-quality early childhood education and care	Anne Mitchell; Louise Stoney; Mildred Warner (Cornell) lead researcher on the Child Care Bureau–funded grant, Linking Economic Development and Child Care	
Alliance for Early Success (formerly Birth to Five Policy Alliance)	To act as a "catalyst for state policy action" for children	Lisa Klein, PhD, executive director (former chair was Joan Lombardi); formerly at the Kauffman Foundation	Buffet Early Childhood Fund; Gates; Harris; Heising-Simons; Kaiser; Kellogg; Packard
American Federation of Teachers (AFT)	Labor union – issued a policy statement in support of ECE in 2003	Randi Weingarten, president	
BUILD Initiative	Supports development of state early childhood development systems in 10 states	Susan Hibbard, interim executive director	Created by the Early Childhood Funders' Collaborative that includes Gates; Harris; Kellogg; Pritzker; Schott; Schumann, among others
Child Care Aware of America (National Association of Child Care Resource and Referral Agencies)	Mission is to ensure all families have access to high-quality affordable child care	Lynette Fraga, executive director	Funding sources not listed
Child Trends	Early childhood research institute with HQ in Bethesda, MD		Number of funders including Casey; Gates; Grant; Harris; Kellogg; MacArthur; Mailman; McCormick; Mott; Pew as well as national and state govt depts and other advocacy organizations

Child Welfare League of America (CWLA) National Child Day Care Task Force	Advocates for better federal policy and adequate funding for high-quality and accessible child care	Christine James-Brown, CEO	Some foundation funders, including Casey and MacArthur; along with corporate supporters and member agencies
Center for Law and Social Policy (CLASP)	Mission to improve the lives of low-income people; child care and early education has been a strong research focus	Olivia Golden, executive director; Christine Johnson-Staub, senior policy analyst, child care and early education; former director of Policy Mark Greenberg is now Acting Assistant Secretary, Administration for Children and Families, US Dept of Health and Human Services	Foundation funding includes Gates; Kellogg
Children's Defense Fund (CDF)	Goal to improve policies and programs for children, especially vulnerable children with motto "leave no child behind"	Marian Wright Edelman, president; Geoffrey Canada, board chair (president of the Harlem Children's Zone)	Funded by a number of foundations and corporations and individual donations
Committee for Economic Development (CED)	Business-led policy think tank; early learning is one of its primary areas of research and advocacy related to education; policy studies: *Why Child Care Matters* (1933); *Preschool for All* (2002)	Steve Odland, CEO; James Rohr, executive chair Early Learning Project Subcommittee	Has commissioned research by James Heckman
Council of Chief State School Officers (CCSSO)	Issued policy statement in 2009 re: the "quiet crisis" in early childhood; supports integrated quality state early childhood systems aligned with K–3 programs, esp. for those most at risk	Terry Holliday, president; Chris Minnich, executive director	Partnered with a number of corporations

(Continued)

Table 4.5. Advocacy organizations and policy entrepreneurs that focus on early childhood education and development (Continued)

Organization	Mission	Lead Actor(s)	Foundation Support
Early Childhood Data Collaborative (ECDC)	Goal to coordinate state ECE data	Carlise King, executive director; members: Center for the Study of Child Care Employment, UC Berkeley; Council of Chief State School Officers; Data Quality Campaign; NCSL; NGA Center for Best Practices; Pew	Funding from Alliance for Early Success; Packard; and Pew
Educare Learning Network	Program of early learning practices implemented in partnership with schools, Head Start, Early Head Start, foundations to provide programs of full-day, full-year and with evaluation conducted		Ounce of Prevention Fund; Buffet Early Childhood Fund; Gates; Harris; Kaiser; Kellogg
Families and Work Institute	Provides research on workplace issues, youth, and early childhood; conducts a number of ongoing projects	Ellen Galinsky, president and co-founder	Receives funding from a number of corporate sponsors and foundations including Carnegie; Casey; Mailman; MacArthur; and other non-profits
Fight Crime: Invest in Kids	Organization of police chiefs, sheriffs, prosecutors, attorneys general, and others advocating for early childhood program investments	David Kass, president	Funding from Casey; Gates; Harris; Kellogg; McCormick; Packard; Pew; Pritzker, among others
First Five Years Fund	Mission is to advance federal investment in early childhood education for disadvantaged young children	Kris Perry, executive director (former executive director of First Five California)	Buffet Early Childhood Fund; Gates; Harris; Heising-Simons; Kaiser; Kellogg; Packard; Pritzker
Institute for Women's Policy Research (IWPR)	As part of its mission it advocates for high-quality affordable child care, an early childhood system, and strengthening the early childhood sector and workers	Heidi Hartmann, president; Barbara Gault, executive director and VP	Number of foundation funders including Casey, Gates, Kellogg and Mott; along with support from labour unions and other NGOs

National Association for the Education of Young Children (NAEYC)	Professional org. whose mission is to promote professional practice and working conditions in early childhood education; support early childhood programs; promote excellence in early childhood education	Carol Brunson Day, president; Rhian Evans Allvin, executive director	Number of foundation funders including Carnegie; Casey; Joyce; Kellogg; Mailman; McCormick-Tribune
National Black Child Development Institute (NBCDI)	National advocacy organization for children of colour with focus on early care and education and child welfare	Cindra Taylor (interim president and CEO); founding president was Evelyn Moore (who was a teacher in the Perry Preschool study)	Est'd by the Black Women's Community Development Foundation; no info on current funders
National Center for Children in Poverty (NCCP), Columbia University Mailman School of Public Health, Department of Health Policy and Management	Mission to promote the economic security, health, and well-being of low-income families and children; as part of that goal it conducts research and advocacy related to early learning and care	Renée Wilson-Simmons, director	Many foundation funders including Casey; Foundation for Child Development; Harris; Kellogg; Mailman; MacArthur; Packard; some corporate donors and govt depts; some individual donors
National Conference of State Legislatures (NCSL)	Bipartisan organization that provides support to state govts; policy innovation across state govts; and voice of states to the federal govt; has est'd a child care and early education legislative network	Robyn Lipkowitz, program director, Children and Families Program; Julie Poppe covers early childhood care issues	Since 2011, Alliance for Early Success has funded an Early Learning Fellows program to expand knowledge base of legislators and staff re: early years research and policy
National Education Association (NEA)	Professional organization and labour union; supports free, publicly funded, quality kindergarten programs in all states; mandatory full-day kindergarten; optional free, publicly funded, quality pre-kindergarten programs for all 3- and 4-year-old children; public funding as per K-12 funding	Dennis Van Roekel, president; John Stocks, executive director	Most funding comes from membership dues

(Continued)

Table 4.5. Advocacy organizations and policy entrepreneurs that focus on early childhood education and development (Continued)

Organization	Mission	Lead Actor(s)	Foundation Support
National Governors Association (NGA)	Mission to improve state govt; share best practices; and lobby Washington; Center for Best Practices develops a number of resources related to early childhood governance	David Moore, director of the Center for Best Practices; Albert Wat is a senior policy analyst in the education division (formerly at Pew/Pre-k Now)	Funding support from foundations and governments; specific project grants funded by foundations as well
National Head Start Association (NHSA)	Represents Head Start programs; mission is to support the Head Start field in early child development	Vanessa Rich, board chair	Funding not specified
National Women's Law Center	As a women's advocacy organization, major focus has been on child care and now prekindergarten and Head Start, including workforce and policy issues	Nancy Duff Campbell, founder and co-president; Helen Blank, director of Child Care and Early Learning	Funding from many foundations including Casey; MacArthur; Mailman; Packard; Schott, among others; many corporate donors and other NGOs
New America Foundation	Public policy institute; early education initiative as part of the education policy program	Anne-Marie Slaughter, president and CEO; Lisa Guernsey, director, Early Education Initiative	Funding from many foundations including Carnegie; Casey; Foundation for Child Development; Gates; Joyce; MacArthur; Mott; Pritzker, among others; some govt funding; other NGOs
Next Generation	Two principal missions: climate change and children and families; focus on California in particular	James Steyer, Co-founder; Ann O'Leary, vice-president & director, Children & Families Program	Co-founder and funder Tom Steyer
Ounce of Prevention Fund	Mission to ensure that all children – particularly low-income – have quality early childhood experiences in the first five years of life	Diana Mendley Rauner, president	Founded by the Irving Harris Foundation; partnered with the Alliance for Early Success; funding also from Gates; Kellogg; Pritzer

Pre-K Now	10-year campaign (2001–11) of Pew Charitable Trusts	Libby Doggett, director (now Deputy AssistantSecretary for Policy and Early Learning at the US Department of Education)	Pew Charitable Trusts
ReadyNation (formerly Partnership for America's Economic Success)	Organization of business leaders advocating for children and youth policies as part of human capital investment to strengthen the economy	Sarah Watson, national director (former director of Pew's national pre-kindergarten campaign)	Est'd through Pew funding; plus many other foundations; funders include Buffet; Heising-Simons; MacArthur; Pew; Pritzker; Schott; Schumann; among others
Too Small to Fail/ Clinton Foundation	Mission to improve the health and well-being of children zero to five; focus on research on brain development, early learning, and health	Hillary Clinton, co-chair; Patti Miller, director	Clinton Foundation and Next Generation; partnered with American Academy of Pediatrics, PBS Parents, Sesame Workshop, Univision, and Zero to Three
Urban Institute	Conducts economic and social policy research; although it does not have an explicit policy focus on early childhood education currently, it has conducted a number of studies and written reports as part of children and youth, education, and families focus	Sarah Rosen Wartell, president	Established by the Lyndon Johnson administration; funding ongoing from govt but also foundations and private sponsors; foundation funders include Casey; Kaiser; and Mott
Voices for America's Children (formerly National Association of Child Advocates); closed in 2013	Mission to advocate for children at the federal, state, and local levels; one main area is early childhood education	N/A	Funding from member organizations as well as foundations including Casey, Packard, among others
Zero to Three	Mission to ensure all babies and toddlers have "a strong start in life"	Matthew Melmed, executive director	Funding from several foundations including Buffet; Harris; Mailman; McCormick; Pritzker, among others; along with corporate and private sponsors

Sources: Information gathered from organization websites and author interviews.

remainder of this chapter documents the parallel diffusion of ideas in the neighbouring country of Canada.

Branching Out of the Policy Network – Canada

It would be far from accurate to suggest that the Canadian policy community was influenced entirely by actors and events in the United States. But many political leaders and policy officials have echoed the statement by Manitoba's Minister of Education, Citizenship, and Youth, Peter Bjornson, who said at a meeting of the Ministers of Education of the Americas that "evidence from numerous research studies and evaluations of existing programs have shown time and again that investment in early childhood education and care is a crucial component of a person's overall development" (Council of Ministers of Education, 2007, p. 9). Public officials in Canada draw on the longitudinal analyses and the cost–benefit work of Heckman and others in making the case for program interventions. As the next chapter's ideational process tracing demonstrates, even when the source of ideas is international, such as from the OECD, many of those ideas regarding early learning at the international level have been influenced by US research and policy. And many of the policy trends in Canada mirror events in the United States even while the extent of policy change in Canada – with the exception of Quebec – is less extensive than in the United States.

The child care advocacy community in Canada, however, has been very active at the federal and provincial and even local levels for decades (Prentice, 2001; Timpson, 2001). Both the Child Care Advocacy Association of Canada and the Canadian Child Care Federation have been active in policy work, as have a number of provincial advocacy groups and Childcare Resource and Research, whose director is Martha Friendly. Many of the national labour unions, such as the Canadian Labour Congress and the Canadian Union of Postal Workers, have also been strongly supportive of expanding funding and support for child care policies and programs since the 1960s. Women's organizations, including the National Action Committee on the Status of Women, have also been strong supporters of a national universally accessible high-quality publicly funded system of early childhood education and care. Many of these organizations have had fairly good access to government policy networks over the years, including supportive cabinet ministers and even prime ministers. Child care has been the subject of a federal Child Care Task Force (1984–6) and a special Parliamentary

Committee (1985–7) and received strong endorsement in the submissions to the federal Royal Commission on the Status of Women in 1970. Yet there has been little policy change nationally.

The year 1995 marked a watershed in Canada with the cancellation of the federal Canada Assistance Plan (CAP), which had provided funding for child care as part of federal transfers to provinces for those on social assistance, and the creation of the Canada Health and Social Transfer (CHST) block fund, which did not specifically earmark funds for child care (Friendly and White, 2007; Timpson, 2001). At the same time, a number of government programs emerged at the federal and provincial levels that emphasized early childhood development and parental support programs: the federal Community Action Program for Children (CAP-C) and the Canada Prenatal Nutrition Program in 1994, and Aboriginal Head Start on reserves in 1995 (Doherty, 2007), as well as provincial programs such as Ontario's Healthy Babies, Healthy Children; Ontario's Early Years Centres; Healthy Child Manitoba; and PEI's Healthy Child Development program. Federal, provincial, and territorial officials cooperated to create the National Child Benefit in 1998 (Simmons and Graefe, 2013). Critics label these shifts as emphasizing children to the neglect of women (Dobrowolsky and Jenson, 2004); but they also reveal increased attention to the early years.

By the late 1990s, various federal officials had begun paying attention to research – some generated in Canada, but much that was emerging in the United States – on the factors that contribute to strong child development. Academic research by Canadians started to appear around that time (e.g., Keating and Hertzman, 1999), as did the widely distributed McCain–Mustard report completed for the Ontario government (McCain and Mustard, 1999). Health Canada issued a discussion paper in July 1999 that discussed the components of an early child development system (Health Canada, Childhood and Youth Division, 1999). A second paper, prepared by the federal/provincial/territorial advisory committee on population health, circulated in September 1999 for the FPT conference of health ministers in Charlottetown, PEI. Human Resources and Development Canada (HRDC) also began to study determinants of early child development. That ministry's Applied Research Branch commissioned a number of studies (e.g. Cleveland and Hyatt, 1997; Doherty, 1997; Kohen, Hertzman, and Brooks-Gunn, 1998; Lefebvre and Merrigan, 1998) and held a national conference on 27–9 October 1998 in Ottawa that brought together a number of researchers, including contributors to the National Longitudinal Survey of Children and

Youth, as well as officials from HRDC and Statistics Canada (HRDC, 1998). The Applied Research Branch continued to commission a number of other studies (e.g., Connor and Brink, 1999a, 1999b; Seifert, Canning, and Lindemann, 2001), including a summary report from the conference that promoted a number of early interventions (HRDC, 1999). HRDC then launched its Early Years Initiative in 1999, the goal of which was to "enhance knowledge about community factors that influence the early development of children" though a number of funded pilot projects throughout the country (HRSDC, n.d., p. 3).

In September 2000 the federal government, along with provincial and territorial governments (save for Quebec), signed the Federal–Provincial–Territorial Agreement on Early Childhood Development, wherein the federal government agreed to transfer $2.2 billion over five years and the provincial and territorial governments agreed to use federal funding to improve and expand services in four priority areas: healthy pregnancy, birth, and infancy; parenting and family supports; early childhood development, learning, and care; and community supports (CICS, 2000). In March 2003, in an effort to direct monies to child care programs, the federal human resources minister, Jane Stewart, committed to the Multilateral Framework on Early Learning and Child Care (MFA) with provincial and territorial ministers responsible for social services (except Quebec). The federal government agreed to provide $900 million over five years, beginning in 2003, to support provincial and territorial government investments specifically in early learning and child care (CICS, 2003). In 2003 the federal human resources department was also briefly reconfigured and renamed under the federal Liberal governments of Jean Chrétien and Paul Martin (2003–2006) to include Human Resources and Skills Development Canada (HRSDC), which was to focus on workforce-related aspects of HR; and Social Development Canada (SDC), which was to focus on social support programs for children, families, and seniors.

As influences on these shifts in children's policy, federal officials interviewed cited the literature on human capital development and the work of researchers such as Fraser Mustard, as well as the availability of data generated by the National Longitudinal Survey of Children and Youth (NLSCY), which Statistics Canada began in 1994. Also, a national network of organizations had emerged in the late 1990s under the aegis of the National Children's Alliance to press for policy changes. This group of around fifty organizations[10] bringing a variety of perspectives on early childhood was established in the spring of 1996 and began to have monthly meetings to share information and best practices on how to improve policies for children nationally in Canada. And it met with members of the federal cabinet as well as MPs and administrative officials responsible for children at the federal level.

Also, by the mid- to late 1990s, a number of Canadian research institutes had begun to actively publicize work that made explicit connections between early childhood development research and best policy practices. One of the main organizations was the Canadian Policy Research Networks (CPRN), founded in 1994 by Judith Maxwell, former chair of the then-defunct Economic Council of Canada, and funded by several federal departments. The organization dissolved in December 2009, but before it did, in the space of fifteen years it published a plethora of policy studies on a number of themes, one of the main areas being children, youth, and families, under the directorship of Jane Jenson, a professor of political science at the University of Montreal (CPRN, 2009). The Head of CPRN, Judith Maxwell, described the origins of the research:

> In November '96 we held a workshop in the Laidlaw offices in Toronto and we had probably 12 or 15 people there, including some researchers, several people from the federal government and from the provincial government at Queen's Park and probably some community people … And we brainstormed the design of the project at that meeting and then we raised the money; as I said the core of it came from the Laidlaw Foundation, but we also had other foundations, like the Lawson Foundation and I think HRDC as it was then called and a couple of provinces eventually came in as well. And then if you look at the Blueprint [Jenson and Stroick, 1999], it is actually the summation of I think eight or nine different studies at frequent intervals and the last study came out – the big sort of technical synthesis report – came out in January or February of 2000. So over a three-year period, we probably had five or six different roundtables, reviewing specific pieces of research as they were completed.[11]

Many of the research studies CPRN produced drew on comparative policy examples, especially in Europe, and particularly in France (O'Hara, 1999; Phipps, 1999), as was similarly happening in the United States (Neuman and Peer, 2002; Richardson and Marx, 1989; Waldfogel, 2001). The focus of the CPRN studies was quite broad – the enabling conditions for healthy early child development, which encompassed adequate income, effective parenting, and supportive community environments (Avard and Tipper, 1999; Jenson and Stroick, 1999).

Another influential organization was the Canadian Institute for Advanced Research (CIAR, now CIFAR), founded in 1982. It has been sponsoring research on the determinants of health for many years (e.g. Mustard, 1991). One of CIFAR's earliest projects was a population health program that ran from 1987 to 2003 and that explored social determinants of health. CIAR's human development program, which ran from 1993 to 2003, stemmed directly from the population health program to examine social factors that affect not just health but also development, including child development. The former head of that organization, Dr Fraser Mustard, was the author of a number of the reports on the importance of early years, including the widely cited McCain–Mustard Report (1999), written for the Ontario government's Early Years Study (see also the follow-up report by McCain, Mustard, and Shanker, 2007) and co-authored a report with Frances Picherack (Mustard and Picherack, 2002) on the state of early child development in British Columbia.

Leading members of the business and financial community, including David Dodge, former deputy finance minister and then governor of the Bank of Canada, credit Mustard's CIFAR work as "instrumental in expanding the frontiers of our knowledge in this area" (Dodge, 2003, p. 4). Some of the leading population health and child development researchers in the country were affiliated with CIFAR's projects. All became "friends of Fraser Mustard" and academic champions for early child development programs. As one interviewee stated, the scientific research was useful to present when critics tried to reduce ECEC to "babysitting." Indeed, some credit Prime Minister Paul Martin's conversion to the importance of early years to Fraser Mustard (White, 2011a). Liberal MP John Godfrey, who served as chair of the House of Commons subcommittee on children and youth at risk for much of the Chrétien government years, similarly argues that his own conversion occurred as a result of reading Mustard's work (White, 2011a).

While Canadian foundations are not generally as large or well-endowed as US ones, it is clear that some have managed to be quite influential. Besides CIFAR, for example, there is the Invest in Kids Foundation, which sponsored a huge public education campaign in Ontario in the late 1990s and early 2000s with the message "The Years Before Five Last the Rest of Their Lives." The Atkinson Charitable Foundation is a major funder of early childhood education and development projects, including the Atkinson Chair in Early Childhood and Society at the University of Toronto, as well as pilot projects for creating a seamless day for children in early years programs, such as Toronto's First Duty pilot project. Other foundations include the Laidlaw Foundation and the Lawson Foundation. Even Status of Women Canada (1986) functions somewhat like a foundation in its sponsorship of research that promotes women's equality, including balancing work and family life.

The Laidlaw Foundation in particular provided crucial funding for research on children and youth, some of which was published under the aegis of the foundation itself. Some of the rest was published under the aegis of the Canadian Council on Social Development, the Social Planning Council of Metropolitan Toronto, the Canadian Institute of Child Health, the Vanier Institute of Child Health, Campaign 2000, the Centre for Studies of Children at Risk at McMaster University, and CPRN, as mentioned above (for a complete list, see Gilbert and Zemans, 2001, pp. 163–6).

An academic research network also started to build. Richard Tremblay, a professor of pediatrics, psychiatry, and psychology at the University of Montreal, is the director of the Centre of Excellence for Early Child Development; he is also one of the directors of the Strategic Knowledge Cluster on Early Child Development, which involves a number of early child development researchers, including co-director Michel Boivin at Laval University; Jane Bertrand, who is a faculty member at George Brown College in Toronto and researcher with the Early Years Study, and who is the program director for the Margaret and Wallace McCain Family Foundation; Carl Corter, Professor Emeritus at the Jackman Institute of Child Study, OISE/University of Toronto; Magdalena Janus, who is an associate professor in the Department of Psychiatry and Behavioural Neurosciences and Clinical Epidemiology and Biostatistics at McMaster University in Hamilton, Ontario, and who is also affiliated with the Offord Centre for Child Studies; Jennifer Jenkins, a professor in the Department of Human Development and Applied Psychology at the University of Toronto and Atkinson Chair in Early Child Development and Education; and Ray Peters, Research Director of the Research Coordination Unit, Queen's University, of Ontario's Better Beginnings, Better Futures Demonstration Project.

In BC, the Human Early Learning Partnership (HELP) is a research network based at the School of Population and Public Health at the University of British Columbia. It receives funding from the BC government and the Lawson Foundation, among others. The founding director was Clyde Hertzman, the Canada Research Chair in Population Health and Human Development and professor in the School of Population and Public Health at UBC. It is also connected to the Forum for Early Child Development Monitoring, another research network involving individuals and organizations across Canada, which focuses on early child development monitoring and involves the Atkinson Centre for Society and Child Development, University of Toronto; the Centre of Excellence for Early Child Development; the Offord Centre; the Strategic Knowledge Cluster on Early Child Development; and Healthy Child Manitoba, among others.

Hertzman and co-author Dan Keating, former Atkinson Charitable Foundation Chair in Early Childhood Development and Education, OISE/University of Toronto, and now at the University of Michigan School of Education, co-edited *Developmental Health and the Wealth of Nations*, which brought together research that examined the social dimensions of economic growth and child and family well-being (Keating and Hertzman, 1999). Other research and policy statements on the human capital benefits of early years programs began to appear from David Dodge, as well as Charles Coffey, the RBC Financial Group's executive vice-president for government and community affairs (Coffey, 2003). Coffey was also the co-chair of the Commission on Early Learning and Child Care for the City of Toronto with Margaret McCain (Coffey and McCain, 2002). Craig Alexander, senior vice-president and chief economist of TD Bank Group, has also made public statements in support of early childhood education based on returns on investment (e.g., Alexander, 2012). University of Toronto Rotman School of Management professor Daniel Treflar stated the case for early years programs in an op-ed in the *Ottawa Citizen* (Treflar, 2004).

The broader consensus that was emerging within the policy community focused on a number of early years programs to support early childhood development; but again, just as in the United States, the specific policy recommendations that had emerged by the end of the 2000s focused on early childhood education, certainly with "and care" added, but with varying emphases on the latter while integrating the two sets of policies and programs. At its 2003 annual meeting, the Canadian Child Care Federation (CCCF) approved a formal change of its mission from improving quality in child care services for Canadian families to "achieving excellence in *early learning* and child care" (emphasis added). The Integration Network at the Institute of Child Study at OISE (e.g. Colley, 2005) was explicitly "established to address ... the abrupt division for kindergarten-age children between 'care' programs in child care centers and 'education' in public kindergarten." By August 2007 even the Child Care Advocacy Association of Canada, which had long supported the expansion of universal publicly funded, not-for-profit child care for children ages 0 to 12, stated that "the place to start is with three to five year old children [either] within the school system [or] in community-based licensed centres, preschools and family homes" (CCAAC, 2007, p. 4). That policy shift to focus on early learning in kindergarten and pre-kindergarten came with a price: K–12 education is an exclusive provincial responsibility in Canada, and this significantly lessens the case for federal involvement, as chapter 7 documents.

Conclusion

This chapter had documented the presence and nature of scientific and policy ideas and mapped the early childhood policy network to demonstrate the scope and substance of ideational diffusion and ideational change. Documenting the scope and substance of the main ideas animating the efforts of the policy community and the expanding policy network is not done to claim that the network's structure is the source of the change; nor is it done to explain why the network has developed as it has. Rather, it is to demonstrate the effects of network actors' interactions in promoting particular policy ideas and the diffusion of ideas "over time and space" (Fisher, Leifeld, and Iwaki, 2013; Paterson et al., 2014, p. 13). Ideational theory leads us to predict, though, that it is not just the frequency of exposure to these ideas that leads policy makers to rethink their approach to early years programs. The source of authority matters, as does policy framing.

The chapter began by tracing shifts in scientific understandings of childhood and tracking the ways in which those scientific understandings became popularized. It also documented the main change agents that emerged in those early years to influence future policy. The most significant shift in discussions around policies and programs for children has been the privileging of universal programs and those that emphasize early childhood education in particular. That privileging of these particular policy ideas is based on presumptions about the developmental benefits of early years programs based on US-based longitudinal studies. The evidence base of the policy consensus also rests on claims grounded in neuro-scientific and developmental psychology studies – albeit with deepening disputes over whether and to what extent those scientific studies support particular policy recommendations (White, Prentice, and Perlman,2015). Other "angles" to the increasing scientific consensus include human capital development claims and the economics of anti-poverty programs and, more recently, maternal employment.

An epistemic community of professionals has clearly emerged whose members share "a commitment to a common causal model and a common set of political values" (Haas, 1990, p. 41) regarding best policy practices, and who spread these ideas by attending conferences and sharing their ideas. These actors, as a community, are catalysts for policy change in this policy arena; so are a host of US foundations and advocacy organizations. They comprise a very active knowledge regime whose messages reached a host of decision makers both domestically and around the globe. Indeed, one Canadian federal official interviewed in the mid-2000s claimed that the scientific grounding and evidence base for policy making would make policy change a "no-brainer."

As later chapters document, however, the characteristics of the idea (principled versus instrumentally rational arguments) matter in persuading policy makers to adopt early years programs. Scientific consensus and actor mobilization are not enough; what also matters are the "frames" that actors use when discussing and advocating for these policies. Insofar as political and social change occurs, what matters is not only (or primarily) the degree of mobilization, but also *how* that mobilization occurs – that is, what arguments are marshalled, what ideas are brought to the table, and how arguments are framed (Fischer and Forester, 1996; Fischer, 2003; Lakoff, 2002; Lakoff and Johnson, 1980). The next chapter documents the travelling "up" of these ideas to the transnational and international levels. The extent of the landing "down" at the state and provincial levels in the United States and Canada is documented in the two subsequent chapters.

Chapter Five

Transnationalization and Internationalization of ECEC Ideas[1]

This chapter documents the role that transnational policy actors (either as communities of experts and/or policy advocates) as well as international organizations (IOs) have played in promoting ECEC policy change in industrialized countries. It traces the development of these norms at the international level – norms that have been generated domestically by actors and organizations within the United States and some European countries and then diffused to the IO level. The findings lend evidence to claims by world society and sociological institutionalist scholars (Boli and Thomas, 1999; Finnemore, 1996a, 1996b; Finnemore and Sikkink, 1998; Meyer et al., 1997) that cultural homogenization is occurring at the transnational and international levels around the idea of early child development and especially around the importance of early childhood education and care. That homogenization is not unanimous: while human capital development goals are powerful motivators for such policy prescriptions as part of broader economic development and prosperity goals, other norms are emerging – for example, that early childhood education is "good" for children (regardless of the demonstrated economic benefits), a key component of children's rights, and supportive of other policy goals such as gender equality.

The chapter also demonstrates that international norms are diffusing to domestic policy makers rather unevenly across welfare states. A significant constraint on ideational transfer from the international or transnational to the domestic policy level is the willingness of national governments to regard those actors and organizations as sources of legitimate policy advice (Acharya, 2004; Cortell and Davis, 1996, 2000). Some national governments may regard the authority of IOs with suspicion or may regard IO endorsement as a reason *not* to adopt a policy domestically. Thus, even if policy ideas become normative at the international level, there can be varying levels of receptivity to those ideas within domestic policy processes.

While IOs may not directly affect decision making, they can through their reports and conferences facilitate the spread of ideas of best practices among member countries; IOs can also *create* an epistemic community. IOs thus may not be *authoritative* actors but rather *epistemic* actors. Shifts in beliefs and practices at the international level can do much to inform domestic best practices and policies. But as Weyland (2006, p. 4) notes in the case of pension reform in Latin America, "nations retain a considerable margin of choice in deciding whether to adopt a foreign model or not" (see also Orenstein, 2008; Risse-Kappen, 1994). One can argue that a "culture shift" has occurred when ideas have become so widespread that they become taken for granted – normative, that is, principles of "right action" (Boli and Thomas, 1999) – and so popular that they affect domestic policies and practices. So it is important to probe whether the ideational shifts that are traced in this chapter have policy traction in the countries under study, namely the United States and Canada.

The Transnationalization and Internationalization of Domestic ECEC Policy Ideas

Research and advocacy organizations and actors in the United States have developed a dense policy network over the past two decades in the area of the early years. That network has become transnational in scope, with ideas diffusing through both research linkages and advocacy work.[2] The transnational character of policy advocacy is important (see also Klotz, 2002; Kollman, 2007). Keck and Sikkink (1998, p. 1) contend that "by building new links among actors in civil societies, states, and international organizations, they multiply the channels of access to the international system." This network has developed an increasingly scientific set of arguments in support of early childhood education interventions in particular. As will be demonstrated, the principal policy idea to emerge is that early childhood education is a policy solution to broader human capital development challenges.

The cross-jurisdictional diffusion of scientific studies of early childhood development, education, and care can be traced back to the 1960s. Welshman (2010, pp. 90–1), for example, notes that the introduction of Project Head Start in the United States garnered a lot of attention in other countries, such as the United Kingdom. The OECD- and Ford

Foundation–sponsored conference in 1969 on education for disadvantaged children included a presentation by Head Start evaluator Edward Zigler, and the conference had UK attendees such as Alan Little and George Smith, who co-authored a follow-up paper for the OECD that documented educational projects for the disadvantaged in the United States (Welshman, 2010, p. 90). Welshman (2010, p. 90) notes that the educational priority areas or EPAs introduced in the United Kingdom in the late 1960s "drew on US action-research projects, language development kits and tutorial methods." The UK Conservative government in the 1980s drew on Head Start and other programs in the United States to justify expanding nursery education in the United Kingdom (Welshman, 2010, pp. 90–1). The Blair government was also influenced by US research (Kirp, 2007, p. 231). Norman Glass, deputy director of the Public Services Directorate in HM Treasury under the Blair government, contends that the idea of Sure Start, launched in 1998, emerged from a review of services for young children under the Comprehensive Spending Review, which the Blair government undertook after winning the 1997 election. Glass (1999, p. 259) notes that "there was evidence from programmes like Head Start and the Perry Pre-School programme in the United States, as well as experimental programmes in this country that comprehensive early years' programmes could make a difference in children's lives" (see also Sylva and Pugh, 2005).

This kind of direct ideational transfer is not always visible, however. As Paterson and colleagues (2014, p. 425) note, policy ideas do not necessarily "find immediate homes in already existing polities like nation-states." Existing authorities are often "slow to take up the idea or actively resist ... it" (Paterson et al., 2014, p. 425). Ideas may first need to find a home at the international level.

IOs are playing an increasingly important role in promoting policy ideas, although there are disputes in the literature about the extent of their influence on substantive policy making at the domestic level.[3] IOs are perceived as influential because they can facilitate the negotiation of conventions, which are then binding on country governments that ratify them; or because they provide advice to governments underpinned by their expertise and broader legitimacy with regard to economic and other policies; or because they can build in policy requirements as part of loan conditions and have leverage owing to expertise and influence on bilateral lending policies. IOs can alter "the behavior of states and nonstate actors by changing incentives for their decisions" (Barnett and Finnemore, 2004, p. 7).

Some scholars dispute whether IOs can exercise these "harder" forms of power, especially in developed countries; others argue that "softer" tools at IOs' disposal are just as persuasive. Increasingly, researchers are tracking IOs' influence on domestic policy through "softer" forms of governance such as *surveillance* – that is, the monitoring of compliance with goals or benchmarks that member states set for themselves through international bodies (Marcussen, 2006, p. 198) – and *peer review* – that is, the examination and assessment of state policy by other states (Pagani, 2002). Finally, IOs are seen as creators and transmitters of norms. Finnemore (1993, p. 594) argues that by creating a policy forum in which issues can be debated, IOs can provide "an arena in which norms and convergent expectations about international behavior are developed." These norms then shape the identity of the countries involved in the IOs and define what it means to be a member of the organization (e.g., Meyer et al., 1997).

In the area of ECEC, certain IOs such as the OECD and the World Bank have tended to be influential because of the expert knowledge they hold (e.g., Barnett and Finnemore, 2004, chapter 3). IOs' framing of policies as "best practices" can sometimes overcome traditional antipathy towards programs, and that policy framing can be useful when more intrusive mechanisms such as loan requirements are not an option (e.g., Cortell and Davis, 1996). IOs, along with domestic and transnational policy actors, can thus be ideational entrepreneurs, working to shift policy thinking on childhood, the nature of learning, and the kinds of programs necessary for successful childhood and adult lives. The development of these norms has the potential to help overcome domestic normative resistance to state-funded child care and ECE programs. They thus can provide crucial forums for new ideas around ECEC and perhaps persuade policy makers and the public to shift from viewing child care as a private good and early education as unnecessary (Bennett, 2003), to seeing both as essential, integrated public services.

IOs' attention to ECEC policy is somewhat surprising. The international aspects of early childhood policy seem less obvious than, for example, peace and security (e.g., Ruggie, 1998), trade and economic and financial sector coordination and management (e.g., Pauly, 1997), climate change and pollution control (Bernstein, 2001; Haas, Keohane, and Levy, 1993), and even science and scientific research coordination (Finnemore, 1993). The IO that would appear to have the most potential interest in this issue because of ECEC's connection to both effective parental employment and children's lifelong learning – the ILO – has typically paid little attention to these issues. Its research program has historically included collecting data on maternity and parental leave but not a lot of work on ECEC.[4] The OECD, in contrast, has established the largest research program and has been most visible in the industrialized countries in promoting these policies, although labour market issues have driven other IOs such as the EU to try to coordinate action under international and regional trade agreements (Linos, 2007) and the World Bank has increasingly paid attention to ECEC policy as part of a human capital development agenda.

Why, though, would traditionally economic and financially focused IOs such as the World Bank and the OECD care about these issues? The next section provides an ideational process tracing of IOs' position on ECEC, focusing on the European Union (EU), the International Labour Organization (ILO), the Organization of American States (OAS), UN agencies – particularly the UN Children's Fund through the instrument of the Convention on the Rights of the Child, and the UN Educational, Scientific, and Cultural Organization (UNESCO) – and the World Bank.

The Importance of IOs in Promoting ECEC Norms

One of the older organizations to focus on ECEC issues is the Consultative Group on Early Childhood Care and Development (CGECCD), which was formed in the 1980s from a group of donor funding agencies including the Ford Foundation, the Bernard Leer Foundation, and UNICEF. The Ford Foundation and the Bernard Leer Foundation hosted a conference in May 1983 that involved a number of IOs, including UNESCO, UNICEF, the US Agency for International Development (USAID), and the International Development Research Centre (IDRC) from Canada. Researcher Robert Myers presented a report that formed the basis for an inter-agency organization with funding from the Ford Foundation, UNICEF, USAID, and the High/Scope Foundation (CGECCD, n.d). A follow-up meeting in October 1984 brought additional organizations to the consultative group: the Carnegie Corporation, the World Bank, the Aga Khan Foundation, and the World Health Organization (WHO). The Consultative Group has a broad agenda that focuses on improving children's lives in developing countries and is explicitly focused on evidence-based policy making (CGECCD, n.d.).

In 1986 the European Commission began major research on ECEC policy when it established the Childcare Network as part of the EU's

Second Equal Opportunities Program (European Commission Network on Childcare, 1996). The network consisted of a coordinator and country experts from member states. In 1991 it was renamed the European Commission Network for Childcare and Other Measures to Reconcile Employment and Family Responsibilities for Women and Men. It produced a number of reports (e.g., European Commission Childcare Network, 1990; European Commission Network on Childcare, 1994) and drew a lot of attention within the European policy community not just to the issue of child care but also to parental leave, men as carers, and reconciling work and family life.

A survey of these and other documents produced by IOs has uncovered four different sets of ideas regarding early childhood education and care. The following section provides details on those differing ideas and the authoritative actors promoting them.

ECEC as Part of Human Capital Development

All of the IOs reviewed[5] have endorsed to some extent the policy prescriptions that best reflect the human capital development paradigm. These IOs have always recognized that education is an important foundation for a country's economic success, although only recently have they paid attention to *early* childhood education. For example, in 1990, the countries participating in the UN's World Conference on Education for All,[6] while declaring that "learning begins at birth," also stated that "early childhood care and initial education ... can be provided through arrangements involving families, communities, or institutional programmes, as appropriate," and that the "main delivery system for the basic education of children outside the family is primary schooling" (UNESCO, World Education Forum, 2000, p. 76). In 2000, in contrast, the countries participating in the UNESCO World Education Forum in Dakar, Senagal, committed to "expanding and improving comprehensive early childhood care and education, especially for the most vulnerable and disadvantaged children," as part of its six Education for All goals (UNESCO, World Education Forum, 2000, p. 8). That commitment to expanding and improving ECEC did not go as far as the explicit target of 2015 by which "all children, particularly girls, children in difficult circumstances and those belonging to ethnic minorities, have access to complete, free and compulsory primary education of good quality" (UNESCO, World Education Forum, 2000, p. 8).

UNESCO (2006, ch. 5) justifies the need for such programs based on arguments that the early years are important for children's brain development, that early childhood programs can enhance development and provide an important way to equalize children's primary education experiences and overcome economic disadvantage and exclusion, and that investments in early childhood produce economic gains for countries. The Organization of American States (OAS, 2007) justifies its hemispheric commitment to early childhood education by stating that "childhood is a decisive phase in the human life cycle and a comprehensive approach to it will allow us to overcomes the challenges of poverty, inequity and social exclusion." The World Bank is the strongest proponent of the human capital development view of ECEC (see, e.g., World Bank, 2015; Young, 2002, 2007); it also endorses a broad range of early child development (ECD) programs, including child health, child nutrition, and early childhood education and care (Young, 2002, p. 1).

This human capital development perspective is rooted in a belief in the positive relationship between early childhood education and other development programs and success throughout children's lives in the form of improved employment and earnings, better health outcomes, and less social assistance dependency and crime – all the positive outcomes identified in the longitudinal studies in the United States. Further arguments to support investments as part of a human capital development strategy include the view that globalization prods governments to pay attention to human resource needs. In order to be competitive in a globalized world of free-flowing capital, labour markets need to be flexible and able to adapt. A knowledgeable and adaptable workforce is necessary because "the only real asset that most advanced nations hold is the quality and skills of their people" (Esping-Andersen, 2002, p. 28); thus industrialized economies depend more and more on being able to "mobilize the productive potential of those who today are children" (Esping-Andersen, 2002, p. 28). If schools fail to create that workforce, then governments will need to adopt strategies and policies to make sure that their workforces adapt through job retraining. But "remedial policies once people have reached adulthood are unlikely to be effective unless these adults started out with sufficient cognitive and social skills. A social investment strategy directed at children must [therefore] be a centerpiece of any policy for social inclusion" (Esping-Andersen, 2002, p. 30).

The 2006 OECD *Starting Strong II* report (Annex D) contains a summary of some of the international research that has accumulated to support public investment in ECEC. It is based in part on cognitive neuro-scientific claims about the benefits of early learning on young children as well as the cost-effectiveness of these programs. Indeed, the World Bank (e.g. Young, 2007, p. iii) states explicitly that "evidence- and population-based instruments and measures to monitor, evaluate, and compare ECD [early childhood development] interventions over time and across settings" are needed because "the leveraging of enhanced policies and investments in early childhood development depends on being able to assess and document, consistently and rigorously, the need for ECD programs across communities and the outcomes for children and families participating in these programs."

Those cost–benefits analyses also factor heavily into the persuasiveness of the policy recommendations (e.g., World Bank, 2015), with the message being that if these programs did not deliver future positive economic returns, they would not be worth doing. Cost–benefits analyses are often at the root of decisions as to whether programs should be delivered in a targeted or universal manner, and whether governments should commit resources broadly to early child development programs writ large such as child health and child nutrition, or more specifically to early childhood education and care. All IOs but the World Bank have declared their support for universally accessible ECE programs as a principal instrument in a human capital development strategy. Some, such as the EU (European Council, 2002), have established explicit target dates by which they wish to see governments achieve comprehensive early childhood development; others, such as the OAS's (2007) hemispheric commitment to early childhood education, merely ask governments to "increase quality comprehensive early childhood education coverage, in accordance with each member state's possibilities and with the long-term goal of universalizing its integral care for the very young."[7]

ECEC as Part of a Social Pedagogical Approach to the Child

Human capital development is not the only perspective underlying IOs' research and policy recommendations. This in some ways complicates the message that IOs send and may affect the extent to which country governments adopt IOs' recommendations.

The early childhood development perspective promoted by the World Bank (Young, 2002, 2007) can promote a targeted approach to ECEC services or a universal approach with targeting for the most disadvantaged groups. This perspective emphasizes the goal of promoting all children's overall developmental needs: meaning their health and physical development; emotional well-being and social competence; positive attitude towards learning; good communication skills; and cognition and general knowledge (e.g., NEGP, 1997). Bennett (2003) contends that ECD concern for the "whole child" and for childhood as a sui generic period of life underlies the social pedagogical approach, as does the notion of the child as learner. The child as learner means not just in the purely cognitive way, although many human capital arguments conceive of learning as "school readiness" and achieving a certain level of literacy and numeracy by a certain age.

Bennett (2005, pp. 6–7) distinguishes between social pedagogical and school readiness approaches by looking at countries' curriculum frameworks. He argues that a country's underlying approach to ECEC cannot be discerned simply from a curriculum – that is, the plan of instructional activities to inculcate learning; we must also examine the overall framework, which includes three broad sets of quality indicators: structures, orientation, and interaction. Structural factors include the amount of investment in the system, child/staff ratios, staff levels of certification and professional development, and the infrastructure for programs (i.e., buildings, resources, and so on). Orientation factors include the kinds of legislation, regulation, national curriculum, staff standards, and so on in place, as well as that staff's understanding of the principles and purposes of ECEC. Integration factors include the quality of relationships in services and the interaction between staff and children.

The OAS's (2007) statement on early childhood education emphasizes some of these broader social pedagogical criteria. Objective (e) recommends the coordination of "educational sectors and institutions with other national, local, and subnational authorities responsible for providing protection, nutrition, health, culture, and social welfare-related components in such a way as to guarantee the provision of comprehensive early childhood care." Objective (f) speaks to strengthening the preparation and professional development of all educators, including "teachers, families, and communities." Objective (g) calls for the formulation of "policies and educational, inter-institutional, and inter-sectoral coordination strategies for the successful transition of children between the different stages in early childhood." And Objective (h) calls for mechanisms to evaluate the quality of ECEC programs. Similarly, in its review of ECEC policies around the world, the Education for All global monitoring report emphasizes issues of quality and effectiveness in ECEC programming (UNESCO, 2006, chs. 7, 8). The World Bank

(2015), in contrast, is much less committal as to what the "right" ECEC program design is.

ECEC as Part of Children's Rights

The idea of ECEC as a right tends to be promoted mainly by the United Nations (Bellamy and UNICEF, 2001; UNICEF, 2007). For example, the Dakar Framework for Action adopted by the participant countries during UNESCO's 2000 World Education Forum justified its Education for All commitments on the basis of a number of human capital investment rationales (as discussed above), but also articulated a rights-based approach to education – that is, "all children, young people and adults have the human right to benefit from an education that will meet their basic learning needs in the best and fullest sense of the term," and education "is the key to sustainable development and peace and stability within and among countries, and thus an indispensable means for effective participation in the societies and economies of the twenty-first century, which are affected by rapid globalization" (UNESCO, World Education Forum, 2000, p. 8). In addition, Article 5.3 of the Program of Action that emerged from the UN International Conference on Population and Development in Cairo in 1994 states that "governments, in cooperation with employers, should provide and promote means to facilitate compatibility between labour force participation and parental responsibilities … Such means could include … day-care centers … kindergartens … paid parental leave."

Currently, three international conventions recognize child care as a human right (Davis, 2005). Article 11 of the UN Convention on the Elimination of All Forms of Discrimination Against Women (1981), adopted in 1979, deals with employment rights for women. It commits state governments to eliminate discrimination against women in employment and to ensure equal employment opportunities with men. Article 11(2) specifically commits country governments to provide maternity leave protection and paid maternity leave, and Article 11(2)(c) commits those governments "to encourage the provision of the necessary supporting social services to enable parents to combine family obligations with work responsibilities and participation in public life, in particular through promoting the establishment and development of a network of child-care facilities."

Article 18(2) of the UN Convention on the Rights of the Child, adopted in 1989 (Convention, 1989), commits country governments to "render appropriate assistance to parents and legal guardians in the performance of their child-rearing responsibilities and shall ensure the development of institutions, facilities and services for the care of children." Article 18(3) in addition states that "States Parties shall take all appropriate measures to ensure that children of working parents have the right to benefit from child-care services and facilities for which they are eligible." Finally, Davis (2005, p. 147) notes that the International Covenant on Economic, Social, and Cultural Rights (ICESCR), which recognizes that "everyone has a right to work and to have an equal opportunity to be promoted in employment," has also been interpreted to include child care.

Outside the UN, some other IOs have picked up the discourse of rights. For example, while the education ministers in the member countries of the OAS (2007) have committed to developing comprehensive early childhood education programs on the basis of human capital investment concerns, they also state that "equitable and timely access to quality and integral education adapted to global and local contexts and global realities is a human right, a public good, and a political priority."

Unlike the human capital development paradigm, rights arguments do not impose attendant duties and responsibilities on the part of children to learn or be economically successful. Rather, these rights declarations impose obligations on states to provide these services. But without appeal to cost–benefit rationales, and without acceptance from governments of the moral imperative to act, it has been difficult to persuade country governments to comply. The United States in fact has not ratified any of the three major UN conventions; its view is that "it has little to learn from human rights practices of other nations" (Davis, 2005, p. 148). Australia, which has ratified CEDAW, has entered a reservation to the article that commits countries to implement paid maternity leave (Brennan, 2007b, p. 41). Countries that have ratified are supposed to submit reports to the UN Committees monitoring compliance (Davis, 2005). Under Canadian law, though, these international treaties have no legal effect domestically until they have been adopted as part of Canadian law. Thus, there is no mechanism, other than shaming, to ensure compliance with these conventions.[8]

ECEC as Part of Gender Equality

One could say that all of the IOs reviewed have endorsed to some extent the notion that "the relative lack of investment in childcare and parental leave policies tends to undermine the position of women in the labour market" as well as affect the overall economy by way of higher unemployment (with parents dropping out of the labour market) and a lower income-tax base (Bennett, 2003, pp. 33, 36). The sacrifices in labour market participation that primarily women make in order to care for children are extremely costly for those workers and their families. They result in considerably lower earnings accumulated over a lifetime, as well as lower pension earnings and health and other benefits coverage (Gornick and Meyers, 2003). They are also costly to governments, which are increasingly faced with labour shortages. There are thus points of overlap with the human capital development argument. As Esping-Andersen and colleagues (2002, pp. 10–11) argue, "gender equality policies should not be regarded as simply a concession to women's claims. If society is not capable of harmonizing motherhood with employment, we shall forego the single most effective bulwark against child poverty – which is that mothers work. We shall, additionally, face very severe labour force shortages or, alternatively, a shortage of births. And, as women now tend to be more educated than men, we shall be wasting human capital."

The extent to which IOs make gender equality a central part of their policy research and recommendations varies greatly, however. The EU has gone furthest in pushing for ECEC programs to promote the reconciliation of work and family life (e.g., European Commission, 2006). The focus of EU policy until 2000 was maternity and parental leave rights and benefits.[9] Lewis and Campbell (2007, p. 7), though, argue that since 2000, the EU's focus "has switched from parental leave to promoting childcare provision," although "childcare services have been the subject of a 'target' … rather than a Directive as was the case for parental leave." In the 2002 meeting of the Council of Ministers in Barcelona, the EU encouraged member countries "to remove disincentives to female labour force participation and strive, taking into account the demand for childcare facilities and in line with national patterns of provision, to provide childcare by 2010 to at least 90% of children between 3 years old and the mandatory school age and at least 33% of children under 3 years of age" (European Council, 2002, p. 12). By 2006, the OECD (2006, p. 78) estimated that about five countries – Belgium (Flanders region), Denmark, France, Norway, and Sweden – had definitely achieved the target set by the Barcelona meeting, and Finland had as well, if one excludes children under the age of one (as almost all parents take parental leave).[10]

The ILO has also been a major promoter of child care and paid maternity leave as important programs in promoting gender equality at work.

The member countries of the ILO adopted its first convention on maternity protection in 1919 (Convention no. 3). The convention endorsed a program of twelve weeks of maternity protection with benefits "sufficient for the full and healthy maintenance of herself and her child." The convention covered all women working in industry and commerce. In 1952 the ILO member countries ratified a revised convention (no. 103) that extended the twelve-week program to all women workers. The member countries also passed Recommendation 95, which recommended that the leave period be extended to fourteen weeks (six week prior to birth and eight weeks afterward) at 100 per cent of prior wages. The 2000 ILO convention (no. 183) endorsed the extended leave period of fourteen weeks with benefit levels of not less than two-thirds of previous earnings. The 2000 ILO Recommendation (no. 191) endorsed a leave period of eighteen weeks with 100 per cent wage replacement.

With regard to child care, in 1981, the participating countries in the ILO passed Convention 156 concerning workers with family responsibilities. Article 5(b) of C156 declared that "all measures compatible with national conditions and possibilities shall further be taken … to develop or promote community services, public or private, such as child-care and family services and facilities." Part 5 of the accompanying Recommendation 165, Workers with Family Responsibilities, details a number of recommendations regarding child care to "encourage and facility the establishment, particularly in local communities, of plans for the systematic development of child-care and family services and facilities" (ILO Bureau for Gender Equality, 2006). Of the liberal welfare states, only Australia has since ratified the convention.

The OECD has also tackled ECEC as part of its research agenda on policies to promote the reconciliation of work and family life, mainly through its Babies and Bosses project (OECD, 2005, 2007; see also Mahon, 2006). Bennett (2003, p. 40) contends that "in most countries, policy for under-threes still emphasizes expansion of services as a necessary support for maternal employment in a strong economy, rather than as a public service that can benefit both children and parents." The UN (e.g., UNESCO, 2006), in contrast, tackles the issue as one of equal education for all, that is, girls and boys, women and men.

IOs' Domestic Policy Influence

There is strong evidence that IOs increasingly view early childhood education and care programs as a principle of "right" action – that is, normative – albeit with variation in the specific basis of that norm. The question is to what extent IOs influence countries' domestic policy agendas either directly or indirectly, and liberal welfare states in particular, as drivers of cultural change. The next section provides an extended study of one IO's influence on Canada.

Case Study: The OECD's Influence

The OECD has had the most visible ECEC research program among the IOs, and its research reports have received a lot of media attention in Canada (e.g., Canada NewsWire, 2006; Crane, 2006; Monsebraaten, 2004; Philp, 2004), although much less so in the United States.[11] Porter and Webb (2008, p. 44) identify the OECD as a "paradigmatic example of an identity-defining international organization" whose "primary impact comes through efforts to develop and promote international norms for social and economic policy" through its studies, reports, and data. As Grek (2009, p. 24) notes, the OECD, unlike the EU, does not have legal instruments at its disposal. And unlike the World Bank or the IMF, it does not have financial levers to promote particular policies. Its influence, rather, comes through the mechanism of peer review – the examination and assessment of state performance by other states (Pagani, 2002) – such that it can pressure states to adopt the changes it recommends. Grek (2009, p. 24) also notes the influence of its annual ranking exercises, which include the International Indicators of Educational Systems (INES) project, begun in 1988, which produces reports such as "Education at a Glance" and PISA.

The OECD became interested in education issues as part of its attention to human capital development under its mandate to "promote policies designed … to achieve the highest sustainable economic growth and employment and a rising standard of living in Member countries, while maintaining financial stability, and thus to contribute to the development of the world economy" (Article 1 of the OECD Convention, 1960). Henry and colleagues (2001, p. 9) note that the OECD's educational focus became structurally embedded in the organization in 1968 with the establishment of the Centre for Educational Research and Innovation (CERI) and the creation of the Education Committee in 1970. Lifelong learning became the principal theme of both CERI and the Education Committee in the mid-1990s (Henry et al., 2001, p. 52).

As Mahon (2006, p. 180) notes, the OECD has always been a champion of active labour market policies and considered child care in relation to employment (OECD, 1990). By the early to mid-1990s, the OECD (again) had begun to highlight the importance of promoting employment and employability, especially for the less-skilled and the long-term unemployed (e.g., OECD, 1994a). It focused attention on two strategies: "employment-oriented social policies," including "active labour market policies," and a "life-long learning" strategy so as to ensure that children became productive economic actors as adults, and not marginalized (OECD, 1999, p. 3; see also OECD, 2001b, p. 13). ECEC was seen as the key program: that is, early childhood development was the foundation of lifelong learning and development, and "when sustained by effective fiscal, social and employment measures in support of parents and communities, early childhood programming would help to provide a fair start in life for all children, and contribute to educational equity and social integration" (OECD, 2006, p. 3). Below, I trace through the process by which that idea emerged and consider the actors who promoted it.

In 1992 the Ministerial Council of the OECD commissioned the Secretariat of the OECD to conduct a major study on the issue of high and persistent unemployment in the member countries. The secretariat released its concluding report, *The OECD Jobs Study: Facts, Analysis, Strategies*, in 1994 (OECD, 1994b). According to that report, "increasing the provision of early childhood education programmes, especially for children from disadvantaged backgrounds, is part of a long-term strategy improving labour force skills and competencies" (OECD, 1998; see also Recommendation 8 of the 1994b report). One year after that study was released, the OECD's Centre for Educational Research and Innovation (CERI) released a report, *Our Children at Risk*, which recommended that countries adopt proactive measures for children in their early years so as to prevent school failure (OECD CERI, 1995). Then, in 1996, the ministerial meeting of the Education Committee, *Making Lifelong Learning a Reality for All*, focused on early childhood education as well as ways to provide the foundations for lifelong learning. The ministers' communiqué articulated the goal of improving access and quality in early childhood education and care (OECD, 1996). The 1997 OECD secretary-general's note summarizing the policy conference Beyond 2000: The New Social Policy Agenda, also highlighted the view that preventative policies, especially in the early years, should be given greater emphasis in countries' social protection systems (OECD, 1997, p. 11).

The Education Committee of the OECD included early childhood education and care in its 1997–8 program of work (OECD, 1998).

It held an informal meeting of early childhood education and care policy experts in January 1998. Subsequently, it announced its proposal for a thematic review of the early learning and care practices of those member countries that had agreed to participate in the review (Australia, Belgium, the Czech Republic, Denmark, Finland, Italy, the Netherlands, Norway, Portugal, Sweden, the United Kingdom, and the United States).

The goal of the thematic review of ECEC policies and programs was to "provide cross-national information to improve policy-making and planning in early childhood education and care in all OECD countries" by reporting on countries' programs and policies, including regulations and governance, staffing issues, program content, and financing (Bennett, 2003, p. 22). Its major report, *Starting Strong* (2001) was based on a comparative analysis of those country studies (OECD, 2001b). The Education Committee then conducted a second round of reviews (of Austria, Canada, France, Germany, Hungary, Ireland, Korea, and Mexico). In 2006 it released its second major report, *Starting Strong II*, which reviewed the progress the original countries had made in achieving the goals set out in the first *Starting Strong* report and incorporated the new data from the second round of country reviews (OECD, 2006).

It is important to remember that the diffusion of ECEC policy ideas occurred not just from the OECD to country governments but also from domestic policy experts and advocates to the OECD. Inclusion of that scientific expertise was a crucial part of the *Starting Strong* project. Not coincidentally, at about the same time that the *Starting Strong* project began, the OECD's Centre for Educational Research and Innovation (CERI) launched its Learning Sciences and Brain Research project in order to "discover what insights cognitive neuroscience might offer to education and educational policy and vice-versa" (OECD CERI, 2002, p. 9). One of its research tasks was to investigate the importance of the early years of a child's life to successful lifelong learning (OECD CERI, 2002, p. 12). The OECD sponsored three academic conferences; the first of these, on early learning in 2000, involved a number of academic experts. The second phase of the project (OECD CERI, 2007) involved a number of country governments' ministries of education as well as the US National Science Foundation. The corpus of research cited in the 1998 OECD document suggests that the first *Starting Strong* review was informed mainly by US research. The second *Starting Strong* report (OECD, 2006, ch. 9 and Annex D) also presented evidence supporting the importance of the early years to children's success in life.

One of the principal actors behind convincing the OECD to launch the *Starting Strong* project was Abrar Hasan, who was head of the Education and Training Division of the Directorate for Education, Employment, Labour and Social Affairs. Two other principal actors were the co-authors of the 2001 *Starting Strong* report: Michelle Neuman, who at the time was an administrator in the OECD's Education and Training Division and is now the special adviser on early childhood care and education for UNESCO (Neuman, 2007) and was on the 2007 EFA Global Monitoring Report team (UNESCO, World Education Forum, 2006); and John Bennett, a consultant in the OECD's Education and Training Division (OECD, 2001b, p. 4), who also co-wrote *Starting Strong II* with Collette Taylor from Australia's Queensland University of Technology (OECD, 2006, p. 5). Bennett had been the director of the Early Childhood and Family Unit at UNESCO from 1989 to 1997 and then worked as a consultant for the Starting Strong Network that emerged after the *Starting Strong* project ended. This network is made up of country government representatives (currently organized and managed by the Flemish governmental agency, Kind en Gezin) and has the following mandate: to develop, share, and disseminate information "on experiences, research and good practice of countries in the field"; to serve "as a clearing house of new policy research in the field and identify ... new areas for fruitful policy research and analysis"; to identify "data development needs and contribut[e] to the development of methodology for developing such data"; to organize workshops on certain policy themes; and to facilitate "contacts among researchers, policy makers and practitioners, and with international networks in related fields" (Starting Strong Network, 2008). The network thus provided a base from which international epistemic communities could wield influence.

In terms of the specific ideas promoted, while the origins of the *Starting Strong* project were grounded in human capital development thinking, the principal actors involved in the project promoted those ideas in conjunction with broader social development goals, as evidenced in the documents they produced. That broader message may also account for why the OECD has not been as successful in persuading government officials to adopt their best practices recommendations.

The 2001 *Starting Strong* report (p. 3) contends that the OECD study took "a broad and holistic approach to studying children's early development and learning." From its survey of the initial group of participating countries' policies, it identified eight key elements of a "successful" ECEC policy: (1) "a systemic and integrated approach to policy development and implementation"; (2) "a strong and equal partnership with the education system"; (3) "a universal approach to access, with particular attention to children in need of special support"; (4) "substantial public investment in services and the infrastructure"; (5) "a participatory approach to quality improvement and assurance"; (6) "appropriate training and working conditions for staff in all forms of provision"; (7) "systematic attention to monitoring and collecting data collection"; and (8) "a stable framework and long-term agenda for research and evaluation" (OECD, 2001b, p. 11).

In addition to fulfilling an educational purpose – that is, determining what countries do best – the OECD reports offer policy recommendations. The 2006 *Starting Strong* report (p. 4) recommends that governments, in building their own ECEC systems, (1) "attend to the social context of early child development"; (2) "place well-being, early development and learning at the core of ECEC work, while respecting the child's agency and natural learning strategies"; (3) "create the governance structures necessary for system accountability and quality assurance"; (4) "develop with the stakeholders broad guidelines and curricular standards for all ECEC services"; (5) "base public funding estimates for ECEC on achieving quality pedagogical goals"; (6) "reduce child poverty and exclusion through upstream fiscal, social and labour policies and ... increase resources within universal programmes for children with diverse learning rights"; (7) "encourage family and community involvement in early childhood services"; (8) "improve the working conditions and professional education of ECEC staff"; (9) "provide freedom, funding and support to early childhood services"; and (10) "aspire to ECEC systems that support broad learning, participation and democracy." These recommendations fall more into the social pedagogical framework that Bennett (2005) identifies than into human capital development.

While the vision of a successful ECEC strategy offered in the 2001 *Starting Strong* report and the specific recommendations outlined in the 2006 *Starting Strong II* report were not radical for some OECD countries, for many others that vision and those recommendations *were* radical, to say the least. Most liberal welfare states, for example, are far from having established "a universal approach to access" as well as "substantial public investment in services and infrastructure." Liberal market approaches tend to predominate, even in countries such as the United Kingdom, which has increased public ECEC spending over the past ten years. Indeed, a market-based and particularly a large corporate-based system can be a hindrance to even the most benign of the OECD's recommendations, such as accumulation of data on quality, staffing, and so on. Some companies may claim that such information is private and "proprietary" company information.

Mahon (2006, pp. 173–4, 179) observes that "the OECD operates as an important source of transnational policy knowledge construction and dissemination," especially at times when "states are involved in a process of 'unlearning' old policies … and learning new ones." The OECD's power lies in its peer review function. As Pagani (2002, p. 5) notes, "peer review is characterized by dialogue and interactive investigation" with country officials, which can influence those officials' thinking during the process. Porter and Webb (2008) argue that through its knowledge production function, the OECD is also engaged in norm creation.

The other useful part of the OECD exercise was highlighting cross-national policy trends, the implication being that there are leaders and laggards. As Pagani (2002, p. 5) notes, peer review can lead to "peer pressure" – that is, the level of public scrutiny exercised during the process and after completion, along with "comparisons and, in some cases, even ranking among countries," and domestic media attention and public opinion shifts, can pressure change. The OECD study was the first to highlight discrepancies in ECEC provision between liberal welfare states and those of continental Europe. The only other large cross-national research project – by the European Commission Network on Childcare and Other Measures to Reconcile Employment and Family Responsibilities – surveyed only those countries belonging to the European Community at the time (e.g., European Commission Childcare Network, 1990; European Commission Network on Childcare, 1996). As Pagani (2002, p. 6) argues, "peer pressure does not take the form of legally binding acts, as sanctions and other enforcement mechanisms. Instead, it is a means of soft persuasion which can become an important driving force to stimulate the State to change, achieve goals and meet standards."

The OECD's 2001 *Starting Strong* report (p. 8) identified seven trends: "1) expanding provision toward universal access; 2) raising the quality of provision; 3) promoting coherence and co-ordination of policy and services; 4) exploring strategies to ensure adequate investment in the system; 5) improving staff training and work conditions; 6) developing appropriate pedagogical frameworks for young children; and 7) engaging parents, families and communities." The extensive data reported in the two OECD studies and in the country background reports and country notes allowed policy researchers and advocacy organizations in Canada, for example, to highlight Canada's comparatively poor performance (e.g., Friendly et al., 2007). In countries where governments tend to be much more willing to borrow policy ideas from other jurisdictions, including IOs, that shaming can resonate among domestic policy officials and be picked up by advocacy groups and the media. Indeed, while Canada and the United States were both chastised as laggards in the OECD (2001b) report, the media gave that criticism much greater play in Canada; I have not discovered similar attention in the United States. This reflects cross-national differences regarding the extent to which countries view themselves as part of international society.[12] In fact, one House of Representatives staff person, when asked whether the House's focus in the mid-2000s on the quality and effectiveness of federal programs such as Head Start was influenced by reports such as the OECD's, stated that House discussions and decisions were being driven solely by internal politics and partisan debate between Republicans and Democrats regarding what role, if any, the government should be playing in the delivery of early childhood development programs and services.

But as Pagani (2002, pp. 12–13) argues, for peer review and peer pressure to be effective, there must be "convergence among the participating countries on the standards or criteria against which to evaluate performance," and there must be mutual trust and credibility with regard to the examiners chosen to conduct the review. In the case of Canada, some public commentators (e.g., Wente, 2004, p. A19) questioned the credentials of the people who conducted Canada's review. Wente claimed that the country note had been written by "two of Canada's leading daycare lobbyists," which was incorrect but served to undermine the credibility of the international team of examiners.[13] One interviewee also reported that the final version of the OECD country note had required some negotiation and massage. This interviewee said that the first version of the country note had been much harsher, especially with regard to ECEC services for Indigenous peoples in Canada, but that the report had been reworked, given that federal and provincial governments were in the midst of negotiating policy changes.[14] All of these factors may have resulted in less peer pressure.

The PISA Effect

Another way the OECD may be contributing to policy change has been labelled "the PISA effect" (e.g., Jensen, 2009), which relates to how countries are performing on cross-national comparable educational assessments such as the OECD's PISA or the US Department of Education's TIMSS. The United States has been collecting comparative data since 1995 and every four years hence. The OECD first reported its results in 2000 and has reported every three years since. The results of those assessments reveal that Canada and Australia perform consistently above average – indeed, near the top of the international rankings – whereas the United States performs consistently at or below average on both PISA and TIMSS. The results for New Zealand and the United Kingdom vary. In the 1999 TIMSS results, New Zealand and England performed similarly to the United States on mathematics achievement of eighth-graders, but while New Zealand and the United States performed similarly on science achievement, England performed better – similarly to Australia and Canada (US Department of Education, National Center for Education Statistics, 2001). On PISA assessments, however, New Zealand performs consistently well above average, similarly to Australia and Canada, whereas the United Kingdom performs poorly (although not as poorly as the United States, which ranks at or below average among the participating countries (see Table 3.1).

A number of researchers have written about the impact that PISA results have had on national education policies – for example, about PISA "surprise" in relation to Finland's excellent performance; PISA "shock" in Germany in relation to its relatively middling performance; and PISA "promotion" in the United Kingdom, where the government touted results even though there was little media reaction or policy response (Breakspear, 2012, p. 6; see also Ertl, 2006; Grek, 2009). Regardless of the prevalence of "PISA shock" or "PISA complacency," the fact that there is PISA at all is significant. Cross-national performance evaluations suggest a new norm – that student performance in reading, math, and science is one measure of whether a state is modern or not (Meyer et al., 1997) – and suggest a growing importance of connecting human capital goals with primary- and secondary-level educational performance (Martens and Niemann, 2010, p. 9).

One would expect that countries that perform relatively poorly on these international rankings would be more likely to suffer "shock" and subsequently be willing to invest public funding in education, including early childhood education, as a means to improve student test scores. The OECD (2004c, p. 243) has found in particular that "in the majority of countries, students who report that they attended pre-school for more than one year show a statistically significance performance advantage in mathematics over those without pre-school attendance." Even when one adjusts for socio-economic background so as to take into account that children from socio-economically more advantaged families are more likely to benefit from pre-school education, "in more than half of the OECD countries, a considerable effect remains." The same is true with reading literacy.

Martens and Niemann (2010, p. 2) find, though, that country reactions bear little relation to their actual performance on PISA. In fact, the media in the United States, Canada, New Zealand, and the United Kingdom (along with Norway) paid the least attention to PISA results in the 2000, 2003, and 2006 evaluations (Martens and Niemann, 2010, p. 4), despite wide variation in PISA performance. Canada and New Zealand are two of the most highly ranked countries in terms of PISA performance, but the lack of media coverage suggests PISA "complacency" and certainly widely divergent levels of public investment in early childhood education. The United Kingdom and the United States similarly have poured significant resources into expanding early childhood education, despite reported public and media "complacency" towards PISA results (Martens and Niemann, 2010; Knodel, Martens, and Niemann, 2013).

As Martens and Niemann (2010, p. 16) point out, the United States has been aware of problems in its education system for decades. The US Department of Education and the National Commission on Excellence in Education flagged concerns in the 1983 report *A Nation at Risk*, and every president since has placed education reform at the top of the policy agenda (Martens and Niemann (2010, p. 17). And it was the United States that pressured the OECD to provide comparative education data, one part of which was the creation of PISA. So the causal arrow may, in fact, be reversed. Martens and Niemann (2013, p. 315) note that US federal policy makers only began to notice PISA rankings after the 2010 PISA result, which included Shanghai for the first time.

Conclusion

The timing of and commonalities in the broad direction of policy recommendations suggest that ECEC ideas have become normative at the IO level. International organizations are playing key roles in shifting thinking about childhood, the nature of learning, and the kinds of programs necessary for successful childhood and adult lives. That shift in thinking is necessary in order to overcome domestic resistance to state-funded child care and early childhood programs, especially in traditionally liberal welfare states. International organizations are not the creators of those ideas; rather it appears they are popularizers of ideas that are bubbling up from the domestic (and increasingly transnational) epistemic communities, which spread these ideas by attending conferences and sharing their ideas with one another and with decision makers, including IOs. IOs, as authoritative actors, provide the authoritative evidence that these policies are needed for a host of reasons including human capital development, social development, gender equality, and children's rights.

While this global norm generation is important, it is not as effective domestically as would be expected by world society theorists (Ramirez and Boli, 1987; Meyer, et al., 1992). Instead, variation in policy uptake lends weight to theoretical arguments (Acharya, 2004; Ha, 2008; Hay, 2000; Risse-Kappen, 1994) that domestic policy factors are also important when accounting for the specific patterns in ECEC provision in liberal welfare states, particularly in the North American countries of Canada and the United States. It is to those domestic policy factors that our attention now turns.

PART THREE

From Ideas to Policy Change

Constructing Early Childhood Education and Care Policy Shifts in the United States

"Two and a half years ago, biology researchers at MIT were discussing their work with an outside advisory committee. What could help you in your job, they were asked. One simple answer came from the women in the room: child care. David H. Koch, a billionaire philanthropist and MIT graduate known as much for his conservative activism as for his generosity, had attended dozens of these meetings, but had never been so moved. 'I got a tear in my eye,' he said. Koch, who had already given the Massachusetts Institute of Technology about $150 million for research and faculty positions, decided to spend $20 million more on day care."

Carolyn Y. Johnson, "David Koch Funds Day Care at MIT,"
Boston Globe, 4 October 2013

"The business of educating four-year-olds should be the responsibility of the parents, not the state."

Oklahoma Republican Governor Frank Keating's veto speech
regarding SB 1100, the Common Education Reform Initiative to
expand 4-year-olds' access to pre-kindergarten, 14 June 1996

These quotes illustrate diametrically opposed views of child care and early childhood education in the early twenty-first century, of whether these programs are needed, and of whether governments should provide them. Remarkably, both of these views are expressed by conservative political actors: David Koch is an American business person and well-known as a major contributor to conservative organizations and campaigns and to the Republican Party. Oklahoma governor Frank Keating, a Republican, uttered those words just two years before he signed legislation to extend kindergarten to all 4-year-olds in the state.

That policy change made Oklahoma the leading state in the provision of pre-kindergarten in the United States, with the highest enrolment levels of 4-year-olds and the most extensive use of a public delivery mechanism through public schools.

Previous chapters have documented that a large part of these ideational shifts came about via changed scientific understandings of the child, family, education, and the role of the state vis-à-vis the family. As this chapter demonstrates, though, there is no direct link between the proliferation of scientific studies and policy adoption. Many national- and state-level public officials have voiced support for early childhood development policies and programs, particularly pre-school; many policy makers and advocates appear to believe that if you build early childhood education programs of any kind, children will excel on any number of indicators. In some instances, though, public officials seem immune to the evidentiary arguments. There is thus a growing disjuncture between the scientific evidence related to best practices around early years and the policies that are being adopted in various jurisdictions in the United States.

Understanding the connection between science and evidence-based policy making and policy outcomes, I argue, means going beyond typical explanations of interest mobilization, policy diffusion, and policy learning to consider the specific ideational features of these policies and the change elements at work. The changes that have occurred do not follow typical patterns, as chapter 3 demonstrated, nor is there strong evidence of rational policy diffusion or "learning" from one jurisdiction to another. Rather, a more complex pattern of policy change can be discerned, where a confluence of ideas, actor mobilization, and political "moments" yield policy change in a certain number of jurisdictions; this change then builds up until a more widespread policy change can be discerned. Various strategies to induce change include a series of incremental changes such as the introduction of targeted programs that were subsequently universalized in Georgia and Oklahoma; a series of lawsuits in New Jersey; and ballot initiatives in Florida and California. The changes occurred because actors came up with the "right" idea and then used the "right" policy frames to induce policy change. These "right" ideas and frames are those that appeal to widely held assumptions about how the world works and that solve particular policy challenges.

Explanations for successful universal pre-k policy adoption, therefore, do not adhere to any simple causal mechanism. Policy change is occurring in the United States in fits and starts, and change in one jurisdiction does not necessarily trigger changes in other jurisdictions. Successful strategies in one state, such as litigation to expand pre-k, have not worked in other states: litigation was successful in New Jersey but not widely replicated in other states. Thus far, Oklahoma is the only state that has chosen to deliver UPK through public schools. It is not immediately apparent why a cigarette tax worked to fund First Five in California (Rose, 2010, p. 155), but not a coffee tax in Seattle (Kershaw, 2003). The success of a particular strategy is also difficult to predict. Instead, change appears to occur rather sporadically; but it tends to be most evident where actors mobilize language to offer effective solutions to policy problems that fit with prevailing norms and ideological frameworks. The pertinent question for researchers, therefore, is how and why particular ideas resonate in particular contexts.

This chapter analyses the discursive tools used to try to persuade policy makers and the public to accept early years funding and delivery. Successful advocacy typically involves presenting a rationale for policy investment rooted in instrumentally rational or evidence-based arguments. Then various institutional venues are targeted in order to induce policy change. Successful adoption occurs when political leadership has a degree of autonomy to usher through changes and protect policy investments from detractors, and when the public exhibits strong trust in the state to act. But at the heart of policy change is changed perceptions of policy. This chapter thus begins with an analysis of ideas and strategic framing.

Why Does Framing Matter?

Many people – from politicians, to pundits, to party organizers and strategists, to academics – argue that framing can change the way people view an object (Benford, 1997; Chong and Druckman, 2007; Fischer, 2003; Gamson, 1992; Goffman, 1974; Lakoff, 2002; Lakoff and Johnson, 1980; Zaller, 1992). Many models of the policy process, from Baumgartner and Jones's (1993) punctuated equilibrium model, to Kingdon's (1984) policy streams approach, to Sabatier and Jenkins-Smith's (1993) advocacy coalition framework, rest at least in part on the importance of policy images and frame effects. But how do we know that framing matters?

Gamson (1992) describes framing as how events or activities in society come to be understood by political elites and the public. Frames provide order and meaning to those events in a selective way. Framing rests on the behavioural theory that people can only attend to so many pieces of information at one time. Individuals' limited cognitive capacity will lead them to focus on certain aspects of a problem or to perceive some aspect of an issue differently depending on how an issue is presented to them (Tversky and Kahneman, 1981). Weyland (2006) argues, therefore, that policy learning often does not take place in a comprehensively rational way. Policy makers, like all decision makers, are limited by and respond to cognitive heuristics such as *availability* (i.e., information that is immediate and striking), *representativeness* (i.e., a mistaken assumption of how representative data are); and *anchoring* (i.e., placing a lot of weight on initial information or values, which affects how one views subsequent information).

People are presumed to have beliefs and preferences, so frames appeal at both a strategic level and at the normative level. They can be viewed as "rhetorical weapons," but as Druckman (2010, p. 282) argues, frames "also live inside the mind; they are cognitive structures that help individual citizens make sense of the issues" (quoting Kinder and Sanders, 1996, p. 164). Strategic framing can be used to generate competing and inconsistent preferences or to get people to act against their preferences. According to Druckman (2010, p. 282), "when a frame in communication affects an individual's frame in thought, it is called a framing effect." Receptivity to frames depends on how the frames interact with individuals' world views and political predispositions.

Framing is a different discursive technique than priming or persuasion, Chong and Druckman (2007, p. 114) argue. Priming works to call attention to an issue through, for example, repetition that works to give it greater weight. Persuasion, in contrast, works to change people's beliefs about an issue, or their opinion or evaluation of it (Chong and Druckman, 2007, p. 115).

One key framing mechanism is a focusing event that can get voters to attend to long-term consequences and accept policies made according to what Alan Jacobs (2011) labels policy investment logics. For example, poor PISA scores in the United Kingdom and the United States drew voters' and policy makers' attention to the need for investments to improve education and reduce poverty. And certainly that depiction of the institutionally favourable policy process captures accurately some of the jurisdictions that have adopted universal pre-school such as Georgia and Oklahoma. But that characterization does not hold in the state of California in the mid-2000s and in some Canadian cases, as the next chapter reveals. In those cases, rational policy discussion was overridden by the strong assertion of principled beliefs about the appropriate role of the state and its relationship to the family, and about the meaning of childhood.

Ideational (or Discursive) Characteristics That Can Cause Policy Shifts

As other researchers and policy advocates have observed, policy makers' and the public's concern for children is affected by complicated and often conflicting beliefs about "parental responsibility, the roles of women and men, the role of government in helping families, and the extent of society's obligation to its least advantaged citizens" (Sylvester, 2001b). The public tends to view families as responsible for the care and support of their own children; concomitantly, public support for child care as instrumental to parental employment seems to have grown, although there is no consensus that the *state* in particular needs to provide such services (in contrast to more favourable views of state funding and provision of primary and secondary and even tertiary education in some countries). Views on early childhood education or "pre-school" are shifting, though, as documented in previous chapters. While some see the education of young children as primarily a parental responsibility, others are increasingly advocating for formal programming for younger children.

Two sets of frames have therefore come to dominate policy discussions in the United States: child care is part of welfare reform to help poor, single mothers into the workforce; and early childhood education is needed to lift children of poor families out of poverty and help those children be "school ready." In the United States, something about the idea of early childhood education in particular is persuasive in both an instrumental and a constitutive sense in a way that previous policy frames were not (such as "child care as vital to gender equality"). For decades, women's groups tried to frame child care on principled and practical grounds as pivotal to women's equality, with little success (Michel, 1999; Timpson, 2001). That framing, and child care as a universal right and benefit for all children, have been relatively unsuccessful in liberal welfare states.

A huge amount of framing research began to emerge in the late 1990s and intensified in the 2000s to determine just what messaging *does* work in the United States. Voices for Illinois Children and Market

Strategies, Inc., in a presentation to the National Governors Association meeting in Washington, DC, in September 2001, presented the results of their public opinion research, which revealed that a majority of the public thought that the years 0 to 3 were "the most important age[s] for developing a child's capacity to learn." But they also uncovered what they labelled as a "values war," especially among the older generation, who perceived dual-income families as merely "dumping kids in day care" and as an affront to their perceived values of parenthood (although a majority of those surveyed also acknowledged that two incomes are a necessity). The presenters coached the governors to "avoid cues which trigger this kind of resentment" and to "keep focus on 'those who truly need it'" (Voices for Illinois Children / Market Strategies Inc., 2001). The presenters reported that typically child care was seen as babysitting "rather than true education" and thus "using language such as 'early education' helps." And they noted that there is a "widespread perception that 'kindergarten teachers can tell the difference' between kids with a mother at home and those who have been 'warehoused' in day care." The three messages to the governors were that the public displayed "some suspicion about putting birth-to-3-year-olds in the public education system"; that "full-day kindergarten is not seen as a high priority – or even necessarily desirable"; and that "universal programs must be voluntary and it is important to emphasize this" (Voices for Illinois Children / Market Strategies Inc., 2001).

A plethora of other strategic research emerged in the 2000s regarding how to message early years programs (see, e.g., Berkeley Media Studies Group, 2004; Blood, 2000; Dorfman and Woodruff, 1999; McManus and Dorfman, 2002; the Build Initiative's list of resources on early childhood's strategic communications http://www.buildinitiative.org/Resources/CategoryLanding/tabid/208/cid/169/smid/603/tmid/412/Default.aspx; and ReadyNation's strategic messaging website http://www.strongnation.org/readynation). One of the biggest strategic frame analysis organizations is the FrameWorks Institute. In 1998 the Benton Foundation published a number of essays by researchers such as George Lakoff and Susan Nall Bales (the founder of the FrameWorks Insitute) on framing of children's issues (Benton Foundation, 1998). It followed with a second document published in partnership with the Coalition for America's Children and funded by the Annie E. Casey Foundation (Coalition for America's Children, 1999). In 1999, Bales founded the Washington-based FrameWorks Institute, which focused on strategic frame analysis. It began to focus on early child-hood development issues explicitly in 2001 when it began a year-long study into what the American public thought about school readiness. It expanded its analysis to track how specific language and communications around early years influences public opinion and policy preferences (such as the use of the terms "day care" or "school readiness" (FrameWorks Institute, 2005) and to consider this policy in light of other issues, such as poverty (FrameWorks Institute, 2009). The institute has garnered a huge amount of foundation funding and is working alongside a plethora of research institutes, foundations, and advocacy organizations.[1] One project in particular has been ongoing since 2009 as a joint initiative with the National Scientific Council on the Developing Child, the Center for the Developing Child at Harvard University, and the National Forum on Early Childhood Program Evaluation to help the scientific community communicate research on early childhood development more effectively.[2] Researchers have noted the challenges of communicating to policy makers and the broader public some of the complex findings from this neuroscience research, such as the concept of neural plasticity (Kendall-Taylor and Haydon, 2013; Shonkoff and Bales, 2011).

Other organizations that have explored strategic frame analysis for early childhood include Cultural Logic LLC, based in Providence, Rhode Island, whose principal research includes early childhood development (along with two other projects, one on the architecture of government and the other on climate change); and the Communications Consortium Media Center, based in Washington, DC, which has focused on family policy and children's issues since 1988. In addition, a number of university-based research institutes and centres have focused research on framing children's issues. For example, UCLA's Center for Communications and Community under the founding Director Frank Gilliam focused a lot of research on early childhood framing. Gilliam is also a senior fellow at the FrameWorks Institute. In the early 2000s the David and Lucile Packard Foundation funded the Berkeley Media Studies Group's project on media advocacy around child care. And in the early 2000s, the Annenberg Public Policy Center of the University of Pennsylvania received a grant from the David and Lucile Packard Foundation to analyse early childhood messaging (Falk, 2003; Slass, 2003). The Pew Foundation has also done work on messaging to the business community and others (see, e.g., Watson, 2011).

Child Care, Early Childhood Development, or Early Childhood Education? Which Frames Work?

Child Care and Early Childhood Development

The challenges against the "child care" or "day care" frame extend far back in US history. That challenge is neatly captured in a statement by Lee R. Frankel of the United Hebrew Charities at a 1905 National Federation of Day Nurseries (NFDN) conference where he declared that day nurseries are only makeshift and "the great issue is the family, and the proper place for development is in the home" (NFDN, 1905, p. 36, as quoted in Michel, 1999, p. 73). Conservative groups still take that position. The National Association of Evangelicals declared that any federal government child care program would "detract from parents' God-given responsibility for child care" (as quoted in Cohen, 2001, p. 112). Numerous conservative groups and individuals have voiced sustained and vociferous opposition for decades to the idea of government child care funding, including Phyllis Schlafly of the Eagle Forum; Gary Bauer and William Malloy, Jr, of the Family Research Council; Robert Rector of the Heritage Foundation; and Beverly LaHaye of Concerned Women for America (Cohen, 2001, p. 102).

More surprisingly, the idea of early childhood development also provokes negative responses. Cohen (2001) argues that it was the focus on early child development that killed the 1971 Comprehensive Child Development Act. In the late 1960s, advocates pushed to universalize the Head Start program introduced in 1965. Child development experts such as Bruno Bettelheim, Urie Bronfenbrenner, Bettye Caldwell, and Edward Zigler testified before Congress in the late 1960s about the importance of child development programs for the first years of life (Cohen, 2001, p. 26). The idea of universalizing Head Start connected early years programs to child development concerns explicitly, rather than child care per se.

President Richard Nixon at first seemed very supportive of more comprehensive child development legislation. He stated publicly in 1969 that "so crucial is the matter of early growth that we must make a national commitment to providing all American children an opportunity for healthful and stimulating development during the first five years of life" (as quoted in Cohen, 2001, p. 44). Haskins (2005, p. 146) notes that Nixon made a number of organizational changes in government. His administration consolidated children's programs under the Department of Health, Education and Welfare and created the Office of Child Development, appointing Ed Zigler as its head.

Although originally supportive of a broad, developmentally based child care policy, the president turned against the legislation out of what appears to have been principled opposition; however, his decision also reflected intra-party politics and budgetary concerns. The major emphasis in the 1971 child care bill was not support for working mothers, narrowly cast to include only poor mothers, but rather child development and education for *all* children "as a matter of right" (s. 1512, p. 4) (Phillips and McCartney, 2005, p. 109). That emphasis on state intervention for all children, not just those in need, contributed to the bill's defeat (Cohen, 2001). The bill emphasized universality, proposing to provide "the legislative framework for eventual universally available child development programs for all families who need and want them" (Steinfels, 1973, p. 187, quoting a speech in Congress by Senator Walter Mondale, 6 April 1971).

During congressional hearings, conservative religious groups argued quite vehemently that child care undermined the traditional family and that it should not be publicly supported. Some in Congress argued that child care was a communist plot, designed to Sovietize America (Steinfels, 1973, p. 191). The bill passed both Houses late in 1971. By then the Nixon administration was firmly against the bill, as were conservative religious groups.

According to Cohen (2001, ch. 2), Nixon vetoed the legislation largely because of concerns about costs (Haskins [2005, p. 146] notes as well federal concerns about allowing local governments to control funds) but also because conservative legislators were concerned that it would harm children by emphasizing "Soviet-style child-rearing techniques" and thereby supplanting the traditional family. Faced with these challenges, including the possibility of a primary election challenge in 1972, Nixon vetoed the legislation using rather passionate rhetoric: "For the Federal Government to plunge headlong financially into supporting child development would commit the vast moral authority of the National Government on the side of communal approaches to child-rearing over against the family-centered approach" (as quoted in Steinfels, 1973, p. 19; Cohen, 2001, p. 51).

Haskins (2005, p. 147) notes that the word "communal" evokes fears of "communistic" approaches to child development; but it also connotes the opposite of individual maternal caregiving in the home.

Bowlby's (1952) attachment theory was raised to argue that children in the hands of anyone other than the mother would experience separation anxiety, which would negatively affect their social and emotional development. Phillips and McCartney (2005, p. 109) contend that "this veto went well beyond divorcing child-care goals from child development goals. It explicitly pitted child care against the family in a zero-sum equation that, to this day, fuels public ambivalence about the relation between parental and 'other' care."

Ideological opposition remained so strong that when Congressman Brademas and Senator Mondale tried to revive modified child care legislation in 1974 and 1975, they were subjected to an anonymous smear campaign – thousands of letters and leaflets were distributed that accused the members of Congress of harbouring Communist sentiments and of trying to introduce a "'soviet-style system of communal child rearing'" (Cohen, 2001, p. 57). The first Bush administration was supportive of child care; even so, the Child Care and Development Block Grant (CCDBG) legislation passed in 1990 was targeted to low-income families. That act provided federal transfers to states to provide child care support for families earning less than 75 per cent of the state median income; however, the parents had to be working or in job training or another education program (Cohen, 2001, p. 129).

By the time of the Clinton administration, federal legislators had conceded that child care funding was a necessary part of policies to encourage parental employment. The year 1996 marked a historic shift in thinking about both child care and social assistance policy in the United States with the end of Aid to Families with Dependent Children (AFDC) and the creation of Temporary Assistance for Needy Families (TANF) (Mink, 1998). The Personal Responsibility and Work Opportunity Reconciliation Act (PRWORA) of 1996, which established the TANF block grant to help states pay for welfare programs, included another grant to help states subsidize child care costs for families receiving social assistance. That linking of child care to welfare reform was a pivotal victory for Democratic lawmakers, given that Republican leaders originally intended to "gut" child care funding as well (Cohen, 2001, p. 180, quoting Senator Christopher Dodd).

Interviewees reported therefore that TANF marked a significant shift in policy makers' views of child care funding. The strong work imperative built into the program led policy makers to accept the idea that families needed access to child care in order to participate in the labour market. The inclusion of child care in the final legislation represented a compromise on the part of Democratic and Republican members of Congress; it also signalled a growing consensus that programs that required single parents to work also required that funding be provided for child care (Haskins, 2001, p. 26, Table 2.1). Since the TANF reforms, attention to child care has declined on the policy agenda, replaced by efforts to expand and indeed universalize early childhood education.

Early Childhood Education

Early childhood development's focus on the "whole child" (spanning the ages 0–12) can be deemed too expensive and too all-encompassing compared to pre-school programming. Conservative commentator Chester Finn (2009, p. 40), in *Reroute the Preschool Juggernaut*, captures this sentiment when he argues that "particularly when dealing with small children, adults must certainly attend to 'the whole child' and his/ her varied developmental needs. Nevertheless, in today's pre-K policy context, what matters most is a program's effectiveness in imparting essential school-readiness skills to its young participants, principally in the cognitive domain."

As chapter 2 demonstrated, the big cultural shift has been away from the romantic notion of childhood as innocent, natural, and non-educational towards the view that pre-school is an appropriate age to begin a child's formal education. Because education is a state responsibility, state executives and legislatures are key players in pushing for UPK reforms. The National Governors Association started to come on board to the idea of pre-school in the early 1990s as it became increasingly concerned about school readiness (Cohen, 2001, p. 253). Cohen's (2001) book details very well the activities of the NGA in the mid- to late 1990s on these issues. The NGA clearly had functional reasons for supporting pre-school program interventions, including "reducing illiteracy, enhancing school readiness, and improving academic achievement" (Cohen, 2001, p. 273). Governors began to see it as increasingly in their interests to seek ways to achieve these goals. Watson (2011, 6) reports that at least six governors called for early childhood investments in their 2010 State of the State addresses "specifically because of the impact on economic growth or workforce development."

From an educational perspective, expansion occurred as a result of increasing federal and state involvement in education. Institutional (including funding) responsibility has been predominantly local in the United States, delegated to local school districts for reasons such as more efficient delivery of educational services and greater democracy through local administration (Mintrom, 2000, p. 14). In recent years, however, state involvement has increased because local funding and administration has created huge disparities in educational services as a result of variation in the property tax bases on which school districts rely. State funding is increasingly used to equalize funding across school districts. But at the same time, increased state funding has led to increased demands for accountability in the spending of those funds (Mintrom, 2000, p. 15). Also, federal introduction of the US Educate America Act in 1994 and the No Child Left Behind Act in 2001 has put pressure on public schools to improve overall student performance and close achievement gaps between more and less advantaged students (Manna, 2006; McGuinn, 2006; Vinovskis, 2009).

Pre-kindergartens give the impression of offering high standards and better pay while incorporating both education and care into their programs. Whether that is the case or not in mixed markets for pre-school seems beside the point. Rose (2010, p. 95) notes, in fact, that some advocates have lobbied for the term "educare" to improve the image of child care. And for-profit child care chains, such as KinderCare Learning Centers (note the name) and Bright Horizons, see their value-added as providing working parents with child care that has a strong early childhood education component. And, of course, pre-kindergarten is not fully substitutable for child care, as funding may only be provided for part-day programs or they may not run in the summer; also, they do not serve the youngest children.

Changes in Public Opinion

Public opinion surveys in the United States from the early 2000s reveal that a majority of the public still believed then that "parents should be the primary influence on their children's lives" and that "it is best if mothers can be home to care for the very young" (Sylvester, 2001a, 55, citing the results of a poll of 2,021 respondents in California in 1999). A 2013 Pew survey still found that 51 per cent of those surveyed thought that children were better off if mothers were at home – but only 5 per cent of those surveyed thought the same of fathers at home (Pew Research Center, 2013, p. 2). In a 2012 Pew survey, only 18 per cent of respondents thought that "women should return to their traditional roles in society"; however, only 21 per cent of respondents thought that the trend towards mothers of young children working outside the home was a good thing for society (Pew Research Center, 2013, p. 6). And 74 per cent of those surveyed thought that the increasing number of women working for pay had made it harder for parents to raise children (Pew Research Center, 2013, p. 7).

But a majority of those polled in the early 2000s supported public funding for child care to support low-income families (Sylvester, 2001a, p. 57; see also Dorfman and Woodruff, 1999; McManus and Dorfman, 2002). Public opinion surveys reveal strong and growing support for state investment in early childhood education. A 2001 public opinion survey of 3,230 voters completed for the National Institute for Early Education Research found that 64 per cent of respondents strongly agreed and 23 per cent agreed that state governments should provide "funding and financial support for preschool programs so that all parents who want to can afford to enroll their children" (Peter D. Hart Research Associates / Market Strategies, 2001, p. 2). A 2013 survey of 800 voters in the United States found that 86 per cent of respondents, when presented with a list of national priorities, agreed that "ensuring children get a strong start" was a priority, following "increasing jobs and economic growth" and just ahead of "improving the quality of our public schools" (First Five Years Fund, n.d.). A 2011 national survey of 1,024 likely voters found that 61 per cent of respondents would not support reductions in K-through-12 education to reduce the federal budget.

Compared to programs such as transportation (22 per cent of respondents said no reductions, 49 per cent supported minor reductions) and job training (28 per cent said no reductions, 52 per cent supported minor reductions), K-through-12 education programs had the highest support for "no reductions" (First Focus / Greenberg Quinlan Rosner Research, 2011). State public opinion surveys report similar results. The 2007 Louisiana Early Childhood Public Opinion Survey, with 658 respondents, found that 71 per cent believed that "the state is doing too little to prepare children to succeed in school"; 67 per cent said that "only about half or fewer of children begin kindergarten with the knowledge and skills they need to do their best in school" (Nagle and Goidel, 2007, p. 1).

More and more opinion makers from both the left and the right are endorsing early childhood education. In a 2008 *New York Times* column titled "Fresh Start Conservatism," conservative columnist David Brooks (2008) called for new economic policies to support American workers. Besides policies to foster two-parent families, he called for early childhood education: "There could be nurse-home visits for children in chaotic homes so that they have some authority in their lives. Pre-school should be radically expanded and accountability programs put in place." In a 2014 column about the killing of the unarmed black teen-ager Michael Brown, *New York Times* columnist Charles Blow (2014) wrote that discrimination against black and Latino students starts early, and the first example he gave was that "access to preschool programs is not a reality for much of the country."

Of course, vociferous opposition still exists in some quarters to these various programs. Their opponents' framing focuses on link-ing pre-school and child care programs. In 2009, Chester Finn of the Hoover Institution published *Reroute the Preschool Juggernaut*, in which he wrote: "Most preschool programs serve a day-care function, too, affording parents a place where their daughters and sons will be cared for, given snacks and games as well as a cognitive boost, while they themselves work (or do chores or sip tea)" (p. 21). Finn distinguished child care from pre-school and seemed to be suggesting that child care is socially undesirable if it simply provides parents with a break from their childrearing obligations ("sipping tea" instead of raising one's children). Finn (2009, 23) argues that the state does not have a "compel-ling interest in paying for day care for the children of working parents unless they would be unable to work *without* that subsidy and therefore have to turn to welfare, crime, or some other socially costly alternative" (emphasis in original). Nor does society have a "compelling interest in paying for pre-K education except insofar as it demonstrably and dura-bly" upgrades "its human talent across the board, as well as [narrowing] harmful and unjust learning gaps and [ensuring] that everybody has a fighting chance to develop their intellect and skills to the maximum."

Some conservatives have also expressed opposition to kindergarten. In 2012, for example, during the Belknap County Convention meeting to discuss the design of a new jail, New Hampshire State House Represent-ative Bob Kingsbury reportedly stated that he was working on a theory that there is a connection between local crime rates and communities that offer public kindergarten. He then declared that "we're taking children away from their mothers too soon" (in Drapcho, 2012). He also insisted that the rise in crime was linked to a decline in gun ownership and to boxing not being offered as a sport in school. In a follow-up interview published in the *Huffington Post*, Celock (2012) reports that Kingsbury

> did acknowledge that other factors can contribute to higher rates of crime
> and kindergarten classes are just one of them. But he mentioned having

read an article showing the impact of moving young children out of London during World War I. "In World War I, London was being bombed by the Germans and they sent the children out of the city," Kingsbury said. "That was a disaster for England."

Kingsbury did not believe that child care or pre-school programs were to blame, since they are voluntary in nature:

"Children go to kindergarten at the point of a gun," Kingsbury said. "Children go to day care and it's not the same; there is no point of a gun." Kingsbury said he believes that teachers are partially to blame but the rise in crime is not the fault of teachers. Instead he blamed attorneys and the courts for what he called a lack of discipline and rules in schools and for prohibiting teachers from disciplining students as in previous decades. (Celock, 2012)

Conservatives thus raise concern about pre-schools and kindergartens becoming the new child care centres, raising all the anti-institutionalization rhetoric associated with the latter.

But the public is increasingly embracing the idea of educationally grounded pre-school as an important educational experience for young children. Some child care and early childhood development experts worry about the emphasis on rote memorization of the alphabet and number recognition over play-focused curriculums in many centres (Fuller, 2007; Gopnik, 2011). But many parents seem to embrace the idea of pre-school education. In one – perhaps extreme – case, the *New York Times* in 2011 reported that a New York City parent had launched a lawsuit against her daughter's $19,000 per year pre-school because it did not prepare her daughter for the intelligence test the child would have to take in order to be admitted into New York's private school system (Anderson, 2011). The *Globe and Mail* reported that the parent felt "the place was no more than a 'big playground' teaching mere shapes and colours and therefore damaging her kid's educational future" (Pearce, 2011).

Policy Change at the US State Level

The above discussion demonstrates the extent to which ideas around universal ECEC have shifted in the United States. While early years education is still deeply contested, more and more of the public and policy makers accept the idea of it. These shifts in ideas are the causal mechanism behind policy changes; but ideas spread unevenly, which raises further puzzles as to the specific mechanisms of diffusion. The extensiveness of culture change can really only be observed in hindsight. The rest of this chapter therefore maps the scope of policy change at the US state level as well as some of the change mechanisms.

Observations at the state level are important because pre-school involves a policy area under state and local authority. Advocates' efforts have been heavily devoted to state kindergarten and pre-school expansion, in what Karch (2009) and others have labelled *venue shifting*, building on many already existing programs such as voluntary pre-k and Head Start. Over the past two decades the vast majority of US states – forty-two out of fifty as of 2015, according to the National Institute for Early Education Research (Barnett et al., 2016, p. 6) – have introduced or expanded early childhood education programs, and these programs enrol children younger than age 5 either part-day or full-day. By 2015, more than one-quarter (29 per cent) of all 4-year-olds in the United States were attending a pre-school program (Barnett et al., 2013, p. 6), and more than 75 per cent of children in kindergarten were attending a full-day program in the United States (Children's Defense Fund, 2014). Three states – Georgia, Oklahoma, and Florida – have opened these programs to all students, not just children from low-income families. States that have committed to UPK, at least on paper, include Florida, Georgia, Illinois, New York, Oklahoma, Vermont, and West Virginia (Squires, 2014). But only a handful of those states – Florida, Oklahoma, and Vermont, along with the District of Columbia – have over 70 per cent of 4-year-olds enrolled, and only Oklahoma delivers its pre-k program in public schools (as opposed to a variety of providers, as is typical in other states).

Broad enrolment figures mask unevenness in access (Libassi, 2014, p. 1). While forty-five states and the District of Columbia have adopted Common Core standards for kindergarten math and language arts, and those standards are based on the assumption that kindergarteners are going to school for the full day, only twelve of the states that have adopted the Common Core standards *require* that school districts provide full-day programs at no charge for all children. Thirty-five US states do not make kindergarten attendance mandatory, and five states do not have in place any legislation requiring districts to offer kindergarten. The Children's Defense Fund (2014) reports that only eleven states and the District of Columbia require schools to offer full-day kindergarten by statute: Alabama, Arkansas, Delaware, Louisiana, Maryland, Mississippi, New Mexico, North Carolina, South Carolina, and West Virginia. Workman (2013) lists Tennessee and Oklahoma but not New Mexico as offering full-day programs, and she notes that New Jersey's *Abbott* district kindergartens are full-day (see below). Program length varies from 2.5 to 7 hours per day, and when the program is part-day, some parents are expected to pay for the other part of the day.

Very few of the pre-primary programs in place can be rated as successful in terms of access and quality indicators. Indeed, some states that have not committed to UPK provide greater access to programs than those that have declared a commitment to UPK: access in Wisconsin and Iowa is better than in Georgia or New York, for example (Barnett et al., 2013, p. 13). In terms of access to pre-kindergarten, the highest-ranked states include Florida, Oklahoma, Vermont, Wisconsin, West Virginia, Iowa, and Georgia (see Table 3.2).

Some states such as Illinois, with its Preschool for All initiative in 2006, New York, and West Virginia, have committed to UPK but have not delivered, leaving major cities such as Chicago and New York to initiate their own programs. Other states, such as Arkansas, Colorado, and South Carolina, have explicitly targeted funding to low-performing schools as opposed to committing to UPK, while others, such as North Carolina and Tennessee, target at-risk children. In terms of spending on pre-kindergarten, in addition to DC, New Jersey, which does not provide universal access, is the highest-ranked state, along with Connecticut, Rhode Island, Oregon, Minnesota, and Alaska, none of which make top ten lists in terms of access (see Table 3.2). And the NIEER reports that many states have cut UPK spending as a result of recent economic downturns (Barnett et al., 2013). On quality measures, except for Alaska, Rhode Island, Minnesota, and Washington State, there is little overlap between state spending and quality rankings. Oklahoma ranks in the top ten states for access and quality but twenty-fifth in terms of state spending; Florida ranks at the very top in terms of access but thirty-fifth in terms of spending and near the bottom in terms of quality. And in terms of funding, some states provide less money for kindergarten than they allocate for grade one students (Libassi, 2014, pp. 1–2). To pay for pre-kindergarten expansion, Florida uses a voucher system, Arkansas uses a beer tax, Arizona a tobacco tax, and California a cigarette tax; Georgia, Kentucky, North Carolina, and Tennessee all use lottery funds. In California, a tax on high incomes failed, as did a coffee tax in Washington State (NIEER, 2005).

Explaining Policy Change at the US State Level: Political Leadership, Instrumentally Rational Argumentation, and State Capacity and Legitimacy to Act

What explains these cross-jurisdictional investment patterns? As chapter 3 documented, the patterns of investment do not map easily with theories of policy innovation that focus on political interests or diffusion mechanisms. Policies and programs have emerged in both Democrat- and Republican-dominated states, in both small and large states, in both rich and poor states, and in non-regionally contiguous states such as Oklahoma and Florida. A multitude of actors are involved in advocating for early years programs, including philanthropic foundations such as PEW Charitable Trusts (Bushouse, 2009), advocacy groups and think tanks such as Rob Reiner's I Am Your Child Foundation / Parents' Action for Children, provider associations such as the National Association of Child Care Resource and Referral Agencies (NAC-CRRA), teachers' unions such as the National Education Association (NEA), business associations such as the Committee for Economic Development, and anti-crime groups such as Fight Crime: Invest in Kids. While some research suggests that much of the impetus behind universal pre-k is advocacy-driven (Bushouse, 2009; Fuller, 2007; Kirp, 2007), a major ballot initiative failed in California despite the efforts of a host of policy advocates, including Rob Reiner's Parents' Action for Children. Bushouse (2009) notes that strong advocates and foundations were non-existent in the early adopter states of Oklahoma, Georgia, New York, and West Virginia. She notes as well that in the early adopter states, media coverage was virtually non-existent. Conversely, an active media discussion in California managed to highlight opposition ideas (Jacobson, 2009).

A number of mechanisms appear to be at work in convincing the public and policy makers to invest. Important factors seem to include (1) arguments for policy investment rooted in instrumentally rational reasons, (2) political leadership with a degree of autonomy to usher through changes, and (3) institutionalization to protect policy investments from detractors. Political autonomy and trust in political leadership are especially important in jurisdictions where the public regards investment with suspicion. And as Patashnik and Zelizer (2013, pp. 1076–7) argue, some strategic choices on the part of policy makers can undermine successful implementation. These include (1) meagre resources or delayed resource flows that prevent strong institutionalization and supportive constituencies, (2) divisive enactment or narrow margins of victory that encourage revisiting an issue in later years, and (3) and failure to uproot the opposition's base of support because of policy changes as a result of "layering" rather than "displacement" of new rules on top of old ones.

Political leadership and policy entrepreneurship played a role in UPK policy initiatives in the early adopter states. State actions have involved a variety of policy entrepreneurs, including state governors in Georgia (Zell Miller), Illinois (Rod Blagojevich), and New Mexico (Bill Richardson); legislatures in New York, Oklahoma, and West Virginia; and a variety of change mechanisms such as lawsuits in New Jersey and a ballot initiative on a constitutional amendment in Florida (Bushouse, 2009; Karch, 2013; Rose, 2010).

Once policy makers have been convinced of the logic of the action, then the key factor in preventing policy backtracking (Patashnik, 2008; Patashnik and Zelizer, 2013) is some kind of institutionalization mechanism such as passage of a constitutional amendment guaranteeing provision, or some kind of mechanism to secure longer-term financing. All of these factors were present in the early UPK adopter states of Georgia and Oklahoma but were not present in New York, Illinois, and West Virginia. In Georgia, policy institutionalization occurred through the use of state lottery funds. In Oklahoma, the state provided funding at the same level as grade school, securing public provision through schools. Other states have experimented with other institutional mechanisms such as "sin" taxes (e.g., Arkansas's beer tax and California's cigarette tax). And in New Jersey, litigation was a prominent factor.

Instrumental Rationality, Politically Autonomous Leadership, and Policy Institutionalization

Georgia and Oklahoma launched reform efforts with a relative degree of autonomy from the public and thus little political opposition. Both of these cases also provide evidence of the importance of grounding policy arguments in instrumental reasoning and functional logics. Bushouse (2007, p. 2) notes that three of the four states that later pioneered universal pre-k (Georgia, Oklahoma, and West Virginia) were members of the Southern Regional Education Board (SREB). In 1988 the SREB released *Goals for Education: Challenge 2000*. As Bushouse (2007, p. 2) writes, "the report, developed over a nine-month period by a commission of 17 Southeastern educators and politicians, called for providing free preschool and full-day kindergarten to all at-risk children and requiring readiness tests before children enter first grade." There was certainly a functional rationale behind this policy. Bushouse (2007, p. 2) writes: "Consensus was building across the Southern region that reliance on luring industry with the inducements of cheap labor, no unions, and low taxes was insufficient for continued economic growth. The new thinking was that the path to improve the attractiveness of Southern locations for companies was to invest in building strong public school systems. This would achieve two objectives: (1) it would create a better educated workforce and (2) strong public schools would attract professional workers to relocate to Southern states."

Georgia was the first to implement UPK, and it did so under the political leadership of Zell Miller. There is evidence that Miller was aware of brain research and cost–benefit analyses of pre-k programs (Ackerman at al., 2009; Bushouse, 2009). He was also a skilled policy entrepreneur. He based his 1990 gubernatorial campaign on promised education reforms (including a targeted pre-kindergarten program), to be paid for by lottery funds, in order to improve the state's educational performance (Ackerman et al., 2009, p. 4). He presented his plan for a targeted pre-k program as a constitutional amendment to voters in 1992. Given the massive revenues generated by the lottery and the positive academic results from the targeted program, the state made the program universally available in 1995, thus universalizing funding without broad public debate.

Oklahoma also incrementally expanded its pre-kindergarten program. It suffered from poor education performance and loss of school enrolments, and thus from 1980 to 1990 the state ran a pilot program for some 4-year-olds. It expanded that program in 1990 based on positive education performance outcomes in the pilot (Ackerman et al., 2009, p. 5). Four-year-olds were able to enrol in state kindergarten programs, but not on the basis of the same funding as 5-year-olds. In 1998 the state legislature agreed to equalize funding for 4-year-olds and thus effectively created a program for 4-year-olds within the public schools.

Neither of these UPK initiatives was subject to broad public debate. Bushouse (2007, 2009) notes that strong UPK advocates and charitable foundation support were non-existent in the early adopter states of Oklahoma, Georgia, New York, and West Virginia. Media coverage was virtually non-existent as well. In this regard, an active discussion in the media during California's UPK ballot initiative managed to highlight opposition ideas (Jacobson, 2009). But the institutionalization of the funding mechanism in Georgia (with lottery funds), and the delivery agents (public schools) in Oklahoma, ensured program longevity in those states.

The other states – Illinois, New York, and West Virginia – that have declared support for UPK neither subjected plans to broad public debate nor put in place enabling conditions to ensure funding for further program expansion. Illinois lost a champion in Governor Rod Blagojevich, who signed UPK legislation in 2006 but was impeached and removed from office in 2009 as a result of a political scandal. New York signed UPK legislation in 1997 under the leadership of Assembly Speaker Sheldon Silver that proposed to have a UPK system in place within five years (Rebell et al., 2013). Champions in the New York state legislature and governor's office have waxed and waned, however; Governor George Pataki attempted to eliminate UPK budget appropriations entirely in his 2003–4 budget (Mitchell, 2004, p. 12). Governor Eliot Spitzer was a champion but quickly lost office also due to scandal. West Virginia passed legislation in 2002 to get UPK by 2012 but so far has not truly universalized pre-k. But unlike Illinois and New York, West Virginia ranks fairly high in terms of access and state spending (see Table 3.2).

In these three states, legislative action has not yet brought about universality, despite initial policy enthusiasm,[3] because of the lack of mechanisms to institutionalize UPK. For example, the New York legislation authorized state spending on part-day (2.5 hour) programs for 4-year-olds, but phased in implementation over five years and distributed the funding based on district wealth and need factors. That scattering of funds and the fact that the state did not deliver on its per student funding commitments over the five-year time period meant that only about one-third of districts were participating by 2003–4 (Rebell et al., 2013, p. 11), in addition to some targeted programs receiving experimental pre-k grants that had been in place since 1966 (Mitchell, 2004). In 2007, then-governor Spitzer proposed a new funding scheme that would make all districts eligible for funding; also, expenditures would be doubled over four years so that by 2010–11, all students in high-need, low-achieving school districts would be eligible for a full-day program (Rebell et al., 2013, p. 11). That plan was implemented, but the 2008 global financial crisis led the state to freeze further increases in 2010 and to reduce overall allocations. Rebell and colleagues (2013, p. 11) report that the funding formula for pre-kindergarten is so complicated that it is difficult to know precisely how much funding each district should be allocated. The spottiness of coverage means that the program is "universal" in name only.

Lack of institutionalization can easily lead to policy reversals, as seen in Arizona. In 2004, then-governor Janet Napolitano signed legislation that committed the state to phase in full-day kindergarten programs for 5-year-olds. The legislation offered funding to schools with the highest percentage of children from low-income families (measured by eligibility for free and reduced-price meals at schools); the goal was to provide full-day kindergarten to all schools by 2007 (Libassi, 2014, p. 3). But the legislation did not alter the funding formula, which granted schools half the amount for kindergarten programs as for other grades, although it did provide a supplementary fund. In 2006, new legislation eliminated the phase-in plan and immediately made schools eligible for a new funding formula for kindergarten. That formula was improved but still lower than what was offered for grade school; it also eliminated funds for capital improvements to expand spaces in schools (Libassi, 2014, p. 3). Then in 2010, after Napolitano was appointed to head the Department of Homeland Security, Republicans in the Arizona House and Senate, under the new Republican governor Jan Brewer, eliminated state funding for full-day kindergarten. As Libassi (2014, p. 3) argues, because the state did not make kindergarten funding mandatory, and instead relied on budget incentives to schools to expand full-day kindergarten, the program was vulnerable to reversals when opponents were given the political opportunity. Opponents relied on conservative research institute reports such as from the Goldwater Institute, which argued that there was no value-added to full-day as opposed to part-day programs (e.g., Ladner, 2007).

Policy Institutionalization through Litigation

New Jersey, as a result of a number of New Jersey Supreme Court rulings, has been pressured into adopting institutional mechanisms to ensure continuation of pre-kindergarten funding, at first for designated districts, and now universalized to all districts. In a 1973 decision the US Supreme Court refused to recognize any "right" to education in the US Constitution.[4] This prompted education advocates to focus on state constitutions and on litigating educational finance inequities as violations of state constitutions (Rebell, 2011–12, p. 1865). According to Rebell (2011–12, p. 1871), education is one of the only governmental services – unlike police, fire protection, and sanitation – that finds constitutional protection in state constitutions as an "affirmative state obligation." Education advocates have had varying degrees of success using state constitutional obligations to extract ongoing resources for pre-school education, with greatest success in New Jersey. Advocates have also successfully litigated in some other states, including Kansas, North and South Carolina, Colorado, and Washington State (Hunter, 2012), and claims are now before the courts in a number of other states as well.[5] Success is not universal, though; some state courts, such as Pennsylvania's, having ruled that school financing adequacy is a non-justiciable issue (O'Brien, 2013).

In 1975 the New Jersey Supreme Court ruled[6] that the state's relative underfinancing of schools in poorer districts violated the state's constitution, which declares that the New Jersey Legislature "shall provide for the maintenance and support of a thorough and efficient system of free public schools for the instruction of all the children in the State between the ages of five and eighteen years." Then in 1981, the Education Law Center launched a case on behalf of twenty children attending schools in low-income areas (Mead, 2009, p. 3). The *Abbott v. Burke* series of twenty rulings, the first of which was issued in 1985, found that the state's relatively inadequate financing of education in poorer districts violated the state constitution. The first of these cases demanded an administrative review of financing arrangements (Mead, 2009, p. 3). In the second ruling, in 1990, the state was ordered to equalize funding to ensure that poorer districts received the same level of education financing as wealthy districts. As a remedy, the government designated thirty-one "Abbott districts" and developed a more robust formula-based funding program for pre-kindergarten. As a result of later rulings, the state agreed to cover 100 per cent of the costs, rather than requiring districts to provide part of the funds. The state also decided to extend programs to full-day (Rebell et al., 2013).

The 1998 court ruling in *Abbott* stated that in order to provide a "thorough and efficient education," the districts needed to provide supplemental programs, including pre-school, for all 3- and 4-year-olds in the thirty-one Abbott districts (Mead, 2009). The courts have been very directive of the kinds of specific standards that need to be in place to ensure pre-schools of high quality. Those standards include that pre-kindergarten teachers must have certification as early childhood educators, that classes must have a maximum of fifteen children, that programs must use a "developmentally appropriate" pre-school curriculum, and that the services provided must be comprehensive (Rebell et al., 2013, p. 18). In 2008 the state passed the School Funding Reform Act to ensure that Abbott pre-kindergartens would be delivered throughout the state on a full-day basis, with at least 90 per cent of eligible children enrolled by the 2013–14 school year (Rebell et al., 2013, p. 18; Mead, 2009, p. 1). Fiscal constraints have meant, though, that the promise of pre-kindergarten beyond the Abbott districts has not yet been realized.

In North Carolina, litigation has been ongoing since 1994, when boards of education along with parents in low-wealth school districts sued the state on the grounds that lack of state funding for education was a violation of the constitutional right to equal educational opportunity for the state's children (Samuels, 2013). In *Leandro v. State* (1997),[7] the North Carolina Supreme Court upheld the suit, ruling that while school districts do not have a right to equal funding, children have a fundamental state constitutional right to the "opportunity to receive a sound basic education" and that the obligation lies with the state, not school districts. The court then handed the case over to Superior Court Judge Howard Manning to rule whether the state was in fact in violation of that constitutional right. In a series of rulings, the judge determined that the state was in fact violating that right by not adequately educating poor children, and he specified how the state had to meet its constitutional obligations. The state appealed those rulings, and in 2004, in a second court ruling,[8] the North Carolina Supreme Court upheld the judge's ruling. In *Leandro II*, the court ruled that the state was in violation of the constitution and that the right to a sound basic education applied not just to K–12 but also to younger children. The court did not mandate pre-k for all, instead deferring to the government to devise a remedy. The state then created the More at Four program, now called NCPK. In 2011, the state reduced the overall funding for NCPK, capped the number of children to be served by the program at 20 per cent, and instituted a co-payment. Five poor counties in North Carolina challenged these cuts and brought a lawsuit, claiming that cuts to the program violated the constitutional right to a sound, basic education for all children in North Carolina. Judge Howard Manning again ruled in favour of the plaintiffs, saying that the state must provide NCPK to all eligible at-risk 4-year-olds who apply, and that the state should not enforce the cap or any other artificial barrier to deny eligibility. In 2012 the state appealed Judge Manning's ruling, but the North Carolina Court of Appeals upheld Manning's order (Samuels, 2013).

Other court challenges have succeeded in states such as South Carolina, or are presently before the courts.[9] Not all litigation has resulted in victory for the plaintiffs. In Wyoming, for example, the state's high court ruled that the state constitution only obliged the state to provide education to children starting at age 6 (Education Justice, 2014). And other court rulings have affirmed that the state is not obligated to provide pre-k as part of a constitutional duty to provide an adequate and equal education.[10] But as Boylan (2007) notes, these court cases can sometimes inspire legislative action, even after the state has won or has decided to appeal. In South Carolina, for example, the state launched an appeal of the court ruling, but it also created a pilot program to provide full-day kindergarten for at-risk 4-year-olds in school districts involved in the lawsuit. The state had already been offering a half-day program to about 30 per cent of at-risk 4-year-olds, since 1984 (Boylan, 2007, p 41). Arkansas launched its ABC Program in 2003 for at-risk students. A similar court case by the State of Massachusetts did not ultimately yield legislative changes; then-governor Mitt Romney vetoed a bill in 2006 that would have provided pre-k for all 3- and 4-year-olds (Boylan, 2007, p. 43).

Policy Institutionalization through Ballot Initiatives[11]

Two states, California and Florida, have attempted to institutionalize UPK through statewide ballot initiatives. Only the Florida initiative was successful. These cases again help demonstrate the mechanisms that lead to policy change: framing strategies; trust in autonomous political leadership; and policy institutionalization. In California, proponents of UPK focused their arguments on the rationale for investment, and especially the costs and benefits of programs; so did advocates in Florida. In California, however, those instrumentally rational arguments were trumped by oppositional arguments about the state's perceived "failure" to manage resources as well as broader public concerns regarding appropriate levels of state involvement in economic and social policy. Lack of trust in the state to "do the right thing" led to the collapse of the ballot initiative.

California and Florida are large states with large state budgets. At the time of their respective ballot initiatives, they faced similar rankings for academic achievement: a report by the American Legislative Exchange Council ranked California forty-second and Florida forty-third for academic achievement in 2004–5 (LeFevre, 2006). California's electorate normally leans Democratic, and in 2005 the state had a strong pro-UPK advocate – Rob Reiner, a former actor and prominent advocate in California education policy, who founded the I Am Your Child Foundation / Parents' Action for Children. Florida, too, had a policy champion – Alex Penelas, mayor of Miami Dade County at the time, and a Democrat in a state that leans Republican. Given the more Democratic leanings of California and previous successful passage of a ballot initiative on early years programs, it seemed more likely that the ballot initiative would pass in California; yet it was Florida that eventually adopted a universal program while California did not.

Reiner was the chair of First 5 California (or the California Children and Families Commission), established after the passage of the 1998 Proposition 10 ballot initiative – sponsored by Reiner – which implemented a state cigarette tax to fund early childhood development programs. In 2005, Reiner proposed a ballot initiative named the Preschool for All Act, intended for the June 2006 primary ballot, that proposed creating a public, voluntary pre-school program available to all 4-year-olds in the state. The proposal advanced an agenda of half-day (three-hour) pre-k, to be funded by an additional 1.7 per cent state income tax on Californians with annual incomes of over $400,000, or $800,000 for couples.

Before its official inclusion on the ballot, Reiner's initiative attracted high-profile support. In July 2005, the Los Angeles Area Chamber of Commerce announced its support for UPK. According to news articles, this decision was based on research showing early childhood education's positive effects on human capital (N.A., 2005). In December 2005 the Rand Corporation released a report quantifying the social and economic benefits to California of a universal pre-school program; one of its findings, cited repeatedly over the course of the campaign, was that a universal pre-school program would generate a return of $2.62 on every dollar invested (Karoly and Bigelow, 2005).

Reiner's prominence as a well-known actor, director, and producer in Hollywood, and as the head of First 5 California, ensured that the Preschool for All Act received plenty of media coverage. In the months leading up the election, however, the First 5 Commission became embroiled in scandal. Already in 2004, questions were being raised about management of the cigarette tax money: state auditors found in July of that year that most of the funds had not been properly spent (Banks, 2004). In the winter of 2006, the First 5 Commission ran a TV ad campaign touting the benefits of pre-school. This led to questions, from the media and others, about whether this was a case of First 5 funds being used improperly to lobby for Proposition 82 (Morain, 2006a). Because of these conflict-of-interest allegations, Reiner announced on 26 February 2006 that he would be taking a leave of absence from the

First 5 chairmanship for the duration of the UPK campaign (Morain, 2006b). A wide-reaching audit of the First 5 Commission's finances was approved in March, in the lead-up to the ballot; media coverage of the possible misuse of First 5 funds continued until the June election, although eventually the commission was cleared of all charges.

The scandal added fuel to the increasingly popular media narratives regarding government waste and inefficiency. This argument over the state's role in the effective delivery of education gained steam, becoming one of the main organizing principles for the opposition. While many high-profile Democrats continued to support Proposition 82, by late May the print media largely did not: the *LA Times*, the *Orange County Register*, the *San Diego Union-Tribune*, the *San Francisco Chronicle*, and the *San Jose Mercury News* all published editorials endorsing a No vote. Polling data illustrate a decline in public support for the initiative as media coverage increased. A February Field poll found that the Yes campaign enjoyed a 21-percentage point lead, of 55 to 34 per cent; by early April, that lead had shrunk to 13 points (52% to 39%); a few days before the June election a final poll showed that support had plummeted, with 46 per cent opposed and only 41 per cent in favour (DiCamillo and Field 2006a, 2006b, 2006c). Thus, despite the early support, Proposition 82 was defeated at the ballot box.

The California case stands in contrast to the experience of Florida, whose implementation of UPK in September 2005 (following the 2002 ballot initiative) pre-dated the launch of the California initiative by around six months. In Florida the factors aligned to achieve successful policy uptake: rhetoric emphasizing the instrumentally rational reasons for investment was combined with effective leadership – both Democrats and Republicans, including Miami mayor Alex Penelas (D) and governor Jeb Bush (R), supported the pre-K initiative – and trust in the state to deliver the program. The pre-K amendment was bundled as part of a larger education policy with a concurrent Amendment 9, which was aimed at reducing class sizes in Florida schools. Public opinion polls commissioned by print and television media indicated consistent support for the pre-k amendment, ranging from 60 to 66 per cent, in the two months prior to the vote, despite a general lack of media coverage regarding the actual amendment vis-à-vis other issues.

As in California, the Florida amendment drew a wave of inquiry that focused on the role of the state, the state's effectiveness in providing a functioning education system, and the cost of program delivery. Yet while UPK was linked to these discussions by virtue of being framed as "education" policy, it drew little additional public exploration as the less costly initiative. In effect, the bundling of pre-K with Amendment 9 served to innoculate UPK from opposition attacks, and despite the launch of a coordinated campaign against the costly class-size initiative, both Amendment 8 (UPK) and Amendment 9 (class sizes) passed.

The passage of a constitutional amendment committing the state to UPK through the ballot initiative allowed policy discussion to quickly move away from questions of the inherent legitimacy of state action to questions of instrument choice, policy settings, and other implementation concerns. The ballot initiative provided very few requirements regarding UPK delivery beyond a commitment that it be established to meet "high quality standards." In April 2003 the Florida Senate passed a bill requiring that options for the pre-k program be studied and that the Florida State Board of Education establish the Universal Prekindergarten Education Advisory Council, to include representatives from public schools, private pre-school providers, early childhood education advocates, the business community, and the community at large.

The creation of an expert panel to assess the research literature on early childhood education and to develop a set of recommendations for "high quality" pre-kindergarten education forged a direct link between the ballot initiative and the instruments and settings needed to meet voters' "expectations." The council published its report in October 2003. Among other things, it called for specific requirements related to school and teacher accreditation, student–teacher ratios, curriculum design, and student assessment (Universal Prekindergarten Education Advisory Council, 2003).

After the Advisory Council recommendations were released, the policy landscape (and the public discussion) on pre-k exploded. Three legislative plans were released almost simultaneously, none of which entirely met the standards set by the Advisory Council. After a period of legislative competition and debate, a UPK implementation bill was sent to Governor Jeb Bush for approval. The bill largely ignored the recommendations of the Advisory Council; also, it set few standards for curriculum, teacher credentials, or school accreditation, and it provided for only three hours of pre-k per day. This legislation immediately became the subject of much public criticism, both for ignoring the Advisory Council's recommendations and for letting down Florida voters, who had clearly asked the state to establish a "high-quality" program. In July 2004, Governor Bush vetoed the bill, saying that it was not what voters had been promised (North Jones, 2004).

To have legislation in place in time for the 2005–6 school year (as required by the language of the ballot initiative), a special legislative session was held in December 2004. Leading up to this session, polling data showed that nearly two-thirds of likely users supported higher quality standards, including a six-hour day, teacher credentials, and "national-quality standards of instruction." By the end of this session, legislators had passed a new pre-k bill, which, while still providing for only a three-hour day, mandated a smaller student–teacher ratio, set program standards, and provided a budget of $2,500 per child. Despite continued criticism from Democratic lawmakers, ECE advocates, and some media, this bill met with Bush's approval. In contrast to California, then, the ballot initiative institutionalized the public's demand for "high-quality" UPK. As a consequence, the legislature was unable to water down the policy during the implementation phase.

Conclusion

As illustrated by the preceding case analysis, social policies that require significant state budget allocations trigger complex policy discussions regarding *whether* to act and *who* should deliver on the investment. Three key factors – instrumentally rational argumentation; political leadership with a degree of autonomy to act; and rapid institutionalization to protect investments from retrenchment – are important to ensuring ECEC policy changes. Because rationales for ECEC policies and programs rest on two sets of arguments – a *policy investment logic* that leverages the power of evidence-based arguments and instrumentally rational calculations about the costs and benefits of early years investments, and a *cultural logic* that rests on societal and policy makers' views about and trust in the state vis-à-vis the family and market – these sometimes competing logics mean that exposure to these ideas is not in itself sufficient to convince policy makers and the public. Also, the investments must be broadly seen as legitimate areas of state activity, and the political leadership has to be relatively immune from political backlash, or at least the policies have to be sufficiently institutionalized to prevent retrenchment.

This chapter therefore demonstrates important scope conditions for models of policy change focused on frame effects. When policies challenge well-entrenched public values or deeply held principled beliefs, as well as significant budgetary outlays, it is hard to convince both policy makers and the public accept those policy investments. So the key to sustaining significant policy reforms is to ensure that perceptions of the state's legitimacy to act endure; otherwise, policy innovations are vulnerable to erosion or reversal (Patashnik, 2008; Patashnik and Zelizer, 2013). Cultural logics can often trump policy investment logics if the state loses its credibility, either through the loss of political leadership or through a contingent event that becomes a focusing event that galvanizes the opposition. If political leadership can shore itself against opposition, however, this can act as a bulwark against opposition attacks.

Chapter Seven

Constructing Early Childhood Education and Care Policy Shifts in Canada[1]

"We took money out of the hands of the lobbyists, academics and bureaucrats, and we gave it to *the real child-care experts* – their names are Mom and Dad."

Prime Minister Stephen Harper's speech to the Conservative Party of Canada, 1 November 2013, referring to the Conservatives' Universal Child Care Benefit (emphasis added)[2]

"I am delighted to announce that Ontario is moving forward with an extended and integrated full-day early learning program for our province's four- and five-year olds. By giving our kids an early full-day start in school, we are putting them on the road to success and building a stronger Ontario for all citizens. This is *the right thing to do* for our youngest students, their parents – and for the long-term prosperity of our province."

Ontario Premier Dalton McGuinty, in a letter to early learning advocates, 26 October 2009 (emphasis added)[3]

"Darlene Krupa could barely believe her eyes when she read a report that recommended that young Albertans – her little Avery included – attend junior kindergarten. The idea is 'just ridiculous,' she said, adding that her daughter, who turns 4 later this month, is not ready for a pressure-filled school environment."

Mahoney, 2004, p. A1

The three quotes above highlight the paradoxical trends in Canadian early childhood education and care in recent years. Lack of federal interest in developing ECEC policy on the part of the federal Conservative party, which was ideologically opposed to "institutionalized" child care services,[4] and the Conservatives' principled belief in "open federalism" in its years in office (2006–15) (Canada, House of Commons,

2007), meant that very little ECEC policy investment occurred after the 2006 federal election.[5] As this chapter documents, however, even before then, very little substantively had occurred around ECEC policy under both Liberal and Conservative governments until the mid-2000 initiative under then–Prime Minister Paul Martin.

At the provincial level, increased recognition of the importance of early childhood education has spurred provincial investment in many but not all provinces and territories. Social policy investments have triggered significant spending on full-day kindergarten in BC and PEI, as well as full-day junior and senior kindergarten in Ontario. Governments in other provinces, such as Alberta, have considered full-day kindergarten but ultimately declined to fund it. In terms of investments, growth of regulated child care services has slowed across Canada, and provincial funding increases have been only modest (Ferns and Friendly, 2014, p. 2).

This chapter charts these trends in ECEC policy development in Canada and examines the scope and substance of policy change. All three factors that were identified as important in the US case – instrumentally rational argumentation, political leadership with a degree of political and policy autonomy to act, and rapid policy institutionalization – also hold for Canada. Governments act when they determine that it is instrumentally rational – for electoral or for policy purposes – to do so. But as the battles over national funding for child care and over the introduction of full-day kindergarten reveal, part of the policy struggle focuses on what the appropriate policies *are* for children. In those policy battles, absent a shift in framing towards an instrumentally rational logic of social policy investment, strong and autonomous policy leadership, and rapid institutionalization of any policy changes, prevailing cultural norms will stymie policy change, as they have for decades in both Canada and the United States.

This chapter first traces policy developments at the federal level, beginning with the federal government's promised comprehensive ECEC investments in 1993 and following them into the present. It then analyses a number of provincial cases to reveal the policy investments and cultural logics at work in those provinces. As in the United States, Canada's federal structure requires us to explore national policy changes *and* changes at the provincial/territorial level.

National ECEC Policy Trends

The OECD Family Database (2014b, PF3.1.A) notes that as of 2011, Canada remains one of the lowest spenders in the OECD on child care and pre-primary education at 0.20 per cent of GDP – a position it has held since the OECD started tracking ECEC spending data (see Figure 1.1). UNICEF (2008) ranks Canada at the bottom (tied with Ireland) of twenty-five OECD countries in terms of ten benchmarks for ECEC services. At the same time, Canada increasingly stands out in terms of the policy instrument used to deliver full-day kindergarten – namely, funding and delivery via public schools. Unlike governments in Australia, the United Kingdom, and the United States, which have expanded their supply of ECEC services in recent years by investing heavily in the ECEC market, provincial governments in Canada have rejected a multitude of delivery agents, or, in the case of PEI, they have switched kindergarten provision to schools from child care centres (Friendly et al., 2013, p. 10). In the United States, only Oklahoma has chosen a similar public delivery mechanism, in which most pre-k is provided in public schools.

Most provinces (seven as of the time of writing) have also shifted responsibility for child care services from community and social services ministries to education ministries (Ferns and Friendly, 2014, p. 3). This consolidation of child care and education services under an education ministry stands in marked contrast to the situation as of the late 1990s. When the OECD embarked on its *Starting Strong* ECEC study in the late 1990s, Canada was initially excluded from the first round of country reviews.[6] The OECD had deliberately adopted the language of "early childhood education and care" as opposed to "child care," which OECD reports and other studies had until then used (e.g., OECD, 1990; European Commission Childcare Network, 1990; European Commission Network on Childcare, 1996), for it was felt that "child care" did not accurately capture the range of formal services that existed in many OECD countries for children under the age of compulsory schooling, nor did it fully capture the educational thrust behind its *Starting Strong* research agenda. But when the Education Directorate of the OECD contacted country governments to ask them to be part of the review, Canadian officials from Human Resources and Development Canada (HRDC) declined, their reason being that education was a provincial responsibility. Members of the Canadian delegation to the OECD's 2001 Early Childhood Education and Care: International Policy Issues Conference in Stockholm succeeded in persuading the federal government to participate in the second round of reviews, but HRDC had a difficult time persuading provincial governments to allow a federal study in an area of provincial jurisdiction. In the end, only four provinces hosted site visits by the OECD review team: BC, Manitoba, PEI, and Saskatchewan (OECD, 2004b).

The policy vacuum evidenced by this policy narrative is the result of the odd placement of responsibility for child care within government line ministries and also within the Canadian federation. Child care, like health care and education, falls under the exclusive jurisdiction of the provinces. But provincial governments have typically lacked the fiscal resources to fully fund those services through own-source revenue. The federal government has traditionally not "crossed the threshold of the school" and provided dedicated funding for primary and secondary education, although it has done so for tertiary (higher) education and somewhat so for child care.

Similarly to the United States, care outside the home for very young children has long divided public opinion. For most of the twentieth century, child care was regarded primarily as a welfare service to support poor working parents (Prentice, 1992). Centres were mainly private and run by charitable organizations. Nursery schools developed as educational enrichment programs. They appealed especially to the middle class. But because they were educational rather than custodial in nature, these schools were not set up to conform to work schedules.

In 1966 the federal government injected itself into child care under the aegis of the federal Canada Assistance Plan (CAP). CAP consolidated a number of provincial social assistance programs into a national shared-cost program to provide transfers to the provinces to fund provincial social assistance (Osborne, 1985). As part of those transfers, the federal government provided provinces and territories with funds to support the cost of child care for eligible low-income families. Federal conditions, which applied to both service providers and parent-users, determined eligibility.

Governments at the time conceptualized child care as part of social assistance and not as part of a comprehensive early childhood program. In 1970, however, the Royal Commission on the Status of Women in Canada recommended that the federal government conceive of a national child care program that would entail more than simply social assistance. It recommended a program "designed for all families who need it and wish to use it" (Canada, Royal Commission on the Status of Women, 1970, p. 270). One of the report's recommendations was for the federal government to help with the costs of building child care centres (Canada, Royal Commission on the Status of Women, 1970, p. 271). The federal Liberal government under Pierre Trudeau responded by amending CAP regulations so that it would share the full operating costs associated with child care centre delivery, not just salaries and other expenses. As a result, provinces had federal monies available on two fronts: for parent-users, and for service delivery. This funding scheme guaranteed the provinces long-term and automatic funding and required no negotiations and thus was a primary factor in the expansion of child care in the provinces (Krashinsky, 1977, pp. 19–20). The open-ended funding system continued until 1990, when the federal government imposed a cap on CAP in a few provinces. In 1996, the program was cancelled.

Child care funding under CAP was directed at low-income families only. The Canadian government began to talk seriously about federal funding for a broader national child care program in the mid-1980s, when the Trudeau Liberals appointed the ministerial-level Task Force on Child Care. It reported in 1986 (Status of Women Canada, 1986), after the Liberals lost the 1984 election. The newly elected Conservative government under Brian Mulroney continued to focus on child care, establishing a Special Parliamentary Committee. It even tabled Bill C-144, the Canada Child Care Act (Canada, House of Commons, 1988), but the legislation died when Prime Minister Mulroney called the 1988 federal election. The Mulroney government did not revisit the child care issue again after its re-election because of the amount of controversy the proposal had generated from child care advocacy groups themselves, mainly over the overall cap on federal cost-sharing for child care, the directing of funds to commercial child care centres, and the lack of national standards (White, 2001b).

In the 1993 election the federal Liberals under Jean Chrétien campaigned to spend $720 million on child care over three years and to create up to 50,000 new regulated spaces per year for three years, with two caveats: that spaces would only be created in a year following a year of 3 per cent economic growth; and that the program would be introduced only with the agreement of the provinces (Liberal Party of Canada 1993, pp. 38–40). As a result of slow economic growth, that election promise did not bear fruit. Instead, after the 1995 Quebec referendum, the federal government pledged in its 1996 Throne Speech that it would "not use its spending power to create new shared-cost programs in areas of exclusive provincial jurisdiction without the consent of a majority of the provinces." It also stated that "any new program will be designed so that non-participating provinces will be compensated, provided they establish equivalent or comparable initiatives" (Canada, House of Commons, 1996, p. 4).

By the end of the 1990s, the federal government appeared to be backing away from funding national social programs. Then, as mentioned in chapter 4, in 2000, Chrétien's government and provincial and territorial leaders (save Quebec) signed the Federal–Provincial–Territorial Agreement on Early Childhood Development (ECDA in 2000 and the Multilateral Framework Agreement on Child Care in 2003).

Interviews with those in the federal policy community revealed that people in Prime Minister Chrétien's policy circle were sympathetic to the idea of early child development – after all, the Chrétien Liberals had introduced the Canada Prenatal Nutrition Program in 1994, implemented the Community Action Program for Children (CAPC) in 1994, and established Aboriginal Head Start in 1995 (Doherty, 2007). But they were also cautious about major monetary commitments. Still, the federal government was persuaded enough about the importance of early childhood development for human capital development and social equity to initiate these two federal–provincial–territorial agreements. Universal early childhood education and care programs were also part of the Liberal Party's broader policy discussion (see, for example, the National Liberal Caucus Social Policy Committee, 2002).

Prime Minister Chrétien stepped down from office at the November 2003 Liberal party convention. His replacement was Paul Martin, the former finance minister. Martin then faced a federal election in June 2004. By the early 2000s, Canadian public opinion had shifted to view public funding for child care more favourably. For example, one public opinion survey found, in response to the question whether "Canada should have a nationally-coordinated child care plan that ensures that all children have access to quality child care regardless of family income, disability, race or region of the country they live in," that 51 per cent strongly agreed and 39 per cent agreed (Espey and Good Company, 2003, p. 92).

Paul Martin's party made a national child care program a central plank of its election platform, promising to spend $5 billion more over five years if it could reach agreement with the provinces and territories over how that money should be spent (Liberal Party of Canada, 2004, p. 29). The Liberals won the election but only with a minority government. From that election victory to the government's defeat in December 2005, the federal Liberal government worked to reach agreement with provincial premiers to spend the $5 billion. The extended negotiations began shortly after MP Ken Dryden became social development minister in July 2004 and lasted almost until the government fell in a non-confidence vote in December 2005. The government first attempted to reach a multilateral agreement as it had two years earlier with the MFA on child care. When that attempt failed in February 2005, Dryden began to negotiate a series of bilateral agreements. In contrast to the MFA negotiations only two years earlier, this time all of the provinces, *including* Quebec, entered into agreements to spend federal funds (Friendly and White, 2007). The final agreement-in-principle, signed in November 2005 with the New Brunswick government, came just before the Martin government's defeat on a non-confidence motion, which triggered the January 2006 federal election. The Liberal Party's 2006 election platform pledged to make the federal commitment to the program permanent (Liberal Party of Canada, 2006); the federal Conservative Party pledged to cancel the agreements. The Conservatives won the election, and the new government immediately followed through on its pledge, cancelling the agreements after the election victory in January 2006 and introducing in its inaugural Speech from the Throne what it labelled the "choice in child care allowance" as part of its "universal child care" plan (Canada, House of Commons, 2006). Signalling a shift from the policy investment logic of the Liberal government, Diane Finley, the human resources and social development minister, in her remarks during the debate over the April 2006 Speech from the Throne, invoked cultural logics: "*Canadian parents are the real experts on child care. They don't need to be told how to raise their children – least of all by the government*" (emphasis added).

The Policy Investment Logics Underpinning the Liberals' Embrace of ECEC under Paul Martin

Canadian Prime Minister Paul Martin was quoted in a *macleans.ca* interview with Ottawa bureau chief John Geddes on 17 December 2004:

> GEDDES: Social development minister Ken Dryden is expected to deliver big things on early childhood education in 2005. Why are you focusing on nationwide day care rather than just helping parents, no matter how they choose to raise their young kids?
>
> MARTIN: First of all, this is not day care, this is early learning and child care. We want to make sure that children are ready to excel as soon as they go to formal school, regardless of income.

The prime minister's deliberate framing of the Liberal government's plan for a national child care program as "early learning and child care"

(ELCC) demonstrates the significant conceptual shift that had occurred within the federal Liberal government and personally in the prime minister.

One could argue that Martin was already predisposed to the ideas underpinning ECEC because of his interest in human capital development, including "education, training, and research and development" (Delacourt, 2003, p. 76). Martin was one of the authors of the 1993 Liberal election platform (the Red Book), which contained a vague reference to early childhood learning and the explicit child care promise (Liberal Party of Canada, 1993). One individual interviewed stated that it was Chrétien, not Martin, who requested the "stay" on child care out of budgetary concerns, given how poorly the economy was performing. In his 1996 budget speech, ironically amidst further cuts to federal budgets – including transfers to the provinces and the dismantling of CAP – Martin delivered what one interviewee referred to as "the education speech." As part of the strategy for "investing in our future," Martin announced programs to support students; these would include raising the limits on tuition credits and Registered Education Savings Plan contributions, as well as broadening eligibility for the federal Child Care Expense Deduction (CCED) to include students and single parents (Martin, 1996, p. 19). Before taking over the Liberal leadership in December 2003, Martin had held a series of policy round tables covering various policy areas, one of which was ECEC policy. Thus, by the time Martin got to be party leader, "he was primed" to embrace a national "early learning and child care" program. The question is, what did the priming?

A number of interviewees emphasized that science was "very important, especially at the early stages," in persuading policy makers to act. As discussed in chapter 4, federal bureaucrats, mainly in Health Canada and Human Resources and Skills Development Canada (HRSDC), as well as policy advocates in the broader policy community, were active in shifting policy attention to early childhood development. As also mentioned, IO research such as the OECD's *Starting Strong* reports (OECD, 2001b, 2006) was also influential. Indeed, a significant impact of the OECD project in Canada may have been to help link early childhood education and child care in the minds of Canadian federal and provincial policy officials and to draw attention to the need to link child care and education services administratively (although federalism concerns prevent those linkages from being made across levels of government).

More important to the shift in federal policy during the early 2000s was the domestic epistemic community operating within the centralized, executive-dominated Westminster parliamentary system, which was very effective in transmitting ideas to the highest levels of political office. Much of the credit for Prime Minister Martin's conversion to ECEC champion goes to Dr Fraser Mustard personally, and to friends of Fraser Mustard who "harangued" Martin beginning in the mid-1990s regarding the importance of the early years from a developmental health perspective. The OECD's country report on Canada had been completed a few years earlier (although its publication was delayed), and it had been circulating in Ottawa for a long time prior to its publication. It was brought to Martin's attention by Peter Nicholson, the deputy chief of staff for policy in the Martin government and a former special adviser to the OECD secretary-general; and by Liberal MP John Godfrey, chair of the House of Commons subcommittee on children and youth at risk for much of Chrétien's tenure as prime minister, who was appointed to cabinet under the Martin government. One interviewee described the OECD report as "one of the 'proof points' to describing the need" in Canada for a national program, along with human capital development and gender equality concerns.

As an MP, Godfrey had served as chair of the National Children's Agenda Caucus Committee, chair of the National Liberal Caucus Social Policy Committee, and chair of the House of Commons Standing Committee on Children and Youth at Risk, among other posts. Before being elected in 1993, he had played a small role in writing the 1993 Liberal Red Book (Delacourt, 2003, p. 79), whose major authors included Martin, current CIFAR president and CEO Chaviva M. Hošek, Eddie Goldenberg, and Terrie O'Leary, who would go on to serve as Canada's representative to the World Bank and to promote her interest in education (Delacourt, 2003, pp. 74, 76, 126). Nicholson, a former senior policy adviser in the federal government, provincial MPP, Liberal finance critic in Nova Scotia, and senior vice-president with the Bank of Nova Scotia, and Lester Thurow, an MIT economist, also weighed in on the platform at the fall 1991 Liberal conference in Alymer, Quebec (Delacourt, 2003, p. 74). After the Liberals were elected in 1993, these two men's ideas regarding productivity and human capital development were raised to the highest levels of government.

Nicholson became the federal Liberals' "resident brain" and served as the Clifford Clark Visiting Fellow in the finance department in 1994–5 (Delacourt, 2003, p. 86). He also served as a director and member of the research council of CIAR. He then became special adviser to the OECD secretary-general in 2002–3. When Martin became prime minister, Nicholson returned to Canada to become Martin's deputy chief of staff for policy. It was Godfrey and Nicholson who introduced Martin to Dr Mustard.

Interviewees reported that the specific policy frames that resonated most powerfully among senior policy officials in Ottawa were the human capital development and women's labour market equality. A national system of early learning and child care was not conceived of simply as an anti-poverty measure or solely as part of human capital development, but rather as something broader. The federal government's emphasis on "child care" and (more vaguely) "early learning" instead of "early childhood education and care" or "universal pre-k" reflected sensitivity to the fact that the provinces have exclusive authority over primary and secondary education. Also, unlike other social policy areas, primary and secondary education remains a jurisdictionally watertight compartment.

Other actors in Ottawa, such as Landon Pearson, appointed by the Chrétien government to the Senate in 1994, who worked with Godfrey on the National Children's Agenda Caucus Committee, championed ECEC as part of a much broader children's rights agenda based on Canada's ratification of the UN Convention on the Rights of the Child. Claudette Bradshaw, who in 1974 had founded the Moncton Headstart Early Family Intervention Centres, and who after being elected to Parliament in 1997 became Minister of Labour and Minister Responsible for Homelessness during the second Chrétien term, contributed to promoting these broader frames.

The Cultural Logics Underpinning the Federal Conservative Government's ECEC Policy since 2006

The federal Conservative Party had signalled its aversion to child care investments in its 2004 federal election campaign. In response to the Liberal election platform, it committed to a $2,000 per child income tax deduction for all families with dependent children under age 16 (Conservative Party of Canada, 2004, p. 18). In the 2006 election campaign, the Conservatives took a different approach, tackling the idea of "institutionalized" and "socialized" child care head on. The Conservatives pledged to end the Liberal Party's bilateral agreements, introduce a $1,200 taxable allowance for each child under age 6, and provide $250 million in tax credits to employers and associations to create 125,000 child care spaces (Conservative Party of Canada, 2006, p. 31).

Before the election writ was dropped in late 2005, the Conservative opposition issued a number of statements condemning the Liberals' ELCC plan. On 15 February 2005, Conservative opposition leader Stephen Harper moved in the House of Commons "*[t]hat the House call upon the government to address the issue of child care by fulfilling its commitment to reduce taxes for low and modest income families [...] and, so as to respect provincial jurisdiction, ensure additional funds for child care are provided directly to parents.*" In justifying the directing of monies to families rather than programs, Harper stated:

[T]here is one major reason that the Liberal vision of child care will inevitably fail. In listening only to the government funded experts, who dominate the child care debate, the government has completely lost touch with the needs and aspirations of Canadian parents. Parents have made it clear that they want choice and empowerment when it comes to deciding how they can best take care of their children.

Harper then went on to cite the Vanier Institute of the Family study ranking parental preferences for child care options:

Yet the government's preferred option is to make the choice for them, to take parents' tax dollars and plough all available money into one option, that of supporting institutional day care centres, an option that parents themselves rank fifth out of six.

Harper then stated:

Parents with children often indicate that they would prefer to stay at home or work part time in order to care for their children, yet at the same time a high percentage of parents with young children both work outside the home, often full time. I have no doubt that some of those parents would prefer and do prefer access to quality institutional day care, but what these facts tell us is that a large number of those parents would prefer to stay at home, work only part time and spend more time with their children were they able to do so.

Harper then signalled a policy proposal that emerged in the 2006 election campaign:

Is it not possible that part of the reason so many parents with young children work outside the home is that our tax system makes it all but impossible for them to do otherwise? Canada is almost unique in the industrialized world in providing no tax benefits to married couples and almost no tax benefits to families with children, beyond a very low income threshold. Other countries provide tax benefits like income splitting between parents, an additional basic personal exemption for children, or universal per child tax credits or deductions. Canada provides nothing except for the universal national child benefit and tax deductions for institutional care. The Conservative Party certainly supports the existing deductions and the national child benefit program and would like to see this enhanced, but the benefit program does not provide enough assistance for many lower income parents to be able to consider staying at home to raise their children, and it provides next to nothing for parents once they are in the middle income range. Rather than devoting billions of dollars to a child care program that will help only a small group of parents, that will pay for structures rather than services, that will lead to even higher government spending and higher taxes for families, and that runs the risk of conflict with provincial governments, we urge the federal government to devote much of the money to cutting taxes for lower income and middle income Canadians, enhancing the existing tax credits for families with children, extending them to more families, and using tax relief and credits to help support those choices that Canadian parents want to make for their own children.

News media reports during 2004–5 focused the ECEC discussion as a debate over the appropriate role of the state in intervening in early childhood. Thériault (2006) notes the *National Post*'s framing of the debate over the federal proposals prior to the signing of the agreements. The *National Post* ran a series of stories published 7–9 December 2004 on the theme of "the Nanny State."[7] It also published an editorial on 11 December 2004 titled "Say No to the Nanny State." Thériault (2006) argues that all of the stories were pitched to oppose the "one size fits all" approach of the federal Liberal government's ECEC plan. The 7 December 2004 story, written by Peter Shawn Taylor, explicitly endorsed the idea of a tax deduction to allow parents "choice" rather than funding for a national child care system. The same story quoted an UQAM professor, Philip Merrigan, who emphasized that the Quebec child care system tended to benefit middle-class rather than lower-income parents – a class theme picked up in Heather Sokoloff's story the next day. The two stories that ran on 9 December (written by Graham Hamilton and Heather Sokoloff) focused on the poor quality of Quebec's system and on whether child care should be delivered by for-profit or not-for-profit providers. Hamilton argued that Quebec's system cost more because of high wages in the heavily unionized not-for-profit child care sector.

The 2006 federal election campaign sparked a maelstrom of public debate and newspaper commentary regarding the desirability of non-parental care. Major commentary comparing the major party platforms appeared in a number of newspapers (Leblanc, 2005; Sokoloff, 2005).

The Conservatives countered the idea of a national early learning and child care system in their election platform by calling their own proposal "Choice in Child Care Allowance." The platform stated:

> The Liberals and the NDP believe that the only answer to expanding child care in Canada is their one-size-fits-all plan to build a massive child care bureaucracy which will benefit only a small percentage of Canadians. Only the Conservatives believe in freedom of choice in child care. The best role for government is to let parents choose what's best for their children, and provide parents with the resources to balance work and family life as they see fit – whether that means formal child care, informal care through neighbours or relatives, or a parent staying at home. (Conservative Party of Canada, 2006, p. 31)

In contrast, the Liberal Party declared that it would make the funding transfers permanent (Liberal Party of Canada, 2006).

After its federal election victory in January 2006, the minority Conservative government quickly announced – and then notified the provinces – that it was cancelling the intergovernmental agreements the Liberal government had negotiated with each province. According to the terms of the agreements, they provided one year of funding to each province/territory. In place of a national program focused on provinces/territories developing ECEC programs, the Harper government opted for a straight cash payment to parents, as well as a fund to create new child care spaces. The child allowance was included in the May 2006 budget (Canada, Department of Finance, 2006, pp. 99–103), and cheques to parents began to flow in July. The cash payment, the Universal Child Care Benefit (UCCB), cost almost $1.8 billion in the 2007–8 fiscal year (Beach et al., 2009, xxii).

The cancellation of the funding agreements went virtually unchallenged by the ten provincial premiers who had signed them. Instead, the provinces began to explore full-day kindergarten and other policies within their own jurisdictions. The second part of the Conservative child care platform, the Child Care Spaces Initiative, remained rather moribund. In its 2007 budget, the Conservative government introduced a 25 per cent investment tax credit to a maximum of $10,000 per space. It also provided a transfer of $250 million to the provinces/territories, also intended to support the creation of child care spaces (Canada, Department of Finance, 2007, pp. 124–5). Child care space creation did not accelerate under this program, however.

While many advocacy organizations felt that the allowance was a poor substitute for a national ECEC system (Battle, 2006; CCAAC, 2005), as did many individuals in newspaper commentaries, public sentiment was not strongly opposed to the idea, and many families reported liking to receive the $100 per month cheque. A survey of 2,005 Canadians completed by the Environics Research Group (2006), commissioned by the Child Care Advocacy Association, and conducted in May 2006 – just months after the election of the Harper government – found that while a large majority of those surveyed believed that government should play a very (47%) or somewhat (35%) important role in helping parents meet their child care needs (p. 5), and 75 per cent believed strongly (43%) or somewhat strongly (33%) in the national child care program proposed by the Liberal government in 2004, 35 per cent of those polled favoured the Conservative government's $1,200 taxable allowance over funding new child care spaces, while 50 per cent favoured the funding of spaces and 15 per cent stated no preference or stated a preference for both approaches (p. 7). The popularity of the universal "child care" benefit made opposition parties hesitant to attack it, and in the 2008 federal election the federal Liberal party promised not to cancel it (Liberal Party of Canada, 2008).

Concerns about creating a skilled workforce do not have the same resonance in Canada as in the United Kingdom and the United States. As Coulombe (2007) argues, Canada does well not just in terms of overall performance results in cross-national educational assessments but also on other measures such as educational equality of opportunity. That is, the gap between the performance of students from families with high socio-economic status versus low socio-economic status is smaller in Canada than in other industrialized countries. This outcome indicates that "the Canadian school system does a relatively good job of improving the skills of students with a low socio-economic background and, therefore, of reducing socio-economic disparities" (Coulombe, 2007, p. 59). Also, the percentage of students ranked as "poor" performers on the 2003 PISA was lower in Canada than in any other country except Finland. These outcomes suggest that "Canada might well have one of the best public education systems in the world for primary and secondary schooling" (Coulombe, 2007, p. 59), although, as Table 3.1 reveals, student performance on the PISA is declining over time. In the absence of a perceived crisis, however, it is difficult to mobilize policy opinion in support of significant federal early years investment, even for the extremely vulnerable populations in Canada, including Indigenous communities (White, 2014).

Summary and Analysis of ECEC Policy at the National Level

The 2006 election marked a sea change in the direction of child care and ECEC policy development. The defeat of the minority Liberal government and the timing of the election meant that the federal government did not have sufficient time to reframe national policy in order to institutionalize (and insulate) federal early years funding. The vagaries of the election cycle in 1984 and 1988 similarly brought a halt to child care policy discussions, whereas the Blair government in the United Kingdom had three terms in office to secure its policy reforms, and the Howard government four terms in Australia. Elections and changes in government thus stymied policy reforms at the national level.

Partisanship, while important, is not a sufficient explanation for the policy changes observed throughout Canada. While a number of policy changes in Canada occurred under Liberal governments and the PQ in Quebec, the Liberal party is a "big tent" party, especially at the provincial level, and represents a rather broad ideological spectrum. Major expansion of child care funding was attempted in the late 1980s under a federal Conservative government and brought to an end by another federal Conservative government.

Federalism also clearly plays a major role in slowing the pace of policy change in Canada, a constraint that unitary liberal welfare states such as New Zealand and the United Kingdom do not face. Federal governments in Canada, unlike in the United States, are constrained by jurisdictional concerns over investing federal funds in primary and secondary education. Thus, the most significant expansion of early years programs is occurring via provincial action exclusively.

Provincial Initiatives

Within provincial governments, significant reform of the administrative apparatus to deliver early years programs has occurred over the past decade. Previously, responsibility for child care and education rested with two different ministries – usually an education ministry for kindergarten, and a health or social services ministry for child care (Friendly et al., 2007, pp. 195–7). Over the past decade, though, seven provinces have shifted responsibility for child care services from a social services ministry to an education ministry (Ferns and Friendly, 2014, p. 3). This signals a conceptual shift around early years programs.

Each province/territory has a range of programs, including regulated child care centres, part-day nursery schools, home-based regulated family child care, public kindergartens, and a vast web of unregulated child care. The range, quality, and access to ECEC programs vary considerably by region and circumstance. In all provinces except Quebec (discussed below), the public funding model relies heavily on fee subsidies targeted to eligible low-income families, and in some provinces, notably Ontario, many eligible families cannot access a subsidy. This welfare (rather than universal) approach means that the high user fees for regulated child care that are levied to support most of the cost of program operations are a major barrier to access for modest and middle-income parents. The available child care spaces cover only a minority of children, and public kindergarten schedules do not meet the needs of working parents. Across Canada even regulated child care is more likely to be poor to mediocre than excellent (Japel, Tremblay, and Côté, 2005). No province/territory provides sufficient high-quality ECEC programs to serve a majority of children or to meet the UNICEF benchmarks for quality, access, and financing (Friendly and Prentice, 2012). But recent initiatives at the provincial level suggest that some provincial governments are slowly embracing a more holistic approach to early childhood education and care for young children, based on a policy investment logic.

Quebec

It is not surprising that Quebec was an early leader in developing comprehensive early childhood policies and programs. Family policy in general is distinctly more important in Quebec than in the rest of Canada; the "family" in Quebec is regarded as a political and collective object linked to nationalism and social solidarity (Le Bourdais, 1994). Early childhood programs, though, are more than a cultural project; the state's concerns about declining fertility, poverty, and the need to increase women's labour market participation and strengthen the social economy (and reduce rates of social assistance) led to dramatic changes to Quebec's family policy in the 1980s and 1990s (Jenson, 1998, 2009; Tremblay, 2009). These changes culminated in major reforms to family policy as outlined by the then-premier, Lucien Bouchard, and the education minister, Pauline Marois, in the 1997 White Paper on family policy *Nouvelles dispositions de la politique familiale: Les enfants au coeur de nos choix* (Gouvernement du Québec, 1997). The government signalled a number of policy concerns: to "fight against poverty, [and to support] equal opportunity, the development of the social market economy, transition from welfare to the workforce and increased support to working parents" (Premier Lucien Bouchard, 23 January 1997, quoted in Tougas, 2002).

Two years before the White Paper was released, the government had appointed a group of experts with a broad mandate to recommend a redesign of the province's social assistance programs and labour market policies. As Jenson (2009, p. 53) notes, this group of experts did not come to a consensus on all issues but did agree on the importance of new services for children. Camil Bouchard, one of the appointed experts, had been a psychology professor at the University of Quebec at Montreal before becoming a member of the Quebec National Assembly. He had helped author *Un Québec fou de ses enfants ("Quebec, crazy about its children")* in 1991 (Groupe de travail pour les jeunes, 1991). Then in 1996 the premier brought together a number of other actors including employers, labour union representatives, and other non-governmental groups for a Summit on the Economy and Employment. Soon after, the premier announced the new family policy.

In a 1997 speech, Bouchard evoked the language of policy investment when expressing concern about high rates of school failure and students having to repeat a grade. There was, he said, a "direct relation between the length of time in an *école maternelle* and a reduction in the rate of having to repeat a primary grade."[8] The premier linked the new family policy to the goal of improving educational outcomes in the school system; so did the education minister, Pauline Marois, who in a 1997 press release cited "American researchers" who had found six-to-one returns on investment in early years programs.[9]

The White Paper outlined a series of family policy initiatives, including a new child benefit program for low-income families, funding for new early childhood education and child care services, and a new parental leave plan (Gouvernement du Québec, 1997). To pay for the new family policies, the government eliminated other family programs, including the "baby bonus" (Tougas, 2002, p. 10; see also Maroney,

1992). The baby bonus was an advance on income tax credits paid at the birth of each child. When it was introduced, it provided $500 for the first two children and $3,000 for the third and subsequent children (Maroney, 1992, p. 26). Despite increases in the amount of the bonus, it was not having the hoped-for positive effect on the birth rate (Maroney, 1992).

The government's first step in 1997 was to expand from part-day to full-day its voluntary kindergarten programs, making all 5-year-olds eligible (as well as a small portion of 4-year-olds from disadvantaged backgrounds, mostly in the city of Montreal). That same year, the government began introducing substantial funding directly to child care programs for children aged 0 to 4 years, and to school-age programs for 5- to 12-year-olds (Tougas, 2002). This was coupled with the gradual roll-out of across-the-board parent fees of $5 per day for children in child care centres and regulated family child care (increased to $7 per day in 2003 by the provincial Liberal government that followed) and capital funding to encourage expansion of not-for-profit *Centres de la petite enfance* (CPEs) – small local networks of not-for-profit centre-based and family child care (Tougas, 2002, pp. 4–5).

Because the reforms stemmed from an expert group evaluating family policy from an employment and human capital development perspective, as well as a family policy perspective, from the beginning the Quebec government explicitly labelled its programs "educational child care" (Ministère de la Famille et de l'Enfance, 1997; Ministère de la Famille et des Aînés, 2007); thus, educational goals explicitly underpinned its ECEC policy (Ministère de la Famille et de l'Enfance, 1999). However, some of the policy choices by subsequent governments have left government dealing with poor-quality child care overall (Japel, Tremblay, and Côté, 2005; Baker, Gruber, and Milligan, 2008). The newly elected Liberal government in 2003 raised child care fees to $7 from $5 per day, to great public protest (Jenson, 2009, p. 49). Other changes included policy and funding that increasingly favoured the development of for-profit child care services as the Liberal government allowed for-profit centres to be eligible to receive children under the $7-per-day subsidies (Jenson, 2009). Thus, despite significant increases in government expenditures, a significant amount of Quebec's supply of child care services remains in for-profit centres and family child care homes, which provide little or no early childhood development education or training. Indeed, Japel, Tremblay, and Côté (2005) found that for-profit and unlicensed family care were four times more likely to be "inadequate" on quality measures as not-for-profit services.

All of this provides background to the government's decision in March 2013 both to expand the number of centre-based child care spaces and to expand kindergarten programs to all disadvantaged 4-year-olds across the province (Dougherty, 2013). Currently, those programs are only available for a small number of disadvantaged children, mostly in Montreal. The decision to introduce Bill 23 seems rooted in evidence-based policy making. In 2009 the education ministry released a report documenting the challenges of keeping youth in school (Ministère de L'Éducation, du Loisir, et du Sport, 2009). As part of its thirteen-point plan to keep students from dropping out, the ministry highlighted programs to support children, including programs to improve the school readiness of very young children in disadvantaged regions. The report endorsed increasing the number of child care spaces in those regions and providing funding for child care services for families receiving income assistance (Ministère de L'Éducation, du Loisir, et du Sport, 2009, p. 19). Capuano, Bigras, and Japel (2014, p. 1) report, however, that children from families in disadvantaged regions tend not to use government-regulated child care centres; rather, they are overrepresented in poor-quality child care. Focusing assistance on child care subsidies would not reach those children and would not expose them to high-quality pre-school experiences. The government seemed to acknowledge that quality "educational child care" may need to be provided in school settings under a public delivery mechanism, unlike in most jurisdictions in the United States, which have pledged to expand pre-kindergarten.

Ontario

The Liberal government under Premier Dalton McGuinty, elected in 2003, launched a number of reforms to education and children's policy in Ontario that were implemented over a number of years. The new premier committed to improving relations with teachers (after the fraught relations between the previous government under Premier Mike Harris and teachers' unions) and to improving provincial educational standards such as literacy and numeracy rates and high school graduation rates. The government also committed itself to reducing classroom sizes in the primary grades and to improving children's early years experiences (Glaze and Campbell, 2007).

Soon after the election, the government established a new Ministry of Children and Youth Services, which brought together parts of the Ministry of Community and Social Services, Ministry of Health and Long-Term Care, and Ministry of Community Safety and Correctional Services (Ontario MCYS, 2008, p. 2). One of the new ministry's tasks was to develop and implement the province's Best Start strategy, among a number of other programs geared towards improving children's programs and services. Best Start (which included a number of policies and programs for children) was launched in November 2004, building on an earlier Conservative initiative to create a province-wide network of maternal, newborn, and early child development resource centres called Ontario Early Years Centres, which were funded in part by the federal government. Best Start also included an expansion of the child vaccination program, newborn screening for hearing, and well-baby visits, among other services.

The government also created a number of expert panels to advise on best policy practices. Among these were two expert panels on early learning and child care, which reported in 2007. The mandate of the Best Start Expert Panel on Early Learning was to "develop an early learning framework for formal preschool settings that would link with the Junior/Senior Kindergarten program and, ultimately, develop a single integrated early learning framework for children ages two-and-a-half- to six-years" (Ontario Ministry of Children and Youth Services Best Start Expert Panel on Early Learning, 2007). The panel, chaired by Jane Bertrand, executive director of the Atkinson Centre for Society and Child Development at the Ontario Institute for Studies in Education (OISE) at the University of Toronto, produced a curriculum framework, *Early Learning for Every Child Today*, to guide early years programs in the province. A second panel, the Ontario Ministry of Children and Youth Services Expert Panel on Quality and Human Resources (2007), was chaired by Donna Lero, the Jarislowsky Chair in Families and Work at the University of Guelph, and focused on the early learning and the child care workforce.

In late November 2007 the government announced the appointment of Dr Charles Pascal as the Ontario Special Advisor on Early Learning to "recommend the best way to implement full-day learning for four- and five-year-olds" (Ontario Office of the Premier, 2007). The press release made extensive reference to research evidence to justify both Dr Pascal's appointment and the initiative itself.[10] Pascal was a professor of psychology at OISE (Ontario Institute for Studies in Education) / University of Toronto and a former deputy minister in the Ontario government in both Education and Community and Social Services.

Pascal's report, issued in June 2009, recommended full-day early learning for 4- and 5-year-olds as well as seamless integrated services to support all young children (Pascal, 2009b). Pascal was highly aware of the need for a strong research basis to justify intervention: in addition to his report and recommendations, he released a compendium of the research that had informed his recommendations (Pascal, 2009a). The report cited a number of pilot projects and experiments in creating a "seamless day" of programming for children.

But while it adopted Pascal's report, the McGuinty government only partly implemented his recommendations. The government announced that it would introduce full-day kindergarten for all 4- and 5-year-olds across the province, beginning in September 2010, with a multi-year phase-in. The government stated that it would staff the classrooms with a teacher and an early childhood educator. It further announced that parents would have the option to enrol their child in an extended day program before and after regular school hours, in schools where sufficient demand was expressed (Ontario Office of the Premier, 2009). But the province did not take up the idea of seamless day programming, with schools as hubs for a number of early years programs.

On its website, Ontario's education ministry encourages parents to enrol their children in the voluntary program because "research shows that children who participate in full-day kindergarten get a solid foundation for future learning" (Ontario Ministry of Education, 2014b). The ministry also provides a weblink to recent evaluations of the roll-out of full-day kindergarten, despite the mixed results of those evaluations (Ontario Ministry of Education, 2014a).

The program remains extremely popular. In the 2011 provincial election, the roll-out of the early learning program became an election issue, with the Progressive Conservative party declaring before the election its opposition to it. But in response to perceived popular support for the program, part way through the election campaign the Conservatives softened their opposition and declared their support for McGuinty's initiative (Jenkins and Artuso, 2011). Public support for the program remained so high that in 2012, when adviser Donald Drummond recommended the cancellation of full-day kindergarten, the Liberal party branded that recommendation a "non-starter." The Liberal finance minister, Dwight Duncan, and Donald Drummond himself, acknowledged that "there is substantial evidence that investments in early childhood education produce significant *socioeconomic* benefits in the long term"; therefore, for the Liberal government, "full-day kindergarten is the one thing we would want to protect" (Canadian Press, 2012; emphasis added). The Conservative opposition leader again raised objections to full-day kindergarten before the 2014 provincial election (Canadian Press, 2013), which the Liberals won decisively with a majority, ensuring the final phase-in of full-day kindergarten in the province.

Alberta

In 2002 the Alberta Ministry of Learning appointed the Alberta Commission on Learning to conduct a comprehensive review of the province's education system from kindergarten to grade twelve. The nine-member panel was chaired by Patricia Mackenzie, a former teacher and Edmonton city councillor, and had a very broad mandate, unlike some of the other commissions reviewed above, to review not only classroom conditions, hours of instruction, and related issues, but also issues such as the impact of globalization, technology, and demography on education (N.A., 2002). In June 2003 the commission issued its final report, which included ninety-five recommendations, including funding for full-day kindergarten for 5-year-olds and a phase-in of junior kindergarten for 4-year-olds (Alberta's Commission on Learning, 2003).

The Alberta government had previously not been as supportive of kindergarten as other provinces. In the mid-1990s it cut $30 million in public funding for its voluntary kindergarten program (Alberta Ministry of Education, 1993). Municipal school boards made up the difference in a number of ways, in some cases charging parents for the service (Mitchell, 1994, p. D3). By 1996 the Progressive Conservative government under Ralph Klein had agreed to reinstate full funding for kindergarten, heeding the public backlash against the cuts (Laghi, 1996, p. A1).

At first the government did not reject the commission's recommendations (Government of Alberta, 2003). But after the report was released, the government encountered widespread public resistance. Alberta's learning minister, Lyle Oberg, stated that "I was assuming that this was going to be very easy, but it's turned out to not be really easy" (Mahoney, 2003, p. A12). The oppositional sentiment at the time was aptly captured by a statement by a spokesperson for the Alberta Federation of Women United for Families: "At three years old, you need care from your parent. You don't need peers or teachers or whatever" (Mahoney, 2004, p. A2).

The government thus ultimately ignored the commission's kindergarten recommendations. As in California, while the government at first accepted the policy logic of investing in early years programs, and had a modicum of institutional insulation, the public expressed opposition to the idea of state investment in pre-k. But the issue has not gone away in Alberta at the elite policy level. In 2009 a joint report by the Alberta education ministry and the Learning Commission chair, Patricia Mackenzie, issued a Five-Year ACOL Retrospective Report, which restated a number of recommendations from the 2003 report, including again a call for junior and senior kindergarten (Alberta Ministry of Education and Patricia Mackenzie, 2009). In 2012, then-premier Alison Redford announced that her government would begin a new consultation on the Alberta Education Act, including a review of "the learning benefits of full-day kindergarten" and the operational issues surrounding possible implementation (Government of Alberta, 2012). This reflects the reality that a number of Alberta school districts are already paying the full cost of full-day kindergarten based on the popularity of these programs among many parents (Hammer, 2011). In January 2013, however, the Alberta government announced a delay in implementing provincially funded all-day kindergarten (Cuthbertson, 2013), and Premier Redford has since resigned.

Conclusion

This chapter, as did the previous chapter on the US case, demonstrates that despite the high salience of ECEC and the myriad arguments made by both governments and advocates regarding the instrumentally rational logic of investment, when policies are at stake that challenge well-entrenched public values or deeply held moral views, and that represent significant budgetary outlays, policy makers and the public have to be convinced to accept the legitimacy of those investments. Early years debates are as fractious in Canada as they are in the United States and occur both at the cognitive level (What is the evidence basis to achieve a particular policy goal?) and at the normative level (What "ought" the state to do, given principled beliefs about the appropriate relationship between the state and other institutions?). Policy change thus will not occur if actors do not start with what Hall (1993) labels third-order change: shifts in principled beliefs and state goals. Once those shifts are under way, policy windows can remain open if actors succeed in drawing attention away from questions of state legitimacy to focus on instrumentally rational concerns. But policy windows can close if actors cannot maintain the credibility of political leadership and the legitimacy of the state to act under public scrutiny. The specific intra-jurisdictional policy debates and framing strategies of actors become crucial factors in the success or failure of policy initiatives. However, policy reforms can quickly become derailed by policy events that undermine the credibility of political leadership or the state's legitimacy to act, as occurred in the pivotal 2006 federal election.

PART FOUR

Conclusion

Chapter Eight

Conclusion

This book is an explicit exercise in ideational process tracing. It tracks the ideational underpinnings of ECEC policy debates and uncovers the primary logics that have emerged around ECEC policies and programs. It finds that two different logics are at work in UPK policy debates: a *policy investment logic* that leverages the power of evidence-based arguments and instrumentally rational calculations about the costs and benefits of early years investments; and a *cultural logic* that rests on societal and policy makers' views about and trust in the state vis-à-vis the family and market. Differences in institutional and cultural contexts have led to variation in adoption of these programs and policies within these and other liberal welfare states. Powerful cultural narratives discipline both policy actors and the public in certain policy directions. This book affirms the importance of norms and cultural practices with regard to policy and emphasizes that policy makers and the public are motivated and deeply affected by the values they attach to things. Those cultural logics can often trump rational policy investment logics. Thus, policy outcomes are as much about the contests over meaning and identity as they are about interests.

The chapters have demonstrated that policy change has not been easily achieved in either the United States or Canada, despite huge efforts on the part of a number of actors and policy leaders. Instead, policy shifts have occurred in fits and starts, with some government backtracking during times of fiscal restraint and even during good times, and in Canada as a result of election losses. This book has demonstrated as well that while evidence-based policy ideas and other instrumentally rational human capital considerations have been very persuasive, and necessary to convince policy makers to make early years investments, they are not enough to convince all policy makers and the public to support political leaders who champion those ideas.

This book has also identified some of the specific ideational and institutional mechanisms necessary to facilitate policy change around ECEC and other controversial policy issues. Social policies that require significant state budget allocations trigger complex policy discussions of *whether* to act and *who* should act to deliver on the investment; for policy change to occur there must be political leadership that can exercise a degree of autonomy from political and public opposition. In federal countries where policy making is focused on national and regional/state/provincial levels, it is important to focus policy attention at the sub-national level as well. Chapters 6 and 7 have documented the extent of policy change in the United States and Canada and note both the unevenness and the variation in policy adoption at both the national and sub-national levels. Those chapters track the strategies used at the national and state/provincial levels to shift public opinion and policy makers' beliefs, including action by legislators themselves, litigation battles, and state-wide ballot initiatives, as strategies of cultural change. In Canada outside of Quebec, a wave of policy reform at the provincial level has focused almost exclusively on the expansion of full-day kindergarten, to varying degrees of success.

The question remains whether these policy changes simply represent adjustments to policy instruments and existing program settings, or are evidence of more fundamental cultural change or "culture move." I will not be so bold as to offer predictions, but I want to revisit some of the measures outlined in chapter 2 and to pose some questions for future investigation.

The first measure for judging the extent of culture change is the extent of the blurring of the distinctions between early childhood education and care and primary education. In a book by Pianta, Cox, and Snow (2007), Ruby Takanishi, the head of the Foundation for Child Development, wrote in the foreword that "at some point in the 21st century, American public education will begin with 3-year-olds" and high school could finish at grade 10 to "enable young people to pursue advanced vocational education or higher education." The notion that public education could begin at age 3 is not so far-fetched when we observe changes at the US state and Canadian provincial level already under way. In places as diverse as Florida, Georgia, Iowa, Oklahoma, Vermont, West Virginia, and Wisconsin, between 60 and 80 per cent of 4-year-olds can attend pre-kindergarten (Barnett et al., 2013, p. 9).

Figure 8.1. Enrolment rates in early childhood and primary education for 4-year-olds, 2012

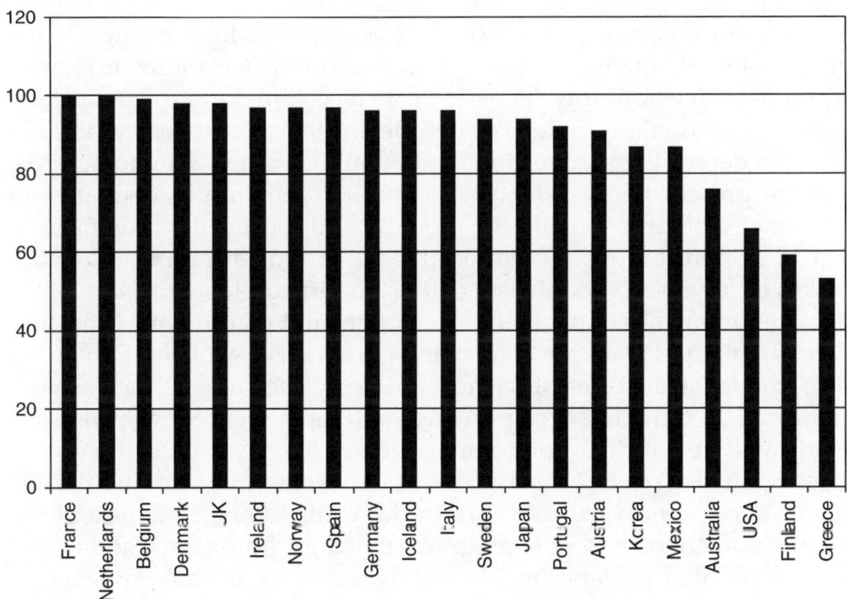

NB: Data for Canada not available; Source: OECD (2014a, p. 327)

Seven states and Washington, DC, provide public funding for full-day pre-k programs that run for at least six hours per day; eleven states plus Washington, DC, provide public funding for full-day kindergarten (Holt, 2014, p. 3). In six provinces (BC, Ontario, Quebec, Nova Scotia, New Brunswick, and PEI), all children can attend full-day kindergarten. The Newfoundland and Labrador government announced in March 2014 that it intends to implement full-day kindergarten by 2016 (Newfoundland and Labrador Ministry of Education, Child, Youth and Family Services, 2014). In Ontario, all 4-year-olds can attend a full-day program delivered in public schools. The BC government has promised but has delayed expanding its full-day program to 3- and 4-year-olds (Hyslop, 2012). Still, both the United States and Canada, along with Australia, rank far behind other OECD countries, including other liberal welfare states, in the number of 4-year-olds enrolled in early learning programs (see Figure 8.1). Surprisingly, given its strong performance on PISA assessments, Finland has low enrolment in early childhood education, although the Finnish government is in the process of reducing the age by which children attend compulsory school from 7 to age 6 (Chandler, 2014).

A second measure of the extent of policy paradigm change is the organizational apparatus that exists to administer these programs. Administrative authority for early years has shifted quite dramatically in many jurisdictions in the past decade. In 1996, Peter Moss and Helen Penn, in describing services for children in the United Kingdom, wrote that "at present, services for young children are both inadequate and irrationally organized ... Both nationally and locally, the present division of responsibility between social services and education authorities makes little sense. Not only is the division difficult to justify, but it perpetuates anomalies of payment, availability and placement." Moss and Penn's (1996, p. 1) calls for "a more integrated service for children under five, under the auspices of a single authority" seem to be increasingly answered. In Canada, seven provinces and territories (New Brunswick, Northwest Territories, Nova Scotia, Nunavut, Ontario, PEI, Saskatchewan) now deliver ECEC services through a single education ministry (Ferns and Friendly, 2014, p. 14). In the United States, because of the plethora of federal and state programs that are administered at the state level, a number of departments and agencies are usually involved in ECEC program delivery, although some states have worked to coordinate services at the state administrative level (Regenstein and Lipper, 2013).

The trend towards decentralized policy development is likely to continue in both the United States and Canada, unlike in the unitary states of the United Kingdom and New Zealand. Even advocacy organizations have adopted a multi-state strategy. Tellingly, in an October 2004 essay in *The American Prospect*, Valora Washington, then-director of Schott Fellowships in Early Care and Education at the Schott Foundation for Public Education, wrote that "the field of early care and education is at a crossroads, where the hoped-for remedy is not a national framework of care but the evolution of 50 unique state solutions" (Washington, 2004). In the United States, at the 2014 White House Summit, the president announced additional funding for states under the Preschool Development Grants program and under federal Head Start and the Early Head Start–Child Care Partnerships program, but federal program funding under Head Start continues to come under challenge from critics who claim that the program fails to prepare children adequately for school (US House Budget Committee Majority Staff,

2014). Meanwhile in Canada, continued federal policy inaction is likely to spur decentralized policy solutions at the provincial and territorial levels. Evidence from this cross-national examination thus suggests the beginnings of policy paradigm change, but with enormous variation, even within the liberal welfare states.

One increasing commonality is that ECEC expansion is occurring within fundamentally liberal welfare norms that privilege private investment (in the United States especially), as well as decentralized policy solutions. The Obama administration as recently as December 2014 announced significant federal investments to encourage ECEC expansion in US states; but that same White House Summit announcement emphasized that a great deal of that investment would occur through public–private partnerships and philanthropic investment from corporations such as The Walt Disney Company and the Lego Foundation (White House Office of the Press Secretary, 2014). As chapter 4 documents, private philanthropic investment has been a major spur to state-level ECEC initiatives in the United States; such investment plays a much smaller role in Canada. But ECEC has always been delivered in mixed markets, and this trend shows no sign of dissipating. Indeed, the Alberta government currently provides kindergarten funding for public, Catholic, charter, and private schools, as well as for approved private, not-for-profit operators (Friendly et al., 2015, p. 82).

The mixed market so evident in early years investments in liberal welfare states can also be observed in other welfare regimes. As Table 8.1 reveals, public funding with hybrid delivery is common not only in pre-primary education but also in primary education in many continental European and Nordic welfare states. Indeed, the process by which early childhood education and care policies and programs are emerging is similar to the pattern for primary education program development (Ansell and Lindvall, 2013; Kaestle, 1983). Education remained largely a private and philanthropic endeavour in most industrializing countries until the mid- to late 1800s. The state's gradual recognition of the importance of education to citizenship and other national values (and national interests) led it to assume responsibility for funding and (usually) delivery, although with a great deal of variation in whether the state funded independent schools.

Such convergence towards mixed delivery methods in ECEC and primary education in the Nordic welfare states especially suggests that the liberal welfare states are no longer outliers. The big question for early years programs in the twenty-first century will be whether liberal

Table 8.1. Percentage of students in pre-primary and primary education by type of school, 2012

		Pre-primary education			Primary education		
		Public	Government-dependent private	Independent private	Public	Government-dependent private	Independent private
Liberal welfare states	Australia	22	78	n/a	69	31	n/a
	Canada	n/a	n/a	n/a	94	6	5
	New Zealand	1	99	n/a	98	n/a	2
	UK	63	31	6	93	3	5
	USA	60	n/a	40	92	n/a	8
Nordic welfare states	Denmark	81	19	n/a	85	15	n/a
	Finland	92	8	n/a	98	2	n/a
	Iceland	88	12	n/a	97	3	n/a
	Norway	54	46	2	98	2	5
	Sweden	83	17	n/a	91	9	n/a
Continental European welfare states	Belgium	47	53	n/a	46	54	n/a
	France	87	12	n/a	85	14	n/a
	Germany	35	65	2	96	4	5
	Italy	70	n/a	30	93	n/a	7
	Netherlands	70	n/a	30	100	n/a	n/a

Source: OECD (2014a, p. 418)

welfare states take on the responsibility not just for funding those services but also for delivering them, as provinces in Canada and the state of Oklahoma are doing, rather than subsidizing private delivery. Will we will see increasing use of a variety of delivery agents?

Important research and policy questions follow from observing this mix of funding and delivery. For scholars of contemporary welfare states, the observation that welfare states of all sorts – not just liberal welfare states – are increasingly reliant on the private sector to deliver education services suggests an important research agenda. Related to the scholarly puzzle of what accounts for this shift in provision, what are the practical implications of relying on a mixture of public and private sector providers? Researchers, largely US-based, have raised questions about the quality of private sector provision. Program quality has important knock-on effects in terms of governments' long-term goal of improving child development outcomes and overall human capital development. Differences in families' use of providers by income raise important concerns about income inequality and access to quality services (Putnam, 2015), as well as concerns about whether the state can achieve other important goals such as student achievement and citizenship education that high-quality education services can provide.

A key issue for future research and policy making, therefore, is the role that governance mechanisms – the rules surrounding financing and provision – play in mediating outcomes produced by different mixes of public and private delivery. While countries are converging on mixed models of program delivery, we can hypothesize that different governance and accountability rules can override differences in the outcomes that would otherwise be produced by private versus public delivery agents because of the way these regulatory and accountability mechanisms incentivize and regulate delivery. A central challenge for researchers and policy makers going forward, therefore, will be uncovering the mechanisms for delivering high-quality programs that produce positive child development outcomes, while recognizing ways to overcome societal and budgetary resistance to program spending.

Notes

Chapter 1

1 For example, on 14 February 2011, in the Iowa Senate, Republican State Senator Mark Chelgren compared Iowa's voluntary pre-school program to Nazi and Communist indoctrination:

> The Chinese are taking 2- and 3-year-olds and educating them. And as a student of history, I also know the Nazis, the Soviets, a whole variety of groups, a whole variety of countries, take their children because it's not just up to age six they're so malleable. The day after they're born is when they learn the most percentage wise. And so what question I have for this body and the question I have in general, if it is all about indoctrinating a child, I would use the exact same arguments that the Nazis used, that we should take children immediately, as soon as we recognize they have potential. What I would challenge us with instead is to put the responsibility on the parents. Because it is parents' responsibility and families' responsibility to make sure that in the formative years of growing as a child, they are taught the values and they are taught and educated by their families and they have that bond, that maternal and paternal bond that is developed during that time. It is not the role or responsibility of this government to take that away from families and to replace it with an indoctrination process by teachers. (J. Jacobs, 2011)

Focus on the Family's website posts the following excerpt by Jill Savage on "The Value of Stay-at-Home Moms":

> What happens at home is central to a child's ability to function through-out his life. Home is where bonding takes place and a child learns to

attach to relationships. When a child can attach, that means they learn to trust people. Learning to trust is essential for having healthy relationships throughout life … With all the diverse roles that home plays in our life, someone has to be on duty to stay true to the construction blueprint … On a construction site, the site manager is an on-site leader. He or she is present every day to make sure plans are followed, jobs are completed, and people are doing what they need to do. The site manager and the general contractor regularly communicate in order to keep the construction plan on task and on time. They confer and strategize together, and then the manager oversees the on-site work … There is so much diversity in what goes on at home that an on-site manager is desperately needed. Someone needs to have the time and energy to invest in each member of the family as well as manage all the different facets of home. That's the essence of the job description *for Mom, the site manager*. (http://www.focusonthe-family.com/parenting/parenting_roles/value-of-stay-at-home-moms.aspx; emphasis added)

These principled beliefs about the role of the state in early childhood and the role of mothers are not limited to the United States. Then-Alberta finance minister Iris Evans declared in a speech to the Economic Club of Canada, Toronto, on 17 June 2009: "When you're raising children, you don't both go off to work and leave them for somebody else to raise, and this is not a statement against daycare. It's a statement about their belief in the importance of raising children *properly*" (O'Neill and Walton, 2009, p. A3, emphasis added).

2 Organized interest groups in the United States that oppose government intervention in early years programs (for varying reasons) include the American Enterprise Institute, the Cato Institute, the Family Research Council, Focus on the Family, the Goldwater Institute, and the Heritage Foundation. See, for example, Cohen (2001); DeBray-Pelot and McGuinn (2009); and Haas (2007). Organizations in Canada include Advocates for Childcare Choice, the Institute for Canadian Values, the Institute of Marriage and Family Canada, Kids First Parents Association of Canada, and REAL Women of Canada. See, for example, McKeen (2006) and Rayside and Wilcox (2011).

3 In 1996, for example, *Newsweek* ran a cover story, "Your Child's Brain" (Begley, 1996) that was so popular, Rose (2010, p. 103) reports that it generated over a million requests for reprints (see also Nash, 1997).

4 See Esping-Andersen (1990) for the original welfare state typology. Other research that identifies liberal welfare states includes Bronfenbrenner

(1992), Myles and Pierson (1997), and O'Connor et al. (1999). Liberal welfare states resemble one another on a number of dimensions: stronger reliance on private schemes to deliver services; stronger emphasis on benefits tied to workforce participation and an increasingly strong emphasis on labour market activation; selective or targeted schemes that exclude certain groups, which leads to gaps in coverage; and lower replacement benefits on programs such as pensions and social assistance (Alber, 2010).

5 Three other provinces (New Brunswick since 1992, and Nova Scotia and Quebec since 1997) offer full-day kindergarten for five-year-olds (Friendly et al., 2015).

6 For excellent country-based histories of early childhood education and care programs and policies, see for example, Brennan (1998) on Australia; Prochner and Howe (2000) and Timpson (2001) on Canada; May (1997; 2001; 2011) on New Zealand; Randall (2000) on the UK; and Beatty (1995), Cohen (2001), Michel (1999), and Vinovskis (2005) on the United States.

7 While the end of the Canada Assistance Plan in Canada also ended explicit national funding for child care, TANF contained specific child care subsidy provisions.

8 Like Ferree and Merrill, I distinguish frames from *discourses*, which are "broad systems of communication that link concepts together in a web of relationships through an underlying logic" (Ferree and Merrill, 2000, p. 455). While Schmidt (2008) and others label these frames, they really are amalgamations of frames connected together with a coherent underlying logic. The *framing process* connotes the process by which "discourses, ideologies, and frames are all connected" (Ferree and Merrill, 2000, p. 456). Framing can have effects on people's preferences and can be used strategically to get people to see what is in their interest. Frame effects can be deeper, however, appealing to both beliefs and preferences (Chong and Druckman, 2007).

9 Policy instruments (Hall, 1993) are the techniques used to achieve policy goals. In the area of pre-school policy, instrument choices revolve around questions such as appropriate teacher credentials, curriculum standards, or the types of permissible providers. Settings refer to distinct levels of instruments, for example, specific student/teacher ratios, or whether teachers need a B.Ed. or simply a certificate in child development.

10 Content analysis involves examining the appearance and frequency of words in government and non-governmental documents, speeches, policy pronouncements, and media reports to determine whether there is variation in the way policies are described across cases (Hardy, Harley, and Phillips,

2004; see also Laver, Benoit, and Garry, 2003). Thematic analysis, in contrast, tries to qualitatively capture patterns within language whose importance is not necessarily revealed through frequency (Braun and Clarke, 2006). Discourse analysis, in turn, rests on the theoretical claims that words can construct a particular meaning and that a relationship exists between the manufacturing of discourse, actors' discursive responses, and the resultant reality (Hardy, Harley, and Phillips, 2004). Discourse analysis helps reveal actors' understanding of the world, which in turn influences their decision making (Fairclough, 1995; Phillips and Hardy, 2002). Discourse analysis thus involves examining how policy makers and the broader community describe a policy and interpreting what words they use (e.g., as positive or negative).

Chapter 2

1 Portions of this section have been published in White (2006, 2009b, 2012, 2017) and White and Friendly (2012).
2 Of course, many researchers have pointed out that no country fits purely within any one regime, and no one model fully captures all the nuances of states' social policy provision. For a review of the research that examines the appropriate categorization of welfare states, see Arts and Gelissen (2002) and Hicks and Kenworthy (2003). For gender-based critiques of Esping-Andersen's work see, for example, Lewis (1992), Orloff (1993), and Sainsbury (1999).
3 Laslett and Brenner (1989, p. 382) define social reproduction as "the activities and attitudes, behaviors and emotions, responsibilities and relationships directly involved in the maintenance of life on a daily basis, and intergenerationally."
4 Some researchers note similar patterns of provision in Ireland, Switzerland, sometimes even the Netherlands, and in the East Asian welfare states of Japan and Korea. For a summary of that research, see Arts and Gelissen (2002, pp. 149–50).
5 For country histories, see ch. 1 n6.
6 See, for example, Grant (1998), Hays (1996), and Hulbert (2003) for reviews of child-rearing advice by American experts throughout the twentieth century; Lewis (1980) and Riley (1983) for reviews of the advice given to mothers in Britain in the early and mid-twentieth century; and Waldfogel (2007) for a review of recent studies on non-maternal child care "harm."
7 Ramirez and Boli (1987, p. 174). See also Kaestle (1983) regarding the development of compulsory schooling in the United States; Axelrod (1997) and Gidney and Millar (2012) in Canada; and Ansell and Lindvall (2013),

Benavot and Riddle (1988), Lindert (2004), and Soysal and Strang (1989) for cross-national comparison of trends.

8 In the Toronto District School Board in Ontario, for example, the Alexander Stirling Public School's lunchroom policy in 2011 stated: "We at Alexander Stirling P.S. believe that it is always best for children to get a break at noon and eat a warm meal at home in a family setting. All students at Alexander Stirling P.S. who have a parent or other adult at home during the lunch hour much go home for lunch … If it is absolutely necessary for your child to stay at school for the lunch hour because you cannot make other arrangements, please complete a lunchroom permission form and return it to the school" (http://schools.tdsb.on.ca/alexanderstirling/policy_lunchroom.htm. Accessed 10 June 2011). A Web search of public schools in Toronto in June 2011 found similarly stated policies, even though most parents were participating in the paid labour force. At one Toronto school with such a policy, fewer than one-quarter of the 550 students reportedly went home for lunch (Gandhi, 2006, p. A1). A Web search five years later found that no such school lunch policies remained in Toronto. Brown Junior Public School's website, for example, states that for students in grades 1 to 6, "while the majority of students stay at school for lunch, some students choose to go home" (http://brownschool.ca/aboutbrown-2/faqs).

But some schools in other provinces still encourage students to go home at lunch. Overlanders Public School in Edmonton states: "We expect students to go home for lunch if there is a parent or guardian at home as students need a break" (http://overlanders.epsb.ca/forparents/lunchnutrition). Prince Rupert, BC's, school district policy as of January 2017 is to encourage students to go home for lunch (sd52.bc.ca/laxkxeen2/wp-content/uploads/2012/09/lunchtime-information.pdf).

9 Even the scholarly works on the subject are infused by this dichotomous view of the programs and services. Contrast Suzanne Helburn and Barbara Bergmann's *America's Child Care Problem: The Way Out* (Helburn and Bergmann, 2002) which focuses on expanding the US child care system to make it more affordable, accessible for working families, and of high quality, with Edward Zigler, Walter Gilliam, and Stephanie Jones's *A Vision for Universal Preschool Education* (Zigler, Gilliam, and Jones, 2006), which focuses much more on expanding early childhood education in the United States. Other models, in contrast, propose more comprehensive and integrated services for children; these include Peter Moss and Helen Penn's *Transforming Nursery Education* (Moss and Penn, 1996). See also,

for example, Friendly and Prentice (2009), Kagan and Cohen (1996), and Lombardi (2003).

10 Details regarding curriculum frameworks in Sweden, New Zealand, Italy, and the US High/Scope project can be found in OECD (2004c). For the Reggio approach, see Edwards, Gandini, and Forman (2012). The latest Swedish pre-school curriculum (Skolverket, 2010) can be found at http://www.skolverket.se/om-skolverket/andra-sprak-och-lattlast/in-english/publication/2.5845?_xurl_=http%3A%2F%2Fwww5.skolverket.se%2Fwtpub%2Fws%2Fskolbok%2Fwpubext%2Ftrycksak%2FBlob%2Fpdf2704.pdf%3Fk%3D2704. The New Zealand early childhood curriculum (New Zealand Ministry of Education, 1996) can be found at: www.education.govt.nz/assets/Documents/Early-Childhood/te-whariki.pdf. Details regarding Canadian provincial curriculum frameworks can be found in Langford (2010).

11 Rhode Island in 1942, California in 1946, New Jersey in 1948, and New York in 1949, followed by Puerto Rico in 1968 and Hawaii in 1969.

12 The Australian education system is comprised of government-run as well as non-government (Catholic and independent) but government-supported programs (Press and Hayes, 2000, p. 58).

13 While compulsory schooling begins at age 6, the OECD (2001b, pp. 14–15) notes that many children are in school by age 5.

14 While compulsory school does not begin until age 6, students can – and most do – enrol in school from their fifth birthday (Meade and Podmore, 2002, p. 1).

15 As devolution has occurred in the UK, variations in provision exist between England, Scotland, Wales, and Northern Ireland, so information in this section pertains mainly to England.

16 The ACTU's support for private, for-profit child care is ironic given strong union opposition to for-profit care in countries such as Canada. See, for example, the Canadian Union of Public Employees' (CUPE) position on for-profit child care: http://cupe.ca/child-care?list=articles&key_i=50&date=&extraKeywords.

17 The Australian Bureau of Statistics (2008) reports a lower percentage of 4-year-olds attending pre-schools: 62 per cent in 2005.

Chapter 3

1 Although world sociology scholars such as Meyer, Ramirez, and Soysal (1992) and Ramirez and Boli (1987) have tracked education spending as part of the development of international norms around what it means for states to be modern.

2 Although Iversen and Stephens (2008) include child care spending along with education spending when analysing the connection between welfare regime and human capital programs. See also Bonoli and Reber (2010) and Jensen (2009, 2011a, 2011b).

3 Functionalist theories of policy change posit that political activity fulfils some function and that policy change occurs as societal needs arise or change, brought on by shifts in technology, the economy, or the labour market (Collier and Messick, 1975; Hall and Soskice, 2001).

4 See Skogstad and Schmidt (2011) for an excellent overview of the domestic and transnational literatures on policy paradigm change.

5 Connecticut legalized civil unions in 2005 and legalized marriage in 2008. Massachusetts legalized marriage in 2004. New Hampshire legalized marriage in 2010. The New Jersey Supreme Court in 2006 ordered the legislature to pass either a civil union or marriage law. The legislature did so in 2012, but the governor vetoed it. The legislature must now try to override the veto. New York legalized marriage in 2011. Vermont legalized civil unions in 2000 and legalized marriage in 2009. One other northeastern state's law on legalization, Maine's, was defeated in a 2009 referendum. One other exception to the northeasten state cluster is Iowa, where a court struck down the gay marriage ban in April 2009 (National Conference of State Legislatures, 2012).

6 For a review of findings of a number of interventions in the United States see, for example, Reynolds et al. (2010) and Shonkoff and Phillips (2000).

Chapter 4

1 "'The school must play a larger role in the development of poor youngsters if they are to have, in fact, "equal opportunity." This often means that schooling must start on a pre-school basis and include a broad range of more intensive services'" (White House, 1964, as quoted in Vinovskis, 2005, p. 40).

2 White and Phillips (2001, pp. 90–1) report that three developmental psychologists – Mamie Clark, Urie Bronfenbrenner, and Edward Zigler – were involved in the creation of Head Start and that "other psychologists such as Jerome Kagan, Jerome Bruner, Benjamin Bloom, and B.F. Skinner were called upon by Sargent Shriver [Head Start founder] or his staff from time to time…"

3 The Baby Einstein company, founded in 1997, became a multimillion-dollar business. It was sold to the Walt Disney Company in 2001. In 2009,

in response to a Federal Trade Commission complaint about the claim that these videos were educational, the Walt Disney Company began to issue refunds to parents (Lewin, 2009).

4 The theme of this cluster of studies is quite distinct from the 1990 National Academies' *Who Cares for America's Children? Child Care Policy for the 1990s* study (Hayes, Palmer, and Zaslow, 1990).

5 Of the three major longitudinal studies, only one – the Carolina Abecedarian study – was of a full-day program. The Perry Preschool and Chicago programs, as well as Head Start, are part-day programs (Jepsen, Troske, and Brasher, 2009, p. ii).

6 The controversy over the publication of this study is detailed well in Phillips and McCartney (2005, pp. 113–15; 123).

7 The Google scholar citation count on the original NBER study as of February 2016 was 602.

8 Not all members of the policy community concurred with this view. For example, in 1988, Douglas Besharov, a resident scholar at the American Enterprise Institute, wrote an op-ed in the *Washington Post*. He quoted Democratic presidential candidate Michael Dukakis and Republican candidate George H.W. Bush: "Michael Dukakis declared in his acceptance speech that it is 'time to see that young families are never again forced to choose between the jobs they need and the children they love.' He has endorsed start-up funding for the Act for Better Child Care, which has a first-year price tag of $2.5 billion. George Bush called child care 'nothing short of a family necessity' and proposed his own $2.2-billion program, a combination of tax relief and grants to the states. Either approach could easily cost $10 billion within a few years and many times that within the decade … Are we really in the midst of a serious child-care 'crisis'? One that requires a major new federal program? Let's look at the facts. Most mothers of small children do not need – or want – full-time licensed day care … Child care may someday be like public schools – available to all families free of charge. But that day is many, many years away. For now, federal policy should focus on the families in greatest need" (Besharov, 1988).

9 Read, for example, George Kaiser's speech on early childhood at the Ounce of Prevention Fund conference, 28 April 2005. Reprinted in the *New York Times Online*: http://www.nytimes.com/2007/02/07/education/07economix2.html?pagewanted=all.

10 For a list of those organizations, see National Children's Alliance (1998) and NCA's website: http://www.nationalchildrensalliance.com/nca/links.htm.

11 See Stroick and Jenson (2000).

Chapter 5

1　Portions of this chapter have been published in White (2011a, 2011b).

2　International Relations (IR) scholars such as Keck and Sikkink (1998, p. 46) label these transnational advocacy networks, comprised of "relevant organizations working internationally with shared values, a common discourse, and dense exchanges of information."

3　Dion (2008), for example, argues that IOs not only establish international norms and provide policy models but also directly influence domestic policy decisions, whereas Weyland (2006) argues that IOs' influence is mediated via domestic institutions.

4　See for example the ILO's social security database at http://www.ilo.org/sesame/IFPSES.SocialDatabase and previously *The Cost of Social Security* (e.g., ILO, 1997), although for recent shifts see, for example, ILO Office of the Director-General (2003) and ILO Bureau for Gender Equality (2006).

5　The World Bank (Young, 2002, p. xi; Young, 2007, p. vii) lists a number of other multilateral agencies involved in its early childhood development symposiums in addition to those mentioned here: the Pan American Health Organization (PAHO), the World Health Organization (WHO), and the US Agency for International Development (USAID), as well as development banks such as the Inter-American Development Bank and the Asian Development Bank.

6　This conference was co-sponsored by UNESCO, UNICEF, UNDP, and the World Bank.

7　Adopted in a plenary session on 16 November 2007 by the Ministers of Education of the member states of the OAS.

8　Nevertheless, in Canada, some academics (e.g., Howe and Covell, 2005), advocacy groups such as the Canadian Child Care Federation (CCCF), and parliamentarians, most visibly Senator Landon Pearson, have worked to persuade Canadian governments to recognize these children's rights in law. In the United States, in contrast, Davis (2005, p. 149) points out that, given the illegitimacy of the international human rights frame in the United States, domestic women's groups have focused their attention exclusively on "domestic standards and paradigms."

9　See Henderson and White (2004) for details on the two EU directives related to maternity and parental leave.

10　Earlier, the European Commission Network on Childcare and Other Measures to Reconcile the Employment and Family Responsibilities of Men and Women (Childcare Network) had recommended that European countries invest at least 1 per cent of GDP in ECEC services (European Commission Network on Childcare, 1996). By the mid-2000s, the OECD (2006, p. 105) estimated that only five countries in Europe achieved that level of investment – Denmark, Finland, France, Norway, and Sweden – and that Hungary and the Flanders region of Belgium were close to that benchmark.

11 A Proquest Newstand search of "child care" and "OECD" yielded over one hundred newspaper and newswire articles in the Canadian press, forty-three of these published between 2004 and 2006, which coincides with the OECD's Country Study of Canadian child care and the OECD's *Starting Strong II* report. The same search yielded no articles in US newspapers during the same time period.

12 For documentaton of the media reports and advocacy organization responses to the OECD (2004b) country report, see CRRU's issue file. Online: http://www.childcarecanada.org/res/issues/oecdthematicreviewcanadareports.html. See, for example, Strang and Chang (1993, p. 250) on the United States' non-participation in international standard setting on social welfare through the ILO, and its refusal to sign the Kyoto Protocol.

13 The OECD's international team consisted of John Bennett from the OECD, Bea Buysse from Belgium, Païve Lindberg from Finland, and Helen Penn from the United Kingdom (OECD, 2006, p. 438). The background report, in contrast, as in all countries, was written by three in-country experts (Doherty, Friendly, and Beach, 2003) and was commissioned by the Government of Canada.

14 Pagani (2002, p. 13) states: "The involvement of the reviewed State in the process and its ownership of the outcome of the peer review is the best guarantee that it will ultimately endorse the final report and implement its recommendations. However, the State's involvement should not go so far as to endanger the fairness and the objectivity of the review. For example, the State under review should not be permitted to veto the adoption of all or part of the final report."

Chapter 6

1 The FrameWorks Institute lists a number of foundation donors and partners, including the Annie E. Casey Foundation, the David and Lucile Packard Foundation, the MacArthur Foundation, the McDonnell Foundation, and the A.L. Mailman Foundation (http://www.frameworksinstitute.org/partners1.html).

2 Visit the FrameWorks Institute website at http://www.frameworksinstitute.org/early-childhood-development.html and Shonkoff and Bales (2011) for details about these initiatives.

3 Mitchell (2004, pp. 9–10) reports that New York State legislators implemented legislation at breakneck speed once State Assembly Speaker Sheldon Silver began to work on education reforms in the fall of 1996. In February 1997 a number of policy advocates held a legislative breakfast in Albany where a panel presented the Carnegie Corporation's report *Years of Promise* (Carnegie Corporation of New York, 1996). At the same venue, a speaker from the Georgia Business Education Roundtable spoke about the recently adopted UPK program in Georgia. By August of that same year, the legislature had enacted the LADDER package of educational reforms that included state financial incentives for full-day kindergarten for 5-year-olds and a commitment to fund pre-kindergarten for 4-year-olds. But because the initiative depended on annual budget appropriations, it was extremely vulnerable to the vagaries of politics and the economy.

4 *San Antonio Independent School District v. Rodriguez*, 411 U.S. 1, 7 (1973).

5 For information on ongoing court challenges, visit the Education Justice, http://www.educationjustice.org/index.html; Education Law Center, http://www.elc-pa.org; and the National Education Access Network, www.schoolfunding.info.

6 *Robinson v. Cahill*, 351 A.2d 713 (N.J. 1975).

7 *Leandro v. State* 488 S.E.2d 249 (N.C. 1997)

8 *Leandro II – Hoke County Bd. of Educ. v. State* 599 S.E.2d 365 (N.C. 2004).

9 *Abbeville County School District v. State*, No. 31–0169, slip op. at 157 (S.C. Ct. C.P. Dec. 29, 2005). See also Hunter (2012) for a list of other states where pre-k litigation has been launched; and Boylan (2007) and Rebell (2012). Visit also the National Education Access Network, http://schoolfunding.info.

10 E.g. *Lake View Sch. Dist. No. 25 v. Huckabee* (*Lake View III*), 91 S.W.3d 472 (Ark. 2002).

11 This section draws heavily on White and colleagues (2015).

Chapter 7

1 Portions of this chapter were published in Friendly and White (2012), White (2011a), White and Prentice (2013), and White and Prentice (2016). Because a lot of the information was gleaned from confidential interviews with people connected to the federal Liberal and provincial government, they have asked that their comments be not for attribution.

2 As quoted by Steven Chase, "Harper Assures Grassroots Conservatives He's Outsider Fighting Elites" *Globe and Mail*, 1 November, http://www.theglobeandmail.com/news/politics/harper-assures-grassroots-conservative-hes-outsider-fighting-elites/article15228311.

3 http://childcarecanada.org/documents/research-policy-practice/09/11/
letter-premier-mcguinty-re-full-day-early-learning.

4 See the Conservative Party of Canada's (2006, p. 31) election platform for a
statement on the party's position on child care.

5 The Harper government after 2006 stated that the federal government
would "place formal limits on the use of the federal spending power for
new shared-cost programs in areas of exclusive provincial jurisdiction"
and would in general respect provincial autonomy in areas of exclusive
provincial jurisdiction (Canada, House of Commons, 2007, p. 8). While
researchers (e.g. Bakvis, 2014) have documented that "open federalism"
has not meant a return to "watertight compartments" in terms of federal/
provincial jurisdictional responsibilities, it has meant little action on the
federal government's part in intergovernmental affairs, and shrinkage in
the overall activity of the state in the realm of social policy.

6 The following information is derived from a presentation given on 15
August 2001 by one of the Canadian delegates to the OECD's Early
Childhood Education and Care: International Policy Issues Conference,
held in Stockholm, Sweden, 13–15 June 2001.

7 The 7 December 2004 story was titled "The Next Medicare? What Can
Taxpayers Expect?"; the 8 December 2004 story was titled "Daycare's
Impact Traces Class Lines – Does Class Matter?"; two stories on 9
December 2004 were titled "Quebec's Sacred Cow Has Quality Issues –
Access vs. Quality" and "Who Should Care for Our Children?"

8 *"Les recherches sont unanimes quant à la relation directe entre la durée de la
fréquentation de l'école maternelle et la réduction du taux de redoublement à
l'école primaire, en plus d'influencer positivement le déroulement ultérieur de
la scolarisation, de l'insertion sociale et du développement de la personnalité.
Parallèlement, au Québec, des études ont révélé que 50% des cas d'abandon
scolaire au secondaire concernaient des enfants ayant accumulé un retard scolaire
dès le primaire et ayant doublé au moins une classe"* (Miville-Deschênes, 1997).

9 *"C'est un effort gigantesque dans les services à la petite enfance qui est proposé dans
les nouvelles dispositions de la politique familiale, un pas que nous devions faire
pour l'avenir de toute la société québécoise. Des chercheurs américains ont, en effet,
évalué que chaque dollar investi dans l'éducation préscolaire procurait en moyenne
$6 d'économies ultérieures pour les fonds publics"* (Miville-Deschênes, 1997).

10 The complete text of the news release is as follows:

> The government has appointed Dr. Charles Pascal to recommend the
> best way to implement full-day learning for four- and five-year-olds, said
> Ontario Premier Dalton McGuinty.

"Research tells us that early learning helps children get off to the best possible start in school – so it's important that we get it right," said Premier McGuinty. "That's why we've appointed one of Canada's leading experts in early childhood education, Dr. Charles Pascal, to get our plan for full-day learning for four- and five-year olds off to the best possible start."

Dr. Pascal is the executive director of the Atkinson Foundation, a charitable foundation dedicated to economic and social justice and Chair of the Education Quality and Accountability Office (EQAO). He has extensive experience in the education sector as a former president of Sir Sandford Fleming College and in taking on significant roles in different provincial governments.

In 1987, he was appointed Chair of the Ontario Council of Regents, the government's chief policy and planning body for the colleges of applied arts and technology. In 1991, he became the Deputy Minister of the Ministry of Community and Social Services and later the Deputy Minister of the Ministry of Education and Training.

A recent Rutgers University study showed that four-year-olds in full-time learning programs scored consistently higher in math and language skills. It found that full-time learning has dramatic and lasting effects on children's learning across a broad range of knowledge and skills.

The McGuinty government has committed to spending $200 million in year three of its mandate and $300 million in year four to make progress on full-time learning for Ontario children.

"We need everyone at their best for Ontario to prosper – and our government will continue building opportunity for parents and investing in the success of children," said Premier McGuinty. "Together, we'll move forward the Ontario way – by working, building and dreaming together." (Ontario Office of the Premier, 2007)

References

Acharya, Amitav. 2004. "How Ideas Spread: Whose Norms Matter? Norm Localization and Institutional Change in Asian Regionalism." *International Organization* 58(2): 239–75. http://dx.doi.org/10.1017/S0020818304582024.

Ackerman, Debra J., W. Steven Barnett, Laura E. Hawkinson, Kristy Brown, and Elizabeth A. McGonigle. 2009. *"Providing Preschool Education for All 4-Year-Olds: Lessons from Six State Journeys."* *Preschool Policy Brief 18 (March).* New Brunswick, NJ: NIEER.

Adams, Gina, and Jodi Sandfort. 1994. *First Steps, Promising Futures: State Prekindergarten Initiatives in the Early 1990s.* Washington, DC: Children's Defense Fund.

Albanese, Patrizia. 2011. "Addressing the Interlocking Complexity of Paid Work and Care: Lessons from Changing Family Policy in Quebec." In *A Life in Balance? Reopening the Family–Work Debate,* ed. Catherine Krull and Justyna Sempruch, 130–45. Vancouver: UBC Press.

Alber, Jens. 2010. "What the European and American Welfare States Have in Common and Where They Differ: Facts and Fiction in Comparisons of the European Social Model and the United States." *Journal of European Social Policy* 20(2): 102–25. http://dx.doi.org/10.1177/0958928709358791.

Alberta Ministry of Education. 1993. *Meeting the Challenge: An Education Roundtable Workbook.* Edmonton.

Alberta Ministry of Education and Patricia Mackenzie. 2009. *Every Child Learns, Every Child Succeeds: Fifth Anniversary Retrospective on Alberta's Commission on Learning Report.* Edmonton: Alberta Learning.

Alberta's Commission on Learning. 2003. *Every Child Learns, Every Child Succeeds: Report and Recommendations.* Edmonton: Alberta Learning.

Alesina, Alberto, and Edward L. Glaeser. 2004. *Fighting Poverty in the US and Europe: A World of Difference.* New York: Oxford University Press. http://dx.doi.org/10.1093/0199267669.001.0001.

Alexander, Craig. 2012. "Early Childhood Education Has Widespread and Long-Lasting Benefits." *TD Economics Special Report* (27 November). http://www.td.com/document/PDF/economics/special/di1112_EarlyChildhoodEducation.pdf.

Alexander, Robin. 2000. *Culture and Pedagogy: International Comparisons in Primary Education.* Oxford: Blackwell.

Almond, Gabriel, and Sidney Verba. 1963. *The Civic Culture: Political Attitudes and Democracy in Five Nations.* Princeton: Princeton University Press. http://dx.doi.org/10.1515/9781400874569.

Anderson, Jenny. 2011. "Suit Faults Test Preparation at Preschool." *New York Times,* 14 March. http://www.nytimes.com/2011/03/15/nyregion/15suit.html.

Andersson, Bengt-Erik. 1992. "Effects of Day Care on Cognitive and Socioemotional Competence of Thirteen-Year-Old Swedish Schoolchildren." *Child Development* 63(1): 20–36. http://dx.doi.org/10.2307/1130898.

Andrews, Kenneth T., and Bob Edwards. 2004. "Advocacy Organizations in the US Political Process." *Annual Review of Sociology* 30(1): 479–506. http://dx.doi.org/10.1146/annurev.soc.30.012703.110542.

Ansell, Ben. 2010. *From the Ballot to the Blackboard.* New York: Cambridge University Press. http://dx.doi.org/10.1017/CBO9780511730108.

Ansell, Ben, and Johannes Lindvall. 2013. "The Political Origins of Primary Education Systems: Ideology, Institutions, and Interdenominational Conflict in an Era of Nation-Building." *American Political Science Review* 107(3): 505–22. http://dx.doi.org/10.1017/S0003055413000257.

Arts, Wil, and John Gelissen. 2002. "Three Worlds of Welfare Capitalism or More? A State-of-the-Art Report." *Journal of European Social Policy* 12(2): 137–58. http://dx.doi.org/10.1177/0952872002012002114.

Ashby, Gerald, Anne Kennedy, and Elizabeth Mellor. 2002. "Early Childhood Services in Australia: Recent Commonwealth and State Initiatives." In *International Developments in Early Childhood Services,* ed. Lorna K.S. Chan and Elizabeth J. Mellor, 7–28. New York: Peter Lang.

Australia, Early Childhood. 2011. *Our Future on the Line: Keeping the Early Childhood Education and Care Reforms on Track. A State of the Sector Report.* library.bsl.org.au/jspui/bitstream/1/2402/1/Our%20future%20on%20the%20line.pdf.

Australian Bureau of Statistics. 2008. *Year Book Australia, 2008.* Online: http://www.abs.gov.au/AUSSTATS/abs@.nsf/bb8db737e2af84b8ca2571780015701e/536AC616F0C145FFCA2573D200107B92?opendocument.

Australian Government. 2009. *Australia's Paid Parental Leave Scheme: Supporting Working Australian Families.* Canberra.

Australian Government (Department of Education, Employment, and Workplace Relations – Office of Early Childhood Education and Child Care). 2010. *State of Child Care in Australia* (April 2010). https://www. mychild.gov.au/documents/state-child-care-australia-2010.

Australian Government Productivity Commission. 2009. *Paid Parental Leave: Support for Parents with Newborn Children*. Inquiry Report no. 47, 28 February. http://www.pc.gov.au/inquiries/completed/parental-support/ report.

Australian Senate (Standing Committee on Education, Employment, and Workplace Relations – References Committee). 2009. *Provision of Childcare*. Canberra: Commonwealth of Australia.

Avard, Denise, and Jennifer Tipper. 1999. *Building Better Outcomes for Canada's Children*. Ottawa: CPRN.

Axelrod, Paul. 1997. *The Promise of Schooling: Education in Canada, 1800–1914*. Toronto: University of Toronto Press.

Baker, Maureen. 1995. *Canadian Family Policies: Cross-National Comparisons*. Toronto: University of Toronto Press. http://dx.doi.org/10.3138/ 9781442672178.

Baker, Maureen, and David Tippin. 1999. *Poverty, Social Assistance, and the Employability of Mothers: Restructuring Welfare States*. Toronto: University of Toronto Press. http://dx.doi.org/10.3138/9781442678668.

Baker, Michael. 2011. "Innis Lecture: Universal Early Childhood Interventions: What Is the Evidence Base?" *Canadian Journal of Economics / Revue Canadienne d'Economique* 44(4): 1069–105. http://dx.doi.org/10.1111/j.1540-5982.2011.01668.x.

Baker, Michael, Jonathan Gruber, and Kevin Milligan. 2008. "Universal Childcare, Maternal Labor Supply, and Family Well-being." *Journal of Political Economy* 116(4): 709–45. http://dx.doi.org/10.1086/591908.

– . 2015. "Non-Cognitive Deficits and Young Adult Outcomes: The Long-Run Impacts of a Universal Child Care Program." NBER Working Paper no. W21571.

Bakvis, Herman. 2014. *Changing Intergovernmental Governance in Canada in the Era of "Open Federalism."* Paper presented at the conference on *Variety and Dynamics of Multilevel Governance in Canada and Europe*, Darmstadt, Germany (12–13 June).

Ball, Stephen J., and Carol Vincent. 2005. "The 'Childcare Champion'? New Labour, Social Justice, and the Childcare Market." *British Educational Research Journal* 31(5): 557–70. http://dx.doi. org/10.1080/01411920500240700.

Banchoff, Thomas. 2005. "Path Dependence and Value-Driven Issues: The Comparative Politics of Stem Cell Research." *World Politics* 57(2): 200–30. http://dx.doi.org/10.1353/wp.2005.0014.

Banks, Gabrielle. 2004. "Use of Prop. 10 Funds Faulted." *Los Angeles Times*, 16 July.

Barnett, Michael, and Martha Finnemore. 2004. *Rules for the World: International Organizations in Global Politics*. Ithaca: Cornell University Press.

Barnett, Steven W. 1983. *The Perry Preschool Program and Its Long-Term Effects: A Benefit–Cost Analysis*. Ypsilanti: High/Scope Educational Research Foundation.

– . 1992. "Benefits of Compensatory Preschool Education." *Journal of Human Resources* 27(2): 279–312. http://dx.doi.org/10.2307/145736.

– . 1993. "Benefit–Cost Analysis of Preschool Education: Findings from a 25-Year Follow-Up." *American Journal of Orthopsychiatry* 63(4): 500–8. http://dx.doi.org/10.1037/h0079481.

– . 1995. "Long-Term Effects of Early Childhood Programs on Cognitive and School Outcomes." *Future of Children* 5(3): 25–50. http://dx.doi.org/10.2307/1602366.

– . 1996. *Lives in the Balance: Age–27 Benefit–Cost Analysis of the High/Scope Perry Preschool Program*. Ypsilanti: High/Scope Educational Research Foundation.

Barnett, W. Steven, Megan E. Carolan, Jen Fitzgerald, and James H. Squires. 2011. *The State of Preschool 2011: State Preschool Yearbook*. New Brunswick: National Institute for Early Education Research.

Barnett, W. Steven, Megan E. Carolan, James H. Squires, and Kristy Clarke Brown. 2013. *The State of Preschool 2013: State Preschool Yearbook*. New Brunswick: National Institute for Early Education Research.

Barnett, W. Steven, Allison H. Friedman-Krauss, Rebecca E. Gomez, Michelle Horowitz, G.G. Weisenfeld, Kirsty Clarke Brown, and James H. Squires. 2016. *The State of Preschool 2015: State Preschool Yearbook*. New Brunswick: National Institute for Early Education Research.

Barnett, W. Steven, and Donald J. Yarosz. 2007. "Who Goes to Preschool and Why Does It Matter?" In *Preschool Policy Brief, no. 15*. New Brunswick: NIEER, Rutgers University.

Battle, Ken. 2006. *The Choice in Child Care Allowance: What You See Is Not What You Get*. Ottawa: Caledon Institute of Social Policy.

Baumgartner, Frank, and Bryan D. Jones. 1993. *Agendas and Instability in American Politics*. Chicago: University of Chicago Press.

Baum, Charles L., II. 2003. "Does Early Maternal Employment Harm Child Development? An Analysis of the Potential Benefits of Leave Taking." *Journal of Labor Economics* 21(2): 409–48. http://dx.doi.org/10.1086/345563.

Beach, Jane, Martha Friendly, Carolyn Ferns, Nina Prabhu, and Barry Forer. 2009. *Early Childhood Education and Care in Canada 2008*. Toronto: CRRU.

Beatty, Barbara. 1995. *Preschool Education in America: The Culture of Young Children from the Colonial Era to the Present*. New Haven: Yale University Press.

Begley, Sharon. 1996. "Your Child's Brain." *Newsweek*, 19 February, 54ff.

Béland, Daniel, Philip Rocco, and Alex Wadden. 2016. *Obamacare Wares: Federalism, State Politics, and the Affordable Care Act*. Lawrence: University Press of Kansas.

Belfield, Clive R., Milagros Nores, Steve Barnett, and Lawrence Schweinhart. 2006. "The High/Scope Perry Preschool Program: Cost–Benefit Analysis Using Data from the Age-40 Follow Up." *Journal of Human Resources* XLI(1): 162–90. http://dx.doi.org/10.3368/jhr.XLI.1.162.

Bellamy, Carol, and UNICEF. 2001. *The State of the World's Children 2001: Early Childhood*. New York: United Nations Children's Fund.

Belsky, Jay. 1986. "Infant Day Care: A Cause for Concern?" *Zero to Three* 6: 1–9.

– . 1987. "Risks Remain." *Bulletin of the National Center for Clinical Infant Programs* 7(3): 22–4.

– . 1988. "The Effects of Infant Day Care Reconsidered." *Early Childhood Research Quarterly* 3(3): 235–72. http://dx.doi.org/10.1016/0885-2006(88)90003-8.

Belsky, Jay, Deborah Lowe Vandell, Margaret Burchinal, K. Alison Clarke-Stewart, Kathleen McCartney, and Margaret Tresch Owen (NICHD). 2007. "Are There Long-Term Effects of Early Child Care?" *Child Development* 78(2): 681–701. http://dx.doi.org/10.1111/j.1467-8624.2007.01021.x.

Belsky, Jay, and David Eggebeen. 1991. "Early and Extensive Maternal Employment and Young Children's Social and Emotional Development: Children of the National Longitudinal Survey of Youth." *Journal of Marriage and the Family* 53(4): 1083–110. http://dx.doi.org/10.2307/353011.

Belsky, Jay, and Michael Rovine. 1988. "Nonmaternal Care in the First Year of Life and the Security of Infant–Parent Attachment." *Child Development* 59(1): 157–67. http://dx.doi.org/10.2307/1130397.

Benavot, Aaron, Yun-Kyung Cha, David Kamens, John W. Meyer, and Suk-Ying Wong. 1991. "Knowledge for the Masses: World Models and National Curricula, 1920–1986." *American Sociological Review* 56(1): 85–100. http://dx.doi.org/10.2307/2095675.

Benavot, Aaron, and Phyllis Riddle. 1988. "The Expansion of Primary Education, 1870–1940: Trends and Issues." *Sociology of Education* 61(3): 191–210. http://dx.doi.org/10.2307/2112627.

Benford, Robert D. 1997. "An Insider's Critique of the Social Movement Framing Perspective." *Sociological Inquiry* 67(4): 409–30. http://dx.doi.org/10.1111/j.1475-682X.1997.tb00445.x.

Bennett, John. 2003. "Starting Strong: The Persistent Division between Care and Education." *Journal of Early Childhood Research* 1(1): 21–48. http://dx.doi.org/10.1177/1476718X030011006.

– . 2005. "Curriculum Issues in National Policy-Making." *European Early Childhood Education Research Journal* 13(2): 5–23. http://dx.doi.org/10.1080/13502930585209641.

–. 2008. "Early Childhood Education and Care Systems: Issue of Tradition and Governance." In *Encyclopedia on Early Childhood Development* [online], ed. R.E. Tremblay, M. Boivin, R. DeV. Peters, and R.G. Barr, 1–5. Montreal: Centre of Excellence for Early Childhood Development. http://www.child-encyclopedia.com/documents/BennettANGxp2.pdf.

Benton Foundation. 1998. *Effective Language for Discussing Early Childhood Education and Policy*. Washington, DC: Benton Foundation and Human Services Policy Center, University of Washington.

Berger, Lawrence M., Jennifer Hill, and Jane Waldfogel. 2005. "Maternity Leave, Early Maternal Employment, and Child Health and Development in the US." *Economic Journal* 115(501): F29–47. http://dx.doi.org/10.1111/j.0013-0133.2005.00971.x.

Berkeley Media Studies Group. 2004. *Making the Case for Early Care and Education: A Message Development Guide for Advocates*. Berkeley: Berkeley Media Studies Group.

Berkman, Michael, and Eric Plutzer. 2010. *Evolution, Creationism, and the Battle to Control America's Classrooms*. New York: Cambridge University Press. http://dx.doi.org/10.1017/CBO9780511760914.

Bernstein, Steven F. 2001. *The Compromise of Liberal Environmentalism*. New York: Columbia University Press. http://dx.doi.org/10.7312/bern12036.

Berry, Frances Stokes, and William D. Berry. 1999. "Innovation and Diffusion Models in Policy Research." In *Theories of the Policy Process*, ed. P.A. Sabatier, 169–200. Boulder: Westview Press.

Berry, Mary Frances. 1993. *The Politics of Parenthood: Child Care, Women's Rights, and the Myth of the Good Mother*. New York: Viking Penguin.

Besharov, Douglas. 1988. "The Politics of Day Care: We're About to Spend Billions on a Dubious Middle-Class 'Crisis.'" *Washington Post*, 21 August. http://www.welfareacademy.org/pubs/childcare_edu/daycare-0888.shtml.

– . 2005. *Head Start's Broken Promise*. Washington, DC: American Enterprise Institute for Public Policy Research.

Bieber, Tonia, and Kerstin Martens. 2011. "The OECD PISA Study as a Soft Power in Education? Lessons from Switzerland and the US." *European Journal of Education* 46(1): 101–16. http://dx.doi.org/10.1111/j.1465-3435.2010.01462.x.

Blau, David. 1999. "The Effect of Income on Child Development." *Review of Economics and Statistics* 81(2): 261–76. http://dx.doi.org/10.1162/003465399558067.

Blood, Margaret. 2000. *Our Youngest Children: Massachusetts Voters and Opinion Leaders Speak Out on Their Care and Education. A Report on Findings from Strategies for Children.* Boston: Stride Rite Foundation.

Bloom, Benjamin S. 1964. *Stability and Change in Human Characteristics.* New York: Wiley.

Blow, Charles. 2014. "Michael Brown and Black Men." *New York Times*, 13 August.

Blyth, Mark. 2001. "The Transformation of the Swedish Model: Economic Ideas, Distributional Conflict, and Institutional Change." *World Politics* 54(1): 1–26. http://dx.doi.org/10.1353/wp.2001.0020.

– . 2002. *Great Transformations: Economic Ideas and Institutional Change in the Twentieth Century.* New York: Cambridge University Press. http://dx.doi.org/10.1017/CBO9781139087230.

Bock, Gisela, and Pat Thane, eds. 1991. *Maternity and Gender Policies: Women and the Rise of the European Welfare States, 1880s–1950s.* New York: Routledge.

Boli, John, and George M. Thomas, eds. 1999. *Constructing World Culture: International Nongovernmental Organizations since 1875.* Stanford: Stanford University Press.

Bonoli, Giuliano, and Frank Reber. 2010. "The Political Economy of Childcare in OECD Countries: Explaining Cross-National Variation in Spending and Coverage Rates." *European Journal of Political Research* 49(1): 97–118. http://dx.doi.org/10.1111/j.1475-6765.2009.01884.x.

Borges Sugiyama, Natasha. 2008. "Theories of Policy Diffusion: Social Sector Reform in Brazil." *Comparative Political Studies* 41(2): 193–216. http://dx.doi.org/10.1177/0010414007300916.

Boushey, Graeme. 2010. *Policy Diffusion Dynamics in America.* New York: Cambridge University Press.

Bowlby, John. 1952. *Maternal Care and Mental Health.* Geneva: World Health Organization.

Bowles, Samuel, Herbert Gintis, and Melissa Osborne Groves, eds. 2005. *Unequal Chances: Family Background and Economic Success.* Princeton: Princeton University Press.

Bowman, Barbara T., M. Suzanne Donovan, and M. Susan Burns, eds. 2001. *Eager to Learn: Educating Our Preschoolers*. Washington, DC: National Academy Press.

Boylan, Ellen. 2007. "High Quality Pre-Kindergarten as the First Step in Educational Adequacy: Using the Courts to Expand Access to State Pre-K Programs." *Children's Legal Rights Journal* 27(1): 34–55.

Braun, Virginia, and Victoria Clarke. 2006. "Using Thematic Analysis in Psychology." *Qualitative Research in Psychology* 3(2): 77–101. http://dx.doi.org/10.1191/1478088706qp063oa.

Breakspear, Simon. 2012. "The Policy Impact of PISA: An Exploration of the Normative Effects of International Benchmarking in School System Performance." OECD Education Working Papers no. 71. Paris.

Brennan, Deborah. 1998. *The Politics of Australian Child Care: Philanthropy to Feminism and Beyond*. New York: Cambridge University Press. http://dx.doi.org/10.1017/CBO9780511597091.

– . 2004. "Child Care and Australian Social Policy." In *Children, Families, and Communities: Contexts and Consequences*. 2nd ed. Ed. Jennifer M. Bowes, 210–27. Melbourne: Oxford University Press.

– . 2007a. "The ABC of Childcare Politics." *Australian Journal of Social Issues* 42(2): 213–25.

– . 2007b. "Babies, Budgets, and Birthrates: Work/Family Policy in Australia 1996–2006." *Social Politics* 14(1): 31–57. http://dx.doi.org/10.1093/sp/jxm003.

Brennan, Timothy. 2006. *Wars of Position: The Cultural Politics of Left and Right*. New York: Columbia University Press. http://dx.doi.org/10.7312/bren13730.

Brinks, Daniel, and Michael Coppedge. 2006. "Diffusion Is No Illusion: Neighbor Emulation in the Third Wave of Democracy." *Comparative Political Studies* 39(4): 463–89. http://dx.doi.org/10.1177/0010414005276666.

Bronfenbrenner, Urie. 1992. "Child Care in the Anglo-Saxon Mode." In *Child Care in Context*, ed. Michael E. Lamb, Kathleen J. Sternberg, Carl-Philip Hwang, and Anders Broberg, 281–91. Hillsdale: Lawrence Erlbaum Associates.

Brooks, David. 2008. "Fresh Start Conservatism." *New York Times*, 15 February.

Brooks, Sarah M. 2005. "Interdependent and Domestic Foundations of Policy Change: The Diffusion of Pension Privatization around the World." *International Studies Quarterly* 49(2): 273–94. http://dx.doi.org/10.1111/j.0020-8833.2005.00345.x.

Brooks-Gunn, Jeanne, Han Wen-Jui, and Jane Waldfogel. 2010. "First-Year Maternal Employment and Child Development in the First Seven Years." *Monographs of the Society for Research in Child Development* 75(2): 7–9.

Broomhill, Ray, and Rhonda Sharp. 2012. *Australia's Parental Leave Policy and Gender Equality: An International Comparison*. Adelaide: Australian Workplace Innovation and Social Research Centre.

Bruer, John T. 1997. "Education and the Brain: A Bridge Too Far." *Educational Researcher* 26(8): 4–16. http://dx.doi.org/10.3102/0013189X026008004.

– . 1998. "The Brain and Child Development: Time for Some Critical Thinking." *Public Health Reports* 113(5): 388–97.

– . 1999. *The Myth of the First Three Years: A New Understanding of Early Brain Development and Lifelong Learning*. New York: The Free Press.

Busch, Per-Olof, Helge Jörgens, and Kerstin Tews. 2005. "The Global Diffusion of Regulatory Instruments: The Making of a New International Environmental Regime." *Annals of the American Academy of Political and Social Science* 598(1): 146–67. http://dx.doi.org/10.1177/0002716204272355.

Busemeyer, Marius R. 2007. "Determinants of Public Education Spending in 21 OECD Democracies, 1980–2001." *Journal of European Public Policy* 14(4): 582–610. http://dx.doi.org/10.1080/13501760701314417.

Bushouse, Brenda. 2007. "Universal Preschool Policy Change in the Pioneer States." Paper presented at the Annual Meeting of the American Political Science Association, 30 August–2 September 2007, Chicago, IL.

–. 2009. *Universal Preschool: Policy Change, Stability, and the Pew Charitable Trusts*. New York: SUNY Press.

Byers, William. 2011. *The Blind Spot: Science and the Crisis of Uncertainty*. Princeton: Princeton University Press. http://dx.doi.org/10.1515/9781400838158.

Campbell, Frances A., Elizabeth P. Pungello, Margaret Burchinal, Kirsten Kainz, Yi Pan, Barbara H. Wasik, Oscar A. Barbarin, Joseph J. Sparling, and Craig T. Ramey. 2012. "Adult Outcomes as a Function of an Early Childhood Educational Program: An Abecedarian Project Follow-up." *Developmental Psychology* 48(4): 1033–43. http://dx.doi.org/10.1037/a0026644.

Campbell, Frances A., and Craig T. Ramey. 1994. "Effects of Early Intervention on Intellectual and Academic Achievement: A Follow-up Study of Children from Low-Income Families." *Child Development* 65(2): 684–98. http://dx.doi.org/10.2307/1131410.

Campbell, Frances A., Craig T. Ramey, Elizabeth Pungello, Joseph Sparling, and Shari Miller-Johnson. 2002. "Early Childhood Education: Young Adult Outcomes from the Abecedarian Project." *Applied Developmental Science* 6(1): 42–57. http://dx.doi.org/10.1207/S1532480XADS0601_05.

Campbell, John L. 2001. "Institutional Analysis and the Role of Ideas in Political Economy." In *The Rise of Neoliberalism and Institutional Analysis*, ed. John L. Campbell and Ove Pedersen, 159–89. Princeton: Princeton University Press.

Campbell, John L., and Ove K. Pedersen. 2001. "Introduction." In *The Rise of Neoliberalism and Institutional Analysis*, ed. John L. Campbell and Ove Pedersen, 1–23. Princeton: Princeton University Press.

– . 2011. "Knowledge Regimes and Comparative Political Economy." In *Ideas and Politics in Social Science Research*, ed. Daniel Béland and Robert Henry Cox, 167–90. New York: Oxford University Press.

Canada, Department of Finance. 2006. *The Budget Plan 2006: Focusing on Priorities: Canada's New Government Turning a New Leaf*. Ottawa.

– . 2007. *The Budget Plan 2007: Aspire to a Stronger, Safer, Better Canada*. Ottawa.

Canada, House of Commons. 1988. Bill C-144. An Act to authorize payments by Canada toward the provision of child care services, and to amend the Canada Assistance Plan in consequence thereof. Second Session, Thirty-Third Parliament. Ottawa.

– . 1996. Speech from the Throne to Open the Second Session, Thirty-Fifth Parliament of Canada. *Debates of the House of Commons of Canada* (Hansard), 27 February. http://www.pco-bcp.gc.ca/index.asp?lang=eng&page=inform ation&sub=publications&doc=aarchives/sft-ddt/1996-eng.htm.

– . 2006. Speech from the Throne to Open the First Session, Thirty-Ninth Parliament of Canada. *Debates of the House of Commons of Canada* (Hansard), 4 April. http://www.pco-bcp.gc.ca/index.asp?lang=eng&page=information &sub=publications&doc=aarchives/sft-ddt/2006-eng.htm.

– . 2007. Speech from the Throne to Open the Second Session, Thirty-Ninth Parliament of Canada. *Debates of the House of Commons of Canada* (Hansard), 16 October. http://www.lop.parl.gc.ca/ParlInfo/Documents/ ThroneSpeech/39-2-e.html.

Canada NewsWire. 2006. "International Report Condemns Tory Approach to Child Care." 20 September: 1.

Canada, Royal Commission on the Status of Women. 1970. *Final Report*. Ottawa.

Canadian Press. 2012. "Schools Need Bigger Class Sizes, Austerity Report Says." 15 February. http://www.cbc.ca/news/canada/toronto/schools-need-bigger-class-sizes-austerity-report-says-1.1241158 .

– . 2013. "Tories Would Freeze Full-day Kindergarten Expansion to Help Fund Public Transit." 19 December. http://globalnews.ca/news/1041099/tories-would-delay-full-day-kindergarten-to-help-fund-public-transit.

Capizzano, Jeffrey, and Gina Adams. 2000. "The Hours That Children under Five Spend in Child Care: Variation across States." In *Series to Assess Changing Social Policies no. B-8, March*. Washington, DC: Urban Institute: 1–11.

Capuano, France, Marc Bigras, and Christa Japel. 2014. "Kindergarten for Four-Year-Olds: A Measure to Promote School and Social Success in Children from Disadvantaged Backgrounds." In *Encyclopedia on Early Childhood Development*, ed. Richard Tremblay, Michel Boivin, and Ray DeV. Peters, 1–5. Montreal: Centre of Excellence for Early Childhood Development and Strategic Knowledge Cluster on Early Child Development.

Carnegie Corporation of New York. 1994. *Starting Points: Meeting the Needs of Our Youngest Children*. New York.

– . 1996. *Years of Promise: A Comprehensive Learning Strategy for America's Children*. New York.

Carneiro, Pedro, and James J. Heckman. 2003. "Human Capital Policy." In *Inequality in America: What Role for Human Capital Policies*, ed. James Heckman and Alan B. Kruger, 77–239. Cambridge, MA: MIT Press.

Cascio, Elizabeth U. 2009. *Do Investments in Universal Early Education Pay Off? Long-term Effects of Introducing Kindergartens in Public Schools*. NBER Working Paper no. 14951. http://www.nber.org/papers/w14951.pdf.

Castles, Francis. 1989. "Explaining Public Education Expenditure in OECD Nations." *European Journal of Political Research* 17(4): 431–48. http://dx.doi.org/10.1111/j.1475-6765.1989.tb00202.x.

– . 1994. "On Religion and Public Policy: Does Catholicism Make a Difference?" *European Journal of Political Research* 25(1): 19–40. http://dx.doi.org/10.1111/j.1475-6765.1994.tb01199.x.

Cato Institute. 2017. "Early Childhood." Washington, DC. https://www.cato.org/research/early-childhood.

CCAAC (Child Care Advocacy Association of Canada). 2005. "Conservative Taxable Allowance Won't Deliver Quality Child Care." 5 December. https://ccaacacpsge.files.wordpress.com/2014/10/contax.pdf.

Celock, John. 2012. "Bob Kingsbury, New Hampshire Legislator, Explains Remarks Linking Kindergarten To Higher Crime." *Huffington Post*, 3 July. http://www.huffingtonpost.com/2012/07/03/bob-kingsbury-new-hampshire-legislator-kindergarten-crime_n_1646369.html.

CGECCD (Consultative Group on Early Childhood Care and Development). n.d. "Origins of the Consultative Group on ECCD." http://www.ecdgroup.com/cg-eccd-history/.

Chamberlain, Alexander F. 1900. *The Child: A Study in the Evolution of Man*. New York: Scribner. http://dx.doi.org/10.1037/13296-000.

Chandler, Michael Alison. 2014. "Finland Working to Expand Early Education." *Washington Post*, 4 March. https://www.washingtonpost.com/local/education/finland-working-to-expand-early-

education/2014/03/04/571aacf8-a3ba-11e3-8466-d34c451760b9_story.
html?utm_term=.4348f878a676.

Child Care Advocacy Association of Canada. 2007. *Priority for Prosperity:
Replace Patchwork and Wishful Thinking with Focused Public Investment in Child
Care. Summary of the CCAAC's 2008 Federal Budget Consultation.* Ottawa.

Children's Defense Fund. 2014. "The Facts about Full-Day Kindergarten."
http://www.childrensdefense.org/child-research-data-publications/data/
the-facts-about-full-day.pdf.

Chong, Dennis, and James N. Druckman. 2007. "Framing Theory." *Annual
Review of Political Science* 10(1): 103–26. http://dx.doi.org/10.1146/annurev.
polisci.10.072805.103054.

CICS (Canadian Intergovernmental Conference Secretariat). 2000. *First
Ministers' Meeting Communiqué on Early Childhood Development.* Ref.
800–038/005. 11 September. http://www/scics.ca/en/product-produit/
news-release-first-ministers-meeting-communique-on-early-childhood-
development/.

–. 2003. *Multilateral Framework on Early Learning and Child Care.* Ref. 830–
779/005. 13 March. http://www.scics.ca/en/product-produit/framework-
multilateral-framework-on-early-learning-and-child-care/.

Cleveland, Gordon A., and Douglas E. Hyatt. 1997. *Subsidies to Consumers or
Subsidies to Providers: How Should Governments Provide Child Care Assistance?*
R-97–7E. Ottawa: Applied Research Branch of Strategic Policy, Human
Resources Development Canada.

Coalition for America's Children / Benton Foundation. 1999. *Effective
Language for Communicating Children's Issues.* Washington, DC.

Coffey, Charles. 2003. *Never Too Early to Invest in Children: Early Childhood
Education and Care Matters to Business! Report.* Toronto: Voices for Children.

Coffey, Charles, and Margaret McCain. 2002. *Commission on Early Learning and
Child Care for the City of Toronto: Final Report.* Toronto: City of Toronto.

Cohen, Bronwen, Peter Moss, Pat Petrie, and Jennifer Wallace. 2004. *A New
Deal for Children? Reforming Education and Care in England, Scotland and
Sweden.* Bristol: Policy Press.

Cohen, Sally S. 2001. *Championing Child Care.* New York: Columbia University
Press. http://dx.doi.org/10.7312/cohe11236.

Coleman, William D., and Grace Skogstad, eds. 1990. *Policy Communities and
Public Policy in Canada.* Toronto: Copp Clark Pitman.

Colley, Sue. 2005. *Integration for a Change: How Can Integration of Services
for Kindergarten-Aged Children Be Achieved?* Integration Network Project
Discussion Paper. Toronto: Institute of Child Study, OISE / University of
Toronto.

Collier, David, and Richard E. Messick. 1975. "Prerequisites versus Diffusion: Testing Alternative Explanations of Social Security Adoption." *American Political Science Review* 69(4): 1299–315. http://dx.doi.org/10.2307/1955290.

Committee for Economic Development. 1985. *Investing in Our Children: Business and the Public Schools: A Statement.* New York.

– . 1987. *Children in Need: Investment Strategies for the Educationally Disadvantaged.* New York.

– . 2002. *Preschool for All: Investing in a Productive and Just Society.* New York.

Committee on Evaluation of Children's Health, Board on Children, Youth, and Families, Division of Behavioral and Social Sciences and Education, National Research Council, and Institute of Medicine of the National Academies. 2004. *Children's Health, the Nation's Wealth: Assessing and Improving Child Health.* Washington, DC: National Academies Press.

Connor, Sarah, and Satya Brink. 1999a. *The Impacts of Non-Parental Care on Child Development.* W-00–2E. Ottawa: Applied Research Branch of Strategic Policy, Human Resources Development Canada.

– . 1996b. *Understanding the Early Years: Community Impacts on Child Development.* W-99-6E. Ottawa: Applied Research Branch of Strategic Policy, Human Resources Development Canada.

Conservative Party of Canada. 2004. *Demanding Better. Federal Election Platform, 2004.* Ottawa.

– . 2006. *Stand Up for Canada: Federal Election Platform, 2006.* Ottawa.

Consortium for Developmental Continuity. 1977. *The Persistence of Pre-School Effects.* Washington, DC: Department of Health, Education, and Welfare.

Consortium for Longitudinal Studies. 1978. *Lasting Effects after Preschool.* Washington, DC: Department of Health, Education, and Welfare.

– . 1983. *As the Twig Is Bent: Lasting Effects of Preschool Programs.* Hillsdale: Lawrence Erlbaum Associates.

Convention on the Elimination of All Forms of Discrimination against Women, G.A. res. 34/180, 34 U.N. GAOR Supp. (No. 46) at 193, U.N. Doc. A/34/46, entered into force 3 September 1981.

Convention on the Rights of the Child. Adopted and opened for signature, ratification, and accession by General Assembly resolution 44/25 of 20 November 1989; entry into force 2 September 1990, in accordance with Article 49.

Cortell, Andrew P., and James W. Davis, Jr. 1996. "How Do International Institutions Matter? The Domestic Impact of International Rules and Norms." *International Studies Quarterly* 40(4): 451–78. http://dx.doi.org/10.2307/2600887.

– . 2000. "Understanding the Domestic Impact of International Norms: A Research Agenda." *International Studies Review* 2(1): 65–87. http://dx.doi.org/10.1111/1521-9488.00184.

Coulombe, Serge. 2007. "Smart Human Capital Policy: An Alternative Perspective." In *A Canadian Priorities Agenda: Policy Choices to Improve Economic and Social Well-Being*, ed. Jeremy Leonard, Christopher Ragan, and France St-Hilaire, 57–65. Montreal: Institute for Research on Public Policy.

Coulson, Andrew J. 2010. "Head Start: A Tragic Waste of Money." *New York Post*, 28 January.

Council of Ministers of Education. Canada. 2007. *Report of the Canadian Delegation*. Fifth Meeting of Ministers of Education of the Americas, Cartagena, Colombia, 14–16 November.

Cova, Anne. 1991. "French Feminism and Maternity: Theories and Policies 1890––1918." In *Maternity and Gender Politics: Women and the Rise of the European Welfare States, 1880s–1950s*, ed. Gisela Bock and Pat Thane, 119–37. London: Routledge.

CPRN (Canadian Policy Research Networks). 2009. *Farewell: Annual Report 2008–2009*. Ottawa.

Crane, David. 2006. "Canada Lagging on Early Childhood Education." *Toronto Star*, 24 September, A2.

Cravens, Hamilton. 2002. *Before Head Start: The Iowa Station and America's Children*. Chapel Hill: University of North Carolina Press.

Crittenden, Ann. 1984. "A Head Start Pays Off in the End." *Wall Street Journal*, 29 November, 1.

Cunha, Flavio, and James J. Heckman. 2007. "The Technology of Skill Formation." *American Economic Review* 97(2): 31–47. http://dx.doi.org/10.1257/aer.97.2.31.

Cuthbertson, Richard. 2013. "Promise of All-day Kindergarten Pushed Back: Timeline for 50 New Schools Also Delayed by 'Bleak' Fiscal Outlook." *Calgary Herald*, 24 January. http://www.calgaryherald.com/news/Promise+kindergarten+pushed+back/7863279/story.html.

Darlington, Richard, Jacqueline Royce, Ann Snipper, Harry Murray, and Irving Lazar. 1980. "Pre-School Programs and Later School Competence of Children from Low-Income Families." *Science* 208(4440): 202–4. http://dx.doi.org/10.1126/science.208.4440.202.

Davis, Martha F. 2005. "Child Care as a Human Right: A New Perspective on an Old Debate." *Journal of Women, Politics & Policy* 27(1–2): 173–9. http://dx.doi.org/10.1300/J501v27n01_11.

Davison Hunter, James. 1991. *Culture Wars: The Struggle to Define America*. New York: Basic Books.

Dearing, Eric, Kathleen McCartney, and Beck A. Taylor. 2009. "Does Higher Quality Early Child Care Promote Low-Income Children's Math and Reading Achievement in Middle Childhood?" *Child Development* 80(5): 1329–49. http://dx.doi.org/10.1111/j.1467-8624.2009.01336.x.

DeBray-Pelot, Elizabeth, and Patrick McGuinn. 2009. "The New Politics of Education: Analyzing the Federal Education Policy Landscape in the Post-NCLB Era." *Educational Policy* 23(1): 15–42. http://dx.doi.org/10.1177/0895904808328524.

Delacourt, Susan. 2003. *Juggernaut: Paul Martin's Campaign for Chrétien's Crown.* Toronto: McClelland and Stewart.

Department of Finance Canada. 2007. *Aspire to a Stronger, Safer, Better Canada: Budget Plan 2007.* Ottawa. http://www.budget.gc.ca/2007/plan/bpa5a-eng.html#spaces.

DfE (Department for Education). 2011. *Provision for Children under Five Years of Age in England: January 20110.* Statistical First Release. SFR 13/2011. London.

DfEE (Department of Education and Employment, UK). 1998. *Meeting the Childcare Challenge.* London: HMSO.

– . 2000. Curriculum Guidance for the Foundation Stage. London: Qualifications and Curriculum Authority.

Diamond, Sarah. 1995. *Roads to Dominion: Right-Wing Movements and Political Power in the United States.* New York: Guilford Press.

DiCamillo, Mark, and Mervin Field. 2006a. "Feinstein Well Ahead of Mountjoy in US Senate Race. Initial Support for Prop. 82, the Pre-school Initiative." *Field Research Corporation.* Release #2184, 7 March.

– . 2006b. "Prop. 82 (Pre-School Education) Leads but by a Smaller Margin than Two Months Ago. Feinstein Running Comfortably Ahead in US Senate Race." *Field Research Corporation.* Release #2196, 19 April.

– . 2006c. "Voters Moving to the No Side on Prop. 82 (Pre-school Education). Speier Pulls Ahead of Garamendi in Democratic Primary for Lt. Governor." *Field Research Corporation.* Release #2199, 3 June.

DiChiara, Albert, and John F. Galliher. 1994. "Dissonance and Contradictions in the Origins of Marihuana Decriminalization." *Law & Society Review* 28(1): 41–77. http://dx.doi.org/10.2307/3054137.

Dion, Michelle. 2008. "International Organizations and Social Insurance in Mexico." *Global Social Policy* 8(1): 25–44. http://dx.doi.org/10.1177/1468018107086086.

Dobbin, Frank, Beth Simmons, and Geoffrey Garrett. 2007. "The Global Diffusion of Public Policies: Social Construction, Coercion, Competition, or Learning?" *Annual Review of Sociology* 33(1): 449–72. http://dx.doi.org/10.1146/annurev.soc.33.090106.142507.

Dobrowolsky, Alexandra, and Jane Jenson. 2004. "Shifting Representations of Citizenship: Canadian Politics of 'Women' and 'Children.'" *Social Politics* 11(2): 154–80. http://dx.doi.org/10.1093/sp/jxh031.

Dodd, Lawrence C. 1994. "Political Learning and Political Change: Understanding Development across Time." In *The Dynamics of American Politics: Approaches and Interpretations*, ed. Lawrence C. Dodd and Calvin Jillson, 331–64. Boulder: Westview Press.

Dodge, David. 2003. *Human Capital, Early Childhood Development, and Economic Growth: An Economist's Perspective*. Speech at the 14th annual meeting of the Sparrow Lake Alliance, Bayview-Wildwood Resort, Ontario.

Doherty, Gillian. 1997. *Zero to Six: The Basis for School Readiness*. SP-241-02-01E. Ottawa: Applied Research Branch of Strategic Policy, Human Resources Development Canada.

Doherty, Gillian. 2007. "Ensuring the Best Start in Life: Targeting versus Universality in Early Childhood Development." *IRPP Choices* 13(8): 1–50.

Doherty, Gillian, Martha Friendly, and Jane Beach. 2003. *OECD Thematic Review of Early Childhood Education and Care: Canadian Background Report*. Ottawa: Government of Canada.

Dolowitz, David P., and David Marsh. 2000. "Learning from Abroad: The Role of Policy Transfer in Contemporary Policy-Making." *Governance: An International Journal of Policy, Administration, and Institutions* 13(1): 5–23. http://dx.doi.org/10.1111/0952-1895.00121.

Dorfman, Lori, and Katie Woodruff. 1999. *"Child Care Coverage in U.S. Newspapers."* Berkeley: Berkeley Media Studies Group.

Dougherty, Kevin. 2013. "Quebec to Introduce Kindergarten for Disadvantaged 4-Year-Olds." *Gazette* (Montreal), 15 March.

Dowling, Andrew, and Kate O'Malley. 2009. "Preschool Education in Australia." December. http://research.acer.edu.au/cgi/viewcontent.cgi?article=1000&context=policy_briefs.

Drapcho, Adam. 2012. "Kingsbury Tells Fellow Reps There's Link between Kindergarten and Crime." *Laconia Daily Sun*, 9 June.

Drezner, Daniel W. 2005. "Globalization, Harmonization, and Competition: The Different Pathways to Policy Convergence." *Journal of European Public Policy* 12(5): 841–59. http://dx.doi.org/10.1080/13501760500161472.

Drori, Gili S., John W. Meyer, Francisco O. Ramirez, and Even Schofer. 2003. *Science in the Modern World Polity: Institutionalization and Globalization*. Stanford: Stanford University Press.

Druckman, James. 2010. "What's It All About? Framing in Political Science." In *Perspectives on Framing*, ed. Gideon Keren, 279–302. New York: Psychology Press / Taylor and Francis.

Dryzek, John S. 1992. "How Far Is It from Virginia and Rochester to Frankfurt? Public Choice as Critical Theory." *British Journal of Political Science* 22(4): 397–417. http://dx.doi.org/10.1017/S00071234 00006463.

Duchen, Claire. 1986. *Feminism in France: From May '68 to Mitterrand*. London: Routledge and Kegan Paul.

Early Child Care Research Network, National Institute of Child Health, and the NICHD Early Child Care Research Network. 2003. "Does Amount of Time Spent in Child Care Predict Socioemotional Adjustment during the Transition to Kindergarten?" *Child Development* 74(4): 976–1005. http:// dx.doi.org/10.1111/1467-8624.00582.

Early Childhood Australia. 2011. *Our Future on the Line: Keeping the Early Childhood Education and Care Reforms on Track. A State of the Sector Report*. library.bsl.org. au/jspui/bitstream/1/2402/1/Our%20future%20on%20the%20line.pdf.

Education Justice. 2014. "Wyoming." http://www.educationjustice.org/ states/wyoming.html.

Educational Testing Service Statistics and Research Division, Policy Information Center. 2002. *An Uneven Start: Indicators of Inequality in School Readiness*. Princeton: Educational Testing Service.

Edwards, Carolyn, Lella Gandini, and George Forman, eds. 2012. *The Hundred Languages of Children: The Reggio Emilia Experience in Transformation*. 3rd ed. Santa Barbrara: Praeger.

Emmenegger, Patrick, Silja Häusermann, Bruno Palier, and Martin Seelieb-Kaiser, eds. 2012. *The Age of Dualization: The Changing Face of Inequality in Deindustrializing Societies*. New York: Oxford University Press. http:// dx.doi.org/10.1093/acprof:oso/9780199797899.001.0001.

England, Kim, ed. 1996. *Who Will Mind the Baby? Geographies of Child Care and Working Mothers*. New York: Routledge.

Entman, Robert M. 1993. "Framing: Toward Clarification of a Fractured Paradigm." *Journal of Communication* 43(4): 51–8. http://dx.doi.org/ 10.1111/j.1460-2466.1993.tb01304.x.

Environics Research Group. 2006. *Canadians' Attitudes toward National Child Care Policy*. Ottawa: Environics Research Group for the Child Care Advocacy Association of Canada.

Ertl, Hubert. 2006. "Educational Standards and the Changing Discourse on Education: The Reception and Consequences of the PISA Study in Germany." *Oxford Review of Education* 32(5): 619–34. http://dx.doi.org/ 10.1080/03054980600976320.

Espey and Good Company. 2003. *Perceptions of Quality Child Care Final Report*. Toronto.

Esping-Andersen, Gosta. 1990. *The Three Worlds of Welfare Capitalism.* Princeton: Princeton University Press.

– . 1999. *Social Foundations of Postindustrial Economies.* Oxford: Oxford University Press. http://dx.doi.org/10.1093/0198742002.001.0001.

– . 2002. "A Child-Centred Social Investment Strategy." In *Why We Need a New Welfare State,* ed. Gosta Esping-Andersen with Duncan Gallie, Anton Hemerijck, and John Myles, 26–67. Oxford: Oxford University Press. http://dx.doi.org/10.1093/0199256438.003.0002.

Esping-Andersen, Gosta, with Duncan Gaillie, Anton Hemerijck, and John Myles, eds. 2002. *Why We Need a New Welfare State.* Oxford: Oxford University Press. http://dx.doi.org/10.1093/0199256438.001.0001.

European Commission. 2006. *A Roadmap for Equality between Men and Women: 2006–2010.* Luxembourg: Office for Official Publications of the European Communities.

European Commission Childcare Network. 1990. *Childcare in the European Community 1985–1990.* Brussels: The Commission.

European Commission Network on Childcare and other Measures to Reconcile Employment and Family Responsibilities. 1994. *Leave Arrangements for Workers with Children.* V/773/94-EN. Brussels: European Commission.

– . 1996. *A Review of Services for Young Children in the European Union 1990–1995.* Luxembourg: European Commission Directorate General V.

European Council. 2002. *Presidency Conclusions, Barcelona European Council 15–16 March 2002.* SN 100/1/02 REV 1. Brussels.

Evers, Adalbert, Jane Lewis, and Birgit Riedel. 2005. "Developing Child-Care Provision in England and Germany: Problems of Governance." *Journal of European Social Policy* 15(3): 195–209. http://dx.doi.org/10.1177/0958928705054082.

Fairclough, Norman. 1995. *Critical Discourse Analysis: The Critical Study of Language.* London: Longman.

Fairholm, R. 2010. *Early Learning and Care Impact Analysis: Report Prepared for the Atkinson Charitable Foundation.* Milton: Centre for Spatial Economics.

Falk, Erika. 2003. *Analysis of the Messages of the Early Childhood Movement.* Washington, DC: Annenberg Public Policy Center of the University of Pennsylvania.

Fernald, Anne, Virginia A. Marchman, and Adriana Weisleder. 2013. "SES Differences in Language Processing Skill and Vocabulary Are Evident at 18 Months." *Developmental Science* 16(2): 234–48. http://dx.doi.org/10.1111/desc.12019.

Ferns, Carolyn, and Martha Friendly. 2014. *The State of Early Childhood Education and Care in Canada 2012.* Toronto: CRRU.

Ferree, Myra Marx, and David A. Merrill. 2000. "Hot Movements, Cold Cognition: Thinking about Social Movements in Gendered Frames." *Contemporary Sociology* 29(3): 454–62. http://dx.doi.org/10.2307/2653932.

Finn, Chester E. 2009. *Reroute the Preschool Juggernaut.* Stanford: Hoover Institution.

Finn-Stevenson, Matia, and Edward Zigler. 1999. *Schools of the 21st Century: Linking Child Care and Education.* Boulder: Westview Press.

Finnemore, Martha. 1993. "International Organizations as Teachers of Norms: The United Nations Educational, Scientific, and Cultural Organization and Science Policy." *International Organization* 47(4): 565–97. http://dx.doi.org/ 10.1017/S0020818300028101.

– . 1996a. *National Interests in International Society.* Ithaca: Cornell University Press.

– . 1996b. "Norms, Culture, and World Politics: Insights from Sociology's Institutionalism." *International Organization* 50(2): 325–47. http://dx.doi. org/10.1017/S0020818300028587.

Finnemore, Martha, and Kathryn Sikkink. 1998. "International Norm Dynamics and Political Change." *International Organization* 52(4): 887–917. http://dx.doi.org/10.1162/002081898550789.

First Five Years Fund. N.d. *Early Childhood Education Is a Top Priority for Voters, Second Only to Increasing Jobs and Economic Growth.* http://edsource.org/ wp-content/uploads/Poll-Fact-Sheet.pdf.

First Focus / Greenberg Quinlan Rosner Research. 2011. "A Quiet Voice: National Survey Findings." Washington. http://www.gqrr.com/ articles/2011/04/20/a-quiet-voice-national-survey-findings.

Fischer, Frank. 2003. *Reframing Public Policy: Discursive Politics and Deliberative Practices.* Oxford: Oxford University Press. http://dx.doi.org/10.1093/ 019924264X.001.0001.

Fischer, Frank, and John Forester, eds. 1996. *The Argumentative Turn in Policy Analysis and Planning.* Durham: Duke University Press.

Fisher, Dana R., Philip Leifeld, and Yoko Iwaki. 2013. "Mapping the Ideological Networks of American Climate Politics." *Climatic Change* 116(3–4): 523–45. http://dx.doi.org/10.1007/s10584-012-0512-7.

Fitzpatrick, Maria D. 2008. "Starting School at Four: The Effect of Universal Pre-Kindergarten on Children's Academic Achievement." *B.E. Journal of Economic Analysis & Policy* 8(1): 46. http://dx.doi.org/10.2202/1935-1682.1897.

Forry, Nicole D., Elizabeth E. Davis, and Kate Welti. 2013. "Ready or Not: Associations between Participation in Subsidized Child Care Arrangements, Pre-Kindergarten, and Head Start and Children's School Readiness." *Early Childhood Research Quarterly* 28(3): 634–44. http://dx.doi.org/10.1016/j.ecresq.2013.03.009.

Fortin, P., L. Godbout, and S. St-Cerny. 2012. *The Impact of Quebec's Universal Low Fee Child Care Program on Female Labour Force Participation, Domestic Income, and Government Budgets.* Working Paper 2012/02. Research Chair in Taxation and Public Finance at the University of Sherbrooke.

FrameWorks Institute. 2005. *Talking Early Child Development and Exploring the Consequences of Frame Choices.* A FrameWorks Message Memo. http://www.frameworksinstitute.org/assets/files/ECD/ecd_message_memo.pdf.

– . 2009. *Framing Child Poverty by Telling a Development Story.* A FrameWorks Message Brief. http://www.frameworksinstitute.org/assets/files/ECD/child_poverty_message_brief.pdf.

Frede, Ellen, Kwanghee Jung, W. Steven Barnett, Cynthia Esposito Lamy, and Alexandra Figueras. 2007. *The Abbott Preschool Program Longitudinal Effects Study (APPLES). Interim Report.* New Brunswick: NIEER.

Freedman, Estelle B. 2002. *No Turning Back: A History of Feminism and the Future of Women.* New York: Ballantine Books.

Friedrich, Otto. 1983. "What Do Babies Know?" *Time Magazine*, 15 August. http://content.time.com/time/magazine/article/0,9171,949745,00.html.

Friendly, Martha, Jane Beach, Carolyn Ferns, and Michelle Turiano. 2007. *Early Childhood Education and Care in Canada 2006.* Toronto: Childcare Resource and Research Unit.

Friendly, Martha, Bethany Grady, Lyndsay Macdonald, and Barry Forer. 2015. *Early Childhood Education and Care in Canada 2014.* Toronto: Childcare Resource and Research Unit.

Friendly, Martha, Shani Halfon, Jane Beach, and Barry Forer. 2013. *Early Childhood Education and Care in Canada 2012.* Toronto: Childcare Resource and Research Unit.

Friendly, Martha, and Susan Prentice. 2009. *About Canada: Childcare.* Black Point: Fernwood Publishing.

– . 2012. "Provision, Policy, and Politics in Early Childhood Education and Care in Canada." In *New Directions in Early Childhood Education and Care in Canada*, ed. Nina Howe and Larry Prochner, 50–79. Toronto: University of Toronto Press.

Friendly, Martha, and Linda A. White. 2007. "From Multilateralism to Bilateralism to Unilateralism in Three Short Years: Child Care in Canadian Federalism 2003–2006." In *Canadian Federalism: Performance, Effectiveness and Legitimacy*, 2nd ed., ed. Grace Skogstad and Herman Bakvis, 182–204. Toronto: Oxford University Press.

– . 2012. "'No-Lateralism': Paradoxes in Early Childhood Education and Care Policy in the Canadian Federation." In *Canadian Federalism: Performance, Effectiveness, and Legitimacy*, 3rd ed., ed. Grace Skogstad and Herman Bakvis. Toronto: Oxford University Press.

Fuller, Bruce. 2007. *Standardized Childhood: The Political and Cultural Struggle over Early Education*. Stanford: Stanford University Press.

Futrell, Mary Hatwood. 1987. "Public Schools and Four-Year-Olds: A Teacher's View." *American Psychologist* 42(3): 251–3. http://dx.doi.org/10.1037/0003-066X.42.3.251.

Galtry, Judith, and Paul Callister. 2005. "Assessing the Optimal Length of Parental Leave for Child and Parental Well-Being: How Can Research Inform Policy?" *Journal of Family Issues* 26(2): 219–46. http://dx.doi.org/10.1177/0192513X04270344.

Gamson, William A. 1992. *Talking Politics*. New York: Cambridge University Press.

Gandhi, Unnati. 2006. "Eat at Home or in Silence, Students Told." *Globe and Mail*, 21 September, A1.

Garfinkel, Irwin, Lee Rainwater, and Timothy Smeeding. 2010. *Wealth and Welfare States: Is America a Laggard or Leader?* New York: Oxford University Press.

Garrett, Geoffrey, and Barry Weingast. 1993. "Ideas, Interests, and Institutions: Constructing the European Community's Internal Market." In *Ideas and Foreign Policy: Beliefs, Institutions and Political Change*, ed. Judith Goldstein and Robert Keohane, 173–206. Ithaca: Cornell University Press.

Gaunt, Catherine. 2011. "UK and Ireland Top European Table of For-Profit Care Providers." *Nursery World*, 1 November.

Gauthier, Anne Hélène. 1996. *The State and the Family: A Comparative Analysis of Family Policies in Industrialized Countries*. Oxford: Clarendon Press.

– . 2007. "The Impact of Family Policies on Fertility in Industrialized Countries: A Review of the Literature." *Population Research and Policy Review* 26(3): 323–46. http://dx.doi.org/10.1007/s11113-007-9033-x.

Gelb, Joyce. 1989. *Feminism and Politics: A Comparative Perspective*. Berkeley: University of California Press.

Geoffroy, Marie-Claude, Sylvana M. Coté, Charles-Edouard Giguere, Ginette Dionne, Philip David Zelazo, Richard E. Tremblay, Michel Boivin, and Jean R. Séguin. 2010. "Closing the Gap in Academic Readiness and Achievement: The Role of Early Child Care." *Journal of Child Psychology and Psychiatry, and Allied Disciplines* 51(12): 1359–67. http://dx.doi.org/10.1111/j.1469-7610.2010.02316.x.

Gerring, John. 1997. "Ideology: A Definitional Analysis." *Political Research Quarterly* 50(4): 957–94. http://dx.doi.org/10.1177/106591299705000412.

Gidney, R.D., and W.P.J. Millar. 2012. *How Schools Worked: Public Education in English Canada, 1900–1940*. Montreal and Kingston: McGill–Queen's University Press.

Gilbert, Nathan, and Joyce Zemans, eds. 2001. *Making Change: Fifty Years of the Laidlaw Foundation*. Toronto: ECW Press.

Gladwell, Malcolm. 2000. "Baby Steps: Do Our First Three Years of Life Determine How We'll Turn Out?" *The New Yorker*, 10 January, 80–7.

Glass, Norman. 1999. "Sure Start: The Development of an Early Intervention Programme for Young Children in the United Kingdom." *Children & Society* 13(4): 257–64. http://dx.doi.org/10.1002/CHI569.

Glaze, Avis, and Carol Campbell. 2007. *Putting Literacy and Numeracy First: Using Research and Evidence to Support Improved Student Achievement*. Paper presented at the American Educational Research Association Annual Meeting, 11 April. http://www.edu.gov.on.ca/eng/research/litNumfirst.pdf.

Goelman, Hillel. 2004. "We Can Learn Much from Down Under: Nine Lessons on Early Child Care We Can Learn from New Zealand." *Monitor*, November 1. Ottawa: Canadian Centre for Policy Alternatives.

Goffman, Erving. 1974. *Frame Analysis*. New York: Free Press.

Goldstein, Judith, and Robert Keohane, eds. 1993. *Ideas and Foreign Policy: Beliefs, Institutions, and Political Change*. Ithaca: Cornell University Press.

Gopnik, Alison. 2011. "Why Preschool Shouldn't Be Like School." *Slate*, 16 March. http://www.slate.com/id/2288402.

Gormley, William T., Jr. 2012. *Voices for Children: Rhetoric and Public Policy*. Washington, DC: Brookings Institution.

Gormley, William T., Jr, Ted Gayer, Deborah Phillips, and Brittany Dawson. 2005. "The Effects of Universal Pre-K on Cognitive Development." *Developmental Psychology* 41(6): 872–84. http://dx.doi.org/10.1037/0012-1649.41.6.872.

Gornick, Janet C., and Marcia K. Meyers. 2003. *Families That Work: Policies for Reconciling Parenthood and Employment*. New York: Russell Sage Foundation.

Gouvernement du Québec. 1997. *Nouvelles dispositions de la politique familiale. Les enfants au coeur de nos choix*. Québec: Secrétariat du Comité des priorités du ministère du Conseil executive.

Government of Alberta. 2003. "Government Supports 84 Commission Recommendations." News Release, 4 December. http://education.alberta. ca/department/newsroom/news/archive/2003/december/20031204.aspx.

– . 2012. "10-Point Plan for Education: Backgrounder." News Release, 10 January. https://www.alberta.ca/release.cfm?xID=31784C87E013F-07B2-09FF-E745E76F1B9DFC1F .

Grant, Julia. 1998. *Raising Baby by the Book: The Education of American Mothers*. New Haven: Yale University Press.

Gray, Virginia. 1973. "Innovation in the States: A Diffusion Study." *American Political Science Review* 67(4): 1174–85. http://dx.doi.org/10.2307/1956539.

Gregg, Paul, Elizabeth Washbrook, Carol Propper, and Simon Burgess. 2005. "The Effects of a Mother's Return to Work Decision on Child Development in the UK." *Economic Journal (Oxford)* 115(501): F48–80. http://dx.doi.org/ 10.1111/j.0013-0133.2005.00972.x.

Grek, Sotiria. 2009. "Governing by Numbers: The PISA 'Effect' in Europe." *Journal of Education Policy* 24(1): 23–37. http://dx.doi.org/10.1080/02680930802412669.

Groupe de travail pour les jeunes. 1991. *Un Québec fou de ses enfants*. Québec: Ministère de la Santé et des Services sociaux.

Ha, Eunyoung. 2008. "Globalization, Veto Players, and Welfare Spending." *Comparative Political Studies* 41(6): 783–813. http://dx.doi.org/10.1177/ 0010414006298938.

Haas, Eric. 2007. "False Equivalency: Think Tank References on Education in the News Media." *Peabody Journal of Education* 82(1): 63–102. http://dx.doi.org/ 10.1080/01619560709336537.

Haas, Ernst. 1990. *When Knowledge Is Power: Three Models of Change in International Organizations*. Berkeley: University of California Press.

Haas, Peter. 1992. "Introduction: Epistemic Communities and International Policy Coordination." *International Organization* 46(1): 1–36. http://dx.doi. org/10.1017/S0020818300001442.

Haas, Peter M., Robert O. Keohane, and Marc A. Levy, eds. 1993. *Institutions for the Earth: Sources of Effective International Environmental Protection*. Cambridge, MA: MIT Press.

Haider-Markel, Donald P. 2001. "Policy Diffusion as a Geographical Expansion of the Scope of Political Conflict: Same-Sex Marriage Bans in the 1990s." *State Politics & Policy Quarterly* 1(1): 5–26. http://dx.doi.org/ 10.1177/153244000100100102.

Hall, Peter A. 1993. "Policy Paradigms, Social Learning and the State: The Case of Economic Policy-Making in Britain." *Comparative Politics* 25(3): 275–96. http://dx.doi.org/10.2307/422246.

Hall, Peter A., ed. 1989. *The Political Power of Economic Ideas*. Princeton: Princeton University Press.

Hall, Peter A., and David Soskice, eds. 2001. *Varieties of Capitalism: The Institutional Foundations of Comparative Advantage*. Oxford: Oxford University Press. http://dx.doi.org/10.1093/0199247757.001.0001.

Hammer, Kate. 2011. "Alberta Struggles with All-Day Kindergarten." *Globe and Mail*, 14 June.

Hampton, Jim. 2004. *How Florida's Voters Enacted UPK When Their Legislature Wouldn't: A FCD Case Study*. New York: Foundation for Child Development.

Hardy, Cynthia, Bill Harley, and Nelson Phillips. 2004. "Discourse Analysis and Content Analysis: Two Solitudes?" *Qualitative Methods Newsletter* 2(1): 19–22.

Harkin, Tom. 2013. "News From the Senate Health, Education, Labor, and Pensions Committee." n.d. http://www.help.senate.gov/imo/media/doc/Strong%20Start%20for%20America%27s%20Children%20Summary.pdf.

Hart, Betty, and Todd R. Risley. 1995. *Meaningful Differences in the Everyday Experience of Young American Children*. Baltimore: P.H. Brookes.

Hartmann, Heidi, and Young-Lee Yoon. 1996. *Using Temporary Disability Insurance to Provide Paid Family Leave: A Comparison with the Family and Medical Leave Act. Research-in-Brief*. Washington, DC: IWPR.

Haskins, Ron. 2001. "Liberal and Conservative Influences on the Welfare Reform Legislation of 1996." In *For Better and For Worse: Welfare Reform and the Well-Being of Children and Families*, ed. Greg J. Duncan and P. Lindsay Chase-Lansdale, 9–34. New York: Russell Sage Foundation.

– . 2005. "Child Development and Child-Care Policy: Modest Impacts." In *Developmental Psychology and Social Change*, ed. David B. Pillemer and Sheldon H. White, 140–72. New York: Cambridge University Press. http://dx.doi.org/10.1017/CBO9780511610400.008.

Havnes, Tarjei, and Magne Mogstad. 2009. *No Child Left Behind: Universal Child Care and Children's Long-Run Outcomes*. Discussion Paper no. 582. Oslo: Statistics Norway Research Department.

Hay, Colin. 2000. "Contemporary Capitalism, Globalization, Regionalization, and the Persistence of National Variation." *Review of International Studies* 26(4): 509–31. http://dx.doi.org/10.1017/S026021050000509X.

Hayes, Cheryl D., John L. Palmer, and Martha J. Zaslow. 1990. *Who Cares for America's Children? Child Care Policy for the 1990s*. Washington, DC: National Academy Press.

Hays, Sharon. 1996. *The Cultural Contradictions of Motherhood*. New Haven: Yale University Press.

Health Canada, Childhood and Youth Division. 1999. *The Early Child Development System and Its Program Components*. Discussion Paper, version 2. Ottawa.

Hebb, Donald. 1949. *The Organization of Behavior*. New York: Wiley and Sons.

Heckman, James. 2000. *Invest in the Very Young*. Chicago: Ounce of Prevention Fund and the Harris School of Public Policy Studies, University of Chicago.

– . 2006. "Skill Formation and the Economics of Investing in Disadvantaged Children." *Science* 312(5782): 1900–2. http://dx.doi.org/10.1126/science.1128898.

Heckman, James J., Robert J. Lalonde, and Jeffrey A. Smith. 1999. "The Economics and Econometrics of Active Labor Market Programs." In *Handbook of Labor Economics* 3, Part A, ed. Orley C. Ashenfelter and David Card, 1865–2097. http://dx.doi.org/10.1016/S1573-4463(99)03012-6.

Heckman, James J., and Dimitriy V. Masterov. 2004. *The Productivity Argument for Investing in Young Children.* Working Paper no. 5, Invest in Kids Working Group. Washington, DC: Committee for Economic Development.

Heckman, James J., and Dimitriy V. Masterov. 2007. "The Productivity Argument for Investing in Young Children." *Review of Agricultural Economics* 29(3): 446–93. http://dx.doi.org/10.1111/j.1467-9353.2007.00359.x.

Heckman, James J., Seong Hyeok Moon, Rodrigo Pinto, Peter A. Savelyev, and Adam Yavitz. 2010. "The Rate of Return to the HighScope Perry Preschool Program." *Journal of Public Economics* 94(1–2): 114–28. http://dx.doi.org/10.1016/j.jpubeco.2009.11.001.

Hega, Gunther M., and Karl G. Hokenmaier. 2002. "The Welfare State and Education: A Comparison of Social and Education Policy in Advanced Industrial Societies." *German Policy Studies* 2(1): 1–29.

Heichel, Stephan, Jessica Pape, and Thomas Sommerer. 2005. "Is There Convergence in Convergence Research? An Overview of Empirical Studies on Policy Convergence." *Journal of European Public Policy* 12(5): 817–40. http://dx.doi.org/10.1080/13501760500161431.

Heidenheimer, Arnold J. 1973. "The Politics of Public Education: Health and Welfare in the USA and Western Europe: How Growth and Reform Potentials Have Differed." *British Journal of Political Science* 3(3): 315–40. http://dx.doi.org/10.1017/S0007123400007894.

– . 1981. "Education and Social Security Entitlements in Europe and America." In *The Development of Welfare States in Europe and America,* ed. Peter Flora and Arnold J. Heidenheimer, 269–306. New Brunswick: Transaction Books.

Helburn, Suzanne W., and Barbara R. Bergmann. 2002. *America's Child Care Problem: The Way Out.* New York: Palgrave Macmillan.

Hemerijck, Anton. 2013. *Changing Welfare States.* Oxford: Oxford University Press.

Henderson, Ailsa, and Linda A. White. 2004. "Shrinking Welfare States? Comparing Maternity Leave Benefits and Child Care Programs in European Union and North American Welfare States, 1985–2000." *Journal of European Public Policy* 11(3): 497–519. http://dx.doi.org/10.1080/13501760410001694273.

Henry, Miriam, Bob Lingard, Fazal Rizvi, and Sandra Taylor. 2001. *The OECD, Globalisation, and Education Policy.* Amsterdam: IAU Press.

Herbst, Chris M., and Erdal Tekin. 2010. "Child Care Subsidies and Child Development." *Economics of Education Review* 29(4): 618–38. http://dx.doi.org/10.1016/j.econedurev.2010.01.002.

Hicks, Alexander, and Lane Kenworthy. 2003. "Varieties of Welfare Capitalism." *Socio-Economic Review* 1(1): 27–61. http://dx.doi.org/10.1093/soceco/1.1.27.

Ho, Shirley S., Dominique Brossard, and Dietram A. Scheufele. 2008. "Effects of Value Dispositions, Mass Media Use, and Knowledge on Public Attitudes toward Embryonic Stem Cell Research." *International Journal of Public Opinion Research* 20(2): 171–92. http://dx.doi.org/10.1093/ijpor/edn017.

Hobson, Barbara, and Marika Lindholm. 1997. "Collective Identities, Women's Power Resources, and the Making of Welfare States." *Theory and Society* 26(4): 475–508. http://dx.doi.org/10.1023/A:1006827814138.

Hochschild, Jennifer, and Nathan Scovronick. 2003. *The American Dream and the Public Schools.* New York: Oxford University Press.

Hoffman, Andrew J. 2011a. "Talking Past Each Other? Cultural Framing of Skeptical and Convinced Logics in the Climate Change Debate." *Organization & Environment* 24(1): 3–33. http://dx.doi.org/10.1177/1086026611404336.

– . 2011b. "The Culture and Discourse of Climate Skepticism." *Strategic Organization* 9(1): 77–84.

Holt, Alexander. 2014. *Making the Hours Count: Exposing Disparities in Early Education by Retiring Half Day vs. Full Day Labels.* Washington, DC: New America Foundation.

Howe, R. Brian, and Katherine Covell. 2005. *Empowering Children: Children's Rights Education as a Pathway to Citizenship.* Toronto: University of Toronto Press. http://dx.doi.org/10.3138/9781442674387.

HRDC (Human Resources Development Canada). 1997. *Status of Day Care in Canada 1995 and 1996.* Ottawa.

– . 1998. *Investing in Children: A National Research Conference, 1998.* http:// www.hrsdc.gc.ca/eng/cs/sp/sdc/pkrf/publications/nlscy/1998-000093/ default-e.shtml.

– . 1999. *Investing in Children: Ideas for Action.* Report from the National Research Conference held in Ottawa, 27–29 October 1998. Ottawa: Applied Research Branch, Strategic Policy, HRDC.

HRSDC (Human Resources and Social Development Canada). n.d. *Overview of UEY.* Ottawa.

Huber, Evelyn, and John D. Stephens. 2001. *Development and Crisis of the Welfare State: Parties and Policies in Global Markets.* Chicago: University of Chicago Press. http://dx.doi.org/10.7208/chicago/9780226356495.001.0001.

Hulbert, Ann. 2003. *Raising America: Experts, Parents, and a Century of Advice about Children.* New York: Alfred A. Knopf.

Hunt, J. McVicker. 1961. *Intelligence and Experience.* New York: Ronald Press.

Hunter, Molly A. 2012. "Litigation Update: Kansas, South Carolina, Colorado, and More." *Education Justice.* Press Release, 4 September. http://www. educationjustice.org/news/september-4-2012-litigation-update-kansas- south-carolina-colorado-and-more.html.

Hustedt, Jason T., and W. Steven Barnett. 2011. "Financing Early Childhood Education Programs: State, Federal, and Local Issues." *Educational Policy* 25(1): 167–92. http://dx.doi.org/10.1177/0895904810386605.

Hustedt, Jason T., W. Steven Barnett, and Allison H. Friedman. 2010. *The New Mexico PreK Evaluation: Impacts from the Fourth Year (2008–2009) of New Mexico's State-Funded PreK Program.* Working Paper. New Brunswick: NIEER.

Hyslop, Katie. 2012. "BC Child Care Advocates in Geneva to Complain to UN." *The Tyee,* 6 February. http://thetyee.ca/News/2012/02/06/Child-Care-Advocates-in-Geneva.

ICW (Institute for a Competitive Workforce). 2010. *Why Business Should Support Early Childhood Education.* Washington, DC: IWC, US Chamber of Commerce.

ILO (International Labour Organization). 1997. *The Cost of Social Security 1990–1996.* Geneva.

ILO Bureau for Gender Equality and International Labour Standards Department. 2006. *Gender Equality and Decent Work: Selected ILO Conventions and Recommendations Promoting Gender Equality.* Geneva.

ILO Office of the Director-General. 2003. *Time for Equality at Work: Global Report under the Follow-Up to the ILO Declaration on Fundamental Principles and Rights at Work.* Report I (B), International Labour Conference, 91st Session. Geneva.

Inglehart, Ronald. 1990. *Culture Shift in Advanced Industrial Society.* Princeton: Princeton University Press.

Iversen, Torben, and John D. Stephens. 2008. "Partisan Politics, the Welfare State, and Three Worlds of Human Capital Formation." *Comparative Political Studies* 41(4–5): 600–37. http://dx.doi.org/10.1177/0010414007313117.

Jacobs, Alan. 2011. *Governing for the Long Term: Democracy and the Politics of Investment.* New York: Cambridge University Press. http://dx.doi.org/10.1017/CBO9780511921766.

Jacobs, Jennifer. 2011. "Preschool 'Indoctrination' Remark Sets off Senate Debate." *DesMoinesRegister.com,* 15 February, p. B1.

Jacobson, Linda. 2009. *On the Cusp in California: How PreK-3rd Strategies Could Improve Education in the Golden State. Washington, D.C., and Sacramento.* Sacramento: New America Foundation.

Jahn, Detlef. 2006. "Globalization as 'Galton's Problem': The Missing Link in the Analysis of Diffusion Patterns in Welfare State Development." *International Organization* 60(2): 401–31. http://dx.doi.org/10.1017/S0020818306060127.

Japel, Christa. 2008. "Factors of Risk, Vulnerability, and School Readiness among Preschoolers: Evidence from Quebec." *IRPP Choices* 14: 16.

Japel, Christa, Richard E. Tremblay, and Sylvana Côté. 2005. "Quality Counts! Assessing the Quality of Daycare Services Based on the Quebec Longitudinal Study of Child Development." *IRPP Choices* 11(5): 1–42.

Jenkins, Jonathan, and Anthony Artuso. 2011. "Ontario PCs Roll Out Education Platform." *Toronto Sun*, 3 September. http://www.torontosun.com/2011/09/03/ontario-pcs-roll-out-education-platform.

Jensen, Arthur R. 1969. "How Much Can We Boost IQ and Scholastic Achievement?" *Harvard Educational Review* 39(1): 1–123. http://dx.doi.org/10.17763/haer.39.1.l3u15956627424k7.

Jensen, Carsten. 2009. "ESPAnet/JESP Doctoral Researcher Prize Essay: Institutions and the Politics of Childcare Services." *Journal of European Social Policy* 19(1): 7–18. http://dx.doi.org/10.1177/0958928708098520.

– . 2011a. "Capitalist Systems, Deindustrialization, and the Politics of Public Education." *Comparative Political Studies* 20: 1–24.

– . 2011b. "Determinants of Welfare Service Provision after the Golden Age." *International Journal of Social Welfare* 20(2): 125–34. http://dx.doi.org/10.1111/j.1468-2397.2009.00667.x.

Jenson, Jane. 1998. "Les réformes des services de garde pour jeunes enfants en France et al Québec: Une analyse historico-institutionnaliste." *Politique et Sociétés* 17(1–2): 183–216. http://dx.doi.org/10.7202/040105ar.

– . 2009. "Rolling Out or Backtracking on Quebec's Childcare System? Ideology Matters." In *Public Policy for Women*, ed. Marjorie Griffin Cohen and Jane Pulkingham, 49–70. Toronto: University of Toronto Press.

– . 2010. "Diffusing Ideas for after Neoliberalism: The Social Investment Perspective in Europe and Latin America." *Global Social Policy* 10(1): 59–84. http://dx.doi.org/10.1177/1468018109354813.

Jenson, Jane, and Denis Saint-Martin. 2003. "New Routes to Social Cohesion? Citizenship and the Social Investment State." *Canadian Journal of Sociology* 28(1): 77–99. http://dx.doi.org/10.2307/3341876.

Jenson, Jane, and Mariette Sineau, eds. 2001. *Who Cares? Women's Work, Childcare, and Welfare State Redesign*. Toronto: University of Toronto Press. http://dx.doi.org/10.3138/9781442683389.

Jenson, Jane, and Sharon M. Stroick. 1999. "A Policy Blueprint for Canada's Children." In *CPRN Reflexion no. 3*. Ottawa: CPRN.

Jepsen, C., K. Troske, and C. Brasher. 2009. *Estimates of the Costs and Benefits of Expanding the Early Childhood Education Program in Kentucky*. Working paper. Center for Business and Economic Research, University of Kentucky. cber.uky.edu/Downloads/CBER_early_educ_report_final.pdf.

Johnson, Carolyn Y. 2013. "David Koch Funds Day Care at MIT." *Boston Globe*, 4 October.

Jordan, Jason. 2006. "Mothers, Wives, and Workers: Explaining Gendered Dimensions of the Welfare State." *Comparative Political Studies* 39(9): 1109–32. http://dx.doi.org/10.1177/0010414005284215.

Kaestle, Carl. 1983. *Pillars of the Republic: Common Schools and American Society, 1780–1860*. New York: Hill and Wang.

Kagan, Jerome. 2000. *Three Seductive Ideas*. Cambridge, MA: Harvard University Press.

Kagan, Sharon L., and Nancy E. Cohen. 1997. *Not by Chance: Creating a System of Early Care and Education for America's Children*. New Haven: Yale Bush Center on Child Development and Social Policy.

Kagan, Sharon L., and Nancy E. Cohen, eds. 1996. *Reinventing Early Care and Education: A Vision for a Quality System*. San Francisco: Jossey-Bass.

Kahn, Alfred, and Sheila Kamerman. 1976. *Child Care Programs in Nine Countries: A Report Prepared for the OECD Working Party on the Role of Women in the Economy*. Paris: OECD.

Kamerman, Sheila B. 2000. "Early Childhood Education and Care: An Overview of Developments in OECD Countries." *International Journal of Educational Research* 33(1): 7–29. http://dx.doi.org/10.1016/S0883-0355(99)00041-5.

Kamerman, Sheila, and Alfred J. Kahn, eds. 1991. *Child Care, Parental Leave, and the Under 3s: Policy Innovation in Europe*. New York: Auburn House.

Kamette, Florence. 2011. "Organisation of School Time in the European Union." *European Issues Policy Paper* no. 212, 5 September.

Karch, Andrew. 2009. "Venue Shopping, Policy Feedback, and American Preschool Education." *Journal of Policy History* 21(1): 38–60. http://dx.doi.org/10.1017/S0898030609090022.

– . 2010. "Policy Feedback and Preschool Funding in the American States." *Policy Studies Journal: Journal of the Policy Studies Organization* 38(2): 217–34. http://dx.doi.org/10.1111/j.1541-0072.2010.00359.x.

– . 2013. *Early Start: Preschool Politics in the United States*. Ann Arbor: University of Michigan Press. http://dx.doi.org/10.3998/mpub.813135.

Karoly, Lynn A., and James H. Bigelow. 2005. *The Economics of Investing in Universal Preschool Education in California*. Santa Monica: RAND Corporation.

Karoly, Lynn A., Peter W. Greenwood, Susan S. Everingham, Jill Hoube, M. Rebecca Kilburn, C. Peter Rydell, Matthew Sanders, and James Chiesa. 1998. *Investing in Our Children: What We Know and Don't Know about the Costs and Benefits of Early Childhood Interventions*. Santa Monica: RAND Corporation.

Karoly, Lynn A., M. Rebecca Kilburn, and Jill S. Cannon. 2005. *Early Childhood Interventions: Proven Results, Future Promise*. Santa Monica: RAND Corporation.

Kastner, Scott L., and Chad Rector. 2003. "International Regimes, Domestic Veto Players, and Capital Controls Policy Stability." *International Studies Quarterly* 47(1): 1–22. http://dx.doi.org/10.1111/1468-2478.4701001.

Keating, Daniel P., and Clyde Hertzman, eds. 1999. *Developmental Health and the Wealth of Nations: Social, Biological, and Educational Dynamics.* New York: Guilford Press.

Keck, Margaret E., and Kathryn Sikkink. 1998. *Activists beyond Borders: Advocacy Networks in International Politics.* Ithaca: Cornell University Press.

Kendall-Taylor, Nathaniel, and Abigail Haydon. 2013. *Plasticity's Promise: Moving Public Thinking beyond the Container and Other Unproductive Models.* Washington, DC: FrameWorks Institute.

Kenworthy, Lane. 2008. *Jobs with Equality.* Oxford: Oxford University Press. http://dx.doi.org/10.1093/acprof:oso/9780199550593.001.0001.

Kershaw, Sarah. 2003. "Voters in Seattle, Where Coffee Is King, Reject a Tax on Espresso." *New York Times,* 17 September. http://www.nytimes.com/2003/09/17/us/voters-in-seattle-where-coffee-is-king-reject-a-tax-on-espresso.html.

Kilburn, M. Rebecca, and Lynn Karoly. 2008. *The Economics of Early Childhood Policy: What the Dismal Science Has to Say about Investing in Children.* Rand Labor and Population Series Occasional Paper. Santa Monica: RAND Corporation.

Kinder, Donal R., and Lynn M. Sanders. 1996. *Divided by Color: Racial Politics and Democratic Ideals.* Chicago: University of Chicago Press.

Kingdon, John. 1984. *Agendas, Alternatives, and Public Policies.* New York: Longman.

Kirp, David L. 2007. *The Sandbox Investment: The Preschool Movement and Kids-First Politics.* Cambridge, MA: Harvard University Press.

Klapdor, Michael. 2017. "Abolishing the Baby Bonus." Budget Review 2013–2014 Index. Canberra: Parliament of Australia. http://www.aph.gov.au/About_Parliament/Parliamentary_Departments/Parliamentary_Library/pubs/rp/BudgetReview201314/BabyBonus#_ftn3.

Klaus, Alisa. 1993. "Depopulation and Race Suicide: Maternalism and Pronatalist Ideologies in France and the United States." In *Mothers of a New World: Maternalist Politics and the Origins of Welfare States,* ed. Seth Kove and Sonya Michel, 188–212. New York: Routledge.

Klotz, Audie. 2002. "Transnational Activism and Global Transformations: The Anti-Apartheid and Abolitionist Experiences." *European Journal of International Relations* 8(1): 49–76. http://dx.doi.org/10.1177/1354066102008001002.

Knodel, Philipp, Kerstin Martens, and Dennis Niemann. 2013. "PISA as an Ideational Roadmap for Policy Change: Exploring Germany and England in a Comparative Perspective." *Globalisation, Societies, and Education* 11(3): 421–41. http://dx.doi.org/10.1080/14767724.2012.761811.

Knott, Jack H., and Diane McCarthy. 2007. "Policy Venture Capital: Foundations, Government Partnerships, and Child Care Programs." *Administration & Society* 39(3): 319–53. http://dx.doi.org/10.1177/0095399706298052.

Knudsen, Eric I. 2004. "Sensitive Periods in the Development of the Brain and Behavior." *Journal of Cognitive Neuroscience* 16(8): 1412–25. http://dx.doi.org/10.1162/0898929042304796.

Koh, Harold Hongju. 2005–6. "Why Transnational Law Matters." *Penn State International Law Review* 24: 745–53.

Kohen, Dafna, Clyde Hertzman, and Jeanne Brooks-Gunn. 1998. *Neighbourhood Influences on Children's School Readiness. W-98–15E.* Ottawa: Applied Research Branch, HRDC.

Kollman, Kelly. 2007. "Same-Sex Unions: The Globalization of an Idea." *International Studies Quarterly* 51(2): 329–57. http://dx.doi.org/10.1111/j.1468-2478.2007.00454.x.

Kopstein, Jeffrey S., and David A. Reilly. 2000. "Geographic Diffusion and the Transformation of the Postcommunist World." *World Politics* 53(1): 1–37. http://dx.doi.org/10.1017/S0043887100009369.

Korpi, Walter. 2000. "Faces of Inequality: Gender, Class, and Patterns of Inequalities in Different Types of Welfare States." *Social Politics* 7(2): 127–91. http://dx.doi.org/10.1093/sp/7.2.127.

– . 2006. "Power Resources and Employer-Centered Approaches in Explanations of Welfare States and Varieties of Capitalism: Protagonists, Consenters, and Antagonists." *World Politics* 58(2): 167–206. http://dx.doi.org/10.1353/wp.2006.0026.

Koven, Seth, and Sonya Michel, eds. 1993. *Mothers of a New World: Maternalist Politics and the Origins of Welfare States.* New York: Routledge.

Krashinsky, Michael. 1977. *Day Care and Public Policy in Ontario. Ontario Economic Council Research Studies 11.* Toronto: University of Toronto Press.

Kremer, Monique. 2007. *How Welfare States Care: Culture, Gender, and Parenting in Europe.* Amsterdam: University of Amsterdam Press. http://dx.doi.org/10.5117/9789053569757.

Labor Project for Working Families. 2003. *Putting Families First: How California Won the Fight for Paid Family Leave.* http://www.working-families.org/publications/paidleavewon.pdf.

Ladd-Taylor, Molly. 1994. *Mother-Work: Women, Child Welfare, and the State, 1890–1930.* Urbana: University of Illinois Press.

Ladner, Matthew. 2007. *Putting Arizona Education Reform to the Test: School Choice and Early Education Expansion.* Phoenix: Goldwater Institute.

Laghi, Brian. 1996. "Alberta to Start Spending Surplus: Klein to Reverse Kindergarten Cut." *Globe and Mail*, 29 January, A1.

Lakoff, George. 2002. *Moral Politics: How Liberals and Conservatives Think*. Chicago: University of Chicago Press. http://dx.doi.org/10.7208/chicago/9780226471006.001.0001.

Lakoff, George, and Mark Johnson. 1980. *Metaphors We Live By*. Chicago: University of Chicago Press.

Lamb, Michael E., Kathleen J. Sternberg, Carl-Philip Hwang, and Anders G. Broberg, eds. 1992. *Child Care in Context: Cross-Cultural Perspectives*. Hillsdale: Lawrence Erlbaum Associates.

Lange, David. 1988. *Before Five: Early Childhood Care and Education in New Zealand*. Wellington: Department of Education.

Langford, Rachel. 2010. *Innovations in Provincial Early Learning Curriculum Frameworks*. Occasional Paper no. 24. Toronto: Childcare Resource and Research Unit.

Laslett, Barbara, and Johanna Brenner. 1989. "Gender and Social Reproduction: Historical Perspectives." *Annual Review of Sociology* 15(1): 381–404. http://dx.doi.org/10.1146/annurev.so.15.080189.002121.

Laver, Michael, Kenneth Benoit, and John Garry. 2003. "Extracting Policy Positions from Political Texts Using Words as Data." *American Political Science Review* 97(2): 311–31. http://dx.doi.org/10.1017/S0003055403000698.

Lazar, Irving, Richard Darlington, Harry Murray, Jacqueline Royce, and Ann Snipper. 1982. "Lasting Effects of Early Education: A Report from the Consortium for Longitudinal Studies." *Monographs of the Society for Research in Child Development* 47(2–3): 1–151.

Le Bourdais, Céline. 1994. "'Quebec's Pro-Active Approach to Family Policy: 'Thinking and Acting Family.'" In *Canada's Changing Families: Challenges to Public Policy*, ed. Maureen Baker, 103–25. Ottawa: Vanier Institute of the Family.

Leblanc, Daniel. 2005. "Whoa, Baby! Chew on These Child-Care Plans." *Globe and Mail*, 6 December, A4.

Lefebvre, Pierre, and Philip Merrigan. 1998. *Family Background, Family Income, Maternal Work, and Child Development*. W-98–12E. Ottawa: Applied Research Branch of Strategic Policy, HRDC.

– . 2008. "Child-Care Policy and the Labor Supply of Mothers with Young Children: A Natural Experiment from Canada." *Journal of Labor Economics* 26(3): 519–48. http://dx.doi.org/10.1086/587760.

LeFevre, Andrew T. 2006. *Report Card on American Education: A State-by-State Analysis, 1983–1984 to 2004–2005*, ed. M. Warner. Washington, DC: American Legislative Exchange Council.

Legro, Jeffrey W. 2000. "The Transformation of Policy Ideas." *American Journal of Political Science* 44(3): 419–32. http://dx.doi.org/10.2307/2669256.

Leibfried, Stephan, Francis G. Castles, and Herbert Obinger. 2005. "'Old' and 'New' Politics in Federal Welfare States." In *Federalism and the Welfare State: New World and European Experiences*, ed. H. Obinger, F.G. Castles, and S. Leibfried, 307–55. New York: Cambridge University Press. http://dx.doi.org/10.1017/CBO9780511491856.010.

Lenschow, Andrea, Duncan Liefferink, and Sietske Veenman. 2005. "When the Birds Sing: A Framework for Analysing Domestic Factors behind Policy Convergence." *Journal of European Public Policy* 12(5): 797–816. http://dx.doi.org/10.1080/13501760500161373.

Leonhardt, David. 2006. "The Price of Day Care Can Be High." *New York Times*, 14 June. http://www.nytimes.com/2006/06/14/business/14leonhardt.html.

Levin-Epstein, Jodie. 2004. *Taking the Next Step: What Can the US Learn about Parental Leave from New Zealand?* CLASP Work–Life Balance Series Policy Brief no. 1. Washington, DC: Center for Law and Social Policy.

Lewin, Tamar. 2009. "No Einstein in Your Crib? Get a Refund." *New York Times*, 23 October. http://www.nytimes.com/2009/10/24/education/24baby.html.

Lewis, Jane. 1980. *The Politics of Motherhood: Child and Maternal Welfare in England, 1900–1939*. London: Croom Helm.

– . 1992. "Gender and the Development of Welfare Regimes." *Journal of European Social Policy* 2(3): 159–73. http://dx.doi.org/10.1177/095892879200200301.

– . 2003. "Developing Early Years Childcare in England, 1997–2002: The Choices for (Working) Mothers." *Social Policy and Administration* 37(3): 219–38. http://dx.doi.org/10.1111/1467-9515.00335.

Lewis, Jane, ed. 1993. *Women and Social Policies in Europe: Work, Family, and the State*. Aldershot: Edward Elgar.

Lewis, Jane, and Mary Campbell. 2007. "UK Work/Family Balance Policies and Gender Equality, 1997–2005." *Social Politics* 14(1): 4–30. http://dx.doi.org/10.1093/sp/jxm005.

Libassi, C.J. 2014. *Raising Arizona: Lessons for the Nation from a State's Experience with a Full-Day Kindergarten*. Washington, DC: New America Foundation.

Liberal Party of Canada. 1993. *Creating Opportunity: The Liberal Plan for Canada (Red Book)*. Ottawa.

– . 2004. *Moving Canada Forward: The Paul Martin Plan for Getting Things Done*. Ottawa.

– . 2006. *Securing Canada's Success*. Ottawa.

– . 2008. *Richer, Fairer, Greener: An Action Plan for the 21st Century*. Ottawa.

Lindert, Peter H. 2004. *Growing Public: Social Spending and Economic Growth since the Eighteenth Century*. New York: Cambridge University Press.

Lindvall, Johannes. 2009. "The Real but Limited Influence of Expert Ideas." *World Politics* 61(4): 703–30. http://dx.doi.org/10.1017/S0043887109990104.

Linos, Katerina. 2007. "How Can International Organizations Shape National Welfare States? Evidence from Compliance with European Union Directives." *Comparative Political Studies* 40(5): 547–70. http://dx.doi.org/10.1177/0010414005285756.

– . 2013. *The Democratic Foundations of Policy Diffusion: How Health, Family, and Employment Laws Spread across Countries*. New York: Oxford University Press. http://dx.doi.org/10.1093/acprof:oso/9780199967865.001.0001.

Little, Alan, and George Smith. 1971. *Strategies of Compensation: A Review of Educational Projects for the Disadvantaged in the United States*. Paris: OECD.

Lockhart, Charles. 2003. *The Roots of American Exceptionalism: Institutions, Culture, and Policies*. New York: Palgrave Macmillan. http://dx.doi.org/10.1007/978-1-349-73144-2.

Loeb, Susanna, Margaret Bridges, Daphna Bassok, Bruce Fuller, and Russell W. Rumberger. 2007. "How Much Is Too Much? The Influence of Preschool Centers on Children's Social and Cognitive Development." *Economics of Education Review* 26(1): 52–66. http://dx.doi.org/10.1016/j.econedurev.2005.11.005.

Loeb, Susanna, Bruce Fuller, Sharon Lynn Kagan, and Bidemi Carrol. 2004. "Child Care in Poor Communities: Early Learning Effects of Type, Quality, and Stability." *Child Development* 75(1): 47–65. http://dx.doi.org/10.1111/j.1467-8624.2004.00653.x.

Lombardi, Joan. 2003. *Time to Care: Redesigning Child Care to Promote Education, Support Families, and Build Communities*. Philadelphia: Temple University Press.

Lopez, Kathryn Jean. 2003. "Who's Minding the Kids?" *National Review Online Interrogatory*, 1 October. http://www.nationalreview.com/article/208143/who-s-minding-kids-interview.

Love, John M., Linda Harrison, Abraham Sagi-Schwartz, Marinus H. van IJzendoorn, Christine Ross, Judy A. Ungerer, Helen Raikes, Christy Brady-Smith, Kimberly Boller, Jeanne Brooks-Gunn, Jill Constantine, Ellen Eliason Kisker, Diane Paulsell, and Rachel Chazan-Cohen. 2003. "Child Care Quality Matters: How Conclusions Vary with Context." *Child Development* 74(4): 1021–33. http://dx.doi.org/10.1111/1467-8624.00584.

Lynch, Robert G. 2004. *Exceptional Returns: Economic, Fiscal, and Social Benefits of Investment in Early Childhood Development*. Washington, DC: Economic Policy Institute.

– . 2007. *Enriching Children, Enriching the Nation: Public Investment in High-Quality Prekindergarten*. Washington, DC: Economic Policy Institute.

Magnuson, Katherine A., Christopher Ruhm, and Jane Waldfogel. 2007. "Does Prekindergarten Improve School Preparation and Performance?" *Economics of Education Review* 26(1): 33–51. http://dx.doi.org/10.1016/j.econedurev.2005.09.008.

Mahon, Rianne. 2006. "The OECD and the Work/Family Reconciliation Agenda: Competing Frames." In *Children, Changing Families, and Welfare States*, ed. Jane Lewis, 173–97. Chelteham: Edward Elgar. http://dx.doi.org/10.4337/9781847204363.00019.

Mahoney, Jill. 2003. "Junior-Kindergarten Proposal Sparks Division." *Globe and Mail*, 5 December, A12.

– . 2004. "Debate Rages on Early Education." *Globe and Mail*, 3 January, A1–A2.

Manna, Paul. 2006. *School's In: Federalism and the National Education Agenda*. Washington, DC: Georgetown University Press.

Manna, Paul, and Patrick McGuinn, eds. 2013. *Education Governance for the Twenty-First Century: Overcoming the Structural Barriers to School Reform*. Washington, DC: Brookings Institution.

March, James G., and Johan P. Olsen. 1989. *Rediscovering Institutions: The Organizational Basis of Politics*. New York: Free Press.

– . 1996. "Institutional Perspectives on Political Institutions." *Governance: An International Journal of Policy, Administration, and Institutions* 9(3): 247–64. http://dx.doi.org/10.1111/j.1468-0491.1996.tb00242.x.

Marcussen, Martin. 2006. "The Transnational Governance Network of Central Bankers." In *Transnational Governance: Institutional Dynamics of Regulation*, ed. Marie-Laure Djelic and Kerstin Sahlin-Andersson, 180–204. New York: Cambridge University Press.

Maroney, Heather Jon. 1992. "'Who Has the Baby?' Nationalism, Pronatalism, and the Construction of a 'Demographic Crisis' in Quebec, 1960–1988." *Studies in Political Economy* 39(1): 7–36. http://dx.doi.org/10.1080/19187033.1992.11675416.

Marsh, David, and J.C. Sharman. 2009. "Policy Diffusion and Policy Transfer." *Policy Studies* 30(3): 269–88. http://dx.doi.org/10.1080/01442870902863851.

Marshall, Katherine. 2003. "Benefiting from Extended Parental Leave." *Perspectives*. Statistics Canada Cat. no. 75–001-XIE.

Martens, Kerstin, and Dennis Niemann. 2010. "Governance by Comparison: How Ratings and Rankings Impact National Policy-Making in Education." *Transformations of the State Working Papers* no. 139. Bremen: Collaborative Research Center.

– . 2013. "When Do Numbers Count? The Differential Impact of the PISA Rating and Rankings on Education Policy in Germany and the US." *German Politics* 22(3): 314–32. http://dx.doi.org/10.1080/09644008.2013.794455.

Martens, Kerstin, Alessandra Rusconi, and Kathrin Leuze, eds. 2007. *New Arenas of Education Governance: The Impact of International Organisations and Markets on Educational Policymaking.* New York: Palgrave Macmillan. http://dx.doi.org/10.1007/978-1-349-58271-6.

Martin, Paul. 1996. *Budget Speech* (6 March). Ottawa: Department of Finance.

Mathers, Sandra, and Kathy Sylva. 2007. *National Evaluation of the Neighbourhood Nurseries Initiative: The Relationship between Quality and Children's Behavioural Development.* Research Report SSU/2007/FR/022. London: Department for Education and Skills.

Mathers, Sandra, Kathy Sylva, and Heather Joshi. 2007. *Quality of Childcare Settings in the Millennium Cohort Study.* Research Report SSU/2007/FR/025. London: Department for Education and Skills.

May, Elaine Tyler. 1995. *Barren in the Promised Land: Childless Americans and the Pursuit of Happiness.* New York: Basic Books.

– . 1997. *The Discovery of Early Childhood: The Development of Services for the Care and Education of Very Young Children, Mid-Eighteenth-Century Europe to Mid-Twentieth-Century New Zealand.* Wellington: Auckland University Press / Bridget Williams Books.

– . 2001. *Politics in the Playground: The World of Early Childhood in Post-War New Zealand.* Wellington: Bridget Williams Books / New Zealand Council for Educational Research.

– . 2011. *I am Five and I Go to School: Early Years Schooling in New Zealand, 1900–2010.* Dunedin: Otago University Press.

May, Helen, and Linda Mitchell. 2009. *Strengthening Community-Based Early Childhood Education in Aotearoa New Zealand: Report of the Quality Public Early Childhood Education Project.* Wellington: NZEI Te Riu Roa.

McAdam, Doug, and Dieter Rucht. 1993. "The Cross-National Diffusion of Movement Ideas." *Annals of the American Academy of Political and Social Science* 528(1): 56–74. http://dx.doi.org/10.1177/0002716293528001005.

McCain, Margaret, and Fraser Mustard. 1999. *Reversing the Real Brain Drain: Early Years Study Final Report.* Toronto: Children's Secretariat of Ontario.

McCain, Margaret, Fraser Mustard, and Stuart Shanker. 2007. *Early Years Study 2: Putting Science into Action.* Toronto: Council for Early Child Development.

McCarthy, John D., and Mayer N. Zald. 1977. "Resource Mobilization and Social Movements: A Partial Theory." *American Journal of Sociology* 82(6): 1212–41. http://dx.doi.org/10.1086/226464.

McGuinn, Patrick. 2006. *No Child Left Behind and the Transformation of Federal Education Policy, 1965–2005*. Lawrence: University Press of Kansas.

McKeen, Wendy. 2006. "Diminishing the Concept of Social Policy: The Shifting Conceptual Ground of Social Policy Debate in Canada." *Critical Social Policy* 26(4): 865–87. http://dx.doi.org/10.1177/0261018306068479.

McManus, John, and Lori Dorfman. 2002. "Silent Revolution: How US Newspapers Portray Child Care." *Issue 11*. Berkeley: Berkeley Media Studies Group.

McMillen, Stan, and Kathryn Parr. 2004. *The Economic Impact and Profile of Connecticut's ECE Industry*. Storrs: Connecticut Center for Economic Analysis, University of Connecticut School of Business.

McMunn, Anne, Yvonne Kelly, Noriko Cable, and Mel Bartley. 2010. "Maternal Employment and Child Socio-Emotional Behavior in the UK: Longitudinal Evidence from the UK Millennium Cohort Study." *Journal of Epidemiology and Community Health* 64 (Suppl. 1): A32–3. http://dx.doi.org/10.1136/jech.2010.120956.82.

McNamara, Melissa P. 2004. "Research on Day Care Finds Few Timeouts." *New York Times*, 10 February, D7.

Mead, Sara. 2009. *Education Reform Starts Early: Lessons from New Jersey's PreK–3rd Reform Efforts*. Washington: New America Foundation.

Meade, Anne. 2000. "The Early Childhood Landscape in New Zealand." In *Landscapes in Early Childhood Education: Cross-National Perspectives on Empowerment – A Guide for the New Millenium*, ed. Jacqueline Hayden, 83–93. New York: Peter Lang.

Meade, Anne, and Valerie Podmore. 2002. *Early Childhood Education Policy Co-ordination under the Auspices of the Department/Ministry of Education: A Case Study of New Zealand*. UNESCO Early Childhood and Family Policy Series no. 1. Paris: UNESCO.

Melhuish, Edward, and Peter Moss, eds. 1991. *Day Care for Young Children: International Perspectives*. London: Tavistock/Routledge.

Melhuish, Edward, and Konstantinos Petrogiannis, eds. 1996. *Early Childhood Care and Education: International Perspectives*. New York: Routledge.

Melzer, Scott. 2009. *Gun Crusaders: The NRA's Culture War*. New York: NYU Press.

Meyer, John W., John Boli, George M. Thomas, and Francisco O. Ramirez. 1997. "World Society and the Nation-State." *American Journal of Sociology* 103(1): 144–81. http://dx.doi.org/10.1086/231174.

Meyer, John, Francisco O. Ramirez, and Yasmine N. Soysal. 1992. "World Expansion of Mass Education, 1870–1980." *Sociology of Education* 65(2): 128–49. http://dx.doi.org/10.2307/2112679.

Meyers, Marcia K., and Janet C. Gornick. 2003. "Public or Private Responsibility? Early Childhood Education and Care, Inequality, and the Welfare State." *Journal of Comparative Family Studies* 34: 379–411.

Michel, Sonya. 1999. *Children's Interests / Mothers' Rights: The Shaping of America's Child Care Policy.* New Haven: Yale University Press.

Michel, Sonya, and Rianne Mahon, eds. 2002. *Child Care Policy at the Crossroads: Gender and Welfare State Restructuring.* New York: Routledge.

Miller, Edward, and Joan Almon. 2009. *Crisis in the Kindergarten: Why Children Need to Play in School.* College Park: Alliance for Childhood.

Ministère de L'Éducation, du Loisir, et du Sport. 2009. *I Care About School.* Québec.

Ministère de la Famille et de l'Enfance. 1997. *Educational Programs for Child Care Centres.* Québec.

– . 1999. *Family Policy in Québec: Another Step towards Developing the Full Potential of Families and Their Children.* Québec.

Ministère de la Famille et des Aînés. 2007. *Meeting Early Childhood Needs: Québec's Educational Program for Child Care Services Update.* Québec.

Mink, Gwendolyn. 1995. *The Wages of Motherhood: Inequality in the Welfare State, 1917–1942.* Ithaca: Cornell University Press.

– . 1998. *Welfare's End.* Ithaca: Cornell University Press.

Mintrom, Michael. 1997. "Policy Entrepreneurs and the Diffusion of Innovation." *American Journal of Political Science* 41(3): 738–70. http://dx.doi.org/10.2307/2111674.

– . 2000. *Policy Entrepreneurs and School Choice.* Washington, DC: Georgetown University Press.

Mintrom, Michael, and Sandra Vergari. 1998. "Policy Networks and Innovation Diffusion: The Case of State Education Reforms." *Journal of Politics* 60(1): 126–48. http://dx.doi.org/10.2307/2648004.

Mitchell, Alanna. 1994. "Alberta's 'Missing Children.'" *Globe and Mail*, 12 November, D3.

Mitchell, Anne. 2004. *The State with Two Prekindergarten Programs: A Look at Prekindergarten Education in New York State (1998–2003).* Climax: Early Childhood Policy Research.

Mitchell, Linda. 2012. "Markets and Childcare Provision in New Zealand: Towards a Fairer Alternative." In *Childcare Markets, Local and Global: Can They Deliver an Equitable Service?* ed. Eva Lloyd and Helen Penn. Bristol: Policy Press. http://dx.doi.org/10.1332/policypress/9781847429339.003.0006: 97-113.

Miville-Deschênes, Christiane. 1997. "La Politique Familiale: Les Enfants au Coeur des Choixs du Gouvernement." Press release, Cabinet de la ministre de l'Éducation du Québec, 23 January.

Monsebraaten, Laurie. 2004. "Child Care Report Hailed." *Toronto Star*, 26 October.

Montpetit, Eric, Christine Rothmayr Allison, and Frédéric Varone. 2007. *The Politics of Biotechnology in North America and Europe: Policy Networks, Institutions, and Internationalization.* Lanham: Lexington.

Mooney, Christopher Z., and Mei-Hsien Lee. 1995. "Legislative Morality in the American States: The Case of Pre-*Roe* Abortion Regulation Reform." *American Journal of Political Science* 39(3): 599–627. http://dx.doi.org/10.2307/2111646.

–. 1999. "The Temporal Diffusion of Morality Policy: The Case of Death Penalty Legislation in the American States." *Policy Studies Journal: Journal of the Policy Studies Organization* 27(4): 766–80. http://dx.doi.org/10.1111/j.1541-0072.1999.tb02002.x.

Morain, Dan. 2006a. "TV Ads Put Focus on Reiner." *Los Angeles Times*, 20 February.

–. 2006b. "Reiner Takes a Leave from Panel on Children." *Los Angeles Times*, 25 February.

Morel, Nathalie, Bruno Palier, and Joakim Palme, eds. 2012. *Towards a Social Investment Welfare State?* Bristol: Policy Press.

Morgan, Kimberly J. 2005. "The 'Production' of Child Care: How Labor Markets Shape Social Policy and Vice Versa." *Social Politics* 12(2): 243–63. http://dx.doi.org/10.1093/sp/jxi013.

–. 2006. *Working Mothers and the Welfare State: Religion and the Politics of Work–Family Policies in Western Europe.* Stanford: Stanford University Press.

–. 2012. "Promoting Social Investment through Work-Family Policies: Which Nations Do It and Why." In *Towards a Social Investment Welfare State? Ideas, Policies and Challenges*, ed. Nathalie Morel, Bruno Palier, and Joakim Palme, 153–79. Bristol: Policy Press.

Morone, James A. 2011. "Big Ideas, Broken Institutions, and the Wrath at the Grassroots." *Journal of Health Politics, Policy, and Law* 36(3): 375–85. http://dx.doi.org/10.1215/03616878-1270991.

Moss, Peter. 1991. "Day Care for Young Children in the United Kingdom." In *Day Care for Young Children: International Perspectives*, ed. Edward C. Melhuish and Peter Moss, 121–41. London: Routledge.

–. 2006a. "Farewell to Childcare?" *National Institute Economic Review* 195(1): 70–83. http://dx.doi.org/10.1177/0027950106064040.

–. 2006b. "From a Childcare to a Pedagogical Discourse – or Putting Care in Its Place." In *Children, Changing Families, and Welfare States*, ed. Jane Lewis, 154–72. Cheltenham: Edward Elgar. http://dx.doi.org/10.4337/9781847204363.00018.

Moss, Peter, and Helen Penn. 1996. *Transforming Nursery Education.* London: P. Chapman.

Mossberger, Karen, and Harold Wolman. 2003. "Policy Transfer as a Form of Prospective Policy Evaluation: Challenges and Recommendations." *Public Administration Review* 63(4): 428–40. http://dx.doi.org/10.1111/1540-6210.00306.

Mucciaroni, Gary. 2011. "Are Debates about 'Morality Policy' Really about Morality? Framing Opposition to Gay and Lesbian Rights." *Policy Studies Journal: Journal of the Policy Studies Organization* 39(2): 187–216. http://dx.doi.org/10.1111/j.1541-0072.2011.00404.x.

Murnane, Richard J., and Greg J. Duncan, eds. 2011. *Whither Opportunity? Rising Inequality, Schools, and Children's Life Chances*. New York: Russell Sage Foundation.

Mustard, Fraser. 1991. *The Determinants of Health*. Toronto: Canadian Institute for Advanced Research.

Mustard, Fraser, and Frances Picherack. 2002. *Early Childhood Development in BC: Enabling Communities*. Toronto: Founders Network.

Myles, John, and Paul Pierson. 1997. "Friedman's Revenge: The Reform of 'Liberal' Welfare States in Canada and the United States." *Politics & Society* 25(4): 443–72. http://dx.doi.org/10.1177/0032329297025004004.

N.A. 2002. "Newly Appointed Commission Reviews Alberta's Education System." *Airdrie Echo*, 17 July. http://www.airdrieecho.com/2002/07/17/newly-appointed-commission-reviews-albertas-education-system.

– . 2003. "The Latest Information on the Daycare Nation." *Globe and Mail*, 19 July. http://www.theglobeandmail.com/opinion/the-latest-information-on-the-daycare-nation/article1334666.

– . 2005. "Business Group Backs Preschool Initiative." *Los Angeles Times*, 28 July.

Nagle, Geoffrey, and Kirby Goidel. 2007. *The Louisiana Early Childhood Public Opinion Survey*. Baton Rouge: Louisiana Partnership for Children and Families.

Nash, Madeleine J. 1997. "Fertile Minds." *Time Magazine*, 3 February. http://content.time.com/time/magazine/article/0,9171,985854,00.html.

National Children's Alliance (Canada). 1998. *Investing in Children and Youth: A National Children's Agenda*. September. http://www.nationalchildrensalliance.com/nca/pubs/investing.htm.

National Commission on Excellence in Education. 1983. *A Nation at Risk: The Imperative for Educational Reform*. Washington, DC: US Department of Education.

National Conference of State Legislatures (with Shelley L. Smith and Mary Fairchild). 1995. *Early Childhood Care and Education: An Investment That Works*. Washington, DC.

– . 2012. Same-Sex Marriage Laws. http://www.ncsl.org/research/human-services/same-sex-marriage-laws.aspx.

National Education Goals Panel. 1991. *The National Education Goals Report: Building a Nation of Learners*. Washington, DC.

National Governors' Association. 1986. *Time for Results*. Washington, DC.

National Liberal Caucus Social Policy Committee, in collaboration with the Caledon Institute of Social Policy. 2002. *A National Child Care Strategy: Getting the Architecture Right Now*. Ottawa.

NEGP (National Education Goals Panel). 1997. *Special Early Childhood Report*. Washington, DC: NEGP.

Neuman, Michelle J. 2005. "Governance of Early Childhood Education and Care: Recent Developments in OECD Countries." *Early Years Journal of International Research and Development* 25(2): 129–41. http://dx.doi.org/10.1080/09575140500130992.

– . 2007. "Good Governance of Early Childhood Care and Education: Lessons from the 2007 EFA Global Monitoring Report." UNESCO Policy Briefs on Early Childhood no. 40 (September–October 2007). Paris: UNESCO. unesdoc.unesco.org/images/0015/001529/152965e.pdf.

Neuman, Michelle J., and Shanny Peer. 2002. *Equal from the Start: Promoting Educational Opportunity for All Preschool Children – Learning from the French Experience*. New York: French–American Foundation.

New Zealand Ministry of Education. 1988. *Education to Be More: Report of the Early Childhood Care and Education Working Group*. Wellington. (Meade Report).

– . 1996. *Te Whariki Early Childhood Curriculum*. Wellington.

– . 2004. *Review of Regulation of Early Childhood Education: Implementing Pathways to the Future: Nga Huarahi Arataki*. Consultation Document. Wellington.

– . 2007a. *July 2007 Annual Census of Children and Staff at Licensed and/or Chartered Early Childhood Services and License-Exempt ECE Groups*. http://www.educationcounts.govt.nz/statistics/ece/ece_staff_return/licensed_services_and_licence-exempt_groups/17812.

– . 2007b. *Free ECE: Information for Parents*. Wellington.

– . 2008a. "Early Childhood Discretionary Grants Scheme." http://www.tpo.co.nz/index.php?option=com_content&view=article&id=53&Itemid=58.

– . 2008b. *State of Education in New Zealand 2007*. Wellington.

New Zealand Ministry of Labour. 2016. *Parental Leave: Information for Employees*. https://employment.govt.nz/leave-and-holidays/parental-leave.

Newberger, Julee J. 1997. "New Brain Development Resarch – a Wonderful Window of Opportunity to Build Public Support for Early Childhood Education!" *Young Children* 52(4): 4–9.

Newfoundland and Labrador Ministry of Education. Child, Youth and Family Services. 2014. "Full-Day Kindergarten to Be Implemented Province-Wide in 2016." News Release. http://www.releases.gov.nl.ca/releases/2014/edu/0327n12.htm.

NFDN (National Federation of Day Nurseries). 1905. Report of the Conference. New York: Author.

NIEER (National Institute for Early Education Research). 2005. "More States Find Virtue in 'Sin Taxes,' New Way to Pay for Early Education." *Preschool Matters* 3, no. 1. http://nieer.org/archive-item/januaryfebruary-2005-volume-3-number-1.

North Jones, Allison. 2004. "Bush Vetoes 'Flawed' Pre-K Bill." *Tampa Tribune*, 10 July.

O'Brien, Courtney J. 2013. "Early Childhood Education and Its Relation to a 'Thorough and Efficient' Education: Why Pennsylvania Should Adopt the Abbott v. Burke Preschool Mandate." Seaton Hall University papers. http://scholarship.shu.edu/student_scholarship/index.5.html.

O'Connor, Julia. 1993. "Gender, Class and Citizenship in the Comparative Analysis of Welfare State Regimes: Theoretical and Methodological Issues." *British Journal of Sociology* 44(3): 501–18. http://dx.doi.org/10.2307/591814.

O'Connor, Julia S., Ann Shola Orloff, and Sheila Shaver. 1999. *States, Markets, Families: Gender, Liberalism, and Social Policy in Australia, Canada, Great Britain, and the United States*. New York: Cambridge University Press. http://dx.doi.org/10.1017/CBO9780511597114.

O'Hara, Kathy. 1999. *Comparative Family Policy: Eight Countries' Stories*. Ottawa: CPRN.

O'Neill, Katherine, and Dawn Walton. 2009. "Minister Reignites Mommy Wars." *Globe and Mail*, 19 June, A3.

OAS (Organization of American States) Inter-American Council for Integral Development (CIDI). 2007. *Hemispheric Commitment to Early Childhood Education*. Adopted at the ninth plenary session of the fifth meeting of ministers of education, 15–16 November 2007. OEA/SER.K/V CIDI/RME/doc.10/07.

Oberhuemer, Pamela. 2005. "International Perspectives on Early Childhood Curricula." *International Journal of Early Childhood* 37(1): 27–37. http://dx.doi.org/10.1007/BF03165830.

OECD (Organisation for Economic Cooperation and Development). 1960. Convention on the Organisation for Economic Cooperation and Development. (14 December). Paris: OECD.

–. 1990. "Child Care in OECD Countries." *Employment Outlook July 1990*. Paris.

–. 1994a. *New Orientations for Social Policy*. Paris.

–. 1994b. *The OECD Jobs Study: Facts, Analysis, Strategies.* Paris.

–. 1996. *Lifelong Learning for All.* Meeting of the Education Committee at the Ministerial Level, 16–17 January 1996. Paris.

–. 1997. *Beyond 2000: The New Social Policy Agenda.* (Note by the Secretary-General) C/MIN (97) 8. Paris.

–. 1998. *Early Childhood Education and Care Policy: Proposal for a Thematic Review: Major Issues, Analytical Framework, and Operating Procedures.* Paris.

–. 1999. *A Caring World: The New Social Policy Agenda.* Paris.

–. 2001a. *Employment Outlook June 2001.* Paris.

–. 2001b. *Starting Strong: Early Childhood Education and Care.* Paris.

–. 2002. "Women at Work: Who Are They and How Are They Faring?" In *Employment Outlook 2002,* 61–124. Paris.

–. 2004a. *New Zealand, Portugal, and Switzerland,* vol. 3: *Babies and Bosses: Reconciling Work and Family Life.* Paris.

–. 2004b. *Early Childhood Education and Care Policy: Canada Country Note.* Paris.

–. 2004c. *Starting Strong: Curricula and Pedagogies in Early Childhood Education and Care: Five Curriculum Outlines.* Paris.

–. 2005. *Canada, Finland, Sweden, and the United Kingdom,* vol. 4: *Babies and Bosses: Reconciling Work and Family Life.* Paris.

–. 2006. *Starting Strong II: Early Childhood Education and Care.* Paris.

–. 2007. *Babies and Bosses: Reconciling Work and Family Life: A Synthesis of Findings for OECD Countries.* Paris.

–. 2011. *Social Expenditure Database.* https://www.oecd.org/social/expenditure.htm.

–. 2014a. *Education at a Glance: OECD Indictators.* Paris.

–. 2014b. *Family Database.* www.oecd.org/els/social/family/database.

–, CERI (Centre for Educational Research and Innovation). 1995. *Our Children at Risk.* Paris.

–, CERI. 2002. *Understanding the Brain: Towards a New Learning Science.* Paris.

–, CERI. 2007. *Understanding the Brain: The Birth of a Learning Science.* Paris.

–, PISA. 2001. *Knowledge and Skills for Life: First Results from the OECD Programme for International Student Assessment (PISA) 2000.* Paris.

–, PISA. 2004. *Learning from Tomorrow's World: First Results from PISA 2003.* Paris.

–, PISA. 2007. *Analysis,* vol. 1: *PISA 2006: Science Competencies for Tomorrow's World.* Paris.

–, PISA. 2010. *PISA 2009 Results: What Students Know and Can Do – Student Performance in Reading, Mathematics, and Science,* vol. 1. Paris.

–, PISA. 2011. "Does Participation in Pre-Primary Education Translate into Better Learning Outcomes at School?" *PISA in Focus* 2011/1. http://

www.oecd-ilibrary.org/education/does-participation-in-pre-primary-education-translate-into-better-learning-outcomes-at-school_5k9h362tpvxp-en.

–, PISA. 2013. *PISA 2012 Results: What Students Know and Can Do – Student Performance in Reading, Mathematics, and Science*, vol. 1. Paris.

Offen, Karen. 1991. "Body Politics: Women, Work, and the Politics of Motherhood in France, 1920–1950." In *Maternity and Gender Politics: Women and the Rise of the European Welfare States, 1880s–1950s*, ed. Gisela Bock and Pat Thane London, 138–59. London and New York: Routledge.

Ofsted (Office of Standards in Education). 2008. *Early Years Leading to Excellence: A Review of Childcare and Early Education 2005–2008 with a Focus on Organisation, Leadership, and Management* (ref. no. 080044). London.

Olmsted, Patricia, and David P. Weikart, eds. 1989. *How Nations Serve Young Children: Profiles of Child Care and Education in 14 Countries*. Ypsilanti: High/Scope Educational Research Foundation.

Olsen, Darcy Ann. 1997. *The Advancing Nanny State: Why the Government Should Stay Out of Child Care*. Policy Analysis no. 285. Washington, DC: Cato Institute.

–. 1999. *Universal Preschool Is No Golden Ticket: Why Government Should Not Enter the Preschool Business*. Policy Analysis no. 333. Washington, DC: Cato Institute.

–. 2005. *Assessing Proposals for Preschool and Kindergarten: Essential Information for Parents, Taxpayers, and Policymakers*. Phoenix: Goldwater Institute.

Olson, Lynn. 2002. "Starting Early." *Education Week* 21(17): 10–19.

Ontario MCYS (Ministry of Children and Youth Services). 2008. *Realizing Potential: Our Children, Our Youth, Our Future – Strategic Framework 2008–2012*. Toronto.

Ontario Ministry of Children and Youth Services, Best Start Expert Panel on Early Learning. 2007. *Early Learning for Every Child Today: A Framework for Ontario Early Childhood Settings*. Toronto.

–, Expert Panel on Quality and Human Resources. 2007. *Investing in Quality: Policies, Practitioners, Programs, and Parents: A Four-Point Plan to Deliver High-Quality Early Learning and Care Services in Ontario*. Toronto.

Ontario Ministry of Education. 2014a. "Full-Day Kindergarten Study Evaluation." http://www.edu.gov.on.ca/kindergarten/theresearchisin.html.

–. 2014b. "Why Should I Enrol My Child?" http://www.edu.gov.on.ca/kindergarten/whyshouldienrolmychild.html.

Ontario Office of the Premier. 2007. "McGuinty Government Moves Forward on Full-Day Learning for Four- and Five-Year-Olds." News release, 27 November. Toronto.

–. 2009. "Ontario Moves Forward with Full-Day Learning: McGuinty Government Putting Kids and Parents First." News release, 27 October. Toronto.

Opp, Karl-Dieter. 2001. "Norms." In *International Encylopedia of the Social and Behavioral Sciences*, ed. Neil J. Smelser and Paul B. Baltes, 10714–20. Oxford: Elsevier.

Orenstein, Mitchell. 2008. *Privatizing Pensions: The Transnational Campaign for Social Security Reform*. Princeton: Princeton University Press. http://dx.doi.org/10.1515/9781400837663.

Orloff, Ann Shola. 1993. "Gender and the Social Rights of Citizenship: The Comparative Analysis of Gender Relations and Welfare States." *American Sociological Review* 58(3): 303–28. http://dx.doi.org/10.2307/2095903.

–. 1996. "Gender in the Welfare State." *Annual Review of Sociology* 22(1): 51–78. http://dx.doi.org/10.1146/annurev.soc.22.1.51.

–. 2005. *Farewell to Maternalism? State Policies and Mothers' Employment*. WP-05–10. Evanston: Northwestern University Institute for Policy Research.

Osborne, John. 1985. *The Evolution of the Canada Assistance Plan: Appendix to the Nielsen Task Force Report on the Canada Assistance Plan*. Ottawa: Department of National Health and Welfare.

Pagani, Fabrizio. 2002. *Peer Review: A Tool for Co-operation and Change: An Analysis of an OECD Working Method*. OECD General Secretariat, Directorate for Legal Affairs Working Paper SG/LEG (2002)1. Paris.

Pascal, Charles. 2009a. *An Updated and Annotated Summary of Evidence: A Compendium To. With Our Best Future in Mind: Implementing Early Learning in Ontario*. Toronto: Queen's Printer.

–. 2009b. *With Our Best Future in Mind: Implementing Early Learning in Ontario. Report to the Premier by the Special Advisor on Early Learning*. Ontario: Queen's Printer.

Patashnik, Eric M. 2008. *Reforms at Risk: What Happens after Major Policy Changes Are Enacted*. Princeton: Princeton University Press.

Patashnik, Eric M., and Julian E. Zelizer. 2013. "The Struggle to Remake Politics: Liberal Reform and the Limits of Policy Feedback in the Contemporary American State." *Perspectives on Politics* 11(4): 1071–87. http://dx.doi.org/10.1017/S1537592713002831.

Paterson, Matthew, Matthew Hoffmann, Michele Betsill, and Steven Bernstein. 2014. "The Micro Foundations of Policy Diffusion toward Complex Global Governance: An Analysis of the Transnational Carbon Emission Trading Network." *Comparative Political Studies* 47(3): 420–49. http://dx.doi.org/10.1177/0010414013509575.

Pauly, Louis W. 1997. *Who Elected the Bankers? Surveillance and Control in the World Economy*. Ithaca: Cornell University Press.

Pearce, Tralee. 2011. "Ivy League-Minded Mom Sues Preschool for $19,000." *Globe and Mail*, 16 March. http://www.theglobeandmail.com/life/the-hot-button/ivy-league-minded-mom-sues-preschool-for-19000/article612568/.

Pedersen, Susan. 1993. *Family, Dependence, and the Origins of the Welfare State: Britain and France 1914–1945*. New York: Cambridge University Press.

Peisner-Feinberg, Ellen S., Margaret R. Burchinal, Richard M. Clifford, Mary L. Culkin, Carollee Howes, Sharon Lynn Kagan, and Noreen Yazejian. 2001. "The Relation of Preschool Child-Care Quality to Children's Cognitive and Social Development Trajectories through Second Grade." *Child Development* 72(5): 1534–53. http://dx.doi.org/10.1111/1467-8624.00364.

Peng, Ito. 2002. "Social Care in Crisis: Gender, Demography, and Welfare State Restructuring in Japan." *Social Politics* 9(3): 411–43. http://dx.doi.org/10.1093/sp/9.3.411.

Pérez-Peña, Richard, and Motoko Rich. 2014. "Preschool Push Moving Ahead in Many States." *New York Times*, 3 February. https://www.nytimes.com/2014/02/04/us/push-for-preschool-becomes-a-bipartisan-cause-outside-washington.html?_r=0.

Peter D. Hart Research Associates/Market Strategies. 2001. National Institute for Early Education Research National Poll. http://nieer-www1.rutgers.edu/news-events/news-releases/poll-shows-voters-want-states-fund-quality-preschool-all-3-and-4-year-olds.

Peters, Ray DeV., Alison J. Bradshaw, Kelly Petrunka, Geoffrey Nelson, Yves Herry, Wendy M. Craign, Robert Arnold, Kevin C.H. Paker, Shahriar R. Khan, Jeffrey S. Hoch, S. Mark Pancer, Colleen Loomis, Jean-Marc Belanger, Susan Evers, Claire Maltais, Katherine Thompson, and Melissa D. Rossiter. 2010. "The Better Beginnings, Better Futures Project: Findings from Grade 3 to Grade 9." *Monographs of the Social for Research in Child Development* (December): 1–200.

Pew Research Center. 2013. *Breadwinner Moms*. Pew Social and Demographic Trends Report, 29 May. http://www.pewsocialtrends.org/2013/05/29/breadwinner-moms.

Phillips, Deborah, and Kathleen McCartney. 2005. "The Disconnect between Research and Policy on Child Care." In *Developmental Psychology and Social Change: Research, History, and Policy*, ed. David B. Pillemer and Sheldon H. White, 104–39. New York: Cambridge University Press. http://dx.doi.org/10.1017/CBO9780511610400.007.

Phillips, Deborah A., and Sally J. Styfco. 2007. "Child Development Research and Public Policy: Triumphs and Setbacks on the Way to Maturity." In *Child Development and Social Policy: Knowledge for Action*, ed. J. Lawrence Aber, Sandra J. Bishop-Josef, Stephanie M. Jones, Kathryn Taaffe McLearn, and Deborah A. Phillips, 11–27. Washington, DC: American Psychological Association. http://dx.doi.org/10.1037/1486-001.

Phillips, Nelson, and Cynthia Hardy. 2002. *Discourse Analysis: Investigating Processes of Social Construction*. Qualitative Research Methods Series no. 50. Thousand Oaks: Sage. http://dx.doi.org/10.4135/9781412983921.

Philp, Margaret. 2004. "Canada's Child Care Is Failing, OECD Says." *Globe and Mail*, 25 October.

Phipps, Shelley. 1999. *An International Comparison of Policies and Outcomes for Young Children*. Ottawa: CPRN.

Pianta, Robert C., Martha J. Cox, and Kyle K. Snow, eds. 2007. *School Readiness and the Transition to Kindergarten in the Era of Accountability*. Baltimore: Paul H. Brookes Publishing.

Pichault, Camille. 1984. *Day Care Facilities and Services for Children under the Age of Three in the European Community*. Luxembourg: Office for Official Publications of the European Communities.

Pielke, Roger A. 2007. *The Honest Broker: Making Sense of Science in Policy and Politics*. New York: Cambridge University Press. http://dx.doi.org/10.1017/CBO9780511818110.

Pierson, Paul. 2000a. "Increasing Returns, Path Dependence, and the Study of Politics." *American Political Science Review* 94(2): 251–67. http://dx.doi.org/10.2307/2586011.

–. 2000b. "The Limits of Design: Explaining Institutional Origins and Change." *Governance: An International Journal of Policy, Administration, and Institutions* 13(4): 475–99. http://dx.doi.org/10.1111/0952-1895.00142.

–. 2000c. "Not Just What but When: Timing and Sequence in Political Processes." *Studies in American Political Development* 14(1): 72–92. http://dx.doi.org/10.1017/S0898588X00003011.

Pinker, Steven. 2002. *The Blank Slate: The Modern Denial of Human Nature*. New York: Penguin.

Plantenga, Janneke, and Chantal Remery. 2009. *The Provision of Childcare Services: A Comparative Review of 30 European Countries*. European Commission's Expert Group on Gender and Employment Issues. Brussels.

Plantenga, Janneke, and Melissa Siegel. 2004. *Position Paper – Childcare in a Changing World*. Prepared for Child Care in a Changing World conference sponsored by the Dutch Presidency, Groningen, the Netherlands, 21–3

October. http://www.childcarecanada.org/documents/research-policy-practice/05/03/materials-child-care-changing-world-european-conference.

Pontusson, Jonas. 2005. *Inequality and Prosperity: Social Europe vs. Liberal America*. Ithaca: Cornell University Press.

Porter, Tony, and Michael Webb. 2008. "Role of the OECD in the Orchestration of Global Knowledge Networks." In *The OECD and Transnational Governance*, ed. Rianne Mahon and Stephen McBride, 43–59. Vancouver: UBC Press.

Powell, Walter W., and Paul J. DiMaggio, eds. 1991. *The New Institutionalism in Organizational Analysis*. Chicago: University of Chicago Press.

Prentice, Susan. 1992. "Workers, Mothers, Reds: Toronto's Postwar Daycare Fight." In *Feminism in Action: Studies in Political Economy*, ed. Patricia Connelly and Pat Armstrong, 175–200. Toronto: Canadian Scholars' Press.

–. 2009. "High Stakes: The 'Investable' Child and the Economic Reframing of Childcare." *Signs* 34(3): 687–710. http://dx.doi.org/10.1086/593711.

Prentice, Susan, ed. 2001. *Changing Child Care: Five Decades of Child Care Advocacy and Policy in Canada*. Halifax: Fernwood.

Press, Frances, and Alan Hayes. 2000. *OECD Thematic Review of Early Childhood Education and Care Policy: Australian Background Report*. Canberra: Commonwealth Government of Australia.

Press, Frances, and Christine Woodrow. 2009. "The Giant in the Playground: Investigating the Reach and Implications of the Corporatisation of Child Care Provision." In *Paid Care in Australia: Politics, Profits, Practices*, ed. Frances Press and Christine Woodrow, 231–52. Sydney: University of Sydney Press.

Prochner, Larry, and Nina Howe, eds. 2000. *Early Childhood Care and Education in Canada*. Vancouver: UBC Press.

Putnam, Robert D. 2015. *Our Kids: The American Dream in Crisis*. New York: Simon and Schuster.

Raden, Anthony. 1999. *Universal Prekindergarten in Georgia: A Case Study of Georgia's Lottery-Funded Pre-K Program*. Working Paper Series. New York: Foundation for Child Development.

–. 2002. *Achieving Full-day Kindergarten in New Mexico: A Case Study*. Working Paper Series. New York: Foundation for Child Development.

Ramey, Craig T., Frances A. Campbell, Margaret Burchinal, Martie L. Skinner, David M. Gardner, and Sharon L. Ramey. 2000. "Persistent Effects of Early Childhood Education on High-Risk Children and Their Mothers." *Applied Developmental Science* 4(1): 2–14. http://dx.doi.org/10.1207/S1532480XADS0401_1.

Ramirez, Francisco O., and John Boli. 1987. "Global Patterns of Educational Institutionalization." In *Institutional Structure: Constituting State, Society, and the Individual*, ed. G.M. Thomas, J.W. Meyer, F.O. Ramirez, and J. Boli, 150–72. Newbury Park: Sage.

Randall, Vicky. 2000. *The Politics of Child Daycare in Britain*. Oxford: Oxford University Press.

–. 2004. "The Making of Local Child Daycare Regimes: Past and Future." *Policy and Politics* 32(1): 3–20. http://dx.doi.org/10.1332/030557304772860012.

Rauch, Dietmar. 2005. "Institutional Fragmentation and Scandinavian Childcare Variations." *Journal of Public Policy* 25(3): 367–94. http://dx.doi.org/10.1017/S0143814X05000371.

Rayside, David, and Clyde Wilcox, eds. 2011. *Faith Politics and Sexual Diversity in Canada and the United States*. Vancouver: UBC Press.

Reardon, Sean F. 2011. "The Widening Academic Achievement Gap between the Rich and the Poor: New Evidence and Possible Explanations." In *Whither Opportunity? Rising Inequality, Schools, and Children's Life Chances*, ed. Richard J. Murnane and Greg J. Duncan, 91–115. New York: Russell Sage Foundation.

–. 2013. "No Rich Child Left Behind." *New York Times*, 27 April. https://opinionator.blogs.nytimes.com/2013/04/27/no-rich-child-left-behind/?_r=0.

Rebell, Michael A. 2011–12. "Safeguarding the Right to a Sound Basic Education in Times of Fiscal Constraint." *Albany Law Review* 75: 1855–976.

Rebell, Michael A. 2012. "The Right to Comprehensive Educational Opportunity." *Harvard Civil Rights–Civil Liberties Law Review* 47: 47–117.

Rebell, Michael A., Jessica R. Wolff, Nancy Kolben, and Betty Holcomb. 2013. *Making Prekindergarten Truly Universal in New York*. New York: Campaign for Educational Equity / Center for Children's Initiatives.

Regenstein, Elliot, and Katherine Lipper. 2013. *A Framework for Choosing a State-Level Early Childhood Governance System*. Boston: BUILD Initiative.

Reynolds, Arthur J., Arthur J. Rolnick, Michelle M. Englund, and Judy A. Temple, eds. 2010. *Childhood Programs and Practices in the First Decade of Life: A Human Capital Integration*. New York: Cambridge University Press. http://dx.doi.org/10.1017/CBO9780511762666.

Reynolds, Arthur J., Judy A. Temple, Dylan L. Robertson, and Emily A. Mann. 2001. "Long-Term Effects of an Early Childhood Intervention on Educational Achievement and Juvenile Arrest: A 15-Year Follow-Up of Low-Income Children in Public Schools." *Journal of the American Medical Association* 285(18): 2339–46. http://dx.doi.org/10.1001/jama.285.18.2339.

Reynolds, Arthur J., Judy A. Temple, Barry A.B. White, Suh-Ruu Ou, and Dylan L. Robertson. 2011. "Age 26 Cost–Benefit Analysis of the

Child–Parent Center Early Education Program." *Child Development* 82(1): 379–404. http://dx.doi.org/10.1111/j.1467-8624.2010.01563.x.

Reynolds, David, and Shaun Farrell. 1996. *Worlds Apart? A Review of International Surveys of Educational Achievement Involving England.* London: HMSO.

Richardson, Gail, and Elizabeth Marx. 1989. *A Welcome for Every Child: How France Achieves Quality in Child Care: Practical Ideas for the United States.* New York: French-American Foundation.

Riley, Denise. 1983. *War in the Nursery: Theories of Child and Mother.* London: Virago.

Risse, Thomas, Stephen Ropp, and Kathryn Sikkink, eds. 1999. *The Power of Human Rights: International Norms and Domestic Change.* New York: Cambridge University Press. http://dx.doi.org/10.1017/CBO9780511598777.

Risse-Kappen, Thomas. 1994. "Ideas Do Not Float Freely: Transnational Coalitions, Domestic Structures, and the End of the Cold War." *International Organization* 48(2): 185–214. http://dx.doi.org/10.1017/S0020818300028162.

Robertson, Brian C. 2000. *There's No Place Like Work: How Business, Government, and Our Obsession with Work Have Driven Parents from Home.* Dallas: Spence Publishing.

–. 2003. *Day Care Deception: What the Child Care Establishment Isn't Telling Us.* San Fransisco: Encounter Books.

Rochon, Thomas R. 1998. *Culture Moves: Ideas, Activism, and Changing Values.* Princeton: Princeton University Press.

Rolnick, Art, and Rob Grunewald. 2003. "Early Childhood Development: Economic Development with a High Public Return." *Fedgazette* (March). Minneapolis: Federal Reserve Bank of Minneapolis.

Rose, Elizabeth. 2010. *The Promise of Preschool: From Head Start to Universal Pre-Kindergarten.* New York: Oxford University Press. http://dx.doi.org/10.1093/acprof:oso/9780195395075.001.0001.

Rosenberg, Tina. 2013. "The Power of Talking to Your Baby." *New York Times,* 10 April. https://opinionator.blogs.nytimes.com/2013/04/10/the-power-of-talking-to-your-baby/?_r=0.

Ross, Marc Howard. 1997. "Culture and Identity in Comparative Political Analysis." In *Comparative Politics: Rationality, Culture, Structure,* ed. Mark Irving Lichbach and Alan S. Zuckerman, 42–80. New York: Cambridge University Press.

Rueda, David, and Jonas Pontusson. 2000. "Wage Inequality and Varieties of Capitalism." *World Politics* 52(3): 350–83. http://dx.doi.org/10.1017/S0043887100016579.

Ruggie, John Gerard. 1998. *Constructing the World Polity: Essays on International Institutionalization*. New York: Routledge. http://dx.doi.org/10.4324/9780203424261.

Ruhm, Christopher J. 2004. "Parental Employment and Child Cognitive Development." *Journal of Human Resources* 39(1): 155–92. http://dx.doi.org/10.2307/3559009.

Ryan, James E. 2006. "A Constitutional Right to Preschool?" *California Law Review* 94(1): 49–99. http://dx.doi.org/10.2307/20439027.

Sabatier, Paul, and Hank Jenkins-Smith. 1993. *Policy Change and Learning: An Advocacy Coalition Approach*. Boulder: Westview Press.

Sainsbury, Diane, ed. 1999. *Gender and Welfare State Regimes*. Oxford: Oxford University Press. http://dx.doi.org/10.1093/0198294166.001.0001.

Samuels, Christina A. 2013. "N.C. Supreme Court to Decide on Pre-k Funding." *Education Week*, 29 October. http://www.edweek.org/ew/articles/2013/10/30/10preschool.h33.html.

Scarr, Sandra, Deborah Phillips, and Kathleen McCartney. 1990. "Facts, Fantasies, and the Future of Child Care in the United States." *Psychological Science* 1(1): 26–35. http://dx.doi.org/10.1111/j.1467-9280.1990.tb00061.x.

Scheiwe, Kirsten, and Harry Willekens, eds. 2009. *Child Care and Preschool Development in Europe: Institutional Perspectives*. New York: Palgrave Macmillan. http://dx.doi.org/10.1057/9780230232778.

Schmidt, Vivien A. 2008. "Discursive Institutionalism: The Explanatory Power of Ideas and Discourse." *Annual Review of Political Science* 11(1): 303–26. http://dx.doi.org/10.1146/annurev.polisci.11.060606.135342.

Schneider, Anne, and Helen Ingram. 1993. "Social Construction of Target Populations: Implications for Politics and Policy." *American Political Science Review* 87(2): 334–47. http://dx.doi.org/10.2307/2939044.

Schneider, Mark, Paul Teske, and Michael Mintrom. 1995. *Public Entrepreneurs: Agents for Change in American Government*. Princeton: Princeton University Press.

Schulman, Karen, Helen Blank, and Danielle Ewen. 1999. *Seeds of Success: State Prekindergarten Initiatives 1998–1999*. Washington, DC: Children's Defense Fund.

Schweinhart, Lawrence J., Jeanne Montie, Zongping Xiang, William S. Barnett, Clive R. Belfield, and Milagros Nores. 2005. *Lifetime Effects: The High/Scope Perry Preschool Study through Age 40*. Ypsilanti: High/Scope Press.

SCRGSP (Steering Committee for the Review of Government Service Provision). 2008. *Report on Government Services, 2008*. Canberra: Productivity Commission.

Scruggs, Lyle A., and James P. Allan. 2008. "Social Stratification and Welfare Regimes for the Twenty-First Century: Revisiting *The Three Worlds of Welfare Capitalism*." *World Politics* 60(4): 642–64. http://dx.doi.org/10.1353/wp.0.0020.

Seifert, Timothy L., Patricia M. Canning, and B. Lindemann. 2001. *A Study of Family, Child Care, and Well-Being in Young Canadian Families*. W-02–3–1E. Ottawa: Applied Research Branch of Strategic Policy, Human Resources Development Canada.

Sheppard, Kate. 2007. "Pre-K Politics in the States." November. Online: http://prospect.org/article/pre-k-politics-states. *American Prospect*. http://prospect.org/article/pre-k-politics-states.

Shipan, Charles R., and Craig Volden. 2008. "The Mechanisms of Policy Diffusion." *American Journal of Political Science* 52(4): 840–57. http://dx.doi.org/10.1111/j.1540-5907.2008.00346.x.

Shonkoff, Jack P., and Susan Nall Bales. 2011. "Science Does Not Speak for Itself: Translating Child Development Research for the Public and Its Policymakers." *Child Development* 82(1): 17–32. http://dx.doi.org/10.1111/j.1467-8624.2010.01538.x.

Shonkoff, Jack P., and Deborah A. Phillips, eds. 2000. *From Neurons to Neighborhoods: The Science of Early Childhood Development*. Washington, DC: National Academy Press.

Shore, Rima. 1997. *Rethinking the Brain: New Insights into Early Development*. New York: Families and Work Institute.

Silver, Harold, and Pamela Silver. 1991. *An Educational War on Poverty: American and British Policy-making, 1960–1980*. New York: Cambridge University Press. http://dx.doi.org/10.1017/CBO9780511522352.

Simmons, Beth A., Frank Dobbin, and Geoffrey Garrett, eds. 2008. *The Global Diffusion of Markets and Democracy*. New York: Cambridge University Press. http://dx.doi.org/10.1017/CBO9780511755941.

Simmons, Beth, and Zachary Elkins. 2004. "The Globalization of Liberalization: Policy Diffusion in the International Political Economy." *American Political Science Review* 98(1): 171–89. http://dx.doi.org/10.1017/S0003055404001078.

Simmons, Julie, and Peter Graefe. 2013. "Assessing the Collaboration That Was 'Collaborative Federalism,' 1996–2006." *Canadian Political Science Review* 7(1): 25–36.

Skocpol, Theda. 1992. *Protecting Soldiers and Mothers: The Political Origins of Social Policy in the United States*. Cambridge, MA: Harvard University Press.

Skogstad, Grace. 2008. *Internationalization and Canadian Agriculture: Policy and Governing Paradigms*. Toronto: University of Toronto Press.

Skogstad, Grace, and Vivien A. Schmidt. 2011. "Introduction: Transnationalism, Domestic Politics, and Policy Paradigm Development." In *Policy Paradigms, Transnationalism, and Domestic Politics*, ed. Grace Skogstad,

3–35. Toronto: University of Toronto Press. http://dx.doi.org/10.1163/ej.9789004186699.i-358.8.

Skolverket. 2010. *Curriculum for the Preschool Lpfö 98*. Stockholm: Fritzes kundservice.

Skrede Gleditsch, Kristian, and Michael D. Ward. 2006. "Diffusion and the International Context of Democratization." *International Organization* 60: 911–33.

Slass, Lorie. 2003. *Engaging Other Sectors in Efforts to Improve Public Policy in Early Childhood Development*. Washington, DC: Annenberg Public Policy Center of the University of Pennsylvania.

Slaughter, Anne-Marie. 2004. *A New World Order*. Princeton: Princeton University Press.

Smolensky, Eugene, and Jennifer Appleton Gootman, eds. 2003. *Working Families and Growing Kids: Caring for Children and Adolescents*. Washington, DC: The National Academies Press.

Sokoloff, Heather. 2005. "Gulf between Parties Is Size of a Small Child: Liberals, Tories Differ Distinctly on Daycare Options." *National Post*, 5 December, A8.

Sosinsky, Laura Stout, Heather Lord, and Edward Zigler. 2007. "For-Profit/ Nonprofit Differences in Center Based Childcare Quality: Results from the National Institute of Child Health and Human Development Study of Early Childcare and Youth Development." *Journal of Applied Developmental Psychology* 28(5–6): 390–410. http://dx.doi.org/10.1016/j.appdev.2007.06.003.

Soss, Joe, Sanford F. Schram, Thomas P. Vartanian, and Erin O'Brien. 2001. "Setting the Terms of Relief: Explaining State Policy Choices in the Devolution Revolution." *American Journal of Political Science* 45(2): 378–95. http://dx.doi.org/10.2307/2669347.

Soysal, Yasemin, and David Strang. 1989. "Construction of the First Mass Education Systems in Nineteenth-Century Europe." *Sociology of Education* 62(4): 277–88. http://dx.doi.org/10.2307/2112831.

Squires, Jim. 2014. "One State's Bold Step toward the Future." *Preschool Matters Today* NIEER Blog, 6 June. http://preschoolmatters.org/2014/06/06/one-states-bold-step-toward-the-future.

Starke, Peter, Herbert Obinger, and Francis G. Castles. 2008. "Convergence towards Where? In What Ways, If Any, Are Welfare States Becoming More Similar?" *Journal of European Public Policy* 15(7): 975–1000. http://dx.doi.org/10.1080/13501760802310397.

Starting Strong Network. 2008. "About the Network." http://www.startingstrong.net.

Status of Women Canada. 1986. *Report of the Task Force on Child Care* (Cooke Report). Ottawa: Minister of Supply and Services.

Steinfels, Margaret O'Brien. 1973. *Who's Minding the Children? The History and Politics of Day Care in America*. New York: Simon and Schuster.

Stolberg, Sheryl Gay. 2001. "Researchers Find a Link Between Behavioral Problems and Time in Child Care." *New York Times*, 19 April. http://www.nytimes.com/2001/04/19/us/researchers-find-a-link-between-behavioral-problems-and-time-in-child-care.html?rref=collection%2Fbyline%2Fsheryl-gay-stolberg&action=click&contentCollection=undefined®ion=stream&module=stream_unit&version=search&contentPlacement=1&pgtype=collection.

Strang, David, and Patricia M.Y. Chang. 1993. "The International Labour Organization and the Welfare State: Institutional Effects on National Welfare Spending, 1960–1980." *International Organization* 47(2): 235–62. http://dx.doi.org/10.1017/S0020818300027934.

Strang, David, and John W. Meyer. 1993. "Institutional Conditions for Diffusion." *Theory and Society* 22(4): 487–511. http://dx.doi.org/10.1007/BF00993595.

Streeck, Wolfgang, and Kathleen Thelen, eds. 2005. *Institutional Change in Advanced Political Economies*. Oxford: Oxford University Press.

Stroick, Sharon M., and Jane Jenson. 2000. *What Is the Best Policy Mix for Canada's Young Children?* Ottawa: CPRN.

Super, Charles M. 2005. "The Globalization of Developmental Psychology." In *Developmental Psychology and Social Change: Research, History, and Policy*, ed. David B. Pillemer and Sheldon H. White, 11–33. New York: Cambridge University Press. http://dx.doi.org/10.1017/CBO9780511610400.003.

Swank, Duane. 2002. *Global Capital, Political Institutions, and Policy Change in Developed Welfare States*. New York: Cambridge University Press. http://dx.doi.org/10.1017/CBO9780511613371.

Sylva, Kathy, Edward Melhuish, Pam Sammons, Iram Siraj-Blatchford, and Brenda Taggart. 2011. "Pre-School Quality and Educational Outcomes at Age 11: Low Quality Has Little Benefit." *Journal of Early Childhood Research* 9(2): 109–24. http://dx.doi.org/10.1177/1476718X10387900.

Sylva, Kathy, and Gillian Pugh. 2005. "Transforming the Early Years in England." *Oxford Review of Education* 31(1): 11–27. http://dx.doi.org/10.1080/0305498042000337165.

Sylvester, Kathleen. 2001a. "Caring for Our Youngest: Public Attitudes in the United States." *Future of Children* 11(1): 52–61. http://dx.doi.org/10.2307/1602809.

–. 2001b. *Listening to Families: The Role of Values in Shaping Effective Social Policy*. New York: Carnegie Corporation.

Tanaka, Sakiko. 2005. "Parental Leave and Child Health across OECD
    Countries." *Economic Journal (Oxford)* 115(501): F7–28. http://dx.doi.org/
    10.1111/j.0013-0133.2005.00970.x.
Temple, Judy A., and Arthur J. Reynolds. 2007. "Benefits and Costs of
    Investment in Preschool Education: Evidence from the Child–Parent
    Centers and Related Programs." *Economics of Education Review* 26(1): 126–44.
    http://dx.doi.org/10.1016/j.econedurev.2005.11.004.
The Business Roundtable and Corporate Voices for Working Families. 2003.
    Early Childhood Education: A Call to Action from the Business Community.
    http://www.bestbeginningsalaska.org/wp-content/uploads/research_
    calltoactionfromthebusinesscommunity.pdf.
Thelen, Kathleen. 2003. "How Institutions Evolve: Insights from
    Comparative Historical Analysis." In *Comparative Historical Analysis in the
    Social Sciences*, ed. James Mahoney and Dietrich Rueschemeyer, 208–40.
    New York: Cambridge University Press. http://dx.doi.org/10.1017/
    CBO9780511803963.007.
Thériault, Luc. 2006. "The National Post and the Nanny State: Framing
    the Child Care Debate in Canada." *Canadian Review of Social Policy* 56:
    140–8.
Thompson, Michael, Richard Ellis, and Aaron Wildavsky. 1990. *Cultural
    Theory.* Boulder: Westview Press.
Thompson, Ross A., and Charles A. Nelson. 2001. "Developmental Science
    and the Media: Early Brain Development." *American Psychologist* 56(1): 5–15.
    http://dx.doi.org/10.1037/0003-066X.56.1.5.
Timpson, Annis May. 2001. *Driven Apart: Women's Employment Equality and
    Child Care in Canadian Public Policy.* Vancouver: UBC Press.
Tougas, Jocelyne. 2002. *Reforming Quebec's Early Childhood Care and Education:
    The First Five Years.* Working Paper. Toronto: Childcare Resource and
    Research Unit.
Treasury, H.M. 2004. *Choice for Parents, the Best Start for Children: A Ten Year
    Strategy for Childcare.* London: HMSO.
Treflar, Daniel. 2004. "Treating Children Well Strengthens a Nation." *Ottawa
    Citizen*, 4 September, B7.
Treisman, Daniel. 2007. *The Architecture of Government: Rethinking Political
    Decentralization.* New York: Cambridge University Press. http://dx.doi.
    org/10.1017/CBO9780511619151.
Tremblay, Diane-Gabrielle. 2009. "Quebec's Policies for Work–Family
    Balance: A Model for Canada?" In *Public Policy for Women*, ed. Marjorie
    Griffin Cohen and Jane Pulkingham, 271–90. Toronto: University of
    Toronto Press.

Tsebelis, George. 1995. "Decision Making in Political Systems: Veto Players in Presidentialism, Parliamentarism, Multicameralism, and Multipartyism." *British Journal of Political Science* 25(3): 289–325. http://dx.doi.org/10.1017/S0007123400007225.

Tversky, Amos, and Daniel Kahneman. 1981. "The Framing of Decisions and the Psychology of Choice." *Science* 211(4481): 453–8. http://dx.doi.org/10.1126/science.7455683.

UK Office for National Statistics. 2000. "Children under Five in Schools as a Percentage of All Children Aged Three and Four, 1970/71 to 1998/99." *Social Trends* no. 30. https://www.ons.gov.uk/.../social-trends.../social-trends/...30.../social-trends-full-report.pdf.

–. 2007. *Social Trends No. 37*. Houndmills: Palgrave Macmillan.

UNESCO (United Nations Educational, Scientific and Cultural Organization). 2006. *Strong Foundations: Early Childhood Care and Education*. Education for All Global Monitoring Report 2007. Paris.

UNESCO, World Education Forum. 2000. *Education for All: Meeting Our Collective Commitments. The Dakar Framework for Action*. Paris.

–. 2006. *Strong Foundations: Early Childhood Care and Education*. Paris.

UNICEF (United Nations Children's Fund). 2007. *Child Poverty in Perspective: An Overview of Child Well-Being in Rich Countries. Report Card 7*. Florence: Innocenti Research Centre.

–. 2008. *The Child Care Transition: A League Table of Early Childhood Education and Care in Economically Advanced Countries. Report Card 8*. Florence: Innocenti Research Centre.

–. 2012. *Measuring Child Poverty: New League Tables of Child Poverty in the World's Rich Countries. Report Card 10*. Florence: Innocenti Research Centre.

Universal Prekindergarten Education Advisory Council. 2003. *Report and Recommendations to the Florida State Board of Education*. https://www.teachmorelovemore.org/docs/UPKCouncil.pdf.

US Census Bureau. 2005. *Maternity Leave and Employment: Patterns of First-Time Mothers: 1961–2000*. Washington, DC: US Department of Commerce.

US Department of Education, National Center for Education Statistics. 2001. *Highlights from the Third International Mathematics and Science Study – Repeat (TIMSS-R)*. https://nces.ed.gov/pubsearch/pubsinfo.asp?pubid=2001027.

US Department of Health and Human Services, National Institutes of Health, National Institute of Child Health and Human Development. 2006. *The NICHD Study of Early Child Care and Youth Development: Findings for Children up to Age 4 1/2 Years*. Washington, DC: NIH.

US House Budget Committee Majority Staff. 2014. *The War on Poverty: 50 Years Later. A House Budget Committee Report*. Washington: US Congress.

US Treasury Working Group on Child Care. 1998. *Investing in Child Care: Challenges Facing Working Parents and the Private Sector Response.* Washington, DC.

van Kersbergen, Kees. 1995. *Social Capitalism: A Study of Christian Democracy and the Welfare State.* New York: Routledge. http://dx.doi.org/10.4324/9780203429587.

van Kersbergen, Kees, and Philip Manow, eds. 2009. *Religion, Class Coalitions, and Welfare States.* New York: Cambridge University Press. http://dx.doi.org/10.1017/CBO9780511626784.

Vandell, Deborah Lowe, Jay Belsky, Margaret Burchinal, Laurence Steinberg, and Nathan Vandergrift, and the NICHD Early Child Care Research Network. 2010 (May). "Do Effects of Early Child Care Extend to Age 15 Years? Results from the NICHD Study of Early Child Care and Youth Development." *Child Development* 81(3): 737–56. http://dx.doi.org/10.1111/j.1467-8624.2010.01431.x.

Vincent, Carol, Annette Braun, and Stephen J. Ball. 2008. "Childcare, Choice, and Social Class: Caring for Young Children in the UK." *Critical Social Policy* 28(1): 5–26. http://dx.doi.org/10.1177/0261018307085505.

Vinovskis, Maris. 2005. *The Birth of Head Start: Preschool Education Policies in the Kennedy and Johnson Administrations.* Chicago: University of Chicago Press. http://dx.doi.org/10.7208/chicago/9780226856735.001.0001.

–. 2009. *From a Nation at Risk to No Child Left Behind: National Education Goals and the Creation of Federal Education Policy.* New York: Teachers College Press.

Voices for Illinois Children / Market Strategies Inc. 2001. "Communicating the Early Childhood Message." Presentation to the National Governors Association Meeting, 10 September, Washington, DC.

Volden, Craig. 2002. "The Politics of Competitive Federalism: A Race to the Bottom in Welfare Benefits?" *American Journal of Political Science* 46(2): 352–63. http://dx.doi.org/10.2307/3088381.

–. 2006. "States as Policy Laboratories: Emulating Success in the Children's Health Insurance Program." *American Journal of Political Science* 50(2): 294–312. http://dx.doi.org/10.1111/j.1540-5907.2006.00185.x.

Volden, Craig, Michael M. Ting, and Daniel P. Carpenter. 2008. "A Formal Model of Learning and Policy Diffusion." *American Political Science Review* 102(3): 319–32. http://dx.doi.org/10.1017/S0003055408080271.

Waldfogel, Jane. 2001. "International Policies toward Parental Leave and Child Care." *Future of Children* 11(1): 98–111. http://dx.doi.org/10.2307/1602812.

–. 2007. "Parental Work Arrangements and Child Development." *Canadian Public Policy* 33(2): 251–71. http://dx.doi.org/10.3138/cpp.33.2.251.

–. 2010. *Britain's War on Poverty.* New York: Russell Sage Foundation.

Walker, John. 1969. "The Diffusion of Innovations among the American States." *American Political Science Review* 63(3): 880–99. http://dx.doi.org/10.2307/1954434.

Warner, Mildred E. 2009. "(Not) Valuing Care: A Review of Recent Popular Economic Reports on Preschool in the US." *Feminist Economics* 15(2): 73–95. http://dx.doi.org/10.1080/13545700802699512.

Warner, Mildred E., and Zhilin Liu. 2005. "Economic Development Policy and Local Services: The Case of Child Care." *International Journal of Economic Development* 7(1): 25–64.

Washington, Valora. 2004. "Where Do We Go from Here?" (October). *American Prospect.* http://prospect.org/article/where-do-we-go-here.

Watamura, Sarah E., Bonny Donzella, Jan Alwin, and Megan R. Gunnar. 2003. "Morning-to-Afternoon Increased in Cortisol Concentrations for Infants and Toddlers at Child Care: Age Differences and Behavioral Correlates." *Child Development* 74(4): 1006–20. http://dx.doi.org/10.1111/1467-8624.00583.

Watson, Sara. 2011. *Mobilizing Business Champions for Children: A Guide for Advocates.* Washington: Pew Center on the States.

Wedeen, Lisa. 2002. "Conceptualizing Culture: Possibilities for Political Science." *American Political Science Review* 96(4): 713–28. http://dx.doi.org/10.1017/S0003055402000400.

Weingast, Barry R. 1995. "A Rational Choice Perspective on the Role of Ideas: Shared Belief Systems and State Sovereignty in International Cooperation." *Politics & Society* 23(4): 449–64. http://dx.doi.org/10.1177/0032329295023004003.

Welshman, John. 2010. "From Head Start to Sure Start: Reflections on Policy Transfer." *Children & Society* 24(2): 89–99. http://dx.doi.org/10.1111/j.1099-0860.2008.00201.x.

Wente, Margaret. 2004. "The Horrors of Unregulated Daycare." *Globe and Mail,* 16 November, A19.

Westinghouse Learning Corporation. 1969. *The Impact of Head Start: An Evaluation of the Effects of Head Start on Children's Cognitive and Affective Development.* Report presented to the Office of Economic Opportunity.

Weyland, Kurt. 2006. *Bounded Rationality and Policy Diffusion: Social Sector Reform in Latin America.* Princeton: Princeton University Press.

–. 2008. "Toward a New Theory of Institutional Change." *World Politics* 60(2): 281–314. http://dx.doi.org/10.1353/wp.0.0013.

White, Linda A. 2001a. "The Child Care Agenda and the Social Union." In *Canadian Federalism: Performance, Effectiveness, and Legitimacy,* ed. Herman Bakvis and Grace Skogstad, 105–23. Toronto: Oxford University Press.

–. 2001b. "From Ideal to Pragmatic Politics: Child Care Advocacy Groups in the 1980s and 1990s." In *Changing Child Care: Five Decades of Child Care*

Advocacy and Policy in Canada, ed. Susan Prentice, 97–116. Halifax: Fernwood Press.

–. 2004a. "Ideas and Normative Institutionalization: Explaining the Paradoxes of French Family and Employment Policies." *French Politics* 2(3): 247–71. http://dx.doi.org/10.1057/palgrave.fp.8200061.

–. 2004b. "Trends in Child Care / Early Childhood Education / Early Childhood Development Policy in Canada and the United States." *American Review of Canadian Studies* 34(4): 665–87. http://dx.doi.org/10.1080/02722010409481694.

–. 2006. "Institutions, Constitutions, Actor Strategies, and Ideas: Explaining Variation in Paid Parental Leave Policies in Canada and the United States." *International Journal of Constitutional Law* 4(2): 319–46. http://dx.doi.org/10.1093/icon/mol007.

–. 2009a. "Explaining Differences in Child Care Policy Development in France and the USA: Norms, Frames, Programmatic Ideas." *International Political Science Review* 30(4): 385–405. http://dx.doi.org/10.1177/0192512109340055.

–. 2009b. "The United States in Comparative Perspective: Maternity and Parental Leave and Child Care Benefits Trends in Liberal Welfare Regimes." *Yale Journal of Law and Feminism* 21(1): 185–232.

–. 2011a. "Institutional 'Stickiness' and Ideational Resistance to Paradigm Change: Canada and Early Childhood Education and Care (ECEC) Policy." In *Policy Paradigms, Transnationalism, and Domestic Politics*, ed. Grace Skogstad, 202–36. Toronto: University of Toronto Press.

–. 2011b. "The Internationalization of Early Childhood Education and Care (ECEC) Issues: Framing Gender Justice and Child Well-being." *Governance: An International Journal of Policy, Administration, and Institutions* 24(2): 285–309. http://dx.doi.org/10.1111/j.1468-0491.2011.01520.x.

–. 2012. "Must We All Be Paradigmatic? Social Investment Policies and Liberal Welfare States." *Canadian Journal of Political Science* 45(3): 657–83. http://dx.doi.org/10.1017/S0008423912000753.

–. 2014. "Understanding Canada's Lack of Progress in Implementing the UN Convention on the Rights of the Child: The Intergovernmental Dynamics of Children's Policy Making in Canada." *International Journal of Children's Rights* 22(1): 164–88. http://dx.doi.org/10.1163/15718182-02201002.

White, Linda A., Adrienne Davidson, Heather Millar, Milena Pandy, and Juliana Yi. 2015. "Policy Logics, Framing Strategies, and Policy Change: Lessons from Universal Pre-k Policy Debates in California and Florida." *Policy Sciences* 48(4): 395–413. http://dx.doi.org/10.1007/s11077-015-9234-9.

White, Linda A., and Martha Friendly. 2012. "Public Funding, Private Delivery: States, Markets, and Early Childhood Education and Care in

Liberal Welfare States: A Comparison of Australia, the UK, Quebec, and New Zealand." *Journal of Comparative Policy Analysis: Research and Practice* 14(4): 292–310. http://dx.doi.org/10.1080/13876988.2012.699789.

White, Linda A., and Susan Prentice. 2013. "When the Evidence Doesn't Matter: Evidence-Based Policy-Making and Early Learning and Care in Canada." In *Evidence-Based Policy-Making in Canada*, ed. Shaun Young, 93–117. Toronto: Oxford University Press.

–. 2016. "Early Childhood Education and Care Reform in Canadian Provinces: Understanding the Role of Experts and Evidence in ECEC Policy Change in Canadian Provinces." *Canadian Public Administration* 59(1): 24–44. http:// dx.doi.org/10.1111/capa.12156.

White, Linda A., Susan Prentice, and Michal Perlman. 2015. "The Evidence Base for Early Childhood Education and Care Program Investment: What We Know, What We Don't Know." *Evidence and Policy* 11(4): 529–46.

White, H. Sheldon, and Deborah A. Phillips. 2001. "Designing Head Start: Roles Played by Developmental Psychologists." In *Social Science and Policy-Making: A Search for Relevance in the Twentieth Century*, ed. David L. Featherstone and Maris A. Vinovskis, 83–118. Ann Arbor: University of Michigan Press.

White House Office of the Press Secretary. 2013. "Fact Sheet: President Obama's Plan for Early Education for All Americans." 13 February. https:// www.whitehouse.gov/the-press-office/2013/02/13/fact-sheet-president-obama-s-plan-early-education-all-americans.

–. 2014. "Fact Sheet: Invest in US: The White House Summit on Early Childhood Education." 10 December. https://www.whitehouse.gov/the-press-office/2014/12/10/fact-sheet-invest-us-white-house-summit-early-childhood-education.

Whitehurst, Grover. 2013. "New Evidence Raises Doubt on Obama's Preschool for All." *Brown Center Chalkboard*, 20 November. https://www.brookings. edu/research/new-evidence-raises-doubts-on-obamas-preschool-for-all.

Wildavsky, Aaron. 1987. "Choosing Preferences by Constructing Institutions: A Cultural Theory of Preference Formation." *American Political Science Review* 81(1): 3–21. http://dx.doi.org/10.2307/1960776.

Wilson, Richard W. 2000. "The Many Voices of Political Culture: Assessing Different Approaches." *World Politics* 52(2): 246–73. http://dx.doi. org/10.1017/S0043887100002616.

Wincott, Daniel. 2005. "Reshaping Public Space? Devolution and Policy Change in British Early Childhood Education and Care." *Regional & Federal Studies* 15(4): 453–70. http://dx.doi.org/10.1080/13597560500230573.

Wisensale, Steven K. 2003. "Two Steps Forward, One Step Back: The Family and Medical Leave Act as Retrenchment Policy." *Review of Policy Research* 20(1): 135–51. http://dx.doi.org/10.1111/1541-1338.00008.

Woessmann, Ludger, and Paul E. Peterson, eds. 2007. *Schools and the Equal Opportunity Problem*. Cambridge, MA: MIT Press.

Wolf, Frieder. 2009. "The Division of Labour in Education Funding: A Cross-National Comparison of Public and Private Education Expenditure in 28 OECD Countries." *Acta Politica* 44(1): 50–73. http://dx.doi.org/10.1057/ap.2008.19.

Wollons, Roberta, ed. 2000. *Kindergartens and Culture: The Global Diffusion of an Idea*. New Haven: Yale University Press.

Wong, Vivian C., Thomas D. Cook, W. Steven Barnett, and Kwanghee June. 2007. *An Effectiveness-Based Evaluation of Five State Pre-Kindergarten Programs Using Regression-Discontinuity*. New Brunswick: NIEER.

Woodhead, Martin. 1988. "When Psychology Informs Public Policy: The Case of Early Childhood Intervention." *American Psychologist* 43(6): 443–54. http://dx.doi.org/10.1037/0003-066X.43.6.443.

Workman, Emily. 2013. *Kindergarten Policy Characteristics*. Education Commission of the States Report (March). http://www.ecs.org/clearinghouse/01/06/80/10680.pdf.

World Bank. 2015. *Early Child Development*. http://www.worldbank.org/en/topic/earlychildhooddevelopment.

Young, Mary Eming, ed. 2002. *From Early Child Development to Human Development*. Proceedings of a World Bank Conference on Investing in Our Children's Future, Washington, DC, 10–11 April 2000. Washington, DC: International Bank for Reconstruction and Development/The World Bank.

Young, Mary Eming, ed., with Linda M. Richardson. 2007. *Early Child Development from Measurement to Action: A Priority for Growth and Equity*. Washington, DC: The World Bank.

Zachrisson, Henrik D., Eric Dearing, Ratib Lekhal, and Claudio O. Toppelberg. 2013. "Little Evidence that Time in Child Care Causes Externalizing Problems during Early Childhood in Norway." *Child Development* 84(4): 1152–70. http://dx.doi.org/10.1111/cdev.12040.

Zaller, John R. 1992. *The Nature and Origins of Mass Opinion*. New York: Cambridge University Press. http://dx.doi.org/10.1017/CBO9780511818691.

Zigler, Edward. 1987. "Formal Schooling for Four-Year-Olds? No." *American Psychologist* 42(3): 254–60. http://dx.doi.org/10.1037/0003-066X.42.3.254.

Zigler, Edward, and Karen Anderson. 1979. "An Idea Whose Time Had Come: The Intellectual and Political Climate." In *Project Head Start: A Legacy of the*

War on Poverty, ed. Edward Zigler and Jeannette Valentine, 3–19. New York: Free Press.

Zigler, Edward, Walter S. Gilliam, and Stephanie M. Jones. 2006. *A Vision for Universal Preschool Education*. New York: Cambridge University Press. http://dx.doi.org/10.1017/CBO9781139167284.

Zimmerman, Jonathan. 2002. *Whose America? Culture Wars in the Public Schools*. Cambridge, MA: Harvard University Press.

Permission Credits

Parts of this volume have been previously published in the following:

Chapter 2

2006   Linda A. White. "Institutions, Constitutions, Actor Strategies, and Ideas: Explaining Variation in Paid Parental Leave Policies in Canada and the United States." *ICON: International Journal of Constitutional Law* 4(2): 319–46.

2009   Linda A. White. "The United States in Comparative Perspective: Maternity and Parental Leave and Child Care Benefits Trends in Liberal Welfare Regimes." *Yale Journal of Law and Feminism* 21(1): 185–232.

2012   Linda A. White. "Must We All Be Paradigmatic? Social Investment Policies and Liberal Welfare States." *Canadian Journal of Political Science* 45(3): 657–83.

2012   Linda A. White and Martha Friendly. "Public Funding, Private Delivery: States, Markets, and Early Childhood Education and Care in Liberal Welfare States – Australia, the UK, Quebec, and New Zealand." *Journal of Comparative Policy Analysis: Research and Practice* 14(4): 292–310.

2017   Linda A. White. "Which Ideas, Whose Norms? Comparing the Relative Influence of IOs on Paid Maternity/Parental Policies in Liberal Welfare States." *Social Politics* (March).

Chapter 5

2011   Linda A. White. "The Internationalization of Early Childhood Education and Care (ECEC) Issues: Framing Gender Justice and Child

Well-being." *Governance: An International Journal of Policy, Administration and Institutions* 24(2): 285–309.

2011   Linda A. White. "Institutional 'Stickiness' and Ideational Resistance to Paradigm Change: Canada and Early Childhood Education and Care (ECEC) Policy." In Grace Skogstad, ed. *Policy Paradigms, Transnationalism, and Domestic Politics.* Toronto: University of Toronto Press, 202–36.

Chapter 6

2015   Linda A. White, Adrienne Davidson, Heather Millar, Milena Pandy, and Juliana Yi. "Policy Logics, Framing Strategies, and Policy Change: Lessons from Universal Pre-k Policy Debates in California and Florida." *Policy Sciences* 48(4): 395–413.

Chapter 7

2011   Linda A. White. "Institutional 'Stickiness' and Ideational Resistance to Paradigm Change: Canada and Early Childhood Education and Care (ECEC) Policy." In Grace Skogstad, ed. *Policy Paradigms, Transnationalism, and Domestic Politics.* Toronto: University of Toronto Press, 202–36.

2012   Martha Friendly and Linda A. White. "'No-lateralism': Paradoxes in Early Childhood Education and Care Policy in the Canadian Federation." *Canadian Federalism: Performance, Effectiveness, and Legitimacy.* 3rd ed. Eds. Grace Skogstad and Herman Bakvis. Toronto: Oxford University Press, 183–202.

2013   Linda A. White and Susan Prentice. "When the Evidence Doesn't Matter: Evidence-Based Policy-Making and Early Learning and Care in Canada." *Evidence-Based Policy-Making in Canada.* Ed. Shaun Young. Toronto: Oxford University Press.

2016   Linda A. White and Susan Prentice. "Understanding the Role of Experts and Evidence in ECEC Policy Change in Canadian Provinces." *Canadian Public Administration* 59(1): 24–44.

Index